The Making of Modern America

The Nation from 1945 to the Present

SECOND EDITION

Gary A. Donaldson

ROWMAN & LITTLEFIELD PUBLISHERS, INC.
Lanham • Boulder • New York • Toronto • Plymouth, UK

ROWMAN & LITTLEFIELD PUBLISHERS, INC.

Published in the United States of America
by Rowman & Littlefield Publishers, Inc.
A wholly owned subsidiary of The Rowman & Littlefield Publishing Group, Inc.
4501 Forbes Boulevard, Suite 200, Lanham, Maryland 20706
www.rowmanlittlefield.com

Estover Road, Plymouth PL6 7PY, United Kingdom

British Library Cataloguing in Publication Information Available

Library of Congress Cataloging-in-Publication Data

Donaldson, Gary.
  The making of modern America : the nation from 1945 to present / Gary A. Donaldson.—2nd ed.
    p. cm.
  Includes bibliographical references and index.
  ISBN 978-1-4422-0957-2 (cloth : alk. paper)
  ISBN 978-1-4422-0958-9 (pbk. : alk. paper)
  ISBN 978-1-4422-0959-6 (electronic)
  1. United States—History—1945-   I. Title.
  E741.D66   2012
  973—dc23   2012023687

Printed in the United States of America

♾ ™ The paper used in this publication meets the minimum requirements of American National Standard for Information Sciences—Permanence of Paper for Printed Library Materials, ANSI/NISO Z39.48-1992.

·Contents·

· Preface ·

The Making of Modern America is a history of the nation from the end of World War II to the present. It is an attempt to explain how we, the American people, made that journey, how we got to where we are today—the routes we took, the trip we made. These are the events that have shaped us, shaped our nation, and formed our character.

This book is designed to meet the needs of students for a concise narrative of America's recent past. It provides an overview of the most important personalities, trends, and events of that period. It also explores the principal economic, political, social, and international problems the nation has experienced as it moved from the heady days of the postwar years through various waves of economic expansion, promises, hopes, war, and, certainly, the fears and failures of the age.

At the end of each chapter, I have added a reading: an important document, an analysis of an event, a biographical sketch. The purpose is to focus on one point that punctuates the period. Several of these readings are designed to interject into the historical narrative an event that does not fit well, an event that was nevertheless an important part of the national conversation at the time. In addition, there have been many important figures in American history whose accomplishments, deeds, and misdeeds cannot be easily shoehorned into the text as written, but whose impact on history has been enormous. You may find these figures among the readings.

This modern era we are studying is unique in American history—in fact, all of history. Most historical times are best evaluated in retrospect. That is, an era must be judged by its impact (good or bad) on the eras that follow it. The modern era has, of course, no future from which it can be analyzed or judged. This is the primary complaint of those who argue that modern history is, in fact, not history at all, but something else. It is often argued that it is impossible to be accurate and impartial about a historical period that has impacted the historian's life. It may seem like a good argument. But should we, then, not study the recent past? Should we wait for the recent past to become the not-so-recent past? Must we wait for the memory of Betty Friedan to fade before we can study the origins of modern American feminism, or until George McGovern dies before we can take a critical look at the 1972 presidential campaign? Of course not. The immediate past is a historical era like any other. We must study it, analyze it, and evaluate it. Future historians will do the same, and undoubtedly interpretations will change.

This book is the culmination of the reading, writing, and teaching I have done over the past twenty (plus) years at Xavier University in New Orleans. Much of this book was written in the aftermath of Hurricane Katrina, when my university, nearly destroyed by six feet of fetid flood water, was undergoing the arduous and expensive process of rebuilding. Today Xavier thrives. This is a miracle in itself.

I've always felt a need to thank the university, its administration, and most of all the faculty at the Department of History for their continued support of my work over the years.

· 1 ·

Postwar Adjustments

World War II changed America. It revitalized the nation's economy; it altered its social structure; it ended the nation's age-old isolationism; and it thrust the United States onto the world stage as a superpower. Americans seemed to expect the change. They knew instinctively that they were entering a new era that would be different from the years before the war. At the same time, they yearned for a world without the danger and personal sacrifices of war and without the struggles and uncertainties of economic depression. But the return to normalcy was difficult, wracked with labor troubles, runaway inflation, shortages, political uncertainties, and the growing specter of communism at home and abroad.

It should not be surprising that when the war ended the American people had tremendous confidence in the future—in their own futures and that of their nation. Most thought the powerful wartime economy would be retooled and redirected toward consumer needs, that the new economy would provide for everyone, maintain full employment, and make the United States the richest nation in the world. Personal income continued to rise after the war, while inflation was low. Factory production increased, and the gap between rich and poor narrowed unlike any other time in the twentieth century. The birth rate rose rapidly; the death rate declined, health improved, and the median life expectancy increased by five years. Generally, all this translated into optimism, a better life, and a better standard of living for more Americans. It was a dynamic time.

In addition, the war, and the prosperity that followed it, brought on new ways of thinking, new ways of living, and a new attitude toward life and what life might bring. But those years also saw frustrations, fears, and anxiety as events began to unfold throughout the world. New enemies replaced old ones, and aggression, again, had to be dealt with through force. America was changing—more rapidly than most Americans could ever realize.

1

ENTER HARRY TRUMAN, THE
"LITTLE MAN FROM MISSOURI"

On February 20, 1945, Vice President Harry S Truman heard that Franklin Roosevelt was dead. Truman had been in office for only a few weeks, and he had met with the president only once or twice. The prospect of inheriting the weight of the nation from Roosevelt's broad shoulders frightened Truman. "I did not want to think about the possibility of his death as President," Truman wrote in his memoirs. When the rumors turned out not to be true, Truman breathed a sigh of relief. But less than two months later, on April 12, Roosevelt was dead, stricken by a massive brain hemorrhage in Warm Springs, Georgia—and Harry Truman was president of the United States. "Maybe it will come out alright," the new president wrote his mother a few days later.

Franklin D. Roosevelt ("FDR") was a symbol for an age, and on April 12, 1945, that age came to an end. He had carried the nation through two of its greatest crises, the Great Depression and World War II. He had served in the White House for over twelve years: more, by far, than any other president; for many Americans he was the only president they had ever known. At the time of his death, he was as much a world leader as he was a leader of the American people. Roosevelt did not live to see the war's end, but events in Europe and the Pacific were about to reach their climax, and all the goals and aims for which the Allied armies had fought and died were about to be realized in total victory.

But for Harry Truman, on that fateful day in April 1945, the problems seemed to outweigh the prospects. Could the American economy absorb ten million war workers and another twelve million soldiers returning from war? There was great concern that the nation's economy had only briefly flourished because of wartime demands and production, and that the end of the war would bring on a resumption of the Great Depression. Or would the opposite occur? Prominent economists predicted runaway inflation as Americans spent their wartime savings on consumer goods, goods that had been denied them during the war. How, then, would organized labor react to the rising cost of living in an inflationary economy? World affairs seemed even more tenuous. The war had to be brought to a successful conclusion, most likely as a result of a costly invasion of Japan. After the war, how should the Soviets be dealt with in a new world order that was bound to emerge from the ashes? All of this hit Truman hard in April 1945. "I felt like the moon, the stars, and all the planets had fallen on me," he told friends.

Americans also were hit hard by the change in Washington. Roosevelt was urbane and witty, charming and inspiring. Truman was often described as ordinary, a "wooden" speaker, "the little man from Missouri." He had risen from the ranks of the small-time politicians, and had ridden the Kansas City Pendergast political machine into the U.S. Senate. There he had made a name for himself as one of only a few Southern Democrats to stand by Roosevelt and the New Deal through the late 1930s and early 1940s.

Truman had begun his life on the frontiers of western Missouri, where opportunities were few and prospects were bleak. Unlike FDR, who had, by all accounts, led a charmed life, there was for Truman no prominent family name, no family wealth, no Harvard education. He served his country in World War I, and then afterward failed twice at private business before going into politics. At the 1944 Democratic Party convention, when southerners and big-city bosses threatened to revolt unless Vice President Henry Wallace was replaced, Roosevelt relented and accepted Truman on the ticket. The two men had never met.

The war in Europe seemed to end quickly. Following Germany's last gasp at the Battle of the Bulge in late 1944 and early 1945, the Nazi war machine collapsed under the barrage of American and British troops advancing from the west and Soviet armies pinching the Germans from the east. Hitler committed suicide in his bunker on April 30 as Russian soldiers crashed through Berlin.

In the Pacific, the end also seemed near, but many analysts feared that Japan might never surrender, forcing a full-scale (and horribly costly) invasion of the Japanese home islands. In February 1945, American troops took the Japanese-held island of Iwo Jima at great cost, and then attacked Okinawa in April—just four hundred miles from the Japanese mainland. The three-month battle for Okinawa was devastating and seemed to show what the United States might expect if it became necessary to invade Japan. The Japanese threw more than fifteen hundred kamikaze planes at the American fleet, killing nearly five thousand sailors. On the island, American troops suffered a 35 percent casualty rate, the highest of any battle in the war. Seven thousand Americans were killed in the island fighting, and forty thousand soldiers and sailors were wounded. Perhaps the most frightening statistics came from the Japanese side: some 110,000 Japanese died in the fighting.

U.S. control of islands close to Japan allowed for regular and devastating bombing campaigns, made all the more ferocious by the nearly complete destruction of the Japanese air force and its ability to defend itself against bombing attacks. In March 1945, General Curtis LeMay led three hundred American B-29s in a massive firebomb raid of Tokyo, which killed over one hundred thousand people and destroyed much of the city. In the following months, B-29s pounded Japan's cities at will.

Truman came to office just as these monumental events in Europe and Asia were unfolding. Generally uninformed on most issues, he stood back and allowed predetermined decisions to be carried out. His first major wartime decision concerned the use of the atomic bomb. Truman was told about the bomb for the first time just after he took the oath of office on April 12. Then in July, when he was told that the bomb had been successfully tested, he was decisive; he did not hesitate to order the bomb dropped on Japan. He later wrote that he never lost a wink of sleep over the decision. As Truman saw it, the bomb had been devised by his predecessor as a weapon of war for use against the enemy. Several million dollars and thousands of man-hours had been spent in its development and production, and, perhaps most importantly, it would end the war quickly and save the lives of American soldiers. There were those who argued against using the bomb. Several scientists who helped develop it argued that an exhibition of the bomb's power would convince the Japanese to surrender. But Truman held firm to his decision, and on August 6, 1945, a B-29 christened the *Enola Gay* (after the pilot's mother) dropped an atomic bomb over the Japanese industrial city of Hiroshima, killing close to one hundred thousand people, most instantly. Thousands more died in the next days, months, and years from the effects of radiation poisoning. Three days later, a second bomb was dropped on the southern city of Nagasaki, killing almost forty thousand. On August 14, the Japanese asked for peace. The war ended officially on September 2 with the signing of surrender documents on the USS *Missouri* in Tokyo Harbor. The war was over.

The new president believed his place was to fulfill Roosevelt's term in office, to achieve FDR's goals as best he could. To that end, Truman sought to extend the tentacles of the New Deal, and in doing so he carried the liberalism of the New Deal into the postwar age. On September 6, he announced his twenty-one-point program to expand many of the New Deal programs. He called for a full employment bill, an increased minimum wage, national housing legislation, an extension of Social Security, a new public works program, and the establishment of a Fair Employment Practices Commission. To this he added a request for an atomic energy control board, federal aid to education, and national health insurance. It was a broad, aggressive program, and a significant extension of the New Deal. However, only two of Truman's twenty-one proposals passed through Congress within the next two years, in part because Congress was becoming more and more conservative, and in part because the president was willing to compromise his domestic reform package in exchange for his foreign policy initiatives, which were perceived as more important. Conservatives in Congress (from both sides of the aisle) also argued that the nation no longer needed Truman's New Deal–style programs, that the economic difficulties of the Great Depression had passed, and that there were new problems that related more to the proper distribution of abundance than to any need to rev up the economy.

THE POSTWAR ECONOMY AND ITS IMPACT

The war revived the American economy, pulling the nation out of the clutches of the Depression and beginning an era of personal affluence that stretched well into the 1970s. At the end of the war, Americans enjoyed the highest standard of living of any of the world's major nations. Only 7 percent of the world's population lived in the United States, but the nation generated a full 40 percent of the world's income. Real personal income more than doubled during the war years, and because of wartime jobs, income was distributed more evenly after the war than anytime before or since. Everyone, it seemed, had come out of the war with money in their pockets and hopes for the future.

The nation's population at the end of the war was about 140 million, not much different from the prewar years. But in the immediate postwar period, the population began making the major shifts that would define the nation's demographics through the rest of the twentieth century. Perhaps the most significant was that a great mass of Americans flowed out of the rural areas and into the nation's cities, completing a trend that had been ongoing for several decades. Not unlike the early years of the twentieth century, Americans left the farms in droves for the good-paying factory jobs in the upper Midwest, mostly in cities where the war industries had thrived during the war years. Part of this had to do with the advent of new farm machinery that allowed for greater efficiency on the farm—fewer workers could cultivate more land. The excess labor made its way into the northern factories. One great exodus took place in the Deep South, where the invention of the mechanical cotton-picking machine meant an end to the need for the labor that had picked the South's cotton by hand for two centuries. That manual labor, much of it African American, abandoned the South (and its racist institutions) for better jobs in the North and West.

Much of this big population shift was westward—particularly to California. During the war, the population of California increased by 40 percent. Most of those immigrants had followed the rumors of opportunity and wartime jobs associated with the Pacific theater. California was, of course, the point of departure for most American soldiers headed west into the Pacific, and the point of return following the war. Not surprisingly, many stayed in California and the population and the economy there boomed. The population of the state jumped from about seven million before the war to nearly eleven million in the early postwar years. California continued to be a symbol of opportunity for Americans.

The California population boom, as significant as it was, was only the focus of a larger shift to the Sunbelt. States like Florida and Texas, and later Arizona, also surged with population growth. Miami, Tampa, Houston, and Dallas were on the road to rivaling the nation's biggest cities of the Midwest and Northeast. In the early 1960s, when air conditioning became practical, these areas would grow even faster.

These migration patterns changed the very character of the nation. Before the war, wealth in America was distributed unevenly; generally it was held in the hands of a few. America was also a rural nation of farmers, with a few industrial outlets and identifiable urban areas in the Northeast and upper Midwest. The rural life was perceived as something of an American ideal, a lifestyle that built the American character and made it distinct from the rest of the world. But by about 1960 much of that Jeffersonian agrarian ideal was erased from the American psyche. By then, only about 8 percent of Americans worked on farms, down approximately 63 percent from a century earlier. Farming was still hard work, and American farmers fed the world, but the farm life was no longer the cornerstone of the American character.

These population shifts also reshaped American politics. By the late 1940s it had become apparent that voters in northern cities were voting primarily Democratic and outvoting the predominantly Republican rural areas. In response, the Republicans, by the early 1960s, began to abandon their old coalition of Northeastern moderates and Midwestern conservatives for a new coalition that abandoned the moderates and pulled together conservatives from the Midwest and the far West. The shift made for a more conservative Republican Party while turning the Democrats into a party of ethnic groups, organized labor, and voters from the urban-industrial Northeast and upper Midwest. In the process, the white South made a long, slow shift from solidly Democratic to nearly solidly Republican, and African Americans left the party of Lincoln for the Democrats. All this would take time—in fact, many of these patterns would not be apparent until well into the 1960s—but the process got its start in the immediate postwar years with the big wartime and postwar population shifts.

THE AMERICAN FAMILY

One major aspect of the era was the rising birthrate. It first became apparent in 1942 and 1943 as a result of what were called "good-bye babies," those babies conceived just before the father was shipped off to war. But it was when the war ended, and the soldiers returned from duty, that the birthrate really soared. The result was the baby boom. Between 1945 and 1960 the population of the nation grew by almost forty million, an increase of nearly 30 percent, the largest in the nation's history. In the 1950s alone the population grew by twenty-nine million—something like twenty-five births per one thousand people. The growth truly changed the face of the nation.

This unpredictable population increase confronted a housing industry that had been dormant for nearly twenty years. The result was a postwar housing shortage that plagued the entire nation. By 1947, six million families were living with friends or relatives and another half million were living in Quonset huts or other temporary housing provided by the government. One part of the answer was to make money available to these new families (mostly ex-servicemen) to buy new homes. That was provided by the GI Bill of Rights (officially the Servicemen's Readjustment Act) in 1944, through which the federal government guaranteed home mortgages to veterans. The second part of the answer was to build the houses, and guaranteed federal loans made that easy. The result was an unprecedented building boom. Single-family housing starts increased from 114,000 in 1944 to almost 1 million just two years later. By 1950 housing starts

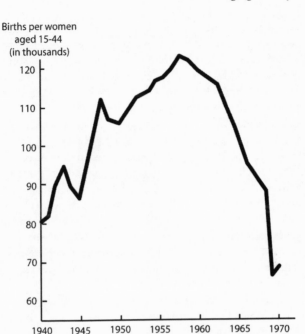

Births per women aged 15-44 (in thousands)

Birthrate, 1940–1970. *Source*: Compiled from U.S. Bureau of the Census, *Historical Statistics of the United States, Colonial Times to 1970*, Bicentennial Edition, Washington, DC, 1975

were up to 1.7 million per year. The growth was a spectacular tribute to American capitalism and the forces of the free market.

As Americans moved from the immediate postwar era into the fifties and the sixties, this baby boom generation would transform the nation, the family, and the American way of life.

THE CHANGING PLACE OF WOMEN

The role of women in American society had been changing since the turn of the twentieth century; that process was accelerated during World War II and into the immediate postwar period. When the war broke out, six million women entered the workforce. By the war's end, over nineteen million women were employed in wage-earning jobs, constituting over 35 percent of the national workforce. In addition, about 350,000 women joined the armed forces as nurses and as WACS (Army), WAVES (Navy), and SPARS (Coast Guard)—newly created military auxiliary units. Wartime propaganda encouraged women to show their patriotism by taking jobs in defense plants. These jobs paid much better than the low-wage jobs traditionally assigned to women, like restaurant workers, laundry workers, and domestic housekeepers. Just before the war, only thirty-six women worked in the nation's shipyards; by war's end, close to 160,000 were employed in all aspects of ship construction. By 1944, 75 percent of these female war workers were married and most had children.

The most enduring symbol representing these women was "Rosie the Riveter," a fictional defense plant worker created by government public relations experts. The hand-drawn Rosie appeared on countless magazine covers throughout the war. Perhaps the most famous Rosie was painted by Norman Rockwell. She appeared on the May 29, 1943, issue of the *Saturday Evening Post*, complete with blue jeans, a rivet gun, big muscles, and welding goggles on her forehead.*

Despite all the patriotic hoopla, these jobs provided little for women in the forms of benefits, pensions, labor contracts, or job security—and certainly not equal pay for equal work. Factory owners and government officials expected women to put in their time only for the duration of the war. Women in the workplace were perceived as a temporary situation for the good of the war effort, and when the war ended the women were expected to give up their jobs and take their place again in the home. The women, however, expected more. Near the end of the war, the Department of Labor recorded that 75 percent of the women working in industry intended to continue working after the war, and of that number, 86 percent expected to stay in their wartime occupations. But they would be disappointed. When the soldiers came home, the women were forced out of their high-paying defense jobs, mostly as a result of pressure to give up those jobs to the men returning from the war—again, they were asked to do their patriotic duty for the good of the nation. Married women particularly were shamed into giving up their jobs and returning to their traditional roles. Within the first year after the war, women's participation in the workforce dropped from 37 to 31 percent.

The baby boom, coupled with a lack of any sort of adequate daycare, added to the exodus of women from the factory back to the home. By 1950, society had begun to romanticize—even celebrate—domesticity, motherhood, and the traditional concepts of the woman in the home, while rejecting the wartime notions of independence, strength, and American women in the workplace. In 1963, Betty Friedan would chronicle much of this in her pathbreaking *Feminine Mystique*. Friedan and her work are discussed more fully in chapter 7.

This trend from the factory to the kitchen, although real, should not be exaggerated. In fact, the number of women in the workplace in 1950 was about eighteen million, only one million or so below the number of women in the

---

*Rockwell borrowed Rosie's pose from one created by Michelangelo of the prophet Isaiah from the ceiling fresco of the Sistine Chapel. Although the reference may have been lost on most Americans, Isaiah warned (740s B.C.) about the dangers his nation of Judah faced from the growing military powers of Assyria and Egypt.

workplace in 1945 and at least five million above the prewar number. It is probably more significant that Rosie the Riveter was forced to turn in her rivet gun for a typewriter or a waitress's apron. In the new postwar economy, working-class families often needed two incomes to make ends meet, while the demand for female office workers and low-paying service jobs grew rapidly. Women in the lower classes continued on the job, but with less fanfare, less money, and less prestige than the women who placed their lives on hold during the war and went to work for the national effort.

TRUMAN, THE ECONOMY, AND ORGANIZED LABOR

Truman entered the White House with a strong 87 percent approval rating owing, most likely, to a combination of anonymity and expectations. The nation seemed to sympathize with his difficult job, while giving him their support at that critical moment in the nation's history. But within eighteen months, Truman's numbers had crashed to a paltry 32 percent—mostly because of his poor handling of the national economy. Truman wanted to expand the New Deal and continue on with FDR's vision, but the economic situation after the war was considerably different than during the Depression years before the war. It was, in fact, really the opposite. The postwar economy boomed. All those fears of a postwar depression evaporated almost immediately as the nation's war industries were switched over to peacetime production to meet the growing demand of consumer goods. Demobilization of the armed forces was rapid, with 8.5 million soldiers (out of 12 million) discharged and sent home within a year. Consumer income was up; production was up. Truman's worries had little to do with the New Deal–era problems of widespread poverty and the burdens of inequality. The concern now was how to distribute the new abundance more equally.

In an attempt to maintain a grip on the economy, Truman decided to carry the wartime wage and price controls into the postwar period, a policy that was immediately unpopular. Not surprisingly, Americans saw the end of the war as a release from all the hardships and sacrifices of the war. Truman, it seemed, wanted to drag that agony on. Workers had socked away 25 percent of their take-home pay in the last two years of the war, and by the summer of 1945 the nation's liquid assets totaled about $140 million—three times the national income in 1932. The nation was an economic explosion waiting to happen. Truman's price controls led to a rapidly growing black market, a flouting of the price-control laws that contributed to the rapid drop in Truman's popularity. Finally, in June 1946 Congress was forced to act. By emasculating the Office of Price Administration (the government agency responsible for implementing and enforcing the controls), Congress lifted nearly all restrictions. The result was an immediate jump in prices, even hyperinflation in some sectors of the economy. The administration feared the worst, but the economy was basically sound. The large infusion of cash spurred business and industry to convert rapidly to peacetime production in order to meet the demand, and production soared.

All of this economic expansion left labor hemmed in, out of the economic loop. During the war, unions had agreed not to strike and not to make demands, all for the war effort. It seemed like a good trade in exchange for good jobs, lots of overtime pay, and even job security. But when the war ended and prices rose, labor appeared ready, willing, and certainly able to shut down the nation's economy in order to achieve economic parity with the rest of the nation's workforce. In fact, they had a good argument. In 1941 the average American laborer's real wage was $28.12 per week. That had risen to $36.72 at the end of the war. But by the fall of 1946, inflation and price hikes (along with a drastic reduction in overtime pay) had pulled union workers' real wages back to the 1941 level. The pie was expanding, but labor's share had remained the same. Industry, however, refused to raise wages. They complained of being stuck with the cost of retooling—from wartime to peacetime production. At the same time, industry was forced to carry much of the burden of Truman's price controls. To become locked in long-term labor contracts in such uncertain economic times was inconceivable to industry leaders. Neither side would budge. Strike was in the air.

The first wave of strikes hit in the spring and summer of 1945, almost immediately after the war in Europe ended. The nation experienced forty-six hundred work stoppages involving five million workers. Then, when the war ended in the Pacific, the bottom seemed to drop out. In September, forty-three thousand oil-refinery workers went out on strike, cutting off one-third of the nation's oil supply. In late November, the United Auto Workers struck General Motors, idling nearly 325,000 workers. Then in January 1946, 750,000 steelworkers walked out; 200,000 electrical workers and another 200,000 packinghouse workers followed.

The fate of the postwar economy (and the nation's prosperity) seemed in jeopardy, and the nation looked to the White House for answers. Truman followed a timeworn method of dealing with labor issues by setting up a blue ribbon committee of labor leaders and industry management to recommend answers. They had none. On April 1, 1946, John L. Lewis, the bushy-browed head of the United Mine Workers, ordered 340,000 soft-coal miners out on strike, which threatened to grind the nation's industry to a halt. Truman would have to act. The big showdown between the president and the unions came in May, when the nation's railroad engineers and trainmen struck, threatening to shut down the nation's commerce. Truman went to Congress, and in a fiery speech asked for the authority to draft railroad workers into the army to keep the trains running. It was a bold move, and probably unconstitutional. But just as Truman spoke, the unions succumbed to the threat and settled the strike. It was a big victory for the president; however, as he would soon see, he had lost the support of organized labor, an integral part of the Democratic Party coalition.

By mid-1946, with the midterm elections approaching in November, Truman's ratings had slipped to just above 30 percent. His obvious mishandling of reconversion (a word used at the time to describe the immediate postwar economy), along with the debilitating strikes (which most Americans either blamed on him or considered him unable to settle), cut deeply into his popularity. Added to that, labor's rank and file had come to see him as anti-union. Even his own party had lost confidence in his ability to win votes. The Democratic National Committee decided in the 1946 campaign that it was better to buy radio time and broadcast some of FDR's old speeches than to send Truman out to campaign for congressional candidates.

The inability of Truman to keep control of the party faithful became all too apparent when, in the 1946 elections, the Democrats lost control of Congress for the first time since 1930. Truman could count himself as the most unpopular president in the twentieth century—and now he had to face a hostile Congress. Democratic Senator J. William Fulbright of Arkansas suggested that Truman was in such an untenable position that he should simply name a Republican Secretary of State (then successor to the presidency in the absence of a vice president) and step aside. From then on, Truman called Fulbright "Senator Halfbright." Truman, however, would hang on for the coming political wars.

ORIGINS OF THE MODERN CIVIL RIGHTS MOVEMENT

World War II unleashed a whole series of social, political, and economic changes in America. Black Americans, after 1945, would stand at the center of many of those changes. Just fifty years before, during the last decade of the nineteenth century, African Americans had little hope for their future. Segregated from the white population and disenfranchised by law, they had been forced into a kind of peonage that kept them powerless—just where white southerners wanted them. There was only one method of protest available: migrate, leave the South for the North where opportunities might be better. The result was the Great Migration, an event that made possible the modern civil rights movement.

The migration of blacks north began to show up in census and statistical reports as early as the 1890s. Over the next twenty years, 200,000 African Americans protested the racism and deplorable situation in the South by migrating to urban centers in the North. In the next decade, from about 1910 to 1920, another half million made the trip, most hoping to get jobs in the war industries. In the 1920s, 750,000 followed those who had gone before. The migrations slowed during the Great Depression, but picked up again as war clouds formed at the end of the 1930s. During the war, as many as one million African Americans moved out of the South in search of wartime jobs. Many found opportunities in the war industry plants in California, where they stayed on after the war.

In the 1930s and 1940s, large numbers of those African Americans who left

The Great Migration of African Americans from the South to the North in the early twentieth century.

the South were pushed out by the new mechanization of agriculture. Owners of large farms could make use of tractors, mechanized cotton-pickers, and other machinery to farm large amounts of land. They no longer needed the same number of tenant farmers or sharecroppers to farm small sections of the land and then share the crop with the owner. These sharecroppers and tenant farmers, both black and white, were pushed off land that their families may have farmed for generations, but did not own. During the twenty years following the beginning of the Great Depression, perhaps as many poor whites moved north and west as did poor blacks—and for mostly the same reasons.

This Great Migration of African Americans out of the South had a huge impact on the nation on several levels, but it was in the political arena that the new black populations in the North had the greatest significance. These African Americans could vote, and for the first time since Reconstruction they could cast their votes in numbers significant enough to influence elections. The jobs these migrants wanted were most often in the large industrial cities of the Upper Midwest, Northeast, and far West. These cities were almost always located in states with the largest electoral votes. Between 1940 and 1947, the number of African Americans in New York City grew from 100,000 to over 800,000; in Chicago from 300,000 to 420,000; in Philadelphia from 300,000 to 415,000; and in Los Angeles from 100,000 to 210,000. By the end of the war African American voters in these cities held the balance of power in close elections that could deliver the big state electoral votes in New York, Illinois, Pennsylvania, and California. The Great Migration, and the political power it brought, would be a significant factor in the advancement of African Americans in the postwar period.

The end of the war brought tremendous optimism to the African American community; the booming postwar economy promised to raise up African Americans along with the rest of the nation—if only relatively. Median black income rose from $1,614 in 1947 to $2,338 in just five years; and as a percentage of white income, black earnings increased from 41 percent in 1947 to 57 percent in 1952. When the war ended, one million more African Americans had civilian jobs than before Pearl Harbor, and those working in government service jobs had jumped from 60,000 to 300,000.

African Americans had other reasons to be optimistic about the future. Over 500,000 blacks had served in the war. The armed services had remained segregated, and black soldiers continued to be led by white (often southern) officers, but in almost all cases black soldiers served with distinction. Perhaps the most noteworthy were the Tuskegee Airmen, who were praised for their action in North Africa and Italy. In the European theater black and white units were often integrated in times of emergency with no discernable concern from either blacks or whites, leading a number of generals to argue that segregation no longer served any real purpose in the armed forces.

At the same time, racism was quickly losing whatever intellectual respectability it once had. At the nation's universities new attitudes toward race began to emerge after the war, particularly in sociology courses where the social problem of America's race relations became a popular theme. Gunnar Myrdal's *An American Dilemma: The Negro Problem and Modern Democracy*, published in 1944, was one of several important works that set out to destroy the turn-of-the-century pseudoscientific beliefs that had been the underpinning of white supremacy. By the mid-1950s, many Americans had come to see the old-time racism as little more than narrow-minded bigotry.

On the world stage, Hitler's racism had turned into a European holocaust. Japan's own racism against its Asian neighbors, particularly the Chinese, was no less brutal than the Nazi death camps. In addition, the growing Cold War pitted the United States and the Soviet Union in competition for the support of the mostly nonwhite Third World, while the Soviets ran an effective propaganda campaign to show the dark-skinned peoples of Africa, Asia, and South America the hypocrisy of American racism. It quickly became clear after the war that if the United States was to be a leader in a multinational world, its racial policies in the South would have to change.

Thus the stage was set. African Americans had gained considerably from the expansion in jobs and income, from service in the military, and from the political power derived from the northern migrations. All this came together in the first few years after the end of the war. For the first time in the nation's history, black Americans had all the tools necessary to launch an aggressive attack on racism. There was tremendous optimism and hope.

Just as the modern civil rights movement began to take its first steps, however, it was thrown back by the Red Scare, the fear of communism that permeated the nation in the late 1940s and early 1950s. The civil rights movement was hardly radical in these years, but unfortunately for blacks it was tagged as radical, with radical goals and radical leadership. This accusation was further fueled by white supremacists, who were prepared to grasp any opportunity to maintain the South's social and political structure. They were able to argue, with some effect, that anyone who championed racial equality or the integration of the races was either a Communist or somehow soft on communism. They also argued that there was a growing Communist movement inside the black community. These tactics kept the civil rights movement at bay through the first half of the 1950s. Civil rights leaders backed away from direct action as a method of protest, fearing the mark of radicalism.

The response was for the movement to adjust its tactics. The promise of direct action was replaced by the old standbys of litigation, legislation, and lobbying—the hallmarks of the NAACP (National Association for the Advancement of Colored People). The association spent the first decade after the war concentrating on fair housing, fair employment practices, voting rights, equal facilities for blacks, and the passage of federal anti-lynching and anti–poll tax laws. Most of this work took place in the nation's courtrooms and state capitols and in the halls of Congress, and was generally invisible to the African American community. But little by little the NAACP chipped away at the walls of segregation and discrimination. For many black Americans the work of the NAACP was slow and inadequate, and delivered only symbolic victories. But by 1945 the NAACP was on the road to a major breakthrough that would change the movement—and America—forever.

In the meantime, there was a series of subtle victories for the civil rights movement. In sports, segregation was voluntary and generally smooth. In 1946 Kenny Washington and Woody Strode signed with the Los Angeles Rams football team. A year later, in possibly the most important civil rights advancement outside of politics and the courts, Jackie Robinson joined the Brooklyn Dodgers and brought an end to segregation in baseball. Robinson's great play on the field, and his strong character off, made him a source of pride for the black community, a true symbol of what the future of race relations in America might become.

At just the same moment, a symbol of southern racism was crumbling. In the 1946 midterm elections, Theodore Bilbo was returned to his Senate seat from Mississippi. A staunch segregationist, Bilbo had won the election by intimidating black voters with such statements as "You and I know what's the best way to keep a nigger from voting. You do it the night before the election. I don't have to tell you more than that." A bipartisan Senate committee refused to allow Bilbo to take his seat until they could review the election. While awaiting the Senate's decision, Bilbo died in August 1947. As Robinson had come to symbolize the hopes and future of African Americans, Bilbo symbolized the racism of the past, still deeply imbedded in southern society, but clearly about to be challenged.

TRUMAN, THE EIGHTIETH CONGRESS, AND THE ELECTION OF 1948

As Truman's poll numbers plummeted, the Democrats split, and then split again. Not surprisingly, the Republicans approached the 1948 presidential election with high expectations. They had come to see their victories in the 1946 congressional elections as a national mandate to dump the New Deal programs and change the direction of the nation. The Republicans in the Eightieth Congress had won their majority in both houses with an effective national campaign that revolved around the phrase "Had enough?" Apparently the answer had been a resounding "yes," although it was not quite clear if voters had had enough of Truman or the New Deal, or both. The Republicans also campaigned hard (really for the first time with significant success) on the topic of anti-communism, insisting that the Washington bureaucracy was awash with Communists.

The Republicans coalesced around Ohio senator Robert Taft, "Mr. Republican," the dour prewar isolationist, the son of a president. Taft was eying his party's nomination, but his lack of public appeal was nearly legendary. Most Americans saw Taft as both dull and arrogant. Those Republicans who opposed him touted a motto that dogged Taft through at least three attempts to win his party's nomination: "Taft can't win." They were probably right.

The relationship between Truman and the Eightieth Congress is legendary in American politics. On domestic matters it was a gloves-off affair, with the president vetoing seventy-five bills (five vetoes were overridden) in the two sessions and with very little accomplished. On foreign affairs, however, the two parties worked together to establish a Cold War foreign policy that endured for over forty years. In the final analysis, the record of the Eightieth Congress benefited Truman more than the Republicans, helping the president ride a surge of popular support to victory in the 1948 election. Congress became Truman's foil. By introducing liberal legislation that he certainly knew the conservative Eightieth Congress would not pass, Truman was able to portray Congress as the political arm of big business, insensitive to the needs of the average American and unwilling to act on much-needed domestic reforms. Truman emerged as the defender of the common man, a fighter against oppression, and the real successor to the New Deal—a program the American people were not prepared to abandon. On foreign affairs, Truman stood up to the Soviets (generally a popular stance with the American people), giving him the image of a strong world leader.

The Republicans seemed to want to jump into the trap. They killed Truman's liberal programs, and then passed a number of bills designed to dismantle the New Deal and aid the wealthy. A Republican bill to cut taxes in the upper income brackets was passed over Truman's veto; and the Republicans excluded several groups from Social Security benefits, overriding two presidential vetoes to get the job done. They turned down Truman's request to expand public power projects in favor of private power interests, and they killed a bill supported by Truman to provide aid to education. A bill to increase the minimum wage failed without so much as a hearing, and a bill to provide housing for veterans met a premature death. Southern Democrats, seeing no real need to follow Truman down to defeat in 1948, supported the Republicans in exchange for their support in killing civil rights legislation. This Republican–Southern Democrat anti-administration coalition was insurmountable, but it allowed Truman to raise his image with the American people as their representative in Washington—in hand-to-hand combat against the forces of big business and privilege.

Perhaps Truman's biggest "victory" over the Eightieth Congress was his veto of the Taft-Hartley Act, a bill designed to curb the excesses of labor and to get some control over the strikes that were sweeping the country. Passed in 1947, Taft-Hartley outlawed closed shops, allowed for court injunctions to end strikes, and banned industry-wide bargaining. It was not harsh, particularly in light of the recent wave of strikes. But the unions called it the "slave labor bill," and it gave Truman the opportunity to get back into labor's good graces. He vetoed the bill, and Congress promptly overrode the veto. Not only did Truman get a law that allowed him to keep the unions under some control, he won back labor's support in the process.

As the 1948 campaign approached, Truman's chief advisors began to counsel the president to shift to the political left and rebuild the old New Deal coalition of the 1930s. The American people, they argued, had not turned their backs on most New Deal programs, and they would continue to support federal aid and intervention into various sectors of the economy. They advised Truman to veto Taft-Hartley, attack the Eightieth Congress, support civil rights, and promote a national health insurance program, fair employment legislation, and federal housing. They identified the various groups from the old New Deal coalition and suggested to Truman how each might be satisfied in order to win their support and votes.

Perhaps Truman's most significant concession was in the area of civil rights in an effort to win black votes. By 1948 a powerful coalition had emerged in the nation's largest cities that included African Americans, liberals, and organized labor, and it was clear that the president would need that support to win in November. This group called for liberal reform, and that included some movement on civil rights. In the late 1940s, however, support for civil rights meant a loss of support from the white South. The question for Truman was, would the South hold if he made concessions to blacks? That is, could he take both the northern big cities and the Solid South? His advisors told him he could, that the South would continue to vote Democratic. Even if a number of southern states deserted him (for the Republicans or possibly a third-party candidate) it would be a good trade if he won the large and closely contested electoral states in the North while losing a few electoral votes in the rural South.

At the same time, several unusually heinous lynchings in the South (some of ex-servicemen) were reported graphically in the national press and brought an outcry from northern whites. In response, Truman created the President's Committee on Civil Rights to look into the nation's race relations. The PCCR deliberated for a year, finally publishing its report, *To Secure These Rights*, in the fall of 1947. This report blamed segregation for the problems that African Americans faced, and then placed the responsibility for solving those problems squarely on the shoulders of the federal government. It called for an end to the poll tax, an end to Jim Crow laws, and the immediate desegregation of the armed forces. It argued for federal legislation to end lynching, and it insisted that federal aid be withheld from both public and private agencies that practiced segregation or discrimination. By February 1948, over one million copies of *To Secure These Rights* had been distributed by the U.S. Government Printing Office, by private printers, and by various interest groups. Truman could not ignore it.

The president responded to the report with a message to Congress in early February 1948 that incorporated many of the recommendations from *To Secure These Rights*. He called for a civil rights division in the Justice Department, the enactment of a federal anti-lynching law, and protection for the right to vote. He also asked for a permanent Fair Employment Practices Commission (FEPC), and he proposed a law that would end discrimination in all interstate transportation services. The Republican Eightieth Congress accommodated Truman by killing all of these proposals and initiatives. African Americans would vote Democratic in November.

All of this set off a shock wave in the South. White southerners saw such an appeal for African American votes to be the beginning of an infringement on their political power, and ultimately an attack on the southern way of life. It also seemed clear that the northern coalition of labor and liberals was about to eclipse the South's place in the Democratic Party. In response, a movement emerged in the South to force the Democrats at their convention to repudiate civil rights and embrace states' rights, which of course included the right to segregate the races. Their plan was simple: If Truman and the Democrats refused to denounce civil rights, southern leaders would leave the party and select alternative candidates for president and vice president. The Democratic Party, they determined, was simply not big enough for white southerners and black liberals.

While the right wing of the Democrats prepared to bolt, the left wing began to coalesce around Henry Wallace, Roosevelt's vice president in his third term. Wallace had agreed to serve as Truman's secretary of commerce, but the two men had conflicted over the issue of U.S.-Soviet relations, and Wallace was asked to leave the administration in the fall of 1946. He immediately became the darling of those liberals who believed that Truman was too conservative. Through 1947

Wallace attained a great deal of popularity, and it seemed possible that he might make a run for the Democratic nomination. But in December 1947 he announced that he would accept the nomination from the Progressive Party. By then, however, Truman was beginning to shore up his left by supporting civil rights and giving labor what they wanted. Wallace was already on a downhill slide into the abyss of American third-party movements. He also accepted support from American Communists (insisting that he would not exclude any group from his coalition of supporters), and he called for rapprochement with the Soviet Union while defending Soviet aggressions in Europe. To many Americans, this sounded like Soviet sympathy just as U.S.-Soviet relations were worsening.

Truman won his party's nomination on the first ballot with no real competition. Democratic liberals forced a strong civil rights plank into the party's platform and the Mississippi delegation, along with about half the delegates from Alabama, left the convention in protest. On July 17, delegates from throughout the South met in Birmingham, Alabama, to form the States' Rights Party, quickly dubbed the Dixiecrats by the press. They nominated South Carolina governor Strom Thurmond for president, and Mississippi governor Fielding Wright for vice president.

The Republicans turned for a second time to New York governor Thomas Dewey. They met at their convention amidst an air of victory; they were certain that they were nominating the next president. Dewey was young, only forty-six. His greatest appeal was among progressive urban voters, particularly in the Northeast. He was, however, not particularly appealing, usually described as standoffish, priggish, and often openly self-important. "You have to know Dewey really well to dislike him," one Republican Party leader said.

Dewey seemed well on the road to victory against the fragmented Democrats, but his overconfidence led him to steer clear of the central issues, and to avoid Truman altogether. His advisors told him just to keep his name before the public as much as possible and the White House would be his. Dewey did nothing more.

Truman attacked the 1948 campaign with a fervor that has become legendary. He traversed the nation on his celebrated whistle-stop tour, traveling 22,000 miles and delivering 271 speeches that were heard by an estimated twelve million Americans across the country. His message was simple: The average American was being hurt by the "do-nothing" Eightieth Congress that had caused high prices, high rents, and a housing shortage. The Republicans had hurt labor, and cut programs that benefited the working classes and farmers. He spoke of "Wall Street reactionaries," and the "economic tapeworm of big business." The people listened. As he left on one of his train trips, Truman's vice presidential candidate, Alben Barkley of Kentucky, yelled at the president as his car pulled away from Union Station in Washington: "Go out there and mow 'em down, Harry." "I'll mow 'em down," Truman replied. "I'll give 'em hell." The exchange was overheard by reporters and made the evening papers. By the time Truman reached the West Coast, people in the crowds were yelling, "Give 'em hell, Harry!"

The polls were unanimous: Dewey would win. In September, pollster Elmo Roper announced that he would no longer poll the nation on the election because Dewey's victory was such a certainty that he refused to burden the country with useless data. Very few, it seemed, believed in Truman—besides Truman. The Democratic National Committee, so certain that Truman would lose, did not even reserve a room for a victory party. But Truman pulled together a convincing win. In the electoral vote, Truman's margin was 303 to 189. The popular vote was closer, 24.2 million to Dewey's 22 million. Thurmond raised 1.2 million votes and took 39 electoral votes in the South. Wallace was ineffectual. The next day, Truman told reporters "labor did it," but Truman lost most of the nation's biggest industrial states. It was the African American votes that made the difference in close voting in California, Illinois, and Ohio; and black voters may have kept Florida, Georgia, and Texas from going to the Dixiecrats. The farm vote in Ohio, Iowa, and Wisconsin helped turn those states over to Truman in close elections.

Truman won the center by purging the conservative white South and the ideological left. The third-party moves by Thurmond and Wallace helped Truman even more. Wallace (with his support from the Communists) allowed Truman to deflect charges from the Republicans of being soft on communism. From the right, the Dixiecrats continued to charge Truman with supporting civil rights. Truman did not deny the charge, and African Americans voted for him in droves. On election night, the Republican Party standard *Chicago Daily Tribune* wrote its well-known headline "Dewey Defeats Truman." A copy was placed on the president's breakfast table by an aide the next morning.

THE FAIR DEAL AND TRUMAN'S SECOND TERM

Truman was vindicated. He reached a high point in his popularity, and the new Eighty-First Congress had a Democratic majority. In his State of the Union address, Truman told the nation that "every segment of our population and every individual has a right to expect from our Government a fair deal." And with that, he gave his program a name, clearly intended as an extension of the New Deal. He called for an immediate increase in the minimum wage, an expansion of Social Security, national health insurance, federal aid to education, low-cost housing, and a repeal of the Taft-Hartley Act. To pay for it, Truman proposed a tax increase. He intended to put a liberal stamp on the next four years.

For several reasons, however, most of the Fair Deal never got past Congress. Although Democrats held a majority in both houses, conservative southerners continued to vote with Republicans on a number of issues in exchange for Republican opposition to civil rights measures. This alliance was successful. It generally

On the morning following Election Day, 1948, an aide (reportedly Clark Clifford) placed a copy of the *Chicago Daily Tribune* on President Truman's chair at breakfast. Truman spent most of the morning holding up the paper for photographers. The *Tribune* and its owner, "Colonel" Robert McCormick, had vehemently opposed Truman's candidacy. *Source*: Bettmann/CORBIS

suppressed Truman's Fair Deal programs and it killed all civil rights initiatives. At the same time, Truman often failed to give his Fair Deal bills the full weight of the presidency. His greatest successes had been in foreign policy, and he was always willing to sacrifice domestic legislation to further his foreign policy agenda. Consequently, several Fair Deal measures opposed by conservatives were allowed to die in order for Truman to receive Republican support for his foreign policy initiatives. But probably the most important reason that the Fair Deal measures did not pass is that the tone of the nation in 1949 was not liberal. The heady days of the New Deal had passed, and the American people were already enjoying much of the prosperity that would be associated with the 1950s. Truman simply may have been trying to push a liberal agenda when the prevailing winds were blowing from the right.

Truman's plan for federal aid to education died quickly, mostly over whether aid should be given to private schools. Southerners also opposed the bill because they assumed that federal aid would be followed by federal regulation, and that might threaten segregation in southern schools. The president's national health insurance plan was popular with the public, but the American Medical Association carried on a national campaign hyping the horrors of "socialized medicine," and Congress killed the bill. Even some of the Fair Deal's successes failed to achieve the administration's goals. Congress passed the president's request for a minimum wage, but it reduced the number of eligible recipients. In the president's most significant victory, the National Housing Act of 1949, Congress authorized the construction of over eight hundred thousand low-income housing units. But fifteen years later, fewer than half of those units had been built or even funded.

The Fair Deal was a failure within the boundaries of U.S. domestic politics in Truman's second term, but it did maintain much of the New Deal in place, and thus extend many of the New Deal programs into another era. The Fair Deal set the agenda for the reforms of the 1960s, particularly in civil rights, federal housing, Medicare, slum clearance, and federal aid to education. Soon the New Deal would become obsolete and unnecessary, when even the most sacred cows of the New Deal era would grow fat and wasteful. But in 1950, the American people were not yet ready to give up the New Deal. One of Truman's many legacies would be to extend Roosevelt's New Deal during a time when the capitalist economic order was expanding rapidly, while still maintaining an extensive social welfare safety net provided by the New Deal programs.

The conservative coalition in Congress also killed Truman's initiatives on civil rights. Legislation outlawing the poll tax, making lynching a federal crime, establishing a permanent Fair Employment Practices Commission (FEPC), and prohibiting segregation and discrimination in interstate transportation all met defeat. Truman, however, seemed determined to do something to fulfill his campaign promises to African Americans. His most significant act was to order the desegregation of the military. In 1950, an administration-appointed committee decreed that all branches of the service should be desegregated at once. The process was generally completed by the early 1950s.

To add to Truman's many problems, some illegal dealings cropped up in Washington, and the administration got stuck with the blame. In 1951 a scandal broke at the Bureau of Internal Revenue (BIR) that resulted in a series of resignations and eventually prosecutions. The public outcry was enormous; the nation's taxpayers were understandably sensitive to corruption in an agency so close to their personal interests. Truman responded by insisting that there really was no scandal, only a few unscrupulous characters who had betrayed the public trust. He was finally forced to put his attorney general, J. Howard McGrath, in charge of an investigation of the BIR. McGrath was perceived as a Truman political crony, and when McGrath stumbled in the investigation and Truman had to fire him, it turned the entire mess into a monumental embarrassment for the president.

Truman's second term seemed to sink into an abyss. Congress was killing his bills as quickly as they were introduced, the war in Korea had reached a stalemate, and there were charges of corruption in Washington that were being blamed on the administration. Perhaps most importantly, the nation was clearly moving to the right. A Gallup poll at the end of 1951 gave Truman the dismal approval rating of 23 percent. As the 1952 campaign approached, the Truman administration began to take on the stench of rotting from within.

CONCLUSION

In the immediate postwar years there was a feeling in America that the hardships had ended, the crusades were over. The United States could finally look to the future, get back to normal, and deal with all the problems that had been pushed aside for decades. America, it seemed, had all the resources and the will to effect its own change and, if necessary, the changes in the world. Hope for the future seemed to be on everyone's mind. The United States, however, had a number of problems, most of which were not yet apparent. When these problems finally emerged, this time of postwar exuberance would be seen as a time of innocence.

Reading: A. Philip Randolph

A. Philip Randolph did not quite fit the mold of the postwar civil rights leader. That movement had its origins in the southern churches, and was led mostly by southern church ministers like Martin Luther King Jr., Ralph Abernathy, and their followers. Randolph was, by most accounts, not a man who counted religion highly in his life: he was older than most of the postwar civil rights leaders, he came from a completely different background, and his objectives were always a bit different than the other leaders of the movement.

Randolph was, primarily, a labor leader. He had founded the Brotherhood of Sleeping Car Porters in 1925, and worked hard his entire life to strengthen that organization within the American Federation of Labor (AFL) and, later, in the Congress of Industrial Organizations (CIO). In 1937, Randolph successfully negotiated a contract with the Pullman Company and brought the Brotherhood of Sleeping Car Porters into the mainstream of the labor movement.

Through his entire life, Randolph was an avowed socialist, who saw the plight of the black man in America as a struggle for equality in the workplace. He founded the radical Harlem newspaper *The Messenger* (later *The Black Worker*), a well-known socialist publication targeting the nation's black working classes. In 1918, Randolph and Chandler Owen (coeditors of *The Messenger*) were charged with breaking the World War I–era Espionage Act for articles they wrote in *The Messenger*; the courts ruled that the articles were seditious and anti-American. In 1919, Randolph argued in *The Messenger* that the black workers should join the International Workers of the World, a radical socialist labor union that advocated syndicalism—the control of industry and government by labor organizations.

Randolph was also an early follower of Marcus Garvey, often introducing him to audiences in New York and supporting his early work and ideas. Garvey promoted an early form of black nationalism and race segregation that grew into a strong back-to-Africa movement. But by 1920, Randolph and others in the civil rights movement of that era began to back away from Garvey and his back-to-Africa schemes. Randolph's disenchantment turned to strong opposition, and he began using the pages of *The Messenger* to launch the "Garvey must go" campaign; finally, he supported a federal investigation of Garvey.

Although Randolph was born in the South, he lived most of his life in Harlem, well outside the rural, church-based, civil rights movement that emerged in the postwar years. Randolph, however, seemed to bridge an important gap between the civil rights movement of the early part of the century (when Garvey was most active in New York, and when W. E. B. DuBois was ascending as a spokesman for African Americans through the magazine *Crisis*) and the postwar movement led by King and others.

Randolph may not have had the same background as the civil rights leaders of the 1950s and 1960s, but in many ways he laid the foundations for their work. That is particularly true of Randolph's dealings with President Roosevelt in 1941. Roosevelt had won the 1940 election with a great deal of black voter support, and Randolph decided that it was time to cash that check. Just before the war began, Randolph (along with Bayard Rustin and A. J. Muste) insisted that Roosevelt issue an executive order creating a fair employment practices committee (FEPC) to ensure that there would be no race discrimination in wartime industries. He also insisted that the armed forces be desegregated. When Randolph threatened a march on Washington of one hundred thousand supporters, FDR relented and agreed to the wartime FEPC (Executive Order 8802), but insisted that Randolph drop his demand to desegregate the armed forces. Much to the disgust of many black radicals in the nation (particularly black newspaper editors), Randolph agreed to call off the march. Throughout the remainder of his life, however, he worked diligently for the desegregation of the military and for a permanent FEPC.

In 1962, Randolph, again along with Bayard Rustin (and many others), planned a second march on Washington, known officially as the March on Washington for Jobs and Freedom. Unlike the planned 1941 march, for which Randolph intended to include only black-led organizations, the 1963 march was to be a collaborative effort of all of the major civil rights organizations, along with the more progressive wing of the labor movement, and other liberal organizations. The march was intended to free up the civil rights bill proposed by the Kennedy administration, which had become bound up in Congress by a coalition of conservative Republicans and Southern Democrats. President Kennedy, like Roosevelt before him, tried to convince Randolph to call off the demonstration, insisting that Congress would be much less likely to act "with a knife to its throat," as Kennedy described the march. The march, however, was a success. More than two hundred thousand demonstrators gathered in front of the Lincoln Memorial on August 28, 1963, where King delivered his famous "I Have a Dream" speech. The Civil Rights Act was finally passed in July 1964.

Randolph died in New York in 1978. He was perhaps best known, between the time of the march on Washington and his death, for opposing the radicalism of the black nationalism and the black power movements, which he believed did little to aid in the cause of the nation's African Americans.

· 2 ·

The Early Cold War

A mericans believed, if only for a short moment, that the victories of World War II had brought an end to world hostilities and conflicts. The United States emerged from the war strong, the world's only nuclear power, while much of the rest of the world was laid waste as a result of the war.

So, it seemed, World War II had been a good war. Americans hailed its end as a total triumph over the very forces of evil, with all goals realized in a complete and moral victory. The sacrifices had been tremendous, but the end of the war had left the United States astride the world, free of any serious enemies, and free to convert its economy to peacetime production.

But all too quickly it became clear that World War II, like most wars, caused as many problems as it solved. The most apparent concern was the huge and dangerous power vacuums exposed by the retreating German army in Europe and the Japanese army in Asia. In Eastern Europe, the Soviets placed friendly governments in Poland, Romania, Bulgaria, and Austria as they pushed the retreating Nazi armies back into Germany; at the war's end, the Soviets occupied every Eastern European capital except Athens. In Asia, Soviet troops were in Iran, Manchuria, and the northern half of Korea. At the same time, Communist insurgencies were trying to topple governments in China, Vietnam, Greece, Turkey, and even Italy. For most Americans, communism and its spread became the new fear.

YALTA AND THE END OF THE WAR

As the war in Europe began to wind down, the representatives of the soon-to-be victorious nations met at Yalta in the Soviet Union. President Franklin Roosevelt met there with Premier Joseph Stalin of the Soviet Union and Prime Minister Winston Churchill of the United Kingdom. It was at Yalta, in February 1945, that the Americans and the Soviets found themselves at loggerheads over the treatment of the postwar world. The agreements at Yalta, as they pertained to postwar Europe, revolved around the disposition of two nations, Poland and Germany.

Stalin demanded that any government in postwar Poland must be friendly to the Soviet Union, and he refused to budge on the point. Roosevelt could do little. Short of declaring war against an ally (an ally that was fully mechanized by then and entirely capable of fielding an army twice the size of the combined armies of the United States and Great Britain), Roosevelt agreed to a compromise on Poland. The government there would be made up of a coalition, one part friendly to the West and one part friendly to Moscow. This government would remain in power only until elections could be held. Stalin agreed, even speculating that elections might be held within a month. Roosevelt then persuaded Stalin to sign an ambiguous and vaguely worded "Declaration on Liberated Europe," which spelled out the formation of governments throughout Eastern Europe that would be "broadly representative of all democratic elements in the population and pledged to the earliest possible establishment through free elections of governments responsive to the will of the people." It was hardly specific and it held Stalin to nothing, but, as FDR told Admiral William Leahy, "It's the best I can do for Poland at this time." He almost certainly planned to push Stalin harder at their next meeting.

All agreed at Yalta that Germany should be dismembered. The Americans,

Participants in the Big Three Conference at Yalta in February 1945: British Prime Minister Winston Churchill, U.S. President Franklin D. Roosevelt, and Soviet Premier Joseph Stalin. The meeting in the Crimea (now the Ukraine) in the Soviet Union determined the shape of postwar Europe. Roosevelt had only a few weeks to live. *Source:* **AP Photo**

the British, and eventually the French would occupy the western zone of Germany and the Soviets would occupy the east. Berlin, inside the eastern zone, was also to be divided east and west. This was intended as a temporary situation, to relieve the obvious problem of a political and security vacuum in Germany.

Roosevelt and Churchill understood the need for an economically viable Germany if Europe were to maintain any economic balance. Certainly, they had learned that lesson from the 1920s, when the postwar German economy collapsed and much of the world suffered. Stalin, however, saw all this differently. He wanted Germany to pay the price for the damage it had inflicted on the Russian people in the war. And he wanted a weak Germany for the future, a Germany that would not again rise and attack the Soviet Union. To that end, he insisted that Germany pay stiff reparations. In addition, he wanted to strip Germany of its industrial might by confiscating its machinery and shipping it to the Soviet Union to rebuild his war-damaged economy there. The decisions at Yalta did not resolve these differences, and that would become a major point of contention in the growing Cold War.

The Yalta agreements pertaining to the Far East were more easily determined. Roosevelt had high hopes of obtaining Stalin's aid in defeating Japan, something that the Soviet leader was willing to do in exchange for a few fairly insignificant concessions in the Far East, mainly influence in Mongolia and Manchuria. Roosevelt also insisted that Stalin recognize Jiang Jieshi (Chiang Kaishek) and the Nationalist Chinese as the only legitimate government in China. This was important to Roosevelt because it denied Soviet support to Mao Zedong and the Chinese Communists. The Nationalists and the Communists had been locked in a bloody civil war since the late 1920s, but during the Japanese occupation of China both groups had moved to the Chinese frontier regions to wait out the war. It was no secret that when the war ended and the Japanese armies left China, the Chinese Civil War would resume. Roosevelt feared that a hot war in Asia between Communist and anti-Communist forces might damage U.S.-Soviet relations—or worse, draw the United States and the Soviet Union into the conflict. Roosevelt hoped that by pushing Stalin to support the Nationalists instead of the Communists that Mao would be too weak to resume the conflict and be forced into a coalition government. Stalin agreed.

Just two weeks after Yalta the Soviets placed a puppet government in Romania, and the failure of the Yalta Conference became apparent. Roosevelt seemed prepared to respond by applying economic pressure on Moscow. He wrote to Stalin of his "astonishment," "anxiety," and "bitter resentment" over the situation, and he admonished the Soviet premier for not allowing the elections he had promised in Poland. To Churchill, FDR wrote of his growing distrust of Stalin and of his intentions to increase the pressure on the Soviets: "Our armies," he wrote, "will in a very few days be in a position that will permit us to become 'tougher' than has heretofore appeared advantageous to the war effort." Just as

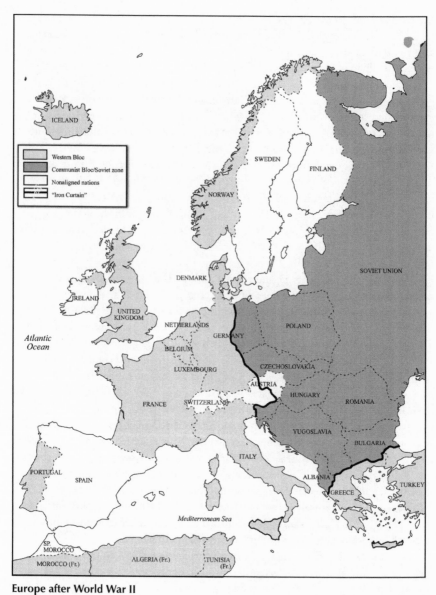

Europe after World War II

the Soviet stranglehold on Eastern Europe grew tighter in mid-April, Roosevelt died, taking with him the hope that goodwill would somehow shape and secure the new order of the postwar world.

HARRY TRUMAN AND THE GROWTH OF CONFLICT

The new president, Harry Truman, had very little experience in foreign policy. To make matters worse, FDR had not bothered to keep his vice president informed on the most significant international issues. Truman even told a friend that all he knew about foreign policy was what he read in the papers. When he came to office, the battle on Okinawa was still raging, while in Europe, American soldiers were moving much more quickly than expected toward Soviet forces racing into Germany from the east. It was the beginning of a new era; the stage was being set for the future, but the new American president was not yet up to the challenge.

Truman's response was natural. He consulted those men who had been closest to Roosevelt. He took the advice of Averell Harriman, FDR's ambassador to the Soviet Union during the war. During his time in Moscow, Harriman had developed a growing distrust of the Soviets. He often spoke of a new "barbarian invasion of Europe," and he told Truman that there were "irreconcilable differences" between the United States and the Soviet Union. Truman also consulted Churchill, who was a virulent anti-Communist. Other Roosevelt advisors, such as Joseph Grew at the State Department, Chief of Staff William Leahy, and Secretary of the Navy James Forrestal, all favored a policy of firmness toward the Soviets. The only Roosevelt insider who saw any possibility of a working relationship with Moscow was Secretary of Commerce Henry Wallace, the man Truman most distrusted (and disliked) in the Roosevelt administration. Although it is certainly true that Stalin gave Truman more than enough cause to develop his own anti-Communist viewpoint, it is small wonder that Truman began moving on his own toward a hard line with Moscow.

Truman got off to a bad start when in May 1945, just after Germany collapsed, he halted all Lend-Lease aid to the Soviet Union. Lend-Lease had been a Roosevelt wartime plan to aid America's allies with supplies and equipment. Truman's move was immediately interpreted by Stalin as diplomatic pressure, and the Soviet leader let Truman know how he felt: "If the refusal to continue Lend-Lease was designed as pressure on the Russians in order to soften them up, then it was a fundamental mistake." Truman sent emissaries to Moscow to smooth out the situation, but the incident added to the growing distrust between the two nations.

Truman and Stalin finally met at the Potsdam Conference outside Berlin in July 1945. Very little was accomplished there. Truman agreed to allow the Soviets to strip eastern Germany of anything it could take (from entire factories to farm

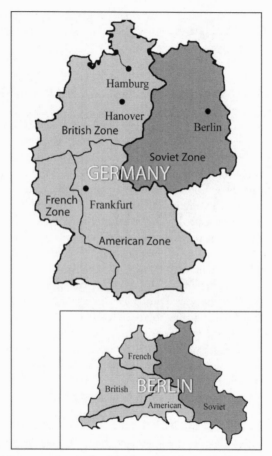

The Division of Germany. Inset: The Division of Berlin inside the Soviet Zone

machinery) in lieu of reparations, a process that had already been completed. And Stalin renewed his commitment to enter the war against Japan. The Potsdam participants all agreed that there was much left to be done, but no final peace conference was ever planned and Truman and Stalin never met again.

It was on the second day of the Potsdam Conference that Truman received word that the nuclear test near Alamogordo in New Mexico had been a success. The president notified Churchill immediately but said nothing to Stalin for several days. The Manhattan Project had been under way since 1942 with the full knowledge and cooperation of the British government, and with the understanding that the two nations would share the atomic secrets. Stalin and the Soviets, however, were left out of the secret transactions. This was an obvious basis for mistrust, but to make matters even worse, Stalin had learned about the project through his own intelligence network as early as 1943 and was fully aware that the Americans and British were sharing the technology. This led Stalin to believe that the West was, again, building a coalition against Moscow.

It is often argued that Truman used the bomb against Japan to intimidate the Soviets—as well as win the war against Japan. Certainly, the use of the bomb hardened the Cold War, whether Truman intended to intimidate the Soviets by its use or not. Stalin immediately began pushing his scientists to produce a bomb to counter the West's new power. Ambassador Harriman noted how the Soviet attitude had changed following the use of the bomb against Japan: The bomb "must have revived their old feeling of insecurity," Harriman told Secretary of State Byrnes in late 1945. "The Russian people have been aroused to feel that they must again face an antagonistic world." Before the end of 1945 the Soviet press had already accused the United States of using the bomb as a threat, or as they called it, "atomic diplomacy." The use of the bomb helped solidify the Cold War.

In September 1945, and then again in December, James Byrnes met with Soviet Foreign Minister Vyacheslav Molotov in an attempt to solve the many growing problems around the world, but again little was resolved. Through 1946 the level of rhetoric increased substantially as the two sides became frustrated by the course of events. In February 1946 Stalin, in a rare public address, called for enormous sacrifices from the Soviet people in the face of growing threats from the West; and he announced a new Five-Year Plan to begin the process of preparing for the eventuality of war. A month later, Churchill replied to Stalin's invective in a speech at Westminster College in Fulton, Missouri. Introduced by the president, Churchill gave testament that the Cold War had begun. "From Stettin in the Baltic to Trieste in the Adriatic," he said, "an Iron Curtain has descended across the Continent." Even though Truman introduced Churchill at Fulton, he never endorsed Churchill's "Iron Curtain" speech and he certainly did not intend it as a break with the Soviets, but Stalin clearly saw it that way. Immediately, he denounced the speech as a "call to war against the USSR." In a public opinion poll taken the same month as Churchill's speech, 71 percent of Americans said they were hostile to Soviet policy, and 60 percent said the United States was being too soft on the Russians.

Almost immediately, it became apparent that the Soviets were trying to fill vacuums left by the war and push their influence out from their borders. One early area of concern was Turkey. During the war Roosevelt and Churchill had both agreed that Stalin should have access to the Mediterranean Sea through the Turkish-held straits, the Dardanelles and the Bosporus. In August 1947, however, Stalin made it clear that he wanted more. He suggested a joint Soviet-Turkish defense of the straits—an obvious plan to build Soviet bases in the region. The U.S. ambassador to Turkey warned Washington that if the Soviets were allowed to dominate Turkey they would spread their influence over the Persian Gulf oil reserves, and perhaps even as far west as the Suez Canal. Truman responded by sending a fleet of warships to the eastern Mediterranean and the Soviets backed away from their pressure on Turkey.

The Soviets also seemed to want to push south into Iran. During the war, the Soviets moved troops into Iran to keep the Germans from grabbing the rich oil reserves there. The situation was discussed at an Allied conference in Tehran in 1943, and it was agreed that the Soviets would withdraw from Iran within six months following the end of the war. When the war ended, however, it appeared that the Soviets were not going to leave. One fear was that Moscow might try to annex northern Iran (the region it occupied) and then place a puppet government in the capital at Tehran. Such a position would allow the Soviets to cast its influence over the entire Middle East. The United States took the issue to the first session of the United Nations, but nothing was resolved. When the six-month deadline passed on March 2, 1946, tensions mounted and a brief war scare spread through Washington when it was learned that the Soviets were moving tanks into northern Iran. Secretary of State Byrnes sent a strongly worded message to the Soviets demanding an immediate withdrawal, but there was no reply. The situation became tense, but the Soviets finally agreed to leave Iran in early May and the episode ended.

In August, following the first atomic bomb attack on Japan, the Soviets rushed into Manchuria to encounter an already defeated Japanese army. Truman intended to hold back the Soviet advances in Asia as much as possible, and to that end he announced that the United States would occupy Japan alone. As the Soviets swept into Manchuria and then into Korea, Washington insisted that the Soviets adhere to earlier agreements and halt their push down the Korean Peninsula. To the surprise of just about everyone, the Soviets stopped their advance, establishing themselves in the northern half of Korea above the Thirty-Eighth Parallel. The United States then moved troops into Korea south of the parallel.

In China, despite the efforts of both the United States and the Soviet Union, the situation began to deteriorate almost immediately following Japan's surrender. No one wanted a resumption of the civil war between the Nationalists and the Communists that had begun in the late 1920s. The Roosevelt-Truman plan was to convince the Soviets to support Jiang Jieshi and the Nationalists, thereby denying aid to Mao and the Communists. Without Soviet aid, the reasoning went, the Communists would be too weak to renew the fight and thus be forced into a coalition government with the Nationalists. Somewhat surprisingly, Stalin agreed and signed the Soviet–Chinese Nationalist Treaty of Friendship and Alliance in mid-August 1945. Stalin and Mao disagreed over their differing visions of the future of world communism mostly because Stalin saw Mao's revolution, supported by the Chinese peasantry, as outside the Marxist-Leninist philosophy that called for a revolution of urban industrial workers against the capitalist classes. This disagreement may have kept the two Communist leaders from joining in an alliance, but it did not prevent Stalin from allowing vast stores of Japanese materiel to fall into Mao's hands as the defeated Japanese troops left

Manchuria. Stalin's motive may have been to fuel the civil war and keep China divided and weak rather than support Mao, but the result was that Mao's forces were strengthened considerably and a resumption of the civil war was a certainty.

Truman, like Roosevelt, feared that a resumption of the Chinese civil war might pit the United States against the Soviets on the Asian continent. Truman tried to prevent a resumption of hostilities by sending emissaries to mediate the differences between the Communists and Nationalists. Jiang, however, believed he could defeat the Communists and he refused to negotiate. American pressure on Jiang forced the two sides to move toward an agreement several times in 1946, but the fighting continued. Finally, in December, U.S. negotiators gave up trying to mediate a settlement and the Truman administration began distancing itself from Jiang and the Nationalists. Despite Jiang's superior numbers, the Nationalist armies suffered a series of disastrous defeats through 1949 and a Communist victory seemed certain. By the end of the year the Nationalists had collapsed and evacuated to Formosa, a large island off the southeast coast of China. There Jiang set up shop claiming to be the only legitimate government of the Chinese people. Truman could only bemoan the loss: "We picked a bad horse," he said. The fall of China would have far-reaching implications for American foreign policy in the Far East, and it would affect American domestic politics for at least thirty years.

Just as events in China reached a climax, the situation in Korea evolved into a Cold War standoff. Immediately after the war, the Americans in the southern zone began a policy of crushing all pro-Communist activity, which allowed for the emergence of a pro-American, anti-Communist police state. When the United States reduced its military presence in the southern zone (a reflection of budget cutbacks in Washington), the vacuum was filled by a Korean constabulary. In May 1948, after several attempts at unification failed, Syngman Rhee, a fierce Korean nationalist and ardent anti-Communist, proclaimed the Republic of Korea under his leadership, with its capital at Seoul. The north responded almost immediately by creating the Democratic People's Republic of Korea with Kim Il Sung as its leader and its capital at Pyongyang. Kim was a staunch Communist with strong ties to both Moscow and to the Chinese Communists, who were still locked in a civil war with the Nationalists just across the Yalu River in China. In Washington, with all eyes reverted to events in Europe, no one seemed to anticipate the growing conflict in Korea.

Another area of growing concern in Asia was Vietnam. This poorly run French colony was occupied by the Japanese in 1941. After the war, Vietnamese nationalists led by Ho Chi Minh demanded independence for Vietnam, but French president Charles de Gaulle announced that France would reoccupy its old colony of Indochina (which included the modern nations of Cambodia, Laos, and Vietnam). On September 2, 1945, in the city of Hanoi in the north, Ho Chi Minh announced Vietnam's independence. At about the same time, French troops began consolidating their positions around Saigon. In November 1946 a

French cruiser opened fire on the port city of Haiphong in the north, killing six thousand civilians. In December, Ho Chi Minh's troops counterattacked, and the first Indochina war began.

It seemed that the Soviets were trying to push into Iran and Turkey, and it was assumed that Communist insurgencies in China, Korea, and Vietnam were directed from Moscow. The obvious response was to try and hold back the Communist tide, to contain all Communist activity.

THE ARCHITECTS OF CONTAINMENT

All of these postwar events brought the United States to the foreign policy of containment. The policy is most often attributed to George Kennan, a counselor at the U.S. embassy in Moscow. In February 1946, Kennan sent what is usually described as a "long telegram" to the State Department in Washington analyzing Soviet foreign policy and recommending that the United States "contain" Soviet expansionist tendencies. Kennan wrote that the Soviets had inherited from the Tsarist Russians a great fear of invasion, first from the eastern barbarians and then from the Europeans in the west. They "have learned," he wrote, "to seek security only in patient but deadly struggle for the total destruction of rival power, never in compacts and compromises with it." In fact, he added, they welcomed conflict because it allowed them to maintain and justify their autocratic rule. The Soviets are, he concluded, both "neurotic" and "insecure." The message to American leaders was clear: The Soviets could not be dealt with through the normal channels of diplomacy. They would have to be handled firmly to keep them contained inside their sphere.

Kennan had not come up with anything new. The Truman administration had, in fact, already implemented a containment policy against the Soviets on several occasions. It was, however, Kennan's analysis of the Soviets as dark, uncompromising, neurotic autocrats that changed the way American foreign policy experts saw the Soviet Union in the immediate postwar period. Kennan's telegram quickly became a must-read among Washington insiders. Kennan was brought back from Moscow to become an advisor to policy makers, and then placed at the head of the Policy Planning Staff, where he set out to reevaluate and set down the American foreign policy of containment.

Containment became an institutionalized policy in Washington as a result of events that were unfolding in the eastern Mediterranean. The Soviet pressure on Turkey, and a growing Communist-sponsored insurgency in Greece, had pushed Britain to its limit in the region. Finally, in late February 1947, London informed Washington that because of economic difficulties they could no longer resist the Soviet probes into Greece and Turkey. It seemed apparent that, if the United States did not step into the breach, the Soviets would expand their influence in the region—and most likely beyond.

On March 12, 1947, the president spoke to a joint session of Congress and laid down the new policy of containment: that the United States would contain all Soviet attempts at expansion. Truman's remarks focused chiefly on the ideological differences between the United States and the Soviet Union. It was an alarmist, black-and-white view of the world. "At the present moment . . . nearly every nation must choose between alternative ways of life," Truman said. "One way of life is based upon the will of the majority, and is distinguished by free institutions, representative government, free elections, guarantees of individual liberty, freedom of speech and religion, and freedom from political oppression. The second way of life is based upon the will of a minority forcibly imposed upon the majority. It relies upon terror and oppression, a controlled press and radio, fixed elections, the suppression of personal freedoms." He insisted that the United States must support "free people who are resisting attempted subjugation by armed minorities or by outside pressures." Then he asked Congress for $400 million in aid to help Greece and Turkey. The bill passed both houses overwhelmingly, public opinion polls showed strong support, and Truman's approval ratings shot up ten points. The message was clear: Anti-communism was popular.

The aid program to block Soviet probes into the eastern Mediterranean succeeded. Soviet pressure on Turkey eased; and with U.S. assistance, the Greek government successfully resisted the Communist insurgency. The initiative become known as the Truman Doctrine, a commitment to aid anti-Communists worldwide, a guide to the Cold War that Truman's successors would follow.

By the time the situation in the eastern Mediterranean had eased, Congress was more concerned with the deteriorating economic conditions in Western Europe. American attempts to aid the European economies through international agencies such as the United Nations Relief and Rehabilitation Agency, the World Bank, and the International Monetary Fund had all failed. Europe remained crippled. The lessons of the prewar era in Central Europe had taught that bad economic times can breed radicalism, and most analysts feared that the conditions in much of Western Europe left the region vulnerable to Soviet influence, even expansion. It seemed especially true in France and Italy, where Communist political parties were gaining strength. At the same time, the United States needed its European trading partners to keep its own economy strong. As the situation in Western Europe worsened, the United States moved to shore up those economies with U.S. dollars. The plan worked, but it drew the line more sharply between the East and the West.

The European Recovery Program (ERP), as it was originally called, was proposed by Secretary of State George Marshall in his Harvard commencement address in June 1947. The offer of aid to Europe was, Marshall said, to facilitate "the revival of a working economy in the world so as to permit the emergence of political and social conditions in which free institutions can exist."

The plan did not distinguish Western Europe from the Soviet-dominated East, but policy makers in Washington clearly had no intention of including the

Soviets, while Moscow was not about to allow their Eastern European satellites to take part in the program. They felt threatened by the harsh wording of the Truman Doctrine, and as the situation between the two sides became increasingly tense, it was inconceivable that the Soviets would accept American aid along with, as they saw it, the strings of American imperialism attached to it. Moscow immediately rejected the U.S. aid and then forced the Eastern European nations under its control to do the same. Czechoslovakia, however, agreed to accept the aid, a move quickly squelched by Moscow that eventually led to a Soviet-sponsored coup there in February 1948. It was also the catalyst that pushed Congress to pass the ERP—by now known as the Marshall Plan. The Soviets responded with their own Molotov Plan for Eastern Europe, but it did little more than force those nations into a tighter dependence on Moscow.

The Marshall Plan was a success. It provided both aid and credit to the Western European nations that was, in turn, used to buy American products, particularly industrial machinery, farm equipment, and other goods. Although the motives of the Marshall Plan have often been questioned, it brought the economies of the Western European nations back to life and bettered the living conditions of millions of people. Through four years, beginning in July 1947, the United States pumped approximately $13 billion (about $130 billion in today's dollars) into the region, boosting the Western European economies (except Germany) to well above prewar levels. The Marshall Plan, however, also created a deep rift between Washington and Moscow, between the now-solid Eastern and Western spheres of influence.

Following the 1947 announcements of the Truman Doctrine and the Marshall Plan, Stalin moved to consolidate his power in Eastern Europe. In May the popularly elected Ferenc Nagy was removed from office in Hungary and Communists seized control. The coup caused a great stir in the United States. In Czechoslovakia the Soviet takeover was even more disturbing. In late 1947 when the Czech government responded to offers of U.S. aid, Soviet troops moved into place along Czechoslovakia's eastern border. The democratically elected government of Eduard Bene fell and the Communists took control on February 25, 1948. Truman saw these events as "exactly the same situation in which Britain and France were faced in 1938–9 with Hitler."

On March 17, Truman went before Congress and asked for universal military training, a resumption of the Selective Service, and a speedy passage of the Marshall Plan. Congress responded by passing the Selective Service Bill and funding a seventy-group air force. There was a sense of urgency.

BERLIN CRISIS AND NATO

While the Soviets tightened their grip on Eastern Europe, the Americans sought to consolidate their power in western Germany. In late May 1948 the United

States, Britain, and France decided to consolidate their three zones of occupation. This was seen by Moscow as an attempt by the West to organize a separate West Germany, a new nation that Stalin most likely believed could become a new threat to the Soviet Union. In early 1948 the United States established a separate currency in western Germany. And that, coupled with the influx of cash from the Marshall Plan, brought rapid economic growth to the western zone. Stalin's reaction to this move was to hold Berlin hostage.

On June 24, 1948, just as the United States was about to extend the currency reform to Berlin, the Soviets blocked the primary highway and train routes from western Germany east into Berlin. In addition, the western sectors of the city were cut from the urban power grid, depriving western Berlin of electricity. Stalin may have been trying to force the Americans into a discussion over the future of Germany. But in Washington, the blockade was seen as an affront, a challenge to the Western presence in Europe, and an attempt by Stalin to snatch control of Berlin. In addition, Truman was in the middle of a presidential election campaign and he was facing an uphill battle against Republicans who were looking for any opportunity to tag him with being soft on communism. Truman seemed to be left with only two choices: concede Berlin or go to war to protect the city. But the president found a third option that both saved Berlin and avoided war. He ordered the air force to maintain an air lifeline to the city, and for nearly a year a fleet of U.S. and British transport aircraft flew around the clock to Berlin's Templehof Airport. The airlift made just under 300,000 flights, delivering to the people of Berlin over two million tons of food and supplies, including 1.5 million tons of coal. At the height of the operation, a transport plane landed in Berlin every minute. The greatest fear was that a humiliated Stalin might launch an attack on the transport planes, and at times tensions were high. But with no interference from the Soviets, the Berlin Airlift became a rousing success, and most of the world saw the United States on the right side of history. On May 12, 1949, the Soviets gave up and lifted the blockade. The Berlin Airlift was the first major confrontation of the Cold War.

The crisis convinced both sides that the problem of the divided Germany was probably impossible to solve. The western allies almost immediately set up a formal West German state, the Federal Republic of Germany, under the staunch anti-Communist Conrad Adenauer. The Soviets responded with the creation of the German Democratic Republic in October. Across the border the armies of the United States and the Soviet Union would stare at each other for another four decades.

The coup in Czechoslovakia and the standoff over Berlin pushed the allies toward a military alliance. Prior to those events, the standoff in Europe had been viewed in Washington as more economic and political than military. But those events, along with the twenty-five Soviet divisions stationed in Eastern Europe, frightened the Western Europeans and they began moving toward an alliance in hopes of defending against what they saw as clear Soviet aggression. In March 1948, just one month following the Czech coup, the United Kingdom, France, and the Benelux countries (Belgium, Netherlands, and Luxembourg) signed the Treaty of Brussels. However, this Western European Union, as it was known, could not counter Soviet power, and almost immediately talks for a new military alliance began, one which would include the United States. In April 1949 the North Atlantic Treaty was signed in Washington creating NATO, the North Atlantic Treaty Organization. It included the United States, Canada, and ten Western European nations. The basis of the pact could be found in Article 5: "An armed attack against one or more members . . . shall be considered an attack against them all." Containment was now backed by military muscle. NATO was America's first binding military alliance. It became a significant step in the nation's emergence onto the postwar world stage, and it symbolized the role of the United States as the Cold War leader of the anti-Soviet coalition. In response, the Soviets set up the Warsaw Pact in 1955, made up of the Communist-controlled nations of southern and eastern Europe.

In late August 1949 came the alarming news that the Soviets had developed an atomic bomb—years before American scientists had predicted. For four years the United States had enjoyed the safety of a nuclear monopoly and the confidence that the nation was secure. Now the Soviets, with the largest land army in the world, was also a nuclear power, and America's security slipped away. Truman responded by pushing the nation's scientists to build a hydrogen bomb, a "superbomb" many times more powerful than the atomic fission weapons used to end World War II. Truman became convinced by physicist Edward Teller and others that if the United States failed to build a hydrogen bomb the Soviets would certainly develop one and use it to blackmail the United States. The project went forward, and U.S. scientists succeeded in exploding a hydrogen bomb in October 1952. If that event offered any security, it was short-lived. The Soviets exploded their own hydrogen bomb less than a year later, in August 1953. An arms race had begun.

COLD WAR IN ASIA AND THE ORIGINS
OF THE KOREA CONFLICT

Just one month after the Soviets tested their atomic bomb, China fell to communism. The two events together shocked America. It seemed that the United States was losing the struggle with the Soviets. The atomic security blanket was gone, and now one of America's chief allies (and the largest population in the world) had fallen to international communism.

In Korea, the Americans and the Soviets had removed their troops from the peninsula, but each had created local armies in their own image to hold the line against the other side. These two hostile armies faced each other across the Thirty-Eighth Parallel, but the world was more interested in events unfolding in Europe. No one in the West saw a conflict coming in Korea—the first major hot spot of the Cold War.

On June 25, 1950, North Korean troops, led by about 150 Soviet-made T-34 tanks, rushed into South Korea without warning. Within two days the South Korean army had been pushed well back from its positions along the Thirty-Eighth Parallel and was beginning to disintegrate. President Truman responded quickly. Within twelve hours of being notified of the invasion, he had made the decision to intervene. "By God," Truman told Secretary of State Dean Acheson, "I'm going to let them have it." He told Secretary of Defense Louis Johnson that he intended to "hit 'em hard."

But Truman's decision was not impulsive. In the charged political climate of 1950 he could have done little else. In late 1949 and early 1950 the situation in the world and at home was changing drastically. In late August 1949 the Soviets had obtained the bomb. In October, Mao inaugurated the People's Republic of China. By the first of the year 1950, Republicans were accusing the Democrats of "losing" China, and of being "soft" on communism. Wisconsin Senator Joseph McCarthy had begun to insist that the administration was harboring Communists in the State Department. Truman could not allow Korea to be "lost."

There were other considerations. Under U.S. leadership the United Nations had condemned the North Korean invasion, and Truman believed that if the UN resolution were not upheld, the United Nations might, as Truman told an aide, go the way of the League of Nations. In his memoirs the president wrote: "The foundations and the principles of the United Nations were at stake unless this unprovoked attack on Korea could be stopped." Truman also believed in the lessons of World War II. In 1938, at Munich, the British had appeased Hitler by allowing him to take the Sudetenland in western Czechoslovakia in exchange for a promise to end all aggressions. He did not. To Truman, and to an entire generation of Americans, that event taught a valuable lesson: appeasement of an aggressor only leads to further demands, and finally an expanded war. He recalled in his memoirs, "I felt that if South Korea was allowed to fall, Communist leaders would be emboldened to override [other] nations."

These were all important reasons for intervention, but perhaps more importantly (and the primary reason American presidents would intervene in other conflicts during the Cold War), Truman realized that if the United States shied away from a forceful response in Korea, American influence abroad would lose ground to the Soviets. For all these reasons, the United States went to war in Korea, just five years after World War II ended. But most Americans did not see Korea for the war it would become. After all, the president insisted on calling it a "police action," and not a war. And this police action was being conducted by a coalition of forces representing the "free world" (as the non-Communist world was called) and under the auspices of the United Nations.

NSC-68 AND THE REDIRECTION OF AMERICAN FOREIGN POLICY

The events of late 1949, particularly the news that the Soviets had developed atomic weapons and the fall of China, pushed Truman to direct his secretary of state, Dean Acheson, to conduct an overview of American foreign policy. The result was National Security Council Paper Number 68 (NSC-68), compiled by the state and defense departments and coordinated by the National Security Council. The document's authors assumed that the Cold War would continue, and that the Soviets would soon achieve the nuclear capability to destroy the United States. They maintained that the conflict with the Soviet Union threatened the very survival of the United States and its institutions. "The assault on free institutions is worldwide now," the report asserted, "and in the context of the present polarization of power a defeat of free institutions anywhere is a defeat everywhere." To that end, NSC-68 argued that the United States should begin a massive rearmament plan and increase its power and that of its allies in the face of the growing Communist threat.

Truman initially rejected NSC-68 as simply too expensive; conservatives in Congress were pushing hard for a balanced budget. At the same time, Truman was confident that America's superior air power (and its ability to deliver nuclear weapons) was sufficient to maintain its military monopoly. But the outbreak of the war in Korea in June 1950 (just two months after NSC-68 was completed) showed that the age of conventional-style warfare had not ended, and that small regional shooting wars might erupt in a number of places simultaneously around the world. In September, four months after the invasion of South Korea, Truman accepted NSC-68 and the United States began an immediate massive arms buildup.

THE COLD WAR COMES HOME

On February 9, 1950, Wisconsin Senator Joseph McCarthy, while speaking to the Republican Woman's Club of Wheeling, West Virginia, grabbed at the issue of Communist subversion in the U.S. government. He claimed to have a list of 205 Communists that he said were working in the State Department with the permission and knowledge of the secretary of state, Dean Acheson. "I have here in my hands," he said, "a list of 205—a list of names that were made known to the secretary of state as being members of the Communist Party and who nevertheless are still working and shaping policy in the State Department." What followed was a sustained attack by McCarthy and others in the Republican Party against what they claimed was an infiltration of Communists into the government and into most aspects of American society.

There were several events that reinforced this fear, particularly the establishment of the People's Republic of China in October 1949 and the Soviet Union's acquisition of the bomb just one month before. Many Americans began to fear that the United States was losing the Cold War, that communism was on the advance. They began to ask questions: How could that happen? McCarthy had an answer: There were Communists in the federal government, he said, who were sabotaging American foreign policy.

The postwar Red Scare did not, however, begin with McCarthy's Wheeling speech. The fear of communism had been growing at least since the end of the war, and even before that. Republicans had tried to link the New Deal, FDR, and organized labor with communism, and in the 1946 mid-term elections the Republicans used the issue of communism to score a big victory that gave them control of Congress—for the first time since 1930.

Anti-communism as a political issue had not escaped Harry Truman. In March 1947 he initiated Executive Order 9855 establishing a loyalty program for federal employees. The order authorized the dismissal of any government employee who associated with various organizations described as Communist, fascist, or simply subversive. An overzealous attorney general's office responded by turning the program into a witch hunt by subjecting every member of the federal government to close scrutiny. Everything was examined, from memberships in organizations to sexual habits and orientation, personal associations, and political affiliations past and present. Malicious gossip, assumptions, and innuendo often became facts, and were entered into the permanent employment record to become grounds for suspicion and dismissal. In the Truman administration, three million federal employees were investigated; 1,210 were fired as a direct result of the program. Of that number, nearly 400 were described as spies. Another 6,000 chose to resign.

The anti-Communist impulse was just as active in other branches of government. In 1945 the prewar Dies Committee (established by Texas congressman Martin Dies to uncover pro-fascist activities in the United States) became the House Committee on Un-American Activities (HUAC). The postwar focus of HUAC, however, shifted to ferreting out Communists. HUAC's most sensational target was the Hollywood movie industry, an entity that many Americans had come to see as a den of loose morals, and filled with leftist writers and producers. In addition, it was becoming increasingly clear that movies had become the prime shaper of national culture and society. Conservative congressmen followed up on these suspicions by making certain that the motion picture industry was not turning out Communist propaganda. In the fall of 1947 HUAC went after the motion picture industry, and there followed several years of sensational attacks by HUAC on Hollywood.

HUAC interviewed "friendly" witnesses, often behind closed doors, like Ronald Reagan, who complained that Communists had tried to take control of the Screen Actor's Guild, and Gary Cooper, who mustered his best "aw, shucks" persona with "From what I hear I don't like it [communism] much because it isn't on the level." As a result of the Hollywood hearings, eight screenwriters and two directors were jailed in 1950 for failure to cooperate with the committee.

Hollywood responded by trying to police itself. Through the 1950s, Hollywood's moviemakers avoided most political issues and any significant criticism of American society. Those who refused to conform, real or suspected, were quietly "blacklisted" and banned from the industry. By 1950, the infamous blacklist had reached 150 names, from John Garfield to Zero Mostel. The blacklist was finally broken in 1960 when blacklisted writer Dalton Trumbo was credited with writing the screenplays for both *Spartacus* and *Exodus*. By most accounts, the blacklists fell into disrepute after that date.

The postwar Red Scare also manifested itself in a series of trials that grew out of a number of high profile spy cases. In 1949 several leaders of the American Communist Party were convicted under the 1940 Smith Act for conspiring in speeches and publications to overthrow the government. Much of the testimony that led to those convictions came from an FBI counterspy inside the Communist Party apparatus named Herbert Philbrick. It was Philbrick who testified that it was, in fact, the objective of the American Communist Party to overthrow the United States government. He wrote a bestseller about his experiences, *I Led Three Lives*, which was made into a movie and then a successful television series by the same name. Philbrick became an early Cold War hero.

In the spring of 1948, HUAC received word that a senior editor at *Time* magazine named Whittaker Chambers had confessed to being a top-level Communist in Washington in the 1930s. In addition, Chambers was willing to testify about his one-time Communist connections, and he agreed to identify his associates—he would name names. Among those Chambers identified as former Communists was Alger Hiss, the director of the prestigious Carnegie Endowment for International Peace. Hiss, if HUAC could prove he was a Communist, would be quite a catch. He was one of the many Ivy League–educated intellectuals who came to Washington in the 1930s to become the enlightened leaders of the New Deal. After clerking for Justice Oliver Wendell Holmes, Hiss rose auspiciously through the State Department maze to the level of director of the office in charge of UN affairs. From there he organized the UN planning conferences at Dumbarton Oaks and San Francisco, and he was with FDR at Yalta. It was the Yalta connection that raised the most eyebrows among HUAC committee members; by 1948 Yalta was being portrayed by conservatives as the great betrayal.

Hiss's rebuttal before HUAC was a firm denial, almost a challenge to the committee to connect him to any aspect of communism. HUAC backed off.

Chambers proved to be a dubious witness, a one-time Communist who had little more to offer as evidence than his "word." But one HUAC member, California Congressmen Richard Nixon, believed that Hiss was lying. Based on Nixon's hunch, a HUAC subcommittee went after Hiss.

Hiss finally sued Chambers for libel. In the trial that followed, Chambers produced a series of documents on microfilm that had been stored in a pumpkin on his farm in Maryland. Chambers claimed that the documents had been given to him by Hiss.

Investigators were able to show that some of the documents had been written on a typewriter once owned by Hiss. In January 1950, Hiss was convicted of perjury and sentenced to five years in prison.

Perhaps the most important aspect of the Hiss case was that it put Nixon into the national spotlight, and identified him as one of the chief Communist hunters in Congress. In 1950, Nixon won a seat in the Senate, and in 1952 he was tapped as Dwight D. Eisenhower's running mate. Nixon would live a life of ups and downs in the political arena, but he would seldom be outside of national politics for the remainder of his life.

Just as the anti-Communist hysteria was reaching its height, just as Joe McCarthy was jumping on the bandwagon, several spies who had penetrated the atomic bomb project in New Mexico were caught. In the fall of 1946 a disgruntled Soviet agent named Igor Gouzenko defected to the West and identified a Soviet spy network in the United States. The roundup produced fifteen spies. In early 1950, the British arrested Klaus Fuchs, a German-born physicist who had worked on the wartime Manhattan Project, and he admitted passing vital information to the Russians. During his interrogations he gave up his accomplices, who in turn fingered Julius and Ethel Rosenberg. It quickly became the popular opinion that the Soviets could not have developed the bomb alone, that they needed some assistance from spies from the West, and that the Rosenbergs (and probably others) had provided the necessary scientific secrets. The Rosenbergs were accused of giving atomic secrets to the Soviets and were tried for espionage and convicted. Judge Irving Kaufman called their actions a "loathsome offense," and accused them of a "diabolical conspiracy to destroy a God-fearing nation." The Rosenbergs continued to maintain their innocence, but despite worldwide appeals for their release they were executed in June 1953. They were, most likely, guilty of espionage, but the significance of the information they passed to the Soviets is still in debate.

By 1950 all the ingredients were in place for a burst of anti-Communist hysteria. The "loss" of China, the Soviet bomb, and evidence of a vast unseen Communist conspiracy all led to a fear that the United States was losing the Cold War to the Soviets. The only element that was missing was leadership, someone who could tap into that fear and feed the frenzy.

McCarthy's Wheeling speech triggered a five-year crusade to hunt down and prosecute Communists in the U.S. government. The accusation by McCarthy and his associates was that Communists had infiltrated the workings of the U.S. government and were responsible for making U.S. policy. It was the answer to the question: Why are we losing the Cold War? In the final analysis, McCarthy uncovered nothing. He found no conspiracy and he sent no Communists to jail. He did, however, drag the nation through its most destructive internal episode since the war. The time is rightly called "McCarthyism."

Joseph McCarthy was little more than a Senate sideliner with a doubtful future. He entered the Senate from his home state of Wisconsin in 1947, and by 1950 he was two years from having to stand for reelection in a state that had gone Democratic in four of the last five presidential elections. Desperately in need of an issue that would keep him in Washington, he stumbled on anti-communism when he received favorable publicity after attacking a Wisconsin newspaper and its editor for what he called "Communist leanings." But McCarthy's Wheeling speech, and the five years of tirades against communism that followed, was little more than jumping into the lead on an issue that was already hot. The Republicans had been using the issue against the Democrats at least since 1946. By the time McCarthy entered the fray, the issue of anti-communism was already old hat.

KOREA, "THE FORGOTTEN WAR"

The American army that went to war in Korea in the summer of 1950 was not the army that had defeated Germany and Japan just five years earlier. Underfunded, badly supplied, and reportedly overweight and poorly trained, the U.S. army of 1950 was a reflection of America's belief that the war to end all wars had been fought and won, and there was little real need to prepare for the next war—certainly not the next conventional war.

The multinational UN army in Korea was made up of soldiers from sixteen nations (out of the sixty UN members). Another thirty nations sent noncombat aid. At any given time in the war, only about 5 percent of the UN troops were from countries other than South Korea and the United States. Slightly more than half of that number came from the British Commonwealth. General Douglas MacArthur commanded all the troops in Korea from his headquarters in Tokyo; and all division-level command and grand strategy was in the hands of American generals. It was clearly an American war, fought under the auspices of the United Nations.

The Korean War was the nation's first limited war of the post–World War II era, and there was some question about its nature, even about what to call it. On June 29, Truman held a press conference intending to define the events in Korea for the American people. He referred to the limited war as a "police action," a term that would return to haunt him as casualty lists began coming in from Korea and photographs began to appear in the press. It was immediately apparent that Truman's "police action" was nothing less than a war of major magnitude and consequences.

The North Korean army, about 135,000 strong, raced across the Thirty-Eighth Parallel and captured the South Korean capital of Seoul in just two days. On June 30 Truman authorized the use of American ground combat forces, and the next day two U.S. Army divisions rushed onto the Korean Peninsula from Japan. But the Americans hardly saved the day. By the first week in August, the U.S. and South Korean troops had retreated to a defensive line about fifty miles around the South Korean port of Pusan. The Pusan Perimeter held for over a month against North Korean attacks while the United States and its UN allies built up their strength inside the perimeter. At the same time, U.S. air power pounded the North Korean lines that stretched far back into North Korea. By early September, MacArthur had built an effective force inside the perimeter and he prepared to take the offensive. In a brilliant strategic move he capitalized on the American air and naval superiority and initiated a daring amphibious landing at Inchon on the Korean west coast near Seoul, deep behind the North Korean lines. The attack was a success, and together with a coordinated attack that burst out of the Pusan Perimeter, the UN forces pushed the North Koreans back north of the Thirty-Eighth Parallel within two weeks.

The stated goal of the "police action" had been achieved; the North Koreans had been contained, pushed back above the Thirty-Eighth Parallel. But as the UN and South Korean troops approached the Thirty-Eighth Parallel, Truman began talking about unifying Korea and of "rolling back" the Red tide. Truman was certainly looking at the upcoming midterm elections, and he saw that a military victory against communism would score big vote numbers for Democratic candidates. He was also being advised that if the North Korean army survived, the military effort would have been in vain, and possibly U.S. troops would have to return at a later date to fight a stronger, perhaps more mechanized North Korean force. And of course, American boys had died in the effort. To many Americans, Truman had a choice: he could either punish the offenders or let them get away with their crimes. He soon came to believe he had to finish the job. On September 11, with the approval of the Joint Chiefs of Staff, Truman authorized U.S. troops to cross the Thirty-Eighth Parallel and invade North Korea with the intention of uniting Korea by pushing the North Korean troops north to the Yalu River on the Chinese border. No one seemed to consider how the Chinese might react to such a move.

On October 9, UN forces headed into North Korea for what they saw as little more than a mopping-up campaign while the North Korean forces disintegrated as they moved. On October 26, several South Korean units reached the Yalu River. Victory was close. By then, however, 250,000 Chinese troops had moved undetected through the lines and infiltrated into North Korea.

The first Chinese attack came on October 25 and obliterated an entire South Korean division. The American command, however, refused to believe it.

Analysts in Tokyo reported that perhaps 40,000 to 80,000 Chinese volunteers had crossed the Yalu and joined the war. MacArthur renewed his offensive and moved troops up to the Yalu. On November 25, a second Chinese wave smashed the UN forces hard, and several South Korean divisions were overwhelmed and torn apart. The next day the Chinese hit again, and then the next day and the next. "The Chinese had come in with both feet," Joint Chiefs Chairman Omar Bradley told Truman. It was, said MacArthur, "an entirely new war."

The situation placed Truman and MacArthur at odds over how the war should be fought. MacArthur insisted that the war be expanded. He wanted a blockade of China's ports, air attacks on Chinese forces and their installations in Manchuria, considerable reinforcements, the use of Jiang Jieshi's troops from Taiwan, and a free hand to use nuclear weapons if necessary. But Truman refused to expand the conflict. In fact, the administration's new objective once the Chinese had intervened was to get out of the situation in Korea as fast as possible while maintaining American integrity. The two opposing objectives produced a conflict between the president and his general. MacArthur, the old soldier who had brought America total victory in the Pacific in World War II, could not see himself fighting brushfires on the Asian continent. Truman, the first president of the new era, had come to see the necessity of a limited war. He knew that conflicts in the nuclear age could spread quickly. Situations were tense all over the world, and an expansion of the Korean War could easily bring in the Soviets and then spread to Europe. Truman was not prepared to preside over World War III.

As the war on the ground escalated, the Truman-MacArthur conflict heated up. In March 1951 Truman planned to make a statement that the United Nations was willing to discuss conditions for settling the war. MacArthur, however, had other ideas. He gave an interview to a British journalist and complained that the administration was restricting his actions to the point that he was not being allowed to win the war. "The situation would be ludicrous," he added, "if men's lives were not involved." That was all Truman could take. On April 9 he assembled his military policy makers: Acheson, Harriman, Marshall, and the members of the Joint Chiefs including their chairman, Omar Bradley. The decision was unanimous. MacArthur would be removed from command. On April 11 Truman announced that General Matthew Ridgway would replace MacArthur.

MacArthur became a symbol for those who felt that the real enemy was the Soviet Union and China, and that the United States, now provoked in Korea, should confront Communist expansionism and "finish the job," as the saying went at the time. Republicans in Congress led those who were outraged by Truman's actions. William Jenner, a Republican senator from Indiana who was riding McCarthy's coattails, said that MacArthur's firing proved that the Truman administration was made up of "a secret coterie which is directed by agents of the Soviet Union." McCarthy himself charged that Truman was drunk when he made the decision to fire MacArthur.

MacArthur's dismissal divided the nation. Either he was an American hero,

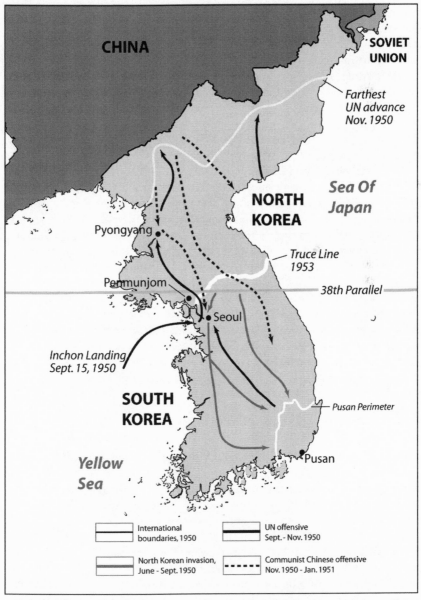

The Korean War, 1950–1953. The Truce Line (at just above the Thirty-Eighth Parallel) continues to divide Korea today.

or he had overstepped his bounds. Some realized the central issue: limited versus total war. Others may have seen the constitutional issue, that military authority must be subordinate to civilian authority. But most Americans saw it in the context of the nation's role in dealing with the expansion of communism. Still others held MacArthur up as a martyr to the cause of anti-communism. Truman's act, necessary as it was, did his administration irreparable damage. He never recovered popularity in the polls, and the issue gave the Republicans an issue for the 1952 campaign.

In Korea, peace talks began in July 1951, but neither side wanted to negotiate from a position of weakness, so the fighting dragged on for another two years. By 1952, the defense budget had jumped to $50 billion from just $13 billion before the war began. Americans grew tired of the war, and it was generally relegated to the back pages of the nation's newspapers. But for the soldiers on the ground, Korea was still cold and the enemy remained dangerous.

The Cold War had turned hot in Korea, but to those who kept a watchful eye on the Soviets, Europe was still the center of attention. In September 1950, the administration announced a plan to rearm West Germany, mostly for the purpose of bringing West Germany into NATO. With memories of the war still fresh in their minds, the other members of NATO complained bitterly. Truman responded by trying to placate the Europeans. He sent another four army divisions to Europe to join the two already there. He also sent Dwight Eisenhower to Paris to head NATO. Although the West German armed forces were integrated into the NATO military force, it was not until 1955 that West Germany became a member of NATO. In 1952 Greece and Turkey were brought into NATO. That allowed the United States to form its military on Russia's southern border.

THE 1952 CAMPAIGN AND THE END OF AN ERA

In November 1951 Truman announced to his staff that he would not run in 1952. He then moved to pick his successor, but all of Truman's choices declined the offer, including Adlai Stevenson, who insisted he wanted to fulfill his term as governor of Illinois. With no heir apparent in the wings, Truman toyed with running for another term, but his advisors convinced him it would be a mistake and he announced in March that he would not run.

The Republicans pinned all their hopes on Eisenhower. But Eisenhower insisted that he was not interested in the nomination. He had left the military in October 1947 and accepted the presidency of Columbia University in New York. Following a virtual writing frenzy, he published his memoirs, *Crusade in Europe*, in the spring of 1948. But he continued to deny any interest in politics—even to himself, in his personal diary. Nevertheless, he maintained important contacts within the inner circle of the Republican Party. In October 1950, Truman asked

Eisenhower to take command of NATO forces in Europe. Ike accepted. As he saw it, it was an opportunity to secure the peace he had won in 1945.

Eisenhower might not have run in 1952 had the Republicans been prepared to nominate a candidate whose beliefs and philosophy were similar to his own. But as the election approached, it appeared that Robert Taft would take the Republican nomination by default, and Eisenhower simply could not abide Taft's prewar-style isolationism. Ike was an ardent internationalist with a strong commitment to collective security. As Taft moved closer to the nomination, Eisenhower moved closer to running.

By the summer of 1951, Republican Party operatives began making pilgrimages to Eisenhower's headquarters in Europe to persuade the general to return to the United States and run. By then the nation was at war in Korea, and they argued convincingly that the nation was in crisis and needed his leadership. With Truman considering another run, and Taft about to take the Republican nomination with no opposition, Eisenhower decided he would enter the race.

In an attempt to keep the Republican Right in line, Eisenhower was prevailed upon to accept Richard Nixon as his running mate. Nixon had made a name for himself as a Communist hunter, but he had managed to avoid much of the stridency of the Red Scare and was considered a respectable figure in the party's right wing.

The Democrats, in their perpetual quest for a new face, finally persuaded Illinois governor Adlai Stevenson to make the run. Truman had looked to Stevenson in 1951, but he had demurred. As the convention approached it looked as though Tennessee senator Estes Kefauver would take the nomination, but most party leaders believed he could not win in the general election. They finally threw their support to Stevenson at the convention and, after three ballots, he took the nomination.

Throughout the campaign the Republicans hit hard at the Democrats for "creeping socialism" and what they called K^1C^2, an acronym for Korea, communism, and corruption. Eisenhower wanted to appeal to voters as the incorruptible candidate, "clean as a hound's tooth," as he said, in the face of what was being perceived as the corrupt atmosphere in Washington. But that image was threatened when the press reported that Nixon had been given a secret slush fund by some California businessmen to meet his campaign expenses. Nixon had tried to present an image to voters as an average guy just trying to make it in a world spoiled by the Democrats. But average guys seldom had $20,000 at their disposal in 1952. Although such a slush fund was not illegal, it presented an image of impropriety, an image Ike refused to tolerate. Eisenhower toyed with dumping his running mate, but the ever-irascible Nixon took advantage of the new medium of television and took his argument to the nation. In what has become known as the "Checkers" speech, Nixon told America about his wife's "respectable Republican cloth coat" and their family dog, Checkers, the only personal gift, he said, he had ever accepted from supporters. "And you know the kids love that dog and I just want to say this right now, that regardless of what they say about it, we're going to keep it." He went on to explain the slush fund, and he managed to convince most of those watching that he had, really, done nothing wrong. The next day, Ike agreed to keep Nixon on the ticket.

If the election was ever in doubt, all doubt faded when, on October 24, just two weeks before the election, Eisenhower announced that if elected, he would go to Korea. It was a tactic the Republicans were saving for the last—a classic October surprise—and it worked famously. The great general would again serve the nation in war. The Democrats could not answer. It brought big votes. Eisenhower won the election by a comfortable margin of over 55 percent of the popular vote, 442 electoral votes, and he brought in a Republican Congress on his coattails. He also broke into the Solid South, grabbing 57 electoral votes there, 18 more than the Dixiecrats had received four years before.

The Republicans were finally in the White House.

Truman left office a very unpopular man, but his stock increased almost immediately, until in the 1970s he reached a near-mythical folk hero status. He remains in the minds of many Americans the simple man from Missouri who stood up to the Russians and who battled for the common man in the face of overwhelming odds, a man who succeeded when all said he could not. Almost certainly, the president who occupied the White House in that turbulent period would have been credited with reshaping the nation and the world. That president happened to be Harry Truman.

CONCLUSION

By 1952 both the United States and the Soviet Union had the bomb, and the armies of both nations faced each other across clearly drawn lines in Europe and Asia. Alliance systems (that in many ways doubled as spheres of influence) were in place. Neither nation trusted the other. Leaders at the Kremlin believed that the United States was attempting to surround the Soviet Union with pro-Western allies. And most Americans had concluded that the Russians were trying to spread their influence and system of totalitarian communism to the rest of the world. Both nations had resigned themselves to a type of containment of the other. And both nations were on the verge of a new phase of the Cold War in which the hearts and minds of the Third World (the rest of the world that was not part of the two spheres of influence) were at stake.

Also by the end of 1952 a massive international arms buildup was under way like none seen before in the history of the world—at least in peacetime. In the United States, it resulted in the rise of a vast military-industrial establishment that was on the verge of controlling parts of the national economy. It was expensive, and liberals, along with budget-minded conservatives, often bemoaned the cost, that every dollar spent on weapons and weapons development was a dollar

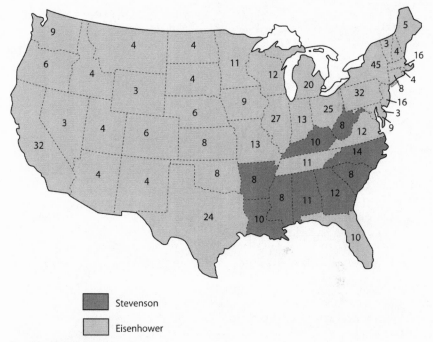

Presidential Election, 1952

that could not be used to help the poor, build roads, balance the budget, or lower taxes. But in fact, the military-industrial complex turned out to be an enormous economic engine. It fueled large sectors of the economy by employing thousands of workers to fill the huge government contracts.

The origins of the Cold War ushered in what one historian would later call the period of "the long peace," in which nuclear weapons were the ultimate deterrent against a war that would have been a holocaust. But in the late 1940s and early 1950s Americans (and probably Russians as well) could not see these events as the origins of a peaceful era. They could only feel the fear, and hope that cool heads in Moscow and Washington would avoid a horrible confrontation.

Reading: Truman and Israel

Truman's decision to recognize Israel in May 1948 would have an impact on U.S. foreign policy and on the Middle East for at least the next sixty years. The policy displaced Palestinian Arabs and enjoined the conflict between the Islamic states of the Middle East and the nation of Israel. For reasons that were related at least in part to the Cold War, Israel would become an important American ally, a reliable friend in a volatile region of the world. At the same time, the United States was becoming increasingly dependent on Middle Eastern oil. That dilemma placed the United States in a very difficult position by the early 1970s.

Following World War I, the British were allowed to control much of the Middle East, including Palestine, under a mandate from the League of Nations. It was during the war, in 1917, that Britain endorsed a plan for a homeland for the Jewish people in Palestine. This Balfour Declaration became official British policy after the war and was included in the peace treaty between Britain and Turkey. Through the 1920s and 1930s the British allowed Jews to settle in Palestine, and by 1939 there were as many as a half million Jews living there, mostly in independent settlements. Many had fled persecution in Nazi Germany.

Around the turn of the twentieth century, many Jews had come to embrace a Jewish nationalist movement known as Zionism; that in turn attracted Arab hostility toward the Jews. By the 1930s these Jewish-Arab conflicts had become so severe that the Jewish settlements in Palestine were turned into armed camps for protection. The British, who did not want to be caught up in the conflict between the Arabs and the Jews, stopped Jewish immigration to Palestine. After the war there was increased pressure on Britain to open Palestine to Jewish refugees displaced by the war, but the British continued to keep the door closed. In response, Jewish militants in Palestine began an insurgency against the British occupiers.

Such was the situation in Palestine when Truman took office in April 1945. And in the greater scheme of world events in that volatile time, the escalating events in Palestine were of little significance. The vast majority of U.S. Jews, however, endorsed Zionism. And many Gentiles agreed, seeing Arab anti-Semitism much the same as Nazi anti-Semitism.

On July 22, 1946, Jewish terrorists bombed the King David Hotel in Jerusalem, a British military compound, killing ninety-one. The British had no real interest in maintaining control of Palestine, and they were not about to become militarily involved against the Jews just a year after the Holocaust ended. Thus they announced their withdrawal, set for May 15, 1948. The British intended that the United Nations take control of Palestine on that day. For the Palestinian Jews, however, that would be the date for independence, the declaration of a Jewish homeland.

Truman was under great pressure to recognize the proposed Jewish state. American Jews had the financial resources to place their position before the administration, as well as the votes to be politically influential. Truman was facing an uphill battle to win the upcoming 1948 presidential election, and there were enough Jews in New York City and the surrounding regions to influence the outcome of the New York state electoral vote. In 1948 New York was the big prize: It carried forty-five electoral votes, more than any other state. Truman's advisors were telling him he needed New York to win, and he needed the Jewish vote to win New York. Truman, a politician first and foremost, certainly saw that the U.S. recognition of the Jewish state in May 1948 would go a long way toward a victory for him in November. At the same time, there was no real opposition to recognition. There was no Arab constituency and no Arab lobby.

But there was opposition to recognition inside the administration, particularly from several State Department officials who saw the future and the need for Arab oil. Truman, however, discounted their opinions.

In November 1947 the United Nations intervened, attempting to resolve the situation in Palestine by proposing a division of the region between the two groups, with Jerusalem designated as a separate entity, a sort of international city occupied by neither side. The Zionists liked it, and agreed; the plan would recognize a Jewish homeland. The Palestinian Arabs rejected the plan.

Truman was under pressure from several directions to recognize the Jewish state. He had a number of Jewish friends from Kansas City who lobbied the cause. Also, the internationally known Zionist and future president of Israel Chaim Weizmann visited the White House on more than one occasion, in an attempt to win over Truman.

At midnight on May 15, 1948 (6:00 P.M. in Washington), the new nation of Israel was born. Truman issued an immediate declaration of recognition. Syria and Lebanon invaded Israel that day; Iraq followed a day later.

It is still not clear whether Truman acted out of political opportunism or moral conviction. Probably both; foreign policy and politics almost always intersect at some level. The United States did not immediately see Israel as an ally or run to its aid against its Arab enemies. That did not come until the Soviet Union, in the mid-1950s, attempted to win friends among the Arab nations.

In the 1948 election, Truman won the Jewish vote in New York, but he lost the state.

·3·

Affluence and Anxiety: America in the 1950s

It was a brave new world in the 1950s. All the postwar reconversion was over, all the economic swings had ended, and it was apparent that the economy was stable and it would stay that way. Eisenhower in the White House was just about as stable as possible. Consequently, Americans seemed to settle down to living their lives. As the economy got stronger, more and more Americans were able to share in the abundance, to buy cars, to buy houses, to live the American dream. Cars and highways made suburban life possible.

Not all of this turned out to be so delightful. There were problems in the 1950s, and most were well hidden.

Perhaps the most important aspect of the 1950s was that it was the first true gasp of the baby boom generation. In several ways the boomers seemed to be looking for something new and different, almost to the point of frustration.

To Americans today the 1950s was an innocent age, when the cars were big and the gas was cheap. When life was less complicated, work was less stressful, and growing up meant simple things like cherry Cokes and Chuck Berry.

THE FAMILY

The baby boom led to a housing demand that caused housing starts to skyrocket in the 1950s. Housing starts in 1944 were a little over 100,000. By 1950 that number had jumped to almost 1.7 million—all to meet the demand of the rapidly growing American family. The leaders in this building boom were the Levitts, a family of builders who had spent the war building tract housing for the military. Their Levittown in Hempstead, New York, on Long Island, was the largest housing development in American history, eventually reaching a total of 17,400 homes that accommodated over 82,000 residents. The first issue of the Levittown community newspaper remarked: "Our lives are held closely together because most of us are within the same age bracket, in similar income groups, live in

55

almost identical houses and have common problems." It was a description of the new generation just coming of age—and the conformity that has marked it.

At first Americans headed to the suburbs to take advantage of low-cost housing often paid for through government-sponsored loans. But the surge to the suburbs exploded in the 1950s as middle-class Americans began to see suburban life as the key to prestige and status and a refuge from all that was wrong with the nation's rapidly decaying cities. Greater space (a yard for the kids), a big house, and better schools all became a necessity for any family that could afford it. Facilitating the rapid growth was the automobile (now readily available through easy bank financing) and government-built roads. It all looked and seemed right, but there was a "crack in the picture window," as John Keats described in his 1956 book by that name.

While it was true that American suburbanites did, in fact, find the tranquility and peace that rural life offered, they had removed themselves from the urbanity and sophistication of the city. Suburban life was neither urban nor rural, and to a number of sociologists and social critics, suburbia had become the new American nightmare instead of the American dream. It was anti-intellectual, materialistic, uncultured, and shallow. Critics of the new lifestyle included Richard and Katherine Gordon (*The Split-Level Trap*, 1961), Keats (*Crack in the Picture Window*, 1956), and William H. Whyte (*The Organization Man*, 1956). In *The City in History* (1961), Lewis Mumford described the American suburb as "a multitude of uniform, unidentifiable houses, lined up inflexibly, at uniform distances, on uniform roads, in a treeless communal waste, inhabited by people of the same class, the same income, the same age group, witnessing the same television performances, eating the same tasteless prefabricated foods, from the same freezers, conforming in every outward and inward respect to a common mold." The flood tide to the suburbs was also lily-white and middle class, leaving mostly African Americans and poor whites in the cities. Quickly, the gap between the city dwellers and the suburbanites widened as the cities lost their tax base and began their journey on the long road to decay. Malvina Reynolds wrote a popular song that, most likely, brought the message home to most Americans:

> Little boxes on the hillside
> Little boxes made of ticky-tacky
> Little boxes on the hillside
> Little boxes all the same
> There's a green one and a pink one
> And a blue one and a yellow one
> And they're all made out of ticky-tacky
> And they all look just the same

At the same time, suburban life often turned women into isolated housewives, often bored, frustrated, and lonely. This new lifestyle, argued Betty Friedan in *The Feminine Mystique* (1963), pushed women to the fringes of society and robbed them of all emotionally fulfilling experiences. The suburbs may have offered space and better schools, but they lacked the city's advantages of cultural enrichment and diversity. It is no wonder that suburbanites flew into a tailspin of conformity and bourgeois smugness.

In the 1950s, America knew that a woman's place was in the home. If there was any question, society was reminded constantly through advertising and in the media. Television, billboards, and print advertising presented America with the perfect woman. She was pretty and popular; she had children, a spic-and-span home, and a successful husband. She was a volunteer, a den mother, a PTA leader. She sang in the church choir, made her own clothes, gave dinner parties, and, most of all, she was devoted to her husband and family. She was Donna Reed, Harriet Nelson, and June Cleaver. The woman's place was in the home, but by the end of the 1950s it was clear that home did not have that much to offer.

Marriage was, of course, the key to domestic success. By 1950 the average age for men to marry was twenty-one; for women it was twenty, the lowest since the turn of the century.

Despite all the affluence, poverty endured. Remarkably, however, it was mostly unseen. As Michael Harrington wrote in *The Other America: Poverty in the United States* (1962), the new suburban middle class had succeeded in removing itself from the sight of poverty. "The very development of American society is creating a new kind of blindness about poverty," he wrote. "In short the very development of the American city has removed poverty from the living, emotional experience of millions upon millions of middle-class Americans. Living out in the suburbs it is easy to assume that ours is, indeed, an affluent society." The newly affluent whites of American suburbia did not see the poverty of the inner-city ghettos, the California lettuce fields, the isolated and unseen hollows of Appalachia, the Indian reservations of the northern Plains, or the rural Deep South. Poverty, it seemed, would remain a part of the national economy—to be rediscovered as a social problem and a political issue in the 1960s.

IT WAS ALL ON TV

In the 1950s television was the wondrous medium of social change. It brought humor, drama, sports, and news directly into the nation's living rooms. The impact was enormous—in fact, almost beyond description. Just after the war, television was little more than a promise made by engineers at RCA that the nation would, someday soon, have moving pictures right in their own homes. By 1947 a few thousand sets had been sold, mostly in the limited markets around New York. But by 1960 there were nearly forty-five million sets in use, and three national networks broadcasting everything from variety and quiz shows to news and sporting events. The nation was hooked up and tuned in. It radically changed entertainment patterns, the conduct of its politics, and the nature of advertising.

Television also began the process of homogenizing the nation's society and culture. Certainly, it informed the nation; by 1961, for the first time, more than half the nation was willing to admit that television was their main source of news. And it entertained. That was, after all, its primary purpose. But was it good entertainment? Many thought it was not, that it was directed at the lowest common denominator in American society. One of those critics was Newton Minow, chairman of the Federal Communications Commission. In 1961 he called television "a vast wasteland." There were others, however, who saw television's potential. Jack Poppele, president of the Television Broadcasters Association, saw the medium "as expansive as the human mind can comprehend." It "holds the key," he said, "to enlightenment which may unlock the door to world understanding." It certainly was potentially enlightening, but at its best early television was lowbrow, aimed directly at the masses—the largest viewing audience, of course, and the group most likely to purchase the products sold during the commercials.

Soap operas, so named because they were at first sponsored primarily by soap companies, provided one of the lowest forms of television entertainment with their long-running stories, superficial dramas, and heart-wrenching tragedies. They came to be associated with the bored white suburban housewife whose only real escape was into the world of *The Guiding Light* and *As the World Turns*. Men in the 1950s often found themselves glued to the TV in the evenings to watch professional wrestling, a pseudo-sport at best that was almost always played for entertainment instead of competition. It was this 1950s genre that gave the nation its first TV star: "Gorgeous George," a handsome, flaxen blond egomaniac who represented the forces of good against evil in the wrestling ring. For the kids there were Saturday morning cartoons, the big weekly event that kept children entertained while parents slept in. Almost immediately, teachers blamed the evil forces of TV for their students' low reading scores and short attention spans.

Perhaps the most enduring television genre from the decade was the situation comedy, or sitcom. Today, Americans look back with a sort of nostalgic awe on these 1950s programs and what is often called "the golden age of television": Lucy conspiring to get into showbiz despite Ricky's insistence that she remain at home; and Ralph Kramden, the New York City bus driver, dreaming up a get-rich-quick scheme in the vain hope of moving up in life. These, of course, were the exceptions. Most 1950s sitcoms were set in almost cliché depictions of the family ideal—or at least what TV producers believed was the family ideal. There were almost always two parents and two or (more typically) three kids, usually in a generic suburb in an unnamed part of the country. The father obviously worked, but the viewers were rarely told where. The mother was a model homemaker with no aspirations beyond that, but she was always witty and firmly in control of her environment. The family often included a teenager who was also a teen idol, a new phenomenon in the 1950s. The best examples of the genre included *Leave It to Beaver*, *The Adventures of Ozzie and Harriet*, *The Danny Thomas Show*, *The Donna Reed Show*, and *Father Knows Best*. They were all optimistic, uplifting, and occasionally funny. It was what Americans wanted to see when they looked at themselves in the mirror.

Other TV genres developed. The comedy-variety show became a television fixture after Milton Berle hit it big in 1949 with *Texaco Star Theater*. The talk show had its birth in 1951 with *Today*, hosted by the easy-mannered Dave Garroway. Essentially a radio show produced for television, *Today* and dozens of shows like it became an American early-morning staple. At about the same time, Steve Allen entered America's bedrooms with his late-night talk show *Tonight*. Allen set the stage for the future of late night by combining light-impact celebrity chit-chat with lowbrow, low-budget comedy routines and sketches.

Perhaps the most popular 1950s programming was the TV game show—a sort of reality TV for the times. There was *What's My Line* and *I've Got a Secret*, game shows popular more for the celebrity panelists than for the guessing games they played. Then there were the game shows on which average Americans tried to win money or prizes. *Queen for a Day* pitted women against each other for prizes as the audience determined, by the volume of their applause, which one had experienced the worst tragedy in her life. *Truth or Consequences* and *Beat the Clock* encouraged people to make fools of themselves on national television. But the biggest audiences came with the big game shows: *The $64,000 Question*, *Dotto*, and the biggest of them all, *Twenty-One*. These shows became hits because America was mesmerized by what appeared to be ordinary people who knew masses of trivia, and who won more and more money as they answered more and more questions. They were fascinated by the policeman who knew art history, the psychologist who knew all there was to know about boxing, the cobbler who knew everything about opera. But it was Charles Van Doren who seemed to capture the imagination of the nation. A Columbia University professor and son of the literary scholar Mark Van Doren, Charles Van Doren, week after week on *Twenty-One*, grimaced painfully to come up with the answers to seemingly unknowable trivia. However, when Van Doren was elevated to national hero status by beating the reigning champ, Herb Stemple (to win the $129,000 prize), Stemple blew the whistle. He told the *New York Times* that Van Doren had been given the answers and admitted he had been paid to throw the game. Van Doren then lied to a congressional committee and finally received a suspended sentence for perjury. The show's producers pointed the finger at the sponsor, Revlon cosmetics, for insisting that the show be rigged in order to make it more dramatic and interesting to viewers.

The game show scandal was one of the most important events in the history of television. It showed that the medium could not be trusted, that it could manipulate the environment to make fake look real. By implication, then, might the networks' news broadcasts be fabricated, slanted, or just inaccurate for dramatic effect—anything to keep the nation watching or to keep the sponsors happy? The networks immediately moved to shore up their credibility in all areas, but particularly in news coverage. News bureaus went to extremes to cover the news as accurately as possible, complete with on-camera evidence that the story being reported was, in fact, the truth. Also as a result of the quiz show scandal, the Federal Communications Commission mandated that each network air one public service program each week and ended advertisers' manipulation of on-air content.

CINEMA IN THE FIFTIES

Movie moguls feared television, and with good reason. In the immediate postwar years, even before television became ubiquitous, theater attendance had dropped by 14 percent. Television threatened to put a small movie theater in every American's living room. Not surprisingly, the two industries saw themselves locked in competition for viewers through the 1950s. It would take a while, but TV and movies would eventually form an alliance that would make money for everyone involved.

One result of this early Hollywood-TV conflict was the emergence of a new crop of movie actors. The movie studios would not allow their contract actors to work in television, so it was the youngest actors who headed into television, many from the New York stage. Rod Steiger, James Dean, Grace Kelly, Paul Newman, Anne Bancroft, Joanne Woodward, Eddie Albert, and Eva Marie Saint all got their starts in television before becoming big film stars. Most were cast in one-performance dramas that were little more than filmed stage plays.

In order to compete with television, Hollywood moved to upgrade its product, to produce movies that could not be made for television. With that came the movie "spectacular," the "epic," with "a cast of thousands." Hollywood also upgraded the movie technology with widescreen Cinemascope and 3-D. The result was not necessarily better movies, just bigger ones. The first movie filmed in Cinemascope was *The Robe* in 1953. From that grew the most memorable genre of the era, the biblical-classic epic, the Cecil B. DeMille–made extravaganza and its innumerable copies. *The Ten Commandments* (1956) led the field, but it was followed closely by *Ben-Hur* (1959), *Spartacus* (1960), and a host of lesser-quality copies. The biggest attack on TV came with Cinerama, a massive process in which the movie is shown by three synchronized cameras onto three adjacent screens simultaneously. The only truly commercial film made with this process was *How the West Was Won* (1962), a Hollywood spectacular that included just about every big actor working at the time. The stampeding buffalo sequence near the end of the film remains one of the most exhilarating film sequences in history—if viewed in Cinerama.

Perhaps the most enduring genre of the 1950s was the horror film. In some ways an outgrowth of 1930s classics like *Frankenstein* and *Dracula* (both produced in 1931), the 1950s horror flicks returned with a number of variations on the original themes—plus the new dimension of outer space, where any creepy creature might attack the good people of Earth. Some of these were well done, and a few, like *War of the Worlds* (1953) and *The Incredible Shrinking Man* (1957), have stood the test of time. But for most critics, the vast majority of 1950s horror films were silly and poorly made. The Japanese film industry produced a number of awful movies for the American market that almost always featured a giant monster in the process of destroying a miniaturized Tokyo. These monsters (Godzilla and Rodan were the most memorable) usually emerged from nuclear test sites—Japanese-inspired irony usually lost on American moviegoers.

An entire group of horror movies was directed at the teenage baby boom audience. The most celebrated were *I Was a Teenage Frankenstein* and *I Was a Teenage Werewolf*, both produced in 1957. In the same genre was *The Blob*, starring a young Steve McQueen, a story that dealt as much with the popular topic of youth alienation as it did with the large, red, viscous "thing" that was devouring a small town's inhabitants. The parents, much to their own peril, refused to listen to the warnings from the teenagers. Not surprisingly, the makers of these movies have been elevated to cult status. Among the most memorable are Sam Arkoff (*I Was a Teenage Werewolf*), Roger Corman (*The Monster from the Ocean Floor*, shot in four days for $12,000), William Castle (*House on Haunted Hill* and *Thirteen Ghosts*, shot in "Illusion-O"), and Edward D. Wood, Jr., who is often credited with making two of the worst movies in history: *Plan 9 from Outer Space* (1959), starring Bela Lugosi and Vampira in a pathetic attempt to mix the horror movie genre with science fiction; and *Glen or Glenda?* (1953), the strange case of a man who could change his sex at will—narrated by Lugosi.

Perhaps the most difficult problem the movie industry faced in the 1950s was censure by the Red Scare and McCarthyism. The climate of the times forbade treatment of controversial topics such as drug addiction, sexual deviation, or even political extremism. Hollywood, however, showed its resiliency by producing a few good movies, often with underlying themes. *High Noon* (1952) has been variously interpreted as a criticism of conformity and also of McCarthyism—despite denials of any such intentions by director Fred Zinnemann. A Western sheriff, played by the indomitable Gary Cooper, must fight the forces of evil alone because he has been abandoned by his town's cowardly citizens. Once he defeats the bad guys at the end of the movie, the town's people rally around him again. The message seemed clear: that those who stand up to McCarthyism (and, more generally, censorship) may have to stand alone, but when victory ultimately comes they will be seen as heroes. John Wayne, certainly a fan of a good Western but also a good friend of the political Right, once said that he thought *High Noon* was the worst movie he had ever seen.

In the classic sci-fi flick *Invasion of the Body Snatchers* (1956) the inhabitants of a small town are turned into emotionless, mindless automatons by giant pods from outer space. To become one of the pod people, as one convert explains, is to be "reborn into an untroubled world, where everyone is the same." Analyses, of course, were varied. Some saw it as a warning against communism; others interpreted it as a criticism of conformity. Undoubtedly, the vast majority who saw it just thought it was a scary movie.

Americans in the 1950s liked to watch movies about the war, in fact to celebrate their victories over evil. John Wayne, as much a soldier as a cowboy, became the American military icon Sergeant Stryker—a soldier's soldier—who was killed at the end of *Sands of Iwo Jima* (1949). Other great war movies included *From Here to Eternity* (1953), starring Burt Lancaster and Deborah Kerr, whose steamy beach scene was extremely sexy for the era, and left little to the imagination.

The American Western was an important genre for the decade, and several were exceptional productions, particularly Howard Hawks's *Red River* (1948) with John Wayne, often at the top of lists of the best Westerns ever made, and John Ford's *The Searchers* (1956) again with Wayne and a strong supporting cast. Alan Ladd starred in the panoramic *Shane* (1953) as the mysterious ex-gunslinger who defends the lowly sodbusters against the powerful cattle barons. The 1950s Western genre produced such enduring cinematic characters as the indefatigable frontiersman, the heartless gunfighter, the stalwart sheriff, the doomed Indian, the cavalry soldier to the rescue, and on and on. By the end of the 1950s the genre had spilled over into television with such familiar Western characters as Matt Dillon, Cheyenne, Paladin, and Maverick.

British director Alfred Hitchcock produced his own personal genre in the 1950s with a series of thrillers, including *Rope* (1948), *Rear Window* (1954), *Vertigo* (1958), and one of the most frightening movies ever made, *Psycho* (1960). *Psycho* is the story of hotel owner/taxidermist Norman Bates, played by Anthony Perkins, who is apparently a normal young man living a normal life in a normal California town. Norman, however, takes on the personality of his dead mother and murders attractive women. For the general public, at least, the word "psycho" entered the national vocabulary, as a noun meaning a mentally deranged killer.

There were several movie icons of the decade, but none quite like Marilyn Monroe. In some ways she defined the era. She started off in Hollywood in dumb blonde bit parts until she hit it big in John Houston's *Asphalt Jungle* in 1950. In 1951 she had a small part in *All about Eve* with George Sanders, who later claimed that he knew Marilyn would be a star "because she desperately needed to be one." In 1955 she made the delightful *Seven Year Itch* opposite the drooling Tom Ewell. A year later she let the world know that she was a serious actress in Joshua Logan's *Bus Stop*. In 1959 she reached her comic peak in Billy Wilder's *Some Like It Hot*, playing wonderfully off Tony Curtis and Jack Lemmon in drag. Her comic performances were appealingly childlike and vulnerable.

COOL CULTURE

A dynamic youth culture emerged in the 1950s. It was the first time the boomers found themselves and insisted they had something to say. Certainly there had been vocal generations of youths before, particularly in the 1920s. But following the hardships of the Great Depression and then the war, it seemed that the nation's youth in the 1950s were ready to explode out of the gate, take on society, and change the nation. The generation that had slogged through the hardships of the previous two decades never quite got it.

Money was undoubtedly at the heart of it all. Teenagers in the 1950s were hardly rich, but they had money to spend, cars to drive, and perhaps too much time on their hands. Their relative affluence turned them into an identifiable demographic: the "teen market." Manufacturers and designers focused a large part of their production on this group, and advertisers targeted their every need and desire.

Fads directed at the young boomers swept the nation. Whatever it was, everyone had to have one. Early in the decade it was Silly Putty, the Slinky, and the Hula-Hoop. Later it was 45-rpm records and transistor radios. By the end of the decade advertisers were selling the wonders of youth to the entire nation, both young and old.

Television certainly had an impact on American youth in the 1950s, but it was the movies that perpetuated the decade's cool culture. The most common image directed at the nation's youth was the cool juvenile delinquent, the kid who was bad on the outside, but good on the inside, often just trying to get along like everyone else. Certainly the most analyzed movie in this genre is the 1955 *Rebel without a Cause*, the story of a troubled young man (James Dean in his first of three roles before his death), whose unspecified problems had forced his family to relocate more than once. The movie's message, however, is that rebellious teenage behavior is a direct result of inadequate parental guidance. The father of Dean's character (played by Jim Backus) refuses to stand up to his wife and "be a man." The father of Natalie Wood's character openly rejects his daughter's affections, and the parents of Sal Mineo's character are absentee and attempt to buy his love by periodically sending him envelopes full of money. A more disturbing film about juvenile delinquency is *Blackboard Jungle*, released in 1955, the same year as *Rebel*. Here an idealistic young teacher, played by Glen Ford, begins his teaching career at a New York inner-city school where his classroom is filled with juvenile delinquents, troublemakers, and gang members. Its disturbing nature, along with its interracial content, caused the movie to be banned in several regions and cities around the country, and occasionally showings brought together rival gangs to "rumble" in the parking lots of theaters. One of the most groundbreaking aspects of the movie was the theme song, "Rock Around the Clock" by Bill Haley and the Comets, one of the first genuine rock 'n' roll songs ever produced. Here again, the kids in trouble complained of a lack of parental guidance. A year earlier in *The Wild One*, a waitress asks the snotty, inarticulate, but definitely "cool" Marlon Brando, "What are you rebelling against?" Brando's predictable response was "What'd ya got?" The new rebels of the era had not yet found a cause to rebel against. That would change.

Juvenile delinquency in the movies translated into something fairly harmless, but in reality it was a problem that would not go away, and it frightened the nation's adults. It was most prevalent in the inner cities, where a nascent gang mentality seemed to be emerging that manifested itself in petty crime, antisocial behavior, and irreverence toward authority and adult supervision. When that behavior became emulated as "cool," at least in physical appearance and attitude, the nation's adults saw a slippery slope of social and cultural deterioration. Studies were conducted, laws were passed, and juvenile delinquency continued to plague the nation's inner cities.

The height of youth cultural expression in the 1950s (as it would be a decade later) was the music. The origins of rock 'n' roll might well be seen as a reaction to the outlandishly bland sounds of late-1940s and early-1950s pop music that ran the gamut from waltzes to novelty songs. Stuck with Perry Como and Rosemary Clooney, it is hardly a wonder that the nation's teenagers by mid-decade had begun experimenting with other forms of music. Young entertainers pulled together an amalgam of the country music style, "rockabilly," African American rhythm and blues, and added a strong electric guitar and a back beat to produce rock 'n' roll. Not unlike jazz, the exact origins of rock 'n' roll remain murky.

As early as 1951 a Cleveland disc jockey named Allen Freed drew a following among white teenagers in the Midwest when he began playing records by black rhythm and blues artists. Apparently Freed first used the phrase rock 'n' roll. But the first true rock 'n' roll superstar came out of the South. In 1954 Sam Phillips, a small-time record producer in Memphis, was looking for what he called a "white man with a black sound" to sell to the youth of white America. He found what he was looking for in Elvis Presley, a nineteen-year-old truck driver from Tupelo, Mississippi, with sullen good looks and a gospel-trained voice. Phillips recorded and released Elvis Presley's first big hit, "That's Alright Mama," a brushed-up rendition of Arthur "Big Boy" Crudup's blues song. Elvis took the R&B that was popular in the black community, gave it a rockabilly style and an occasional gospel cadence, and introduced it to white America. The sound itself seemed to awaken the nation's youth, but perhaps the music's greatest appeal was the raw sexuality that Elvis picked up from R&B. Within a year, Phillips had "sold" Elvis to RCA records, which produced several of Elvis's signature songs: "Heartbreak Hotel," "I'm All Shook Up," and "Don't Be Cruel." His appearances in 1956 and 1957 on the *Milton Berle Show/Texaco Star Theater*, the *Steve Allen Show*, and then the *Ed Sullivan Show* turned him into a national phenomenon. Over the next two years he released a string of fourteen consecutive hits that made him rock 'n' roll's first superstar and made rock 'n' roll the foundation of American youth culture and the primary symbol of youth rebellion.

Elvis was out front, but those who followed were more than just Elvis copiers, and that is what allowed rock 'n' roll to maintain itself and grow. It was, in fact, innovative from the top down. Artists like Chuck Berry and Little Richard (both black R&B artists who made the transition to rock 'n' roll with no difficulty), Buddy Holly, Bill Haley, Jerry Lee Lewis, and Carl Perkins all added something new. The result was an expansion, even an explosion, of style, a need to be different before an audience of teenagers ready to soak up anything with wailing guitar licks and a pounding beat.

THE BEATS

Rebellion seemed to be in the air in the 1950s, and rock 'n' roll seemed to set the stage for that. But at the same time, and in a different part of the country, a genuine counterculture was growing. This counterculture had its antecedents in the black hipsters of the 1930s, a group that had grown out of the Great Migration of African Americans from the rural South to the northern urban ghettos after World War I. They were the second generation of African Americans in the city, and they were openly contemptuous of the white world that oppressed them. Their way of life was hedonistic and punctuated with sexual freedom; their style was sensual and ultimately cool. Their language was jive, their uniform was the zoot suit, their music was jazz, and their drug of choice was marijuana. By the mid-1940s, the zoot suit was replaced by more conservative attire, jazz was replaced by bebop, and marijuana was replaced by heroin. By then, whites living in racially integrated areas like Greenwich Village had caught on to the cool of hip, found the bebop sounds of Charlie Parker, and adopted the drugs and the style of cool. Novelist Norman Mailer called them "the white Negro," but their alienation and their rebellion were against the postwar middle-class values of affluence. And in their rejection of those middle-class norms and values they embraced poverty. They were the Beats, the forebears of the next decade's hippies.

At the Beat epicenter was Allen Ginsberg, a young poet whose remarkable poem "Howl" was a scathing indictment of American materialism. Surrounding Ginsberg was a group of friends and lovers who defined the Beats. Other primary figures included Jack Kerouac and Neal Cassidy, two young adventurers who took off for California, living a life filled with drugs, sex, and jazz. In 1951 Kerouac wrote *On the Road*, a fictionalized account of the trip. The novel spoke to a generation about spontaneity, freedom, adventure, and the mystique of "the road."

Much of the Beat movement was defined by its literature. Ginsburg was a successful poet, Kerouac went on to write two more novels, and there were several other important writers of the movement, including John Clellon Holmes (*Go*, 1952), Chandler Brossard (*Who Walk in Darkness*, 1952), Norman Mailer (*The Deer Park*, 1955), and, later, Lawrence Ferlinghetti (*Her*, 1960) and Ken Kesey (*One Flew Over the Cuckoo's Nest*, 1962). These writers wrote of the darkest side of American society: hedonism, drugs, nihilism, perversion, crime, insanity. They developed their own genre and their own writing style for the era.

ADVANCES IN MEDICAL AND BIOLOGICAL SCIENCE

Postwar Americans had concluded that there were no boundaries to what they could do, what they could accomplish. And that included curing disease. Unquestionably the most heralded medical achievement after the war was the victory over the dreaded infantile paralysis, or polio. In 1952 alone there were 57,628 reported cases of the disease in the United States. In addition, polio crippled and killed untold thousands every year throughout the world. This silent, highly contagious disease paralyzed for life and sometimes killed its victims, mostly young people. It was Jonas Edward Salk whose work defeated the disease. Salk was an epidemiologist who had worked to develop an improved influenza vaccine. In 1947 he continued his work on viruses at the Virus Research Lab at the University of Pittsburgh, eventually shifting his efforts to tackling the polio virus. His work was funded by the March of Dimes of the National Foundation for Infantile Paralysis. After several blind studies, field trials, and volunteer inoculations, the March of Dimes announced in April 1953 that the Salk vaccine was safe and effective. Within two years the cases of polio dropped 90 percent in the United States.

Other medical advances of the immediate postwar era may not have had as much publicity as Salk's polio vaccine, but several are certainly worth noting. In 1953 a British scientist, Francis H. C. Crick, and his American colleague, James D. Watson, discovered the structure of DNA at their research lab at Cambridge University in England. Although it caused barely a blip on the radar of science at the time, Crick and Watson had made one of the most important scientific discoveries in the history of mankind.

In 1960 the Food and Drug Administration approved "the pill," and American sexuality would never be the same. In the early 1950s feminist Margaret Sanger and her wealthy friend Katherine McCormick got together with reproductive biologists Gregory Pincus and Min Chueh Chang to set up the Worcester Foundation for Experimental Biology in Shrewsbury, Massachusetts. By 1954 they had developed norethynodrel, an effective oral contraceptive that had tested well in Puerto Rico and Mexico. By 1957 the G. D. Searle Company had agreed to market the pill as a fertility drug. Following FDA approval in 1960, the drug was marketed as a safe and effective oral contraceptive for women. The pill would have an enormous social impact on the coming decades. It gave women unprecedented control over their fertility, and thus their lives. It also went a long way toward separating sexual activity from reproduction, and that changed the very nature of sex.

There were other significant advances in medicine, several not appreciated until the baby boomers reached advanced age decades later. In the late 1940s a group headed by John Merrill at Brigham Hospital in Boston significantly improved the artificial kidney, opening the door to effective renal dialysis. In 1952 Charles Hufnagel, working at Georgetown University Medical Center, implanted the first effective artificial heart valve in a human. And in the late 1940s and early 1950s researchers at Washington University in St. Louis (along with a number of researchers elsewhere in the nation) determined that excessive cigarette smoking caused lung cancer, opening an entire chapter on causes and prevention of various types of cancer.

Penicillin had been discovered in 1928, but by 1942 there was still only enough penicillin to treat, perhaps, a hundred patients. By the end of the war, however, the United States was producing enough penicillin to meet the needs of the armed forces; after the war, there was enough to meet the needs of the American population. Through the remainder of the decade, researchers discovered other antibiotics, often with specific uses. Streptomycin and isoniazid proved particularly effective against tuberculosis; Chloromycetin, a broad-spectrum antibiotic, combated typhus epidemics in the world's poorest nations; and Aureomycin was a popular antibiotic effective against hundreds of diseases.

The postwar years also saw an interest in anthropology, psychology, and the scientific study of human sexual behavior. Margaret Meade's epic *Coming of Age in Samoa*, first published in the late 1920s, received a rebirth just after the war when it was re-released in paperback. Ruth Benedict's *Patterns of Culture*, first published in the 1930s, received much the same attention. Psychology had not seen such a popularization of the field since Freud. Erik Erikson's *Childhood and Society* (1950) and *Young Man Luther* (1958) explored the concepts of personality development and personality conflicts. B. F. Skinner, a Harvard psychology professor, introduced the psychological concept of behaviorism, arguing that behavior, particularly student behavior, could be controlled and directed by controlling the stimuli.

The nation's curiosity about the mind was surpassed only by its curiosity about the body. The first salvo of the sexual revolution of the next decade was fired by Alfred Kinsey, whose *Sexual Behavior in the Human Male* (1948) changed America's view of sex and sexuality. Kinsey was a zoology professor at Indiana University and the world's foremost expert on, of all things, the wasp. The university needed someone to teach a course on marriage and family, and Kinsey agreed; but lacking any useful published data on human sexual activity, he set out to compile his own. Over a ten-year period he collected and analyzed data on over five thousand males. The report, known almost universally as "The Kinsey Report," was published and became an immediate cultural phenomenon. His data showed that there was a tremendous gap between public perception and the realities of sex, that many of the old social mores were being ignored, and that Americans were seeking and enjoying sex with tremendous gusto. According to

Kinsey's report, men were having extramarital affairs in greater numbers than anyone imagined; sexual activity began, for most Americans, at an earlier age than had been thought; and male homosexuality was more prevalent than presumed. The conclusions were, in fact, startling. The book was later largely discredited, generally because of flaws in the collection of data (almost exclusively from Midwestern white male college students and graduates). Nevertheless, Kinsey's message was clear: America was sexually active. In 1953, Kinsey published *Sexual Behavior in the Human Female.*

If the era had a bible, it was Dr. Benjamin Spock's *Common Sense Book of Baby and Child Care*, first published in 1946. The primary message of "Spock's Baby Book," as it was most commonly known, was that mothers should have confidence in their own natural instincts and common sense, and that it was just as necessary to give comfort and love to a child as to meet basic nutritional needs. Spock provided a basis for a genuine consensus on child rearing in the postwar years.

LITERARY GENRES

One of the primary literary genres of the postwar years was the war novel. Norman Mailer's gritty *The Naked and the Dead* (1948) produced the nation's first postwar literary figure. At age twenty-eight, Mailer shocked the country with his graphic realism, his cynicism, and his profound disillusionment. He wrote about the war in the Pacific, about an army platoon on an arduous and dangerous (but generally meaningless) patrol on an insignificant atoll. Mailer forced his readers to recognize that there were evil forces lurking in the minds of American soldiers, that they did not fight for the high moral principles of achieving a better life and liberty at home. They fought because they were told to, trained to, and because they feared the wrath of their officers if they refused. American soldiers had to kill, and the process was neither pleasant nor humane.

Other war novels included James Jones's *From Here to Eternity* (1951), the story of a free spirit, Private Pruit, who tries and fails to maintain his individuality in the prewar service in Hawaii. *Mister Roberts*, written by Thomas Heggen, tells the story of one sailor's desire to enter the fight against the Japanese. Stuck on the USS *Reluctant* with a mission to transport toilet paper to soldiers of the South Pacific, Mr. Roberts chafed at the bit while he navigated between the swabs and the oppressive and demanding ship's captain.

One of the literary anthems of the postwar era was J. D. Salinger's *The Catcher in the Rye*, published in 1951. It is perhaps the best example of the era's alienation, affluence, and youth neglect. Salinger's protagonist, Holden Caulfield, roams New York City, encountering only phoniness and dishonesty. The novel mocks the hypocrisy, compromise, and conformity of the day. Salinger wrote two more novellas in the early 1960s and then, with no explanation, disappeared into seclusion for the remainder of his life.

The genre of the Southern novel continued on, maintaining its own unique character in the postwar years. William Faulkner continued to write until his death in 1962, and his style was picked up by writers like Robert Penn Warren, whose *All the King's Men* (1946) stands as one of the literary masterpieces of the postwar years. Other major works from Southern writers include Carson McCullers's *The Ballad of the Sad Café* (1951), Flannery O'Conner's *Wise Blood* (1952) and *A Good Man Is Hard to Find* (1955), and Eudora Welty's *The Golden Apples* (1949).

Several important African American writers emerged after the war. Ralph Ellison wrote eloquently in his *Invisible Man* (1952) of the difficulties of being black in a white man's world, a world that refused to recognize his humanity. *Invisible Man* is a landmark in twentieth-century fiction and in African American culture and cultural identity. In 1953 James Baldwin entered the literary scene with *Go Tell It on the Mountain*, a semiautobiographical account about the difficulties of coming of age in Harlem amid the torrents of a lust-driven, religious stepfather. Richard Wright had been one of the pioneers of African American literature in the 1930s with his *Uncle Tom's Children* (1938) and in the 1940s with his masterpiece *Native Son* (1940), which made him the most distinguished African American novelist in that era. In 1945 he published the autobiographical *Black Boy*. The major theme of all three of these writers was the rage and disgust brought on by growing up and living in a white man's world, experiencing the racism, hate, and alienation of being a black man in the United States.

DRAMA AND THEATER

The postwar period was a golden age of drama and theater mainly because of the superb work of two of the nation's greatest playwrights, Tennessee Williams and Arthur Miller. Williams became famous with the production of *The Glass Menagerie* in 1945. It is the story of a fragile, shy girl who seeks escape from reality (and the expectations of her Southern mother) through her assortment of glass animal figurines. It is a tender saga of sadness, unhappiness, and expectations unfulfilled, all topics that fill Williams's dramas. In his highly acclaimed *A Streetcar Named Desire* (first produced in 1947), Williams explores the contradictions of passing Southern gentility and the brutality of the modern world. It is the story of Blanche DuBois, an aging Southern beauty who is forced to confront the brutish reality of her sister's husband, Stanley Kowalski, along with her own past in the seedy Desire slum of postwar New Orleans. Williams scored again in 1955 with *Cat on a Hot Tin Roof*, in which greed, homosexuality, alcohol, and mendacity rip apart a prominent Southern family. Williams continued to produce strong work, including *Sweet Bird of Youth* (1959), *Night of the Iguana* (1961), and *The Milk Train Doesn't Stop Here Anymore* (1963), but his work never again quite reached the level of *Glass Menagerie*, *Streetcar*, or *Cat on a Hot Tin Roof*.

Arthur Miller produced three unsuccessful plays before he hit all the right notes with *Death of a Salesman*, first produced in 1949. It is the story of Willy Loman, an aging salesman whose life has added up to nothing. He is a failure as a husband, as a father, and even as a salesman. His objective in his tragic life has been only to be well liked. Cheating and lying, he tells his sons, are acceptable in a world where getting along is the only objective. Miller not only puts Willy on trial, he puts American society on trial as well. Willy goes along and gets along through compromise, conformity, and even deceit. In the early 1950s Miller found himself the target of the House Committee on Un-American Activities. He fought back with *The Crucible* (first produced in 1953), a drama about the Salem witch trials clearly intended as an allegory for the Red Scare witch hunts of the period.

Eugene O'Neill is usually associated with the prewar, lost generation, but he produced some of his best work after the war, including *The Iceman Cometh* (1946) and *Long Day's Journey into Night*, produced in 1956 following his death in 1953.

Several novels were adapted to the theater, including Thomas Heggan's *Mister Roberts* (1948), Herman Wouk's *The Caine Mutiny* (1954), and Harvey Breit and Budd Schulberg's *The Disenchanted* (1959). In an unusual progression of events, even television plays ended up on the stage, most notably N. Richard Nash's *The Rainmaker* (1955), Paddy Chayefsky's *Marty* (1955), and William Gibson's *The Miracle Worker* (1960).

The dramatists of the immediate postwar period saw the distinction between the promises and the dreams, between the hope for the future and the reality of American life. It was a common thread running through the minds of the nation's intellectuals, playwrights, novelists, and other writers and artists of the postwar years. Their ideas had a major impact on the next decade.

THE NEW AMERICAN RELIGION

There was a discernable religious revival after the war. Americans joined churches in record numbers. In the years just before the war, less than half the adults in the nation said they belonged to a church. By 1960 that number had jumped to over 65 percent. Much of this had to do with the use, by the various religious groups, of modern advertising and marketing techniques, particularly aggressive advertising in the media, the use of giant billboards, and even house-to-house proselytizing. "The family that prays together," Americans were told, "stays together."

Not surprisingly, the nation's postwar religiousness had a distinct Cold War connection. The Soviet Union, the enemy, was a godless entity, and religious leaders in the United States constantly evoked religion as a weapon against communism. If anti-communism can be a religious concept, Americans worshipped at that altar in the 1950s. "Our government makes no sense," Eisenhower proclaimed, "unless it is founded on a deep felt religious faith." And he added in the true Eisenhower manner, "and I don't care what it is." In 1954, Congress decided that it was important to add the phrase "One nation under God" to the Pledge of Allegiance, and the next year it made mandatory the phrase "In God We Trust" on all currency.

The new popular piety had its foundations in the mushrooming suburbia. Similar to the church in rural America in an earlier age, the postwar suburban church was often a place for social gatherings, a meeting place. To belong meant to be a part of the suburban community, to have friends, to make business contacts. It became the focal point of national conformity. To not belong to the community church was to be different, an outsider, a nonconformist, perhaps a Communist or a fellow traveler. The House Committee on Un-American Activities often asked for the religious affiliation of those they suspected of subversive activities, with the tacit assumption that those not affiliated with a legitimate religious group were "godless" Communists. To be perceived as ungodly—a person who refused (or even neglected) to attend church on Sunday—was the wrong way to be judged in postwar America.

The most prominent face of American religion in the postwar years was Billy Graham. A Southern Baptist evangelist whose charisma from the pulpit had a powerful effect on his mass audiences, Graham quickly established himself as the most famous evangelist in the nation—and then the world. By the mid-1950s, Graham was conducting extraordinary mass conversions and huge "crusades" in major U.S. cities, and then around the world. Many of the crusades were televised, and presented to the nation as spectacular affairs. By the end of the 1950s, Graham was as close as the nation would get to a national preacher.

While Graham held his spectacular crusades, Bishop Fulton Sheen, the Auxiliary Bishop of New York, took to television in 1951 to speak to the nation about Catholic theology, the dilemmas of psychology, and the horrors of Soviet communism. To the surprise of most critics, Sheen held his own in a Tuesday night timeslot against the wildly popular *Texaco Star Theater* with Milton Berle ("He uses old material, too," Berle joked). Sheen was best known for his quiet demeanor punctuated by a firm anti-communism. "Stalin," he once said, "must one day meet his judgment." Sheen's network program, *A Life Worth Living*, ran until 1957, and then continued on in syndication as *The Fulton Sheen Program* until the late 1960s.

If Graham and Sheen reflected a more traditional approach to religion in the postwar years, Norman Vincent Peale told the nation that they could find God through what he called "positive thinking," a combination of theology and psychology that entailed mostly good fellowship and good works. Peale's message resonated with those Americans who seemed to be looking for the lighter side of religion. His most famous book, *The Power of Positive Thinking* (1952), remained on the *New York Times* best-seller list for an unprecedented 186 weeks and has sold over seven million copies since it was first published. Americans wanted to be told that their lives were good and that they had achieved their goals, and Peale made them feel good about themselves and about their lives. It was a religion of mass appeal and material success. But many theologians saw Peale's positive thinking as a shallow piety. Theologian Will Herbert, in his book *Protestant, Catholic, Jew* (1956), wrote that the religious conviction of the era was "religiousness without religion, a religiousness with almost [no] kind of content . . . a way of sociability or 'belonging,' rather than a way of reorienting life toward God." And, he added, "By and large, the religion which actually prevails among Americans today has lost much of the authentic Christian (or Jewish) content."

The era had produced two types of religious leaders: Graham, the traditional evangelical of the type that had permeated American history, who took his mission out of the community and put it on television and exposed it to the world; and Peale, who saw the rewards of religious salvation in the foundations of modern psychology and self-assuredness. Graham told all Americans to "examine themselves and renew their own hearts before God." Peale told Americans to "stop worrying and start living."

CONCLUSION

The 1950s stands as a unique era in American history because, unlike other periods of change, the vast majority of American people were touched by the tremendous cultural and social changes that engulfed the nation. Television was, of course, the catalyst for that, for better or worse. It changed the nation, the culture, the politics, the basic social patterns. At the same time, the average American in the 1950s was considerably better off than at any time in the nation's history, and society and culture reflected that abundance in personal wealth and material gain. But running alongside the abundance was the intense anxiety of the Cold War and what that might bring. One response was a fierce conformity that stifled and even strangled various aspects of culture and society at a time when the prosperity might have fueled a new American renaissance.

Reading: A Little Bit of Rock 'n' Roll

America's parents did not like Elvis, particularly after they saw him on *The Milton Berle Show* when he did all the grunting, hair-tossing, and slow, burlesque hip-grinding. He was a certain threat. This was not the sad Elvis of the 1970s, with his dyed hair, sequined peacock jumpsuit, and silver-rimmed aviator glasses. This was the handsome, sexy, crotch-thrusting, hip-swinging twenty-year-old, who could turn up one corner of his mouth (the way bad Elvis impersonators do today) and girls in the front rows would faint—not pretend to faint in the ecstasy of the moment, but go down and out.

If Elvis was "discovered," it was by Sam Phillips, who at his Sun Records in Memphis said he was looking for just the right guy, just the right voice. "If I could find a white man," he said, "who has the Negro sound and the Negro feel, I could make a million." He knew what he was talking about. Phillips had started out recording black R&B artists like Rufus Thomas, "Howlin' Wolf," and Ike Turner. And by the early 1950s it was clear to him (and to others in his business) that black music was gaining a white audience, that it was electrifying white kids all over the country. Elvis made that transition. He carried all the sound that was rock 'n' roll to the white kids who were starved for something new and different. But perhaps more importantly, he showed white America that it was actually possible to be both white and cool.

It was in this time that Elvis was part of Phillips's "Million-Dollar Quartet," including Jerry Lee Lewis, Carl Perkins, and Johnny Cash. All four, according to Perkins, had that Negro sound. Among them it was Perkins who was the writer, with such early standards as "Blue Suede Shoes," "Boppin' the Blues," and "Honey Don't."

In Lubbock, Texas, at the town roller rink, Buddy Holly was making another transition. He was turning rockabilly into rock 'n' roll. He had heard Elvis and had been inspired to bridge the two worlds, to make the transition from his country-western roots to R&B, and then to rock 'n' roll. Holly was more innovative than is usually realized. He was the first to use double-tracking, and he popularized the classic two guitars, bass, and drums setup used by most rock 'n' roll groups, including the Beatles. Holly and the Crickets had a string of hits over just a short three-year period.

For black R&B singers the era was frustrating. Their music had, in fact, been stolen. And all too often, R&B singles were immediately covered by white groups, and almost always sanitized to remove any raunchiness that might offend white parents. Perhaps the two best examples are Joe Turner's "Shake, Rattle and Roll," covered by Bill Haley and the Comets in 1954; and Little Richard's outrageous "Tutti Frutti," turned into a piano-bar tune by Pat Boone. Boone's cover, however, never really overshadowed Little Richard's wild, screaming version, and there are stories that, somehow, Little Richard's music could make black and white kids dance together.

Do-wop was another style that broke into the musical mainstream in the fifties. African Americans have always been able to make art out of "making do." In much the way rap was born (at least in part from young black kids who could not afford instruments), do-wop emerged from a tradition of teenagers comparing voices in urban alleyways. Among the great do-woppers who found their callings on the big-city street corners were The Flamingos ("I Only Have Eyes for You"), Little Anthony and the Imperials ("Tears on My Pillow"), The Dells ("Oh What a Night"), and Frankie Lyman and the Teenagers ("Why Do Fools Fall in Love"). From these grew The Platters, The Pretenders, The Drifters, The Coasters, and the names can go on and on.

If Elvis was a white man who could sing like a black R&B singer, then Chuck Berry was a black singer who could sing—well, like a white man singing like a black singer. If that seems confusing, consider that Chuck Berry's handlers tried hard to keep him off television and minimize his personal appearances in hopes that white parents would think he was, in fact, white. Berry was electrifying in much the same way Elvis was. His infamous duck-walking and his bursts of machine-gun guitar made him the revelation and inspiration of at least the Beatles and the Rolling Stones.

In 1957 the music nearly died. In that year, Little Richard got religion and stopped performing. Chuck Berry violated the Mann Act by transporting an underage girl across the Missouri state line. He eventually served two years in prison. And Jerry Lee Lewis, the "Killer" at the height of his fame, married his thirteen-year-old cousin, Myra. He then went on television to announce it to the world. He never quite realized why America stopped buying his records. Elvis got drafted into the army and went to Europe to fill the ranks of NATO. He left the United States a pounding rocker, and returned a ballad singer and B-movie actor. And then Buddy Holly's plane disappeared into an Iowa cornfield killing everyone on board, including Holly, Richie Valens ("La Bamba"), and the Big Bopper ("Chantilly Lace").

What filled the void were pretty boys, the young singers who met the approval of parents everywhere: Fabian, Frankie Avalon, Paul Anka, and Bobby Darin. Running the show was the always-presentable Dick Clark, whose *American Bandstand* hit the airways in 1959. Clark wore a suit and tie, and the dancing kids were always clean and neat. And parents approved. From 1957 until February 7, 1964, rock 'n' roll lost much of its edge. It was on that day that the Beatles landed at Kennedy Airport.

· 4 ·

The Eisenhower Presidency

After twenty tumultuous years of economic cataclysm, followed by economic experimentation, and then war, economic controls, inflation, labor strife, and then another war, Americans were ready for a change. They were ready for Eisenhower, a president who most believed could return the nation to the good life of prosperity, predictability, and security. Ike was comfortable. In his State of the Union message he used the term "middle way" to describe his approach to domestic issues. It seemed to hit home with the nation. Eisenhower was going to run the nation down the middle of the road. There would be no experimenting and no surprises.

Americans saw Eisenhower as a genial, grandfatherly figure who played bridge and Scrabble in the evenings with his wife and golf on the weekends with his buddies. He had an infectious smile and comforting personality. He seemed to stay above all the political backbiting in Washington. His words were not high-minded and his thoughts, it seemed, were not very complex. Also, his syntax and grammar were often awkward and rambling, all of which seemed to endear him to the average American even more. He was also modest, and there are few things more appealing to Americans than a modest hero. America liked Ike.

But behind the smile and the simple demeanor was a strong, complex figure with his hand on the pulse of the nation and the world, a man with a ferocious temper and well-honed leadership skills who kept the major decisions of the nation to himself. He was intelligent, with a good grasp of politics and the political system. He often worked his will quietly and from behind the scenes. This hidden hand, as Fred I. Greenstein has called Eisenhower's management style, was not a reflection of the simple grandfatherly image he presented to the American people. Stephen Ambrose, in his extensive work on Eisenhower, has pointed out that this was the general's nature. He was a man of simple background and simple disposition. Naturally, he presented that image. At the same time, he had spent his life in the role of leader, decision maker, and diplomat. Not surprisingly, he was comfortable taking the lead and making big decisions. There was nothing contradictory in Eisenhower's character, between the grandfatherly golfer and strong world leader.

EISENHOWER AND DOMESTIC POLICY

Despite Eisenhower's big victory, the Republican Party in 1952 was still a minority party; the vast majority of Americans were registered Democrats. The GOP's message of lower taxes and reduced government spending appealed to the new middle-income Americans, a group whose numbers had grown tremendously as a result of the postwar prosperity. The vast majority of these middle Americans were first-time homeowners who had moved out of the city and into the suburbs. In the early 1950s they were mostly apolitical, neither Republican nor Democrat, conservative nor liberal. If this group had any unifying characteristic at all it was that they wanted to protect their newly acquired wealth and property. Following the 1952 victory the Republicans realized that if they could keep the fires of prosperity burning, these rapidly growing, newly propertied, middle-class suburbanites might become the backbone of a newly rejuvenated Republican Party, a new majority party.

Eisenhower's domestic policy was a general rejection of the Old Guard Republican rhetoric that the New Deal needed to be destroyed and replaced by pre-Depression laissez-faire economics. Instead, he accepted the basic outlines of New Deal reforms, including Social Security, the basic rights of organized labor, and a central role of the government in the economy. At the same time, Eisenhower and the corporate leaders who supported him believed that the New Deal had created a bloated bureaucracy with dangerous socialist tendencies. For Eisenhower moderates, then, the objective was to maintain the gains of the New Deal reforms while reining in the excesses of those specific programs, to find a balance between fiscal restraint and the general welfare. This defined Eisenhower's "Middle Way," and it became the focus of his administration. It was, however, much too liberal for many party conservatives.

One aspect of this balance was to put an end to government programs that conflicted with private enterprise. The Reconstruction Finance Corporation, for instance, was allowed to expire in 1953. The RFC was a relief program that had its origins in the Hoover administration, but it developed into a powerful New Deal agency under Roosevelt. Eisenhower also set out to privatize the nation's public power projects, insisting that public power competed unfairly with private power companies, pushing prices and profits down. In 1954, the Atomic Energy Act placed the development of nuclear power plants into the hands of private utilities. Also, several times the administration refused to support large-scale public power projects, preferring to encourage private ownership of power production. Despite all this, the Tennessee Valley Authority (TVA), a New Deal flagship, remained intact despite deep appropriations cuts from $185 billion in 1952 to $12 million in 1960. Eisenhower called the TVA "creeping socialism" and insisted he would "sell the whole thing if I could." The president also transferred control of offshore oil rights from the federal government to the states, reversing the Truman administration on the issue. The policy spurred offshore drilling by private oil companies, and the Gulf states benefited greatly from the tax revenue produced by the offshore wells. For Ike, these were not attacks on the reforms of the New Deal–Fair Deal era, but a reflection of his desire to encourage private enterprise by removing the federal government from the marketplace.

This policy was also apparent in the administration's efforts to head off all forms of government-sponsored medical programs. Truman had asked Congress for universal health care in November 1945, but that initiative ended when the Republican Congress came to Washington in 1947. Then in 1954, a plan to have the new polio vaccine provided free to all American children came under fire from the administration as "socialized medicine through the backdoor." Using the same fear of socialism-on-the-march, the administration continued to oppose all government-sponsored medical insurance programs, even for the aged and the poor.

In that same vein, Eisenhower intended to get the government out of the agriculture business—something all Republicans seemed to want. But no one knew how to do that without antagonizing farmers. The result was flexible support payments, a plan to tie government payments to the production of a particular commodity. Support payments would rise when production declined, and fall when production increased. The aim was to lower government support payments and make farm products more responsive to market prices. But surpluses continued to rise and prices remained low. In 1956 the Republicans passed the soil bank program, a New Deal–type initiative that paid farmers to take land out of production. But farmers responded by concentrating production on their best land, while pulling their worst land out of production. Soon farmers were producing more on less land than before 1956. In addition, commodity prices, farm income, and the rural population all declined during the decade, while surpluses grew and the cost of the entire program rose dramatically. By 1960, the Eisenhower agricultural program had become a liability for Republicans.

Obviously, America liked Ike—but did they also like the Republicans? That question was mostly answered in 1954 when the Republicans lost control of both houses of Congress (and would not regain control again until Ronald Reagan won control of the Senate in 1980). This setback came despite the administration's ending of the Korean War, general prosperity, and McCarthy's successes at questioning the loyalty of the Democrats. Through the remainder of his administration, Eisenhower found himself in a three-way dance with conservative Republicans on one side and a powerful Democratic Congress on the other. As the decade progressed, the Old Guard Republicans grew weaker (particularly after Taft's death in the summer of 1953) while the Democrats, led by Lyndon Johnson in the Senate and Sam Rayburn in the House, grew stronger. In what has become an almost mythical time in bipartisan cooperation, Eisenhower's Middle Way mostly intersected with the Rayburn-Johnson moderate liberalism.

The result was a flurry of legislation, particularly on welfare programs—a series of bills that Ike liked to call "the floor that covers the pit of disaster." In just two years, between 1953 and 1955, the Democrats pushed through fifty-eight bills with the president's support. To make this bipartisan effort work, Johnson had to fight off criticism from his party's left that believed he was not doing enough to enhance the liberal agenda, while Eisenhower had to deflect the clamor from his party's right that accused him of being much too liberal.

This bipartisanship led to the creation of the Department of Health, Education, and Welfare; an increase in the minimum wage; and an extension of Social Security benefits to more than seven million workers. Eisenhower also signed a bill that authorized construction of thirty-five thousand public housing units. In 1954, after three decades of delay, the two branches also collaborated to approve construction of the St. Lawrence Seaway, connecting the Great Lakes to the Atlantic Ocean. The project was a mammoth undertaking that gave the Midwest, with its immense natural resources and its manufacturing, a deep-water outlet to the Atlantic.

The president also endorsed the Interstate Highway Act of 1956, a plan to build over forty thousand miles of superhighways and freeways. It was to become the largest domestic spending program and the largest public works project in the nation's history. Perhaps Eisenhower's most enduring monument, the new highway system changed the face of the nation while greatly improving its infrastructure. In addition, it made the automobile America's chief means of transportation, a phenomenon that made the United States unique in the world. Automobile manufacturing increased to meet the demand, providing jobs and a real surge in the economy. This mammoth project is an excellent example of the Eisenhower philosophy of governing: the advent of strong bipartisan support to enact policies that nurture a pro-business climate. Eisenhower's secretary of defense, Charles E. Wilson, the former head of General Motors, summed it up best in his famous statement: "I have always assumed that what was good for the United States was good for General Motors." Over the next two decades, Americans demanded increasingly larger cars, and having two cars became a status symbol of the American family. The new highways made it relatively simple, even advantageous, to commute long distances to work, leading to bedroom suburbs and the corresponding lifestyle. But with the change came problems, including the death of the inner city, smog, and rush-hour traffic jams.

A "NEW LOOK" AT FOREIGN POLICY

Eisenhower kept his campaign promise and went to Korea after the 1952 campaign. His promise had been little more than a Republican campaign tactic; obviously the president-elect could do nothing more in Korea than he could from Washington, but his appearance raised troop morale—and also the morale of the

American people, who were, by then, growing tired of the war. Gallup polls had shown that only about 30 percent of the American public approved of the war. Although no anti-war movement arose, it was clear that a strong dissenting opinion was beginning to grow. A limited war of attrition was a difficult commodity to sell.

Eisenhower seemed intent on ending the war as quickly as possible, perhaps realizing that it was increasingly unwinnable in any modern military sense, and a volatile powder keg that might expand into a larger war. He may also have agreed with Omar Bradley's assessment that it was "the wrong war, at the wrong place, at the wrong time, and with the wrong enemy." Finally, in July 1953 the negotiators agreed to a ceasefire that kept Korea divided at roughly the Thirty-Eighth Parallel, about where Korea was divided in June 1950 when the war began. Korea became the "forgotten war," a sort of nasty event best removed from the collective memory. Over the years, Americans came to believe that they had won the Korean War, when in fact the nation could claim little more than a successful containment of Communist aggressions.

Truman's foreign policy had been based primarily on NSC-68, which called for a military buildup to prepare the nation for every type of military challenge, from local conflicts to nuclear war. The strategy was expensive. The U.S. military budget had soared from about $13 billion before the Korean War to $50 billion when Eisenhower took office. The expense had caused a budget deficit of nearly $10 billion. Eisenhower has often been called a moderate and even a liberal on some issues. But on federal spending he was a conservative. He believed strongly in the frugality of limited government and balanced budgets, and he was not going to allow military spending to get out of hand and, as he saw it, destroy the nation's economy. "We must not," he said, "create a nation mighty in arms that is . . . bankrupt in resources."

The result was the "New Look" foreign policy, a plan that would both cut the federal budget while furthering American interests abroad. It was both aggressive and cost-effective, a foreign policy on the cheap. Rather than rely on the expensive ground forces and conventional weapons that were necessary in Korea, Eisenhower and his secretary of state, John Foster Dulles, turned to an aggressive nuclear strategy. "We have adopted a new principle," the president told the nation. "Rather than let the Communists nibble us to death all over the world in little wars, we will rely in [the] future on [our] massive mobile retaliatory powers." This massive retaliation, as it was called, was a warning to Moscow that the United States would respond with its nuclear power as a deterrent against Soviet-sponsored aggression. While reducing its ground forces (and thereby reducing the cost), the United States would build up its weapons-delivery capability by expanding the Air Force from 115 to 137 wings and adding thirty thousand men. The strategy was decisive and inexpensive; and it allowed the president to keep military spending at the reasonable level of about $40 billion per year. To Secretary of Defense Charles Wilson, it was "more bang for the buck." To push the point home to the Soviets, the United States, in March 1954, tested its first hydrogen bomb in the Pacific.

Massive retaliation was at the foundation of the Eisenhower-Dulles New Look foreign policy, but there were other aspects—some announced, some not. The Korean War had taught a number of lessons. One was that the American people were not patient with military conflicts that were indecisive, drawn out, and that took the lives of young men. To that end, Eisenhower and Dulles intended to rely on friendly indigenous forces to fight the Communists, or to give weapons and materiel to America's allies to fight wars in America's interests. Again, the plan was inexpensive. But more importantly, this strategy kept U.S. soldiers out of harm's way, which relieved antiwar sentiment at home.

Another piece of the New Look strategy was what is often called "pacto-mania," a plan to isolate the Communist bloc by convincing the nations surrounding the Soviet Union and China to sign mutual defense treaties with the United States. In Europe, Eisenhower and Dulles accepted NATO as the instrument of defense there. In Southeast Asia, Dulles assembled SEATO, the Southeast Asia Treaty Organization; in the Middle East, it was the Baghdad Pact. By the time Eisenhower left office in January 1961, the Soviet-Chinese Communist bloc was effectively surrounded.

Last in the arsenal of New Look was the unpleasant business of covert military operations, an aspect of the Eisenhower foreign policy that was kept from the American people. The operative force here was the Central Intelligence Agency (CIA), a mostly secret organization of spies created by the National Security Act of 1947. During the Eisenhower administration the CIA grew enormously in size and influence as another means of furthering American interests abroad. CIA-initiated operations generally cost little, and often the results were effective immediately. The initiative worked well within the New Look objective of keeping costs down while maintaining influence and strength abroad.

New Look may have furthered the Eisenhower administration's immediate objectives, but the program had its drawbacks, and those drawbacks were long lasting. New Look was not popular with America's allies, and it frightened its enemies. Massive retaliation turned out to be little more than a threat. Clearly, the United States was not prepared to start a nuclear war over a local conflict, no matter what the ramifications. The use of troops from friendly nations to fight wars in America's interest did not sit well with U.S. allies, who quickly began to see themselves as mercenaries—fighting and dying for U.S. interests. And it soon was apparent in Southeast Asia that U.S.-supplied indigenous troops were not at all adequate to stem the tide of Communist aggressions there. Lastly, CIA covert operations were enormously destructive to the nation's prestige abroad at a time when the United States was striving to be a world leader in the face of totalitarian communism.

New Look sounded ominous, a pattern for plunging the world into the next world war. But Eisenhower was as moderate in his foreign policy as he was in domestic affairs. As world crises emerged, one after another, Eisenhower acted with restraint and caution, never willing to take the country, and the world, to the brink of war. When Soviet tanks rolled into East Germany in 1953 and then into Hungary in 1956, Eisenhower did not respond by annihilating Moscow; and when hostilities escalated in Southeast Asia, he did not attack Beijing. Parts of the Eisenhower-Dulles foreign policy had been spelled out in Republican Party campaign rhetoric. Most of it was simply threat.

A door to the end of the Cold War seemed to open when Stalin died in 1953. The British called for a renewal of good relations between the Soviets and the West, and encouraged a summit conference. Dulles, however, declined the offer partly because a post-Stalin power struggle in Moscow had not yet produced the Soviet Union's next supreme leader. But the obstructions to talks soon passed, and in July 1955 the two sides met at Geneva, the first meeting between the two nations since Potsdam ten years earlier. Very little emerged from Geneva except a short-term friendly exchange that the U.S. press dubbed "the spirit of Geneva." If there was any real achievement it was that the two sides met face-to-face and discussed the issues that divided them. The conference also led to formal cultural, economic, and scientific exchanges between the two nations, leading to better understandings in a few areas.

COVERT OPERATIONS IN IRAN AND GUATEMALA

Much of the Eisenhower-Dulles foreign policy was designed for domestic consumption, but the behind-the-scenes strategy of covert action was no bluff. In 1953, during Eisenhower's first year in office, the CIA pulled off its first political coup—and the impact from it would still be felt a half century later. In 1951 the premier of Iran, Mohammad Mosaddeq, had led an anti-colonial nationalist movement that threatened the power of the Iranian Shah, Mohammed Reza Pahlavi. Mosaddeq had succeeded in whipping up popular feelings against British control of Iranian oil production that resulted in the nationalization of the Anglo-Iranian Oil Company. When Mosaddeq's request for U.S. aid was rejected, he turned to the Soviets. British foreign secretary Anthony Eden then convinced Eisenhower that Mosaddeq was being pulled into the Soviet sphere and that something had to be done immediately. Eisenhower approved "Operation Ajax," an Anglo-American covert operation devised to overthrow Mosaddeq. CIA operatives cobbled together a small anti-Mosaddeq army inside Iran and toppled Mosaddeq, with the final outcome that the Shah was restored to power and the Iranian oil reserves were secured. To show his gratitude, the Shah made certain that the Americans received a portion of the Iranian oil reserves—much to the disappointment of the British, who had hoped to maintain a monopoly on Iranian oil. For Eisenhower it was a quick, cheap, and easy solution to a minor problem that might have developed into a major concern. But to many

Iranians, the American-sponsored coup was an affront to their sovereignty. They resented the Shah, whom they saw as an American puppet; and they felt oppressed by the American-trained and supported secret police, the Savak. In 1979 the Shah was overthrown in a violent revolution. The American-supported Iranian monarchy was replaced with a radical Shiite theocracy that claimed as its first order the hatred of the United States, the Great Satan. The events of the early 1950s created an enemy, not a friend.

Just a year after its success in Iran, the CIA flexed its muscles again, this time in Guatemala. There, Colonel Jacobo Arbenz Guzman had been elected to office in 1951 and had begun a policy of labor and land reforms. But in 1954, when Arbenz moved to confiscate land belonging to the United Fruit Company, Dulles insisted that Guatemala had fallen into the web of international communism. United Fruit was a large American conglomerate and the largest employer in Latin America. Three of the company's primary stockholders included Secretary of State Dulles; his brother, CIA head Allen Dulles; and Walter Bedell Smith, Eisenhower's undersecretary of state, wartime chief of staff, and good personal friend. By most accounts, however, Eisenhower was convinced that Arbenz was headed down the Communist road and would have sought to overthrow him despite the threats to United Fruit. The tipping point came when Arbenz accepted a supply of small arms from Czechoslovakia. Eisenhower responded immediately by authorizing a CIA-directed coup. Not unlike the situation in Iran, the CIA moved in, purchased a local army, and selected an opposition leader, in this case, Colonel Carlos Castillo Armas. Castillo based his opposition force in Honduras, and with the aid of a few World War II–vintage bombers flown by CIA pilots, he prepared to remove Arbenz and take control of Guatemala. After several bombing raids over Guatemala City, Arbenz fled. The Guatemalan coup remained a sore point in U.S.–Latin American relations for years to come.

These events seemed small, but they carried with them an element of the Cold War, a fear that if something was not done immediately the Soviets would take advantage of the chaos and fill the breach first. It would be a pattern of American foreign policy all through the Cold War.

THE SUEZ CRISIS AND AMERICA'S POSTWAR INVOLVEMENT IN THE MIDDLE EAST

The situation in the Middle East in the mid-1950s was extremely complicated, involving both religion and power politics. It was also the area of the world where it was the most difficult for the United States to spread its influence. In 1948 the new nation of Israel was created in Palestine with the support of the United States. The situation generated bitter opposition among the Arab states and they launched a war against Israel, vowing to destroy it. By the mid-1950s, however, the Eisenhower administration had come to see Israel as the cornerstone of its anti-Soviet Middle Eastern foreign policy and continued to support its existence. At the same time, Dulles worked to pull the Middle Eastern states together into an anti-Communist alliance as part of his strategy of surrounding the Soviets with U.S. allies. The result was the Middle East Treaty Organization, linking Turkey, Pakistan, Iran, and Iraq. The Baghdad Pact, as it was better known, was to be the treaty that linked the other pacts, completing the final encirclement of the Soviet Union and China. Turkey was a signatory of both the Baghdad Pact and NATO, and Pakistan had signed both Baghdad and SEATO.

The key to the Middle East was Egypt, by far the strongest Arab power in the region, and its leader, Gamal Abdel Nasser, the freewheeling Arab nationalist who had deposed King Farouk in 1952. The problem with Nasser was that he refused to worship at the altar of anti-communism. "The Soviet Union," Nasser told Dulles, "is more than a thousand miles away and we've never had trouble with them. They have never attacked us. They have never occupied our territory. They have never had a base here." Nasser refused to join the American anti-Communist crusade because of Washington's continued support of Israel.

Nasser denounced the Baghdad Pact as a device of the Western imperialists that was designed to split the Arab world. One month after the Baghdad Pact was signed, Nasser orchestrated an alliance with Saudi Arabia and Syria and immediately announced that if the United States refused aid, he would look for it elsewhere. The threat was clear: He would go to the Soviets. Dulles responded by pulling promised U.S. aid for the construction of the Aswan Dam on the Nile River, the cornerstone of Nasser's economic development plans.

In retaliation, Nasser surprised the world by announcing, on July 26, 1956, that he would nationalize the Suez Canal and use its revenues to build Aswan. He then accepted $500 million in aid from the Soviets, two and a half times the amount offered by the United States and Britain. Nasser was immediately vaulted into the role of leader of the Arab world. The events had allowed the spread of Soviet influence into the Middle East, and the flow of oil was being jeopardized. "Don't think we intend to stand impotent and let this one man get away with it," Eisenhower told a group of congressmen.

Through the summer and fall of 1956 France and England considered a military strike to take back Suez. Israel, fearing a greatly enhanced Egyptian power on its southern border as a result of Soviet aid, was willing to join the attack. On October 29, without consulting Washington, Israel invaded the Sinai and rushed toward the canal. Two days later British and French planes began bombing Egypt, and on November 5, British and French paratroopers invaded. But the world had changed; the old imperialist impulses were dead, and it would be the Cold War superpowers that would step in and define this incident. The Soviets immediately threatened to come to Egypt's aid and refused to take a nuclear strike off the table. Eisenhower, for his part, refused to be dragged into a major conflict by his allies and refused to support the invasion. A ceasefire was quickly signed and all troops pulled back.

The Suez Crisis marked a failure in U.S.–Middle Eastern policy. In order to keep Soviet influence out of the region and retain control of the oil reserves, Eisenhower was forced to turn his back on his European NATO allies and Israel, his strongest ally in the region. The event also greatly increased Nasser's prestige among the Arab states, while intensifying Arab-Israeli tensions. Eisenhower began looking for a new Middle Eastern policy, one that would increase U.S. influence in the region, reduce Nasser's influence, and still contain the Soviets. The result was the Eisenhower Doctrine, a plan to give aid to the nations of the Middle East as a defense against Communist expansion in the region. He requested $200 million in economic aid for the Middle Eastern nations, and he asked Congress for the power to use armed forces against what he called "overt armed aggression from any nation controlled by International Communism." Congress agreed and passed the resolution.

Most Arab states rejected the Eisenhower Doctrine immediately, insisting that it was little more than U.S. influence-building in the region. And Israel denounced it, claiming it would strengthen the Arab nations at their expense. Only Lebanon and Saudi Arabia among the Arab nations accepted it; and Iran (now under the shah's control) also came on board.

But it was not the Soviets that threatened the region. It was Nasser's influence that was spreading, and Nasser's influence that the Eisenhower administration sought to contain. A pro-Nasser rebellion in Jordan threatened the power of King Hussein there. Eisenhower sent $10 million to Hussein and the Sixth Fleet to the eastern Mediterranean to keep Hussein in power. In July 1957 a military coup in Iraq placed a pro-Nasser government in power there and removed a key Arab nation from the Baghdad Pact. In Lebanon, pro-Nasser elements threatened the government. Eisenhower again acted quickly by sending seven thousand U.S. soldiers into Beirut. That force eventually grew to twice that number, including tanks and even tactical nuclear weapons. In an evening address to the nation, the president said he had sent troops to Lebanon to stop Communist aggression, and he compared the situation there to Greece in 1947, Czechoslovakia in 1948, China in 1949, Korea in 1950, and Vietnam in 1954. It was, in fact, little more than inner-Arab strife. The troops left in October. Lebanon had been saved. But many asked: Saved from what?

The Eisenhower-Dulles Middle East policy had gone nowhere. That Soviet influence had been contained was more a testament to Arab nationalism than U.S. foreign policy. Of all the Middle Eastern states, only Israel and the Shah of Iran were true American allies. However, American oil production served everyone, and economic interests in the region soon began to overshadow political interests—at least for the moment.

THE HUNGARIAN CRISIS

As the crisis in the Suez was unfolding, the Soviets seemed to take advantage of the diversion by crushing a revolt in Hungary. In February 1956, at a closed session of the Twentieth Communist Party Congress, Premier Nikita Khrushchev surprised party members by denouncing Stalin for domestic crimes and mistakes in foreign policy. He also hinted that he might loosen the Soviet grasp on Eastern Europe. Poland began an immediate policy of liberalization, even to the point of challenging Moscow's authority. Polish leader Wladyslaw Gomulka called for democracy and threatened an uprising if the Soviets intervened. Khrushchev wavered, and then backed down. It seemed to be a break, and the excitement spread to Hungary, where students took to the streets to demand that the Stalinist Erno Gero be replaced with the liberal Imre Nagy, who promised to replace Hungary's dictatorship with a multiparty democracy. Again, Khrushchev backed down and allowed Nagy to replace Gero. But demonstrations in Budapest continued and became more violent. Movement leaders demanded that Soviet troops leave Hungary, and Khrushchev again relented, ordering a pullback of Soviet tanks to the outskirts of Budapest. Events were intensified by broadcasts from Radio Free Europe and Voice of America that encouraged the revolutionary activity, even to the point of urging the Hungarian people to take up arms.

At just that moment, as Hungary seemed on the road to winning its freedom, on October 28, Israel attacked Egypt and the world looked the other way. Three days later Nagy announced that Hungary would withdraw from the Warsaw Pact, and Khrushchev decided to move. On November 4 and 5 he sent two hundred thousand troops and four thousand tanks into Budapest and crushed the insurgency. The world watched as the battle in the streets turned from brave uprising to bloodbath. Some 40,000 Hungarian citizens, including Nagy, died in the two days of fighting. Another 150,000 left the country.

The image of Soviet communism was stained badly by the events, and the United States used the suppression of the Hungarian uprising as evidence of Moscow's brutality. But the Eisenhower administration also took some heat. After years of boosting the cause of "liberation" and "rollback" of "captive peoples" behind the Iron Curtain, the military reality of the situation was that the United States could do little to aid the peoples of Eastern Europe, and that the calls for "liberation" were always for domestic political consumption, and a sham.

EARLY INVOLVEMENT IN SOUTHEAST ASIA

At the end of World War II, the French hoped to reestablish their presence as a world colonial power. The colonial era in world history was closing, but the French had come to believe that the reestablishment of their colonial empire would aid in their recovery from the war's economic devastations. A major component of that prewar empire had been their Indochina colony in Southeast Asia. By 1946, however, the French attempt to recolonize Indochina had been met with stiff resistance from Vietnamese nationalists, known as the Vietminh. Led by Ho Chi Minh, the Vietminh based their operations in Hanoi in northern Vietnam. By 1950 the French effort was in trouble, mostly because the cost of the war was more than Paris could manage, and the United States had begun to pick up the tab. In that year, the United States pumped in approximately $150 million to shore up the French effort. A year later, that number jumped to $450 million, about 40 percent of the cost of the war. In 1953 the Eisenhower administration pushed that figure to $785 million, and then over a billion dollars the next year, nearly 70 percent of the war's cost. American interests in Vietnam were beginning to grow.

The Vietnamese war against France was a classic independence movement, a fight for freedom from colonial rule. To combat it, France set up a friendly government and claimed that it was the legitimate political entity representing the people of Vietnam, and then operated the government through a puppet. This was intended to turn the Vietnamese nationalist movement into a civil war of two competing nationalist movements, one Communist-inspired and one anti-Communist. Hence the birth of the myth (which the United States inherited and perpetuated) that there were two warring courses of nationalism in Vietnam, and that the French (and later the Americans) supported the legitimate group of nationalists in the south against Communist insurgents in the north. The French attempt to build up this opposing nationalism was never really successful

In 1954 the French had placed an army of sixteen thousand soldiers at Dienbienphu, a large fortress in northern Vietnam near the Laotian border. Dienbienphu was designed to pacify the enemy-held area and maintain a strong French presence in the north. Instead, it became a target for the Vietminh and a trap for the French soldiers defending it. On March 13, Vietminh forces under Vo Nguyen Giap began shelling Dienbienphu from the surrounding mountains, and it quickly became clear that Dienbienphu would fall unless the United States intervened with air support. Eisenhower's advisors encouraged him to launch an attack. At a news conference on April 7, the president talked of dominoes. "You have a row of dominoes set up," he said, "you knock over the first one, and what will happen is the certainty that it will go over very quickly." But Ike had just pulled the United States out of one frustrating land war in Asia, and he was not about to drag the nation into another. When Republican congressmen insisted he strike, he said he would save the French only if the British would help. But London had no stomach for such an endeavor, and Eisenhower backed off. Dienbienphu fell on May 7, and the French walked away from their colonial adventure in Vietnam.

At the Geneva Conference that same year, it was agreed that elections would be held in Vietnam in 1956 and that, until then, a temporary line of demarcation would divide northern Vietnam from the south at the Seventeenth

Parallel. In addition, it was agreed that no foreign nation would introduce troops or establish bases in Vietnam. The United States refused to participate in the conference or recognize the agreement. To shore up U.S. interests in the region, however, Dulles organized a separate mutual defense treaty, the Southeast Asia Treaty Organization (SEATO), signed by Britain, France, Australia, New Zealand, Thailand, Pakistan, and the Philippines. Although South Vietnam, Cambodia, and Laos were forbidden by the Geneva agreements to sign a mutual defense treaty, a protocol was added to the SEATO treaty extending protection to those three countries in the event of an attack. SEATO was a clear threat of a multilateral, U.S.-led intervention in the affairs of Southeast Asia.

The first U.S. military advisors arrived in South Vietnam in February 1955. In October the American-supported Ngo Dinh Diem won a dubious election victory (he received 98.2 percent of the vote) over his opponent, the deposed emperor Bao Dai. Diem was perceived as America's answer to the growing problems in Vietnam. As the saying at the time went, "sink or swim with Ngo Dinh Diem." The United States had a friendly government in place.

The Eisenhower administration realized that a Vietnam-wide free election, as mandated by the Geneva Accords, would be a victory for the popular Ho Chi Minh. "Almost any type of election that could conceivably be held in Vietnam in 1956," a State Department research document disclosed, "would . . . give the Communists a . . . decisive advantage." Thus any attempts to organize an election were ignored by Saigon and Washington.

By the late 1950s Communist guerrillas, or Viet Cong, began organizing and engaging South Vietnamese troops. Late in 1961 the National Liberation Front was formed out of all anti-Diem forces, and Hanoi was again preparing to oust another imperialist power from its territory.

PROBLEMS IN CUBA

Eisenhower's foreign policy suffered a major blow in the last year of his presidency when Fidel Castro and a small band of ardent revolutionaries overthrew the dictatorship of Fulgencio Batista in Cuba. At first, this appeared to be of little significance; Latin American nations changed governments all the time. In fact, Castro came to New York and spoke on U.S. television of his plans for democracy and economic reforms in the poverty-stricken Cuba. But the CIA found Communist infiltration into Castro's inner circle, and CIA head Allen Dulles suggested that the United States withdraw support. Eisenhower, always somewhere in the middle of all things, concluded that both Batista and Castro were unacceptable and began covert operations to find an alternative. In the meantime, he turned down Castro's requests for aid. That was an apparent affront to Castro, who began nationalizing American-owned property in Cuba. Then he accepted aid from Moscow. When Eisenhower responded by placing an embargo on

Cuban sugar, the Soviets agreed to buy all the sugar Cuba could produce. As the situation worsened, the CIA began planning to retake the island using anti-Castro Cubans. Finally, Eisenhower cut all diplomatic ties, and Cuba slipped into the Soviet sphere—just ninety miles off the Florida coast. Soviet Premier Nikita Khrushchev proudly declared the Monroe Doctrine dead and welcomed his new comrade.

Castro's revolution placed a new wrinkle in the cloth of U.S. foreign policy. After 1960 it was assumed that all Latin American revolutions were Communist-inspired, and that if the United States did not act aggressively, the cancer would spread to other Latin American nations. Consequently, the United States tightened its grip on Latin America. Friendly dictators and military juntas, almost always right wing and anti-Communist, became Washington's means of controlling the region. In fact, almost all Latin American revolutionary movements in the last half of the twentieth century were indigenous and nationalistic, and usually hostile to communism. Any left-wing actions usually had more to do with much-needed land reform and a redistribution of wealth than any tilt toward Moscow. In Latin America, as in several other areas of the world, the United States confused revolutions of nationalism with Soviet-dominated communism. It was a serious mistake.

McCARTHYISM, ANTI-COMMUNIST HYSTERIA, AND CONFORMITY AT HOME

Joseph McCarthy had risen on a tide of anti-Communist hysteria that had begun almost immediately after the war and had grown into a near frenzy by 1950. By then a series of events had convinced many Americans that the United States was not winning the Cold War. The "loss" of China to communism, the acquisition of the bomb by the Soviets (much sooner than anyone had expected), and the revelation that a Soviet-sponsored spy network in the United States and Britain had given atomic secrets to Russia fueled the belief that Communists were everywhere. By mid-1950 McCarthy had jumped out in front of the issue and had made it his own.

McCarthy placed his stamp on events by presenting a sense of extreme urgency. He told America that Communists had infiltrated the national government and were gaining strength. He claimed they were directing national policy, and in fact conspiring to take over the nation—as it seemed Communists had taken over other countries. For impressionable Americans the evidence of McCarthy's charges was everywhere.

Of course, McCarthy did not stand alone in making his accusations. Several Republicans, mostly on the right, hoped the issue would embarrass the administration and sweep them back into the seats of power in 1952. Robert Taft pushed McCarthy, telling him that "if one case [doesn't] work, bring up another." House

Minority Leader Joseph Martin praised McCarthy for exposing "the tremendous infiltration of pinks and fellow-travelers into our government." Moderate Republicans, however, were apprehensive. Through all his evidence, subpoenas, and interrogations, McCarthy had produced nothing. In June 1950 Republican Senator Margaret Chase Smith and several other moderates in the party issued the "Declaration of Conscience," deriding McCarthy and his supporters for exploiting "fear, bigotry, ignorance, and intolerance" for their own political gain. Another group of Republicans were afraid that McCarthy's histrionics might backfire and destroy a perfectly good political issue.

All of this was not being confined to Capitol Hill. McCarthy received support from the Hearst, McCormick, and Scripps-Howard newspapers. Rightwing reporters, columnists, and radio commentators like Paul Harvey also sang his praises. The old Roosevelt-haters who had considered the New Deal tainted with socialism believed in what McCarthy was doing. A long list of anti-intellectuals, anti-liberals, Midwestern isolationists, and dozens of right-wing fringe groups supported McCarthy and his efforts.

By the mid-1950s divergence from the mainstream of any sort—social, economic, political, even cultural—might lead to questions of loyalty, to charges of being what McCarthy himself called "communistically inclined." Private businesses often conducted investigations of their employees, and the FBI compiled lists of suspected "travelers." The CIO purged itself of Communists, and college professors throughout the country lost their jobs by the hundreds for having vague associations with liberal groups and causes in the prewar years when antifascism went hand in hand with communism and Communist sympathies. State governments went on their own anti-Communist tirades, firing suspected Communists, demanding oaths of allegiance, and running background checks of just about anyone they wanted. "Communistically inclined" by someone else's definition might cost a career, upset a life. To avoid the spotlight, Americans slipped into conformity. They threw away their Paul Robeson records and red neckties; they stopped drinking vodka and eating Russian caviar. Many denied their pasts and did all they could to fit into the new mainstream to avoid detection for whatever reason. Scholars discovered conformity and conservatism in many university disciplines, including history, economics, and sociology. Hollywood movies found only the good in America, and they warned audiences often of the Communist threat. Dress codes were introduced into schools and businesses, and soon "standing out" became undesirable. It was the new period of conformity, the "paranoid style," as historian Richard Hofstader called it, the "homogenized society," according to another historian, William Leuctenburg. But above all, it was the supreme manifestation of the Cold War at home.

The election of 1952 brought Joe McCarthy a second term in the Senate and at least the appearance that his power was growing. Several senators who had challenged him were booted out in that year's election, including the once-powerful Democrats Millard Tydings of Maryland and William Benton from Connecticut. Both men had led investigations into McCarthy's charges. In addition, Ernest McFarland, an Arizona Democrat and majority leader in the Senate, had also lost his seat. This Republican surge had more to do with Eisenhower's win than with McCarthy's increase in power, but the perception was that opposition to McCarthy and his investigations was a political dead end. In the face of that, many Democrats allowed their hands to be tied and their voices to be silenced. The Republican claim of "soft on communism" had finally worked, and the Democrats backed away from attacking McCarthy. Senate majority leader Lyndon Johnson said, "I will not commit my party to some high school debate on the subject, 'Resolved that Communism is good for the United States,' with my party taking the affirmative."

But McCarthy's reign finally ended, mostly as a result of his ongoing conflict with the army. This conflict had its origins in the summer of 1951 when McCarthy denounced General George Marshall for supporting the Truman administration's failed Far East policy and for favoring a limited war in Korea. McCarthy said that Marshall was part of "a conspiracy so immense and an infamy so black as to dwarf any previous such venture in the history of man." In the fall of 1953 McCarthy demanded that the Department of Defense release the army's confidential files on loyalty and security. The army refused. On March 11, the army issued a detailed report that accused McCarthy and his chief counsel, Roy Cohn, of trying to bulldoze the army into giving an officer's commission to David Shine, McCarthy's sometime "consultant" and a private in the army stationed at Fort Dix. McCarthy hit back by accusing the army of "blackmail" and of trying to sidetrack his investigations into Communist activities inside the army. He lodged forty-six charges against the army. The result was the Army-McCarthy hearings, a televised circus that began on April 22.

For thirty-six days McCarthy continually browbeat witnesses, making wide-sweeping accusations of Communist activity, sympathies, and infiltration. But what Americans saw on their television sets was an uncouth bully, charging and countercharging, name-calling, and continually interrupting the proceedings at crucial points. Near the end of the hearings Senator Stuart Symington of Missouri stood up to McCarthy in a face-to-face confrontation that brought the hearing room to its feet in support of Symington. Time was running out for McCarthy.

Gallup polls taken during the hearings showed McCarthy's numbers sinking fast. Within weeks his popularity, along with his power, evaporated, and the press turned on him with a magnificent ferocity. He quickly became a liability to Republicans, even an embarrassment. When he insisted that a young aide to Joseph Welch, the army's chief counsel, had belonged to a Communist front organization while in college, Welch drove in the last nail. "Have you no sense of decency, sir, at long last?" Welch stared directly at McCarthy and added, "Have you no sense of decency?" It was a turning point; McCarthy never recovered.

Wisconsin Senator Joseph McCarthy, center, and his chief counsel Roy Cohn on the right. *Source*: Popperfoto/Getty Images

No longer afraid of McCarthy or his power, the Senate moved to bring an end to his attacks. In December 1954 the Senate voted 67 to 22 to censure the Wisconsin senator. America's anti-Communist hysteria had come to an end. With his power gone, he passed into obscurity. He died in 1957, before the end of his second term in the Senate. He was forty-nine.

McCarthyism now stands for the entire period from the end of the war until late 1954, even though McCarthy did not get in front of the events until 1950. It included the censure of Hollywood and the press. It encompassed state and local anti-Communist crusades that led to the dismissal of thousands of "subversives" from government jobs. It was the frequent violation of constitutional rights, supported by the argument that the gravity of the threat trumped individual rights. McCarthyism rose out of a fear that was not real, and it declined mostly because the American people finally realized it.

SECOND RECONSTRUCTION: CIVIL RIGHTS IN THE FIFTIES

The nature of race relations in the South in the 1950s was a myth, perpetuated by white southerners and accepted by white northerners. For decades, southerners had told northerners that segregation was a mutual relationship, accepted by both whites and blacks in the South as the proper and mutual social arrangement. Powerful southern senators and congressmen in Washington convinced their northern counterparts that civil rights movements and attempts at desegregation in the South helped no one. And Eisenhower agreed: "I don't think you can change the hearts of men with laws or decisions." But all that changed in the 1950s with the advent of television, accompanied by the direct action of the civil rights movement. Americans could see that blacks in the South wanted equality, demanded it, and would even die for it. That revelation destroyed the support that northern senators and congressmen gave to southern bills that had kept the civil rights movement at bay.

One turning point in the modern civil rights movement was the murder of Emmett Till. There had always been violence against blacks in the South; lynchings had been a social custom, a way, southern whites argued, to keep order. But there was something different about the Emmett Till case. Till's violent death brought the brutality of segregation into the North and, really for the first time, forced northern whites to look directly at it. Till was fourteen in 1955 when he traveled from Chicago to Mississippi to visit relatives. As the story goes, he whistled at a white woman and was later murdered by two white men for the indiscretion. His body was thrown into the Tallahatchie River near Money, Mississippi. The men were acquitted of the crime, but by most accounts they later confessed to friends that they had done it. These events, as heinous as they were, perhaps would have gone unnoticed in the North as just another southern lynching. But Till's mother insisted on having her son's casket open at his funeral to show the brutality of his murder. An estimated fifty thousand people filed past Till's mutilated body. He had been shot and beaten, and his fingers, one ear, and penis had been cut off. A photograph of Till's body began to circulate in the northern press, most notably in *Jet* magazine. Northern whites could no longer deny the brutality of segregation and white supremacy in the South.

BROWN V. BOARD OF EDUCATION OF TOPEKA, KANSAS

The postwar civil rights movement did not begin with the *Brown* decision in 1954, but that case was certainly one of several watershed events. It ended the doctrine of separate-but-equal, as handed down by the Supreme Court in the 1896 *Plessy v. Ferguson* case, and it began the effort to secure equal legal treatment for African Americans. For the next ten years, until the 1964 Civil Rights Act, African Americans and their allies would slowly chip away at de jure (legalized) racial segregation in the South. They would focus on the public schools, the universities, and public facilities. Their methods would be nonviolent: boycotts, sit-ins, and marches.

The road to *Brown* was a long one. Prior to World War II, the greatest victories for African Americans came in the courts, and were led by the work of the NAACP. In 1939, in the case of *Missouri v. Gaines* (*Missouri ex rel. Gaines v. Canada*), the Court ruled that the University of Missouri must provide a separate *and* equal law school for black students, that sending them out of state to receive their education did not meet the requirements of equality. The case was argued before the Court by Charles Houston of the Howard University Law School. In 1950 Houston's student, Thurgood Marshall, successfully argued *McLaurin v. Oklahoma State Regents* before the Supreme Court. The Court held that the University of Oklahoma Law School had not provided equal facilities for its African American students. That same year, in *Sweatt v. Painter*, the NAACP again argued successfully that a separate law school at the University of Texas was not equal, but for mostly intangible reasons such as a lack of opportunity for the black students to interact with their white student colleagues and faculty. These cases were important steps toward overturning *Plessy v. Ferguson* by guaranteeing better education facilities for African American students.

In September 1950 the case that would become *Brown v. Board of Education of Topeka, Kansas* originated when Oliver Brown was told he could not register his daughter at an all-white neighborhood school in Topeka. The case reached the Supreme Court in 1953. By that time the issue before the Court had changed. There was no longer a question that the courts would uphold a demand for equal facilities. The new question was whether the separation of the races—even when the facilities were equal—was a denial of equal protection under the law as guaranteed by the Fourteenth Amendment.

Chief Justice Earl Warren brought a united Court to a unanimous decision on May 17, 1954. The tenor of the decision was clear: The Court saw education at the foundations of equality of opportunity and they agreed that segregated school systems were inherently unequal. "Does segregation of children in the public schools solely on the basis of race," the Court asked, "deprive the children of the minority group of equal education opportunities?" Yes, Warren answered for the Court. "We believe it does. . . . We conclude that in the field of public education the doctrine of 'separate but equal' has no place. Separate educational facilities are inherently unequal."

As important as the *Brown* decision was, it was incomplete. To get his unanimous decision, Warren had agreed to a compromise that excluded from the decision any timetable for implementation. Consequently, few Southern school districts made any immediate moves to desegregate. A year after the initial ruling, the Court handed down what has been called the "second *Brown* decision," ordering desegregation to take place "with all deliberate speed." It was intended as a call to move forward. Instead it seemed to expose the Court's limited powers to enforce broad decisions, and it became an excuse to stonewall. Thurgood Marshall later commented: "I've finally figured out what 'all deliberate speed' means. It means slow."

The initial response from the South was not rebellion. Only one or two southern governors invoked the old southern battle cries of interposition, nullification, and states' rights. Most major southern cities began a slow move toward desegregation of their public schools, generally with the concession that the process was inevitable. But the Eisenhower administration balked at enforcing the Court's decision, and what might have been the beginning of the end of the Jim Crow South turned into a delaying action. Eisenhower did not necessarily want to stand in the way of desegregation. In fact, he had desegregated the District of Columbia and continued Truman's efforts to bring an end to segregation in the armed forces, areas in which he believed he had the authority to enforce desegregation. But Eisenhower held a traditional interpretation of the separation of powers, leading him to believe that he had no such authority to enforce a court decision to desegregate state public schools. He also had no faith in the law as an instrument of social change. Consequently, he kept silent on almost all incidents and issues involving desegregation in the South. He also hoped to pull the South into the Republican Party, a process he considered ongoing through his two administrations. So, with very little support from above, southern moderates who were willing to accept or even aid in school desegregation found themselves isolated and abandoned. Their only reasonable reaction was to back away.

MONTGOMERY AND KING

The history of the modern civil rights movement seems to have begun abruptly when Rosa Parks refused to give up her seat to a white bus patron in Montgomery, Alabama, in December 1955. But, in fact, the Montgomery bus boycott was the result of a growing black awareness and activism since the war, and also the realization in the black community that segregation would collapse against the forces of black unity—particularly if those forces were supported by the power of the federal government.

Every day, around forty thousand African Americans paid a dime to ride the Montgomery city buses. Alabama state law required that the buses be segregated. Blacks in the city found the situation intolerable, and complained regularly to the city commissioners. In the spring of 1954, just after the *Brown* decision was handed down, black leaders threatened to boycott the buses if the practice did not end. The NAACP began to look for an incident that would rally the Montgomery black community and trigger the boycott. For this purpose, they sought a figure of unimpeachable character, someone who could withstand the barrage of attacks that would certainly come.

That was, of course, Rosa Parks. Parks was forty-three, an activist in the local NAACP, and a seamstress in a downtown Montgomery department store. On December 1, she boarded the Cleveland Avenue bus and sat in the fifth row, a portion of the bus open to blacks as long as whites were not left standing. When the whites-only seats filled, Parks and three other black riders were told by the driver to move back. The other black riders complied. Parks did not. The driver threatened to call the police. "You may do that," Parks responded. She was arrested and booked with violation of segregation laws. That evening she was bailed out of jail by the NAACP and the movement had its cause.

Although it was the NAACP, and organizations associated with it, that planned the boycott, it was the ministers in the local churches who moved into the lead of the movement by agreeing to preach the boycott at their Sunday services. From that group Martin Luther King Jr. emerged as the boycott's leader. He was only twenty-six. He had just received his Ph.D. in theology from Boston University, and had recently been appointed minister to the Dexter Street Baptist Church. It would be King who would unite the black community in Montgomery into a powerful force for social change.

King gained inspiration from the basics of Christian thought, the nonviolence and civil disobedience of Henry David Thoreau and from Mohandas Gandhi, whose nonviolent tactics had helped bring an end to British rule in India. He believed (as did others at the time, including theologian Reinhold Niebuhr) that nonviolent direct action might be a useful tool against racial segregation in the South. But King's nonviolent philosophy did not reflect a radical faith. He would show over and over again that he was a cautious leader, satisfied often with incremental progress and compromise.

On December 20, 1956, about a year after Rosa Parks refused to relinquish her seat, the Supreme Court ruled that Montgomery's bus ordinance was unconstitutional. The next morning, King, Rosa Parks, and several members of the local NAACP chapter boarded the first integrated bus in Montgomery's history. By doing little more than ceasing to buy an unsatisfactory product, Montgomery's black community had prevailed. It was a victory for nonviolence.

The victory changed the face of the national movement. Almost immediately, King was catapulted to the role of the movement's primary leader. He received attention in the national press; news reporters covered his speeches; cameras followed him. During the summer of 1956 he embarked on a national speaking tour, bringing more attention to the movement and to himself. By the time the boycott ended, King was out in front of the movement, chosen not only by blacks, but by white liberals as well—northern white liberals with money.

King understood the significance of the press and the need for visibility. That was, in fact, possibly the greatest lesson learned from Montgomery. The northern press was sympathetic to the movement, and a sympathetic press could sway a large northern constituency of wealthy liberals. Through King's leadership, this alliance was forged early and would fuel the movement into the mid-1960s. The key, of course, was to utilize the press—even manipulate it if necessary—and King quickly mastered that skill.

The Montgomery bus boycott became a rallying point. Unlike the *Brown* decision, which seemed to produce more rhetoric and good intentions than results, the boycott was a tangible victory that resulted from southern blacks banding together to force change. It also focused the movement in the South. Through most of the century the movement had been in the hands of civil leagues, like the National Urban League, and legal aid societies like the NAACP. After Montgomery, leadership shifted to a broad network of independent churches that touched nearly every African American in the South.

LITTLE ROCK

The biggest test of the *Brown* decision, and the most important modern test of federal-versus-state power, came in Little Rock, Arkansas, in the fall of 1957. By then it was apparent that governors and other politicians in the South were finding political success by registering their defiance against the *Brown* decision, while moderates on race issues were quickly being isolated. Following the *Brown* decision, it became increasingly clear that being on the wrong side of the race issue could end a political career.

In the summer of 1957 Arkansas Governor Orval Faubus was facing a difficult campaign for a third term. He had won election in 1954 on a platform calling for a progressive, modern Arkansas, but now in 1957 he felt the storm clouds of segregation forming against him. He finally concluded that he had to campaign as a defender of white supremacy or lose the coming election. "If I don't do this," Faubus told a colleague, the segregationists "will tear me to shreds."

Faubus got his chance to prove himself in the fall of 1957 when a federal judge demanded that the Little Rock school system begin the process of desegregation. Faubus announced that he would use the Arkansas National Guard to block the integration of the Little Rock system. The next day, nine African American students attempted to register at Little Rock's Central High School. They were turned away by the National Guardsmen amid a crowd of several thousand jeering whites.

On September 20, a federal judge demanded that Faubus withdraw the troops. He complied, but he replaced them with Arkansas State Police and continued to obstruct the registration of the nine students. On Monday, September 23, the students were allowed to register. When news of that event hit the streets of Little Rock, crowds of angry whites began to form near the school. Violence erupted and white gangs rampaged through the city. Finally, the mayor of Little Rock sent an urgent message to the president: "Situation out of control," he wrote, "and police cannot disperse the mob." Eisenhower responded by federalizing the Arkansas National Guard and sending in one thousand paratroopers from the 101st Airborne Division. On September 25, the nine students entered the school and the incident ended.

The events at Little Rock were important for several reasons. It was, first of all, an important test of federal-versus-state power. It was, in fact, the first use of federal troops to protect American citizens since Reconstruction. It also set the stage for coming civil rights conflicts in which federal authority would always trump the authority of the states. Second, the *Brown* decision was strengthened significantly by the mere fact that the federal government had intervened to enforce the decision. Lastly, the events at Little Rock changed the nation's attitude toward southern racism. The conflict was covered extensively in the press, particularly on television.

The message that went out to the nation following the murder of Emmet Till in 1955 was now the same message that the events in Little Rock projected on television and into the nation's living rooms. It was becoming increasingly clear that the old myth perpetuated by southern whites for northern consumption (that segregation in the South was best for both races) was not true. Among the nine students was fifteen-year-old Elizabeth Eckford. A photograph of her, wearing a white dress and being taunted by white students whose eyes and mouths spewed hatred and viciousness, hit the national press and was repeatedly shown on national news. For many Americans she was a victim, a sweet-looking little girl who wanted nothing more than to go to school and get an education. The leaders of the civil rights movement would learn that the media could be a powerful ally.

THE POLITICS OF CIVIL RIGHTS AND THE CIVIL RIGHTS ACT OF 1957

Civil rights activism, and the violence that was almost certain to come with it, posed a difficult problem for both political parties. Eisenhower had been trying to increase his party's influence in the white South while maintaining Republican black votes from the previous era. The Democrats wanted to continue their influence with the growing black population in the large northern urban centers, while keeping control of white southerners who traditionally voted Democratic. It was in the midst of this ticklish situation that the postwar civil rights movement emerged. One reflection of that was the Civil Rights Act of 1957. On its face, the bill was a compromise, a product of political wheeling and dealing, a vehicle for presidential politics. But in fact, the 1957 Civil Rights Act established an important precedent that would later open the doors to more important bills.

The bill had its origins in the Eisenhower administration as a plan to divide the Democrats and win back black voters in the North who had shifted to the Democratic Party during and after the New Deal era. The election of 1948 had shown that these black voters had come to hold the balance of power in several states with large electoral votes, and Eisenhower hoped to win them back by passing the only civil rights act since Reconstruction. But in 1956, the year it was originally introduced, the bill was killed in the Senate by southern segregationists.

Eisenhower sent the bill to Congress a year later, but this time Senate

Elizabeth Eckford is taunted by local whites as she is turned away from Central High School in Little Rock by National Guardsmen under orders from Arkansas Governor Orval Faubus. In 1999, Ms. Eckford, along with eight others who attempted to enter the school on that day, received the Congressional Gold Medal in the East Room of the White House. *Source*: Francis Miller/Time & Life Pictures/Getty Images

Majority Leader Lyndon Johnson, a Southern Democrat, agreed to take the lead in pushing the bill through the Senate. Johnson was certainly the most powerful Democrat of the late 1950s, and he had his eye on his party's 1960 nomination, but he carried with him the debilitating stigma of being a southern politician who had little interest in issues outside the South. By heading up the passing of this bill, Johnson hoped to rise as a national leader and a potential party nominee.

The nature of the bill reflected the thinking of both Eisenhower and Johnson—and certainly that of many Americans—that the disenfranchisement of southern blacks was at the heart of all racial problems. Once southern blacks received the vote, their political power would be felt and they could demand reforms that would bring an end to segregation and even discrimination. To that end, the 1957 Civil Rights Act created a civil rights division inside the Justice Department and authorized the attorney general to seek court injunctions to stop anyone from interfering with a citizen's right to vote. The bill passed with bipartisan support and displayed a crack, for the first time, in the ability of southern congressmen and senators to stop the passage of such bills. At least in part because of the volatility and the visibility of the incidents in the South, southern congressmen could no longer persuade their northern white brethren to support their cause.

CONCLUSION

Eisenhower's immediate legacy, in the decade or so after his death in 1969, was one of benign neglect. He was a very nice guy who presided over the nation for eight years of general peace and prosperity, but he tolerated McCarthy's antics and fostered the social conformity that was a hallmark of the time he was in office. By the late 1970s Ike's image began to change. He began to be seen as the president the nation wanted and needed in the 1950s, the earth-smoother, the middle roader who worked hard for bipartisanship. He began to be perceived as a president of all the nation, who had spurned partisanship and in-the-mud politics. He came to be known as a decisive leader, whose quiet, behind-the-scenes leadership changed the direction of the nation, and even, quietly, kept McCarthy at bay by denying him access to Executive Department files and information. By the time Stephen Ambrose began writing his biography, Eisenhower had been raised to the level of one of the nation's near-great presidents.

Reading: *Sputnik* and the Space Race

The United States received something of a technological wake-up call in the first week of October 1957, when the Soviet Union announced the successful launch of a satellite into space. Just a month before they had test-fired an intercontinental ballistic missile. These two events together quickly came to represent an American failure, a major defeat that had to be overturned or the United States would lose the Cold War. The strategic implications were ominous. The Soviets had built booster rockets more powerful than anything built by the United States, and they had solved guidance problems that had plagued U.S. scientists. This technology and knowledge gave the Soviets the ability to deliver a nuclear warhead to a target. The Americans were behind in two areas: missile development and space exploration.

Eisenhower tried (mostly unsuccessfully) to reassure the anxious nation by insisting that the Soviet launch was of no real significance. It was fairly apparent, however, that the event had put the Soviets in the lead in several areas. If the Soviets could not yet hit the United States with missiles carrying nuclear weapons, they were trying hard and coming close. It was a frightening thought. Then to make matters worse, America's attempts to match the Soviet accomplishment failed miserably. Two weeks after the Soviet launch, an Atlas rocket exploded on the launch pad at Cape Canaveral in Florida—and the event had been shown on television.

The launch also gave the Soviets an ideological advantage in the propaganda war to win the hearts and minds of the world. Since the war, the Americans had boasted of their technological superiority over the supposedly backward Soviets. That ended. Nations that were straddling the fence between the two Cold War superpowers might now see the Soviets as the winners, the nation (and system) out in front in the competition for technological leader of the world. That could tip the balance of power away from the United States. The United States might well have lost both its technological advantage and its confidence.

Despite Eisenhower's insistence that the event was insignificant, others disagreed. Clare Booth Luce called it "an intercontinental outer-space raspberry to a decade of American pretensions that the American way of life was a gilt-edged guarantee of our material superiority." And Edward Teller, the "father" of the hydrogen bomb, said the Soviet launch was a worse defeat for the United States than Pearl Harbor.

For the first time in his presidency, Eisenhower was attacked by Congress and in the media. The economy had begun to sag, and there was a whiff of corruption in his administration when his special assistant was forced to resign over a bribery scandal. Lyndon Johnson, Texas senator and presidential hopeful for the Democrats, conducted an investigation of the nation's space program.

The event also opened the door to Democratic accusations that the Eisenhower administration had allowed a gap to develop between the U.S. and Soviet military power. Whether it was true or not, John Kennedy would turn that into a political issue in the 1960 campaign and convince voters that he was right.

The satellite was officially known as *Iskustvennyi Sputnik Zemil*, which means "Artificial Fellow Traveler around Earth." Quickly, the American press picked up *Sputnik* (probably because it was the only easily pronounceable word of the three Russian words) and it jumped into the American vernacular.

Eventually, the blame for this perceived failure was placed directly on the nation's public schools. They were criticized for not teaching the basics, particularly in the sciences; for not demanding excellence from their students; and for being overcrowded and obsolete. After *Sputnik*, the education of the nation's youth rose to the level of national security. In 1958 Congress passed the National Defense Education Act, which funded high school math, science, and language programs. Almost immediately, boxes of microscopes began showing up in eighth-grade science classrooms. Congress also established the National Aeronautics and Space Administration (NASA) to coordinate all missile production and space exploration.

Finally, in January 1958 the United States sent a small satellite into orbit. But by then, the Soviets had made another leap by sending up a three-thousand-pound satellite.

Kennedy at Home and Abroad

I t was a popular interpretation that in the 1960 presidential campaign Richard Nixon represented the past while John Kennedy represented the future. Very little about that analogy makes much sense. The two men were about the same age; they had entered Congress at the same time, and, in fact, their backgrounds were surprisingly similar in what they had achieved since they entered public life. Nixon, however, had tried hard to depict himself as an up-by-his-bootstraps figure in an attempt to show that he was a man of the people, as opposed to Kennedy, with his privileged life and lifestyle. Most of that was true. Nixon had not lived in poverty, but as a young boy, life for him had been spare. He had not had the opportunity for an Ivy League education, and he had no storied name to help him through life. And Kennedy had, of course, lived a life in the lap of wealth and privilege. But to the American people, Nixon was tied to Eisenhower and the past—what had gone before. Kennedy was somehow the symbol of the future, of rebirth and hope. As the nation entered the decade, it was these two men who seemed to set the stage for what the future would bring.

ELECTION OF 1960

Most Americans approached the 1960 election with great anticipation. The next president, most agreed, would take the nation into a new era. The Republicans seemed to be in the driver's seat. Eisenhower had steered the country through eight years of general peace and a fairly strong economy, and it was generally agreed that he would be succeeded by his vice president, Richard Nixon. Nelson Rockefeller, the moderate governor of New York, had made some noises about challenging Nixon, but opinion polls in 1959 gave him virtually no chance and he stood down. Nixon certainly looked like a strong candidate. But he was still suffering from his earlier associations with McCarthyism at a time when the

101

nation seemed to want to turn toward moderation and away from the stridency of the Republican Right. Although the McCarthy episode had ended in 1953, many who were linked to it continued to suffer criticism. In the 1956 campaign, Eisenhower tried to ease Nixon off the ticket. By most accounts, Ike hated Nixon's association with McCarthy and the Republican Right and hoped to rid his administration of all vestiges of it. But Nixon prevailed when the president finally realized that he would not go quietly. With that, Nixon was in an almost unbeatable position to grab the 1960 Republican nomination.

The indomitable Nixon rose above all the bad press by reinventing himself as a moderate, particularly on domestic issues. He embraced Eisenhower's middle-of-the road moderation, and he severed most of his ties to the Republican Right. He tried to present himself as the heir apparent to the throne, Ike's second in command, in hopes that the president would give him his blessing and he would coast to the 1960 nomination. But it was not that easy for Eisenhower. He never had much use for Nixon, and he never really embraced him as his successor. At the same time, the position of vice president is often invisible, and Eisenhower had kept many of the big policy decisions to himself, so Nixon's attempt to portray himself as the president's second in command failed to resonate with the American people. One writer called him a "lapdog with a five o'clock shadow."

But in the summer of 1959 Nixon got a big break. While on tour in the Soviet Union he engaged the Soviet premier Nikita Khrushchev in a furious debate in the kitchen of an American model home display in Moscow. Nixon received remarkable media coverage, particularly in *Life* magazine. There was the vice president, standing toe-to-toe with the Russian Bully, at one point with his finger in Khrushchev's face. America loved it, and Nixon's stock soared. He looked like a winner, just a year before the convention.

The Democrats also looked to the 1960 election with a great deal of hope. They had come to the conclusion that the nation liked Ike, but not necessarily the Republicans. The Democrats had controlled Congress since 1954; now they expected to capitalize on that popularity by putting one of their own in the White House. And they were at no loss for candidates. Senator Hubert Humphrey of Minnesota entered the race early, running as a liberal, the successor to the New Deal with a strong civil rights record. Senate Majority Leader Lyndon Johnson ran as the un-candidate, working hard behind the scenes to get the nomination but refusing to announce his candidacy. Senator Stuart Symington of Missouri ran as the compromise candidate with early support from Harry Truman. Adlai Stevenson, the two-time loser, was sniffing around for the nomination again, but despite strong support from liberal intellectuals, the Democratic Party bosses considered him unelectable and shut the door on his candidacy. The frontrunner was John Fitzgerald Kennedy, the good-looking war hero, Pulitzer Prize–winning writer, senator from Massachusetts, and son of Joseph P. Kennedy, "the Ambassador."

Kennedy was not all he appeared to be. His father's money and influence had created an image of youth, vigor, liberalism, and intelligence. But in fact he

U.S. Vice President Richard M. Nixon sticks his finger in the face of Soviet Premier Nikita Khrushchev just before their famous "kitchen debate," a heated verbal exchange at a display of kitchen appliances at the American National Exhibition in Moscow in 1959. The event (and the documenting photos) greatly increased Nixon's stock as the 1960 presidential election approached. *Source*: Hulton Archives/Getty Images

had a conservative voting record in Congress; he had even supported McCarthy in the early 1950s. He suffered from chronic ailments: Addison's disease, malaria, asthma, an ulcer, and a spinal disk problem. And his Pulitzer–Prize winning *Profiles in Courage* was, by some accounts, ghostwritten—or at least partly so.

Kennedy first became a national figure when he made a bid for the second spot on Stevenson's 1956 presidential ticket. He lost to Estes Kefauver, but he immediately began working to win his party's 1960 presidential nomination. He was, however, not universally liked in the party. Party bigwigs like Speaker of the House Sam Rayburn were cool to Kennedy's candidacy because he did not need campaign money and that allowed him to work outside the party structure. Further, he was Catholic, and a lot of the party leadership did not believe a Catholic could win the presidency. Truman disliked Kennedy's father, and feared his influence if Kennedy won the presidency. "It's not the Pope that worries me," Truman said. "It's the pop." Lyndon Johnson saw Kennedy as little more than a rich playboy who would like to be president. And Eleanor Roosevelt told Kennedy, with obvious references to *Profiles in Courage* and his father's influence, "I feel that I would hesitate to place the difficult decisions that the next president will have to make with someone who understands what courage is and admires it, but has not quite the independence to have it."

Kennedy mended fences with most party insiders, and he swept the primaries. His only real challenger was Humphrey, who ran in Wisconsin and West Virginia, losing both to Kennedy. It was in West Virginia that Kennedy addressed the question of his religion, insisting that it would not affect his presidency. "I do not take orders from any Pope, any Cardinal, any Bishop or any Priest." Theodore H. White, in his *The Making of the President, 1960*, wrote, "Over and over again, there was the handsome, open-faced candidate on the TV screen, showing himself, proving that a Catholic wears no horns." He won the primary and was nominated in the summer of 1960. He chose Lyndon Johnson as his running mate.

Immediately following the political conventions, the three television networks invited Kennedy and Nixon to a series of televised debates. With that, presidential campaigning went from the hustings to the television set—and the modern American political campaign was born. Perhaps not surprisingly, the

Democratic presidential candidate John Kennedy reaches toward a sea of outstretched hands during a campaign motorcade. *Source*: Paul Schutzer/Time & Life Pictures/Getty Images

American people in 1960 were more interested in style than substance. Nixon lacked style. Kennedy oozed it.

Kennedy won the election by a squeak—less than one-tenth of one percent (about 118,500 votes). It was the closest popular vote since 1888. But, as is often the case, the electoral vote revealed a different story. Kennedy took twenty-three states with 303 electoral votes. Nixon took twenty-six states and 219 electoral votes. Kennedy was strongest in the urban and suburban North and Northeast, carrying seven of the nation's nine largest states. Nixon was strongest in rural areas and in the West. Kennedy took the African American vote, at least in part because he interceded during the campaign to have Martin Luther King Jr. released from a Georgia prison. Nixon, hoping to draw southern white votes, remained silent during the incident. He won Florida, Tennessee, and Virginia. African American voters kept the remainder of the South safely in the Democratic column.

THE BEST AND THE BRIGHTEST

Kennedy brought with him to the White House a great deal of hope for the nation's future. For many Americans it marked the beginning of a new period in the nation's history. All that seemed to be personified in the new president's inner circle of advisors who were, like JFK, young and energetic. They seemed ready to move mountains and change the world. David Halberstam later called them "the best and the brightest," the leaders of the next generation. Kennedy appointed his brother, Robert, attorney general. At only thirty-six, Bobby was JFK's closest advisor, advocate, and confidant. To reassure the nation's business leaders that he would not hamper business growth, Kennedy appointed a Republican, Douglas Dillon, as treasury secretary. Special counsels Theodore Sorensen and Myer Feldman were thirty-two and thirty-four, respectively; the administration's press secretary, Pierre Salinger, was thirty-five; the president's special assistants, Larry O'Brien and Arthur Schlesinger, Jr., were both forty-six; Special Assistant Kenneth O'Donnell was thirty-six. "Washington seemed engaged in a collective effort to make itself brighter, gayer, more intellectual, more resolute," Schlesinger wrote. "It was a golden interlude. . . ." They were the "Action Intellectuals," cocky, with all the persuasive influence of the American military force, economic power, and technological might behind them.

Kennedy's foreign policy advisors were what one historian called "the containment generation," with ideas born under Truman and nurtured under Eisenhower. The leader of the foreign policy team was Robert McNamara, who was tapped to be secretary of defense. McNamara, a Republican, was the young president at Ford Motor Company, where he had made his name in systems analysis. For McNamara, all answers could be found in the numbers. McGeorge Bundy,

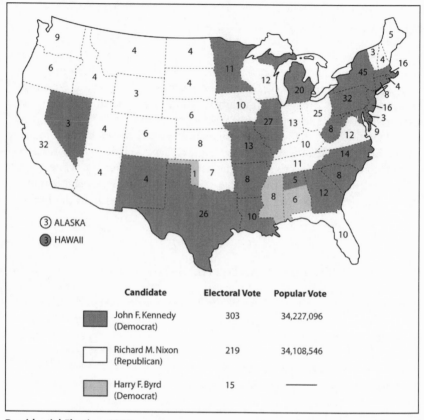

Candidate	Electoral Vote	Popular Vote
John F. Kennedy (Democrat)	303	34,227,096
Richard M. Nixon (Republican)	219	34,108,546
Harry F. Byrd (Democrat)	15	———

Presidential Election, 1960

yet another Republican, was named national security advisor. It was Bundy, perhaps more than any of the other Kennedy whiz kids, who personified the new vigorous blood in Washington. He graduated summa cum laude from Groton, was the first Yale student to achieve a perfect score on his entrance exam, and became dean of Harvard College at only thirty-four. Kennedy often said, "He's the second smartest person I know," but that was probably an insult to Bundy. At forty-one, he was considered too young to be secretary of state, so Kennedy named him special assistant for national security affairs. Secretary of state went to Dean Rusk, the assistant secretary of state for Far Eastern affairs in the Truman administration. Another White House advisor who would greatly influence the new president was Bundy's assistant, Walt Rostow. At forty-one, the same age as Bundy, Rostow was an MIT economics professor who had built a reputation as a grand strategist. For these men, the United States had a special moral mission to save the world in our time.

THE NEW FRONTIER

The new age may have dawned, but governing was something entirely different. As it turned out, Kennedy was not an especially effective domestic leader. Although the new president's record did not show a dedicated liberal, he inherited the Democratic Party's liberal agenda. During his three years in the White House he tried to meet that agenda by introducing a body of liberal legislation that had been ignored by the Eisenhower administration. He called his agenda the New Frontier, a name that gave liberals hope that there was a direct line between JFK and FDR. The New Frontier included an increase in the minimum wage, health insurance for the aged, federal aid to education, and a redevelopment program for poverty-stricken areas. Even though the Democrats held the majority in Congress, a conservative coalition of Republicans and conservative southern Democrats, acting through predominantly southern committee chairmen, kept Kennedy's legislative agenda bottled up. This same conservative coalition had been frustrating liberals and thwarting liberal legislation at least since the end of the war.

Kennedy was, perhaps, most frustrated by his attempt to provide federal aid to education. No one in Congress seemed to be able to rise above the religious issue. Secularists refused to support a bill that funded Catholic schools, while Catholics and their supporters in Congress insisted that any education bill must include support for parochial and private schools. Most frustrating for Kennedy was that his own religion made it difficult for him to support either side. At the time of his death, the National Education Improvement Act was still stuck in committee.

Kennedy's economic policies were more successful. As a senator, he had been a fiscal conservative, willing to challenge most government intervention into the economy. But Walter Heller, the chairman of the Council of Economic Advisors, succeeded in converting Kennedy to Keynesian thinking (the economic philosophy first advanced by British economist John Maynard Keynes that promoted economic growth through federal tax-and-spend policies). Faced with a recession through 1961, Kennedy agreed to adopt Heller's Keynesianism and increase federal spending. At Kennedy's request, Congress raised the minimum wage, broadened Social Security benefits, increased the defense budget dramatically, and approved over $4 billion for federal housing. He also pushed through the Area Redevelopment Act, which allotted federal funds for areas of the country designated as economically distressed. This increased federal spending spurred an economic recovery by the end of Kennedy's first year in office.

But Kennedy was not satisfied; he sought to push the economy harder, beyond recovery to prosperity. In 1962 he sponsored the Manpower Retraining Act, which provided over $400 million in matching grants to retrain workers, and the Revenue Act, which granted $1 billion in tax breaks to businesses to stimulate corporate spending on new machinery and equipment. Later that year, he asked Congress to enact a $13.5 billion cut in corporate and personal income taxes over three years. These tax cuts, along with increased military spending, would pump more money into the economy, generate capital, create deficits, stimulate economic growth, and produce more tax revenue. Like many other proposals, Kennedy's tax cut did not clear Congress before his death, but the economy did recover from the recession and began an extended period of growth mostly because of the administration's increased spending on the military and aerospace. For the three years Kennedy was in office, the economy grew at an annual rate of 5.3 percent and the unemployment rate declined significantly.

The rapid growth and low unemployment, however, spurred inflation. To Kennedy and his economic advisors, the key to holding down inflation was to keep wages and costs in check, particularly in the large industries. In early 1962 Kennedy avoided a potentially inflationary steel strike by persuading steel workers to accept a modest wage increase, thus averting the need for an increase in steel prices. Just two weeks later, however, Roger Blough of U.S. Steel announced a six-dollar-per-ton increase in the price of steel, and other steel companies followed suit. Blough had made statements in the press that he believed Kennedy opposed business and business growth, and the events made it clear that the two men were headed for a clash. The day after Blough's announcement, Kennedy said, "The American people will find it hard, as I do, to accept a situation in which a tiny handful of steel executives whose pursuit of power and profit exceeds their sense of public responsibility can show such utter contempt for the interests of 185 million Americans." Blough said that he had made his decision in the interest of his stockholders. Kennedy responded by rallying the full force of the federal government to pressure big steel to rescind the increase. The Federal Trade Commission threatened to investigate the steel industry for possible price fixing. Attorney General Robert Kennedy announced that he was considering antitrust proceedings against the steel industry. Blough and big steel immediately backed down.

The quarrel with steel was a big victory for Kennedy and for his economic policies that sought to hold inflation in check. And it was generally popular with the American people. But Kennedy had alienated big business, which remained generally pessimistic and distrustful of Kennedy through the remainder of his administration. In May, there was a major stock market crash brought on by a rapid decline in steel stocks. Big business blamed Kennedy and his policies.

Perhaps Kennedy's most enduring legacy has been the development of the space program. Eisenhower's response to *Sputnik* was little more than indifference. Kennedy, however, saw it as a challenge for the nation's future. On May 1, 1960, just four months after taking office and almost immediately after the Soviets launched cosmonaut Yuri Gagarin into orbit around the earth, Kennedy urged the nation to take the lead in space exploration. "I believe," he told Congress, "that this nation should commit itself to achieving the goal, before this decade is out, of landing a man on the moon and returning him safely to earth." He undoubtedly understood that an aggressive and federally funded space program would lead to technological advances and ultimately to long-range weapons development. He also realized that the leader in space exploration would be perceived as the world's most powerful nation in the rivalry with the Soviets. The program to land on the moon, known as Apollo, appealed to the American spirit for adventure, and it was perhaps also the best evidence that the United States was winning the Cold War.

In February 1962 the United States caught up with the Soviets by sending John Glenn into orbit. Kennedy also pushed Congress to pass the Communications Satellite Act, designed to finance and operate a system of telecommunications satellites. Telstar, the first such satellite, was the forerunner of a global system of electronic communications transmissions. These successes encouraged American confidence in its technology and in its resolve to challenge and defeat the Russians. These events also launched the "space race," a new chapter in the U.S.-Soviet arms race.

THE SECOND RECONSTRUCTION—CONTINUED

Following the victory in Montgomery, the civil rights movement quieted for over three years. The reasons are difficult to pinpoint. Eisenhower's reluctance to enforce the *Brown* decision, and the corresponding power southern segregationists gained as a result, may have stifled the movement. Or perhaps the various civil rights organizations and the movement's leaders were unprepared to take the next big steps. Nevertheless, new life was breathed back into the movement on February 1, 1960, when Ezell Blair Jr., David Richmond, Franklin McCain, and Joseph McNeil, four freshmen from the predominantly black North Carolina Agricultural and Technical College, sat down at a Woolworth's lunch counter in Greensboro and asked to be served. "The waitress looked at me as if I were from outer space," one student later recalled. They remained seated and refused to leave. The next day they occupied the seats again, this time accompanied by twenty-five fellow students, and the next day by sixty-three students.

Possibly the most important aspect of the sit-ins was that they gave the press something new to write about, something to cover for the evening news. They quickly picked up the story, spreading the news and the movement like a wildfire throughout the South. Within nine months there were sit-ins in at least sixty cities in nine states involving thousands of young African Americans who chose to defy the South's segregation laws.

At least in this instance, the leadership had fallen behind the movement. The primary civil rights groups at the time, the NAACP, the Southern Christian Leadership Conference (SCLC), and the Congress of Racial Equality (CORE), all tried to get out in front of the movement by organizing the sit-ins and helping the protestors get out of jail. But it was not until the Student Nonviolent Coordinating Committee (SNCC) was formed in April that the sit-ins became actively organized and planned. The original idea was that SNCC would be the student arm of King's SCLC, but almost immediately SNCC's leadership insisted on the organization's independence. That decision came at least in part because the young black activists who formed SNCC were increasingly more militant than King. In fact, they often expressed dissatisfaction with King's willingness to compromise and move cautiously. SNCC soon attracted the most militant civil rights crusaders.

By the end of the year, about seventy thousand people had taken part in sit-ins in over one hundred southern cities and towns. The movement was not always successful, and by no means did it end segregation in the South. But it did instill confidence in those who participated, and it trained young black leaders for the major confrontations that lay ahead. It also reinvigorated the movement and, again, put it on television for the nation to see.

The sit-ins also marked the beginning of Kennedy's commitment to civil rights. The sit-ins began in the middle of the 1960 presidential campaign, and Kennedy, who was nearly unknown in the black community, saw the Republican Party's lack of sympathy for black issues as a vulnerability to be exploited. He openly supported the sit-ins. Then in late October, when King was arrested for a minor traffic violation and sentenced to six months at hard labor in a Georgia penitentiary, Kennedy endeared himself to the African American community by calling King's wife to offer support. Behind the scenes, Robert Kennedy put pressure on an Atlanta judge to release King. The pressure worked and King was released amidst fanfare and press coverage. In a statement printed widely in the press, King's father said, "It's time for all of us to take off our Nixon buttons." In the election, Kennedy took a solid 68 percent of the black vote.

FREEDOM RIDES

Almost by coincidence, one press-worthy event in the civil rights movement seemed to follow another—and the freshness of the stories kept the national press coming. So it was that just as the main thrust of the sit-ins was ending, the freedom rides began. The press simply jumped from one event to the other.

Two buses of riders left Washington, D.C., on May 4, 1962, and headed into the South. Roughly half the group were young African Americans and half were older white pacifists and religious leaders. Their objective was to show that segregation continued in the South despite a 1947 Supreme Court ruling that outlawed segregated seating on interstate buses, and a December 1960 ruling that ordered the desegregation of bus stations and terminals. Their plan was to take integrated buses into the South and at various stops along the way enter segregated terminals. As the buses got deeper into the South, the confrontations between southern whites and the freedom riders escalated. At Anniston, Alabama, one bus was firebombed; and in Birmingham several riders were savagely attacked. All the incidents received heavy news coverage.

All this put Kennedy in a bad position. He was caught between the black voters who had supported him in the 1960 election and southern Democrats who controlled Congress. As the freedom riders attracted more and more violence in the South, Kennedy was faced with a choice: support the riders and antagonize the southern congressmen, or turn his back on the riders in order to curry favor with the southern leadership. Either way it was almost certainly a losing proposition.

The riders went on to Montgomery, where they met with a particularly vicious attack. Kennedy responded by sending in four hundred federal marshals to protect the riders. On May 19, King arrived in Montgomery to lead the movement, and the next evening the marshals clashed with rioters who had trapped King and some others in a church outside of town. On May 24 the last bus headed off to Jackson, Mississippi. They were protected along the way by the Mississippi National Guard, but when they arrived the riders were arrested and sentenced to sixty days in a Mississippi prison.

The freedom rides exposed a rift that was beginning to develop inside the civil rights movement. At the height of the rides, the president had asked King and other leaders in the movement for a "cooling off" period in hopes of ending the violence that was damaging his relationship with Congress. King refused, but he did agree to a "lull." To a growing number of radicals inside the movement there was no difference between the two terms, and they began to see their leader as an instrument of the administration. One radical recalled that he returned from the freedom rides "with the terrible feeling that the angel had feet of clay." In 1962, King and the young radicals still needed each other: The radicals needed King's notoriety and the press coverage he attracted, while King needed the vigor and numbers that the young radical soldiers brought to the movement. That would change.

BIRMINGHAM/BOMBINGHAM

If the movement was on the verge of a split, it was not evident when King and his supporters took on the city of Birmingham in the spring of 1963. The Birmingham city government had made it clear that it would resist desegregation. But to King, Birmingham was the key. He believed that if he could crack Birmingham, the remainder of the South would follow. "As Birmingham goes," he said, "so goes the South." Standing at the gates of the city to do battle with King and the civil rights movement was Eugene "Bull" Conner, the city's long-time police commissioner and enforcer of segregation.

On April 12 King was arrested for defying a court order to stop demonstrating. While in jail, he wrote his *Letter from the Birmingham Jail*, primarily a criticism of white clergymen who had accused him of carrying the movement forward too quickly and too aggressively. To them, the assault on Birmingham was "untimely, unwise, unnecessary, and illegal." King warned of serious problems that might emerge within the movement if he did not receive support from white liberals. "I am convinced," he wrote, "that if your white brothers dismiss us as 'rabble rousers' and 'outside agitators'—those of us who are working through the channels of nonviolent direct action—and refuse to support our nonviolent efforts, millions of Negroes, out of frustration and despair, will seek solace and security in black nationalist ideologies, a development that will lead inevitably to a frightening racial nightmare." King clearly perceived the frustrations and impatience flowing from the young militants, and he saw what the future held if his movement for nonviolent change did not succeed.

On May 2, King organized a march of Birmingham's black children, and by the end of that day the city police had arrested nearly a thousand. The next day Bull Conner, apparently seeing that he was losing the battle, stopped arresting marchers and began a new strategy of attack. He released dogs on the marchers. Others were clubbed and sprayed with seven hundred pounds of water pressure from the city's fire hoses. That night, Americans watched in horror as news reports showed snarling Dobermans ripping the clothes off peaceful demonstrators. The viciousness of the attacks, the shocking display of racism, moved the nation. White Americans in the North again saw that racial conflict in the South was a major social problem that needed to be solved.

Finally, on May 10, a downtown Birmingham group called the Senior Citizens Committee agreed to desegregate the city's lunch counters and hire black workers if King would call off the marches. King agreed. Conner and the segregationists fought back, insisting that those who made the agreement did not represent the city. The next day, the Gaston Hotel, where the movement had set up its headquarters, was firebombed. That same night, King's brother's house was bombed. The violence spread. Seven downtown stores were hit with firebombs. Through the remainder of the summer and into the fall, the violence spread from Birmingham to the rest of the South, engulfing nearly two hundred cities and towns. Southern whites had lost the fight. They knew it, and they were venting their frustrations.

A MOST DANGEROUS TIME

John Kennedy's perception of world events, and thus his foreign policy as president, did not differ greatly from those who had gone before him. Kennedy had matured politically in the 1940s, and like most Americans of his generation he had learned the important lessons of World War II and the early Cold War. In his inaugural address he said that "the torch has been passed to a new generation of Americans—born in this century, tempered by war, disciplined by a hard and bitter peace, proud of our ancient heritage—and unwilling to witness or permit the slow undoing of those human rights to which this nation has always been committed, and to which we are committed today at home and around the world." The United States, he added, is "the watchman on the walls of world freedom." It was clear that the new president was a cold warrior, certainly no less so than the man he had just defeated for the presidency.

Perhaps the most important lesson Kennedy had learned from World War II was that appeasement is only a temporary solution to military aggression. During the Cuban Missile Crisis, he said: "The 1930s taught us a clear lesson: aggressive conduct, if allowed to go unchecked and unchallenged, ultimately leads to war." By 1961, when Kennedy entered the White House, this attitude toward appeasement was a precept, an axiom of American foreign policy that would dictate the nation's actions in dozens of international incidents.

The experiences of the early Cold War had also made Kennedy a devout disciple of containment. He had come to realize the need to contain Soviet aggressions in places like Greece, Turkey, Iran, Korea, and Berlin. He also paid homage to the primary instruments of containment: the Truman Doctrine, the Marshall Plan, and NATO, all designed specifically to stop the spread of communism. In 1956, Senator Kennedy called Vietnam the "finger in the dike of communism."

Kennedy's foreign policy was also directed by the fear of the loss of American influence abroad, as Truman had "lost" China to communism in 1949. When asked to consider reducing aid to Vietnam in 1963, he said: "Strongly in our mind is what happened in the case of China at the end of World War II, where China was lost. . . . We don't want that." Kennedy also believed in the other Cold War shibboleths like monolithic communism, the belief that all of worldwide communism was somehow engineered from the Kremlin; and the domino theory, the Eisenhower-era concept that the fall of one nation to communism meant that surrounding nations would be compelled to accept communism. Kennedy spoke often of "the free world" and the "Communist offensive." "The world," he declared, "cannot exist half slave and half free." By the time Kennedy became president, the American Cold War foreign policy was firmly in place. Kennedy understood it, and he subscribed to it.

Kennedy immediately discarded Eisenhower's doctrine of "massive retaliation," the reliance on nuclear weapons to force a foreign policy agenda. He replaced it with his own policy of "flexible response," a plan to increase the administration's options in dealing with Communist incursions. In 1961 Soviet Premier Nikita Khrushchev placed the United States on notice that Moscow would support what he called "wars of national liberation" in the Third World. This threat placed the United States in direct competition with the Soviets for the soul of the Third World, and that became the target of the Kennedy administration's foreign policy.

Flexible response was designed to confront directly these small conflicts that Khrushchev called "wars of national liberation." It was clear that nuclear power was of little use in fighting these wars. "We intend to have a wider choice," Kennedy told the country in 1961, "than humiliation or all-out nuclear war." Flexible response called for a number of options to deal with a variety of situations from covert activity to conventional warfare, and on to nuclear retaliation if necessary. Flexible response would be expensive (the administration's defense budget rose by $7 billion during his first year in office), but Kennedy and his new advisors were convinced that the United States needed such a plan to deal with the perceived expansionist tendencies of international communism.

To meet the challenge, Kennedy expanded the submarine-launched Polaris missile program, increased army combat divisions from eleven to sixteen, enlarged the Marine Corps and the Air Force, and increased the nation's ICBM capability. By 1963 there were four hundred thousand U.S. troops in Europe. The American buildup was massive, and the Soviets pushed hard to match it.

An important aspect of flexible response was "counterinsurgency," a fighting style designed to take guerrilla warfare directly to the guerrillas—and to win the wars in the Third World that Kennedy expected to fight. The president took a personal interest in this plan, and the result was the celebrated Green Berets, America's premier counterinsurgency force, trained in guerrilla tactics, supposedly equal in fighting ability to any soldier the enemy could field. As counterinsurgency was improved as a form of response, the military became increasingly confident of its ability to fight Communist guerrillas and to show the Communist world that the United States was prepared to confront Khrushchev's so-called wars of national liberation.

The nonmilitary arm of counterinsurgency was the Peace Corps, a sort of peaceful Green Beret force designed to win over the hearts and minds of the Third World. Although this idea can be derided as Cold War motivated, the Peace Corps became the most successful of Kennedy's foreign aid programs. Volunteers, usually young men and women, served two-year terms in Third World countries. In the fall of 1961, Congress appropriated $30 million for the program's first year, and by 1963, five thousand volunteers had served, making significant contributions in education, agriculture, irrigation, and sanitation. If nothing else, the Peace Corps raised the American image around the world to that of an idealistic, selfless nation, even though the program had been founded in the service of the administration's moral crusade to save the world from communism.

Another Kennedy foreign policy strategy was known as "nation building." This initiative had its ideological antecedents in the Marshall Plan, and was born out of the belief that communism is most successful in times of economic hardship. The plan also developed from the assumption that all wars of national liberation were Communist inspired. As Third World nations emerged from colonization in poverty-stricken Africa and Asia, they often fell immediately into the throes of economic or political chaos—and often both. The Kennedy administration hoped that U.S. dollars pumped into these new nations would shore up their economies, control their economic development, and make them less vulnerable to Communist influence.

One example of nation building was the Alliance for Progress, an initiative to strengthen the economies of Latin America in the face of the growing Soviet role in Cuba. The Alliance would provide $20 billion over ten years to the nations of Latin America in exchange for peasant land reform, economic reform, and additional investments from the Latin American nations. At first, the plan was encouraging. There were advances in literacy and health conditions improved, but overall the results were disappointing. It quickly became clear that the economic structure of the Latin American nations could not be changed by simply sending money south. And the plan carried strings, the most important being that the money had to be spent on American-made products, which cost more than goods made in Japan or Europe. American corporations continued to maintain control of economic resources through the region, and the privileged class continued to run the governments. In addition, the Alliance strengthened the old perception of the United States as an imperialist overlord. In the end, the Alliance for Progress did little to improve U.S.–Latin American relations; further, it failed to redistribute income or help the poverty-stricken peasants of Latin America.

CUBA AND THE BAY OF PIGS

The old Democratic Party warhorse Chester Bowles said that the Kennedys came to Washington "sort of looking for a chance to prove their muscle." They got that chance almost immediately when Kennedy chose to follow through on a plan initiated by the CIA in the Eisenhower administration and support an invasion of Cuba by anti-Castro Cuban exiles. The "Bay of Pigs" was Kennedy's first important foreign policy decision as president of the United States, and it was undoubtedly his worst.

Kennedy has often escaped criticism for the Bay of Pigs invasion because the idea was conceived in the previous administration. He was, after all, only carrying out plans that had already been set in motion. But Kennedy had made it clear, even before he took office, that he would support such a plan. During the campaign, he issued a press statement declaring: "We must attempt to strengthen the . . . anti-Castro forces in exile, and in Cuba itself, who offer eventual hope of overthrowing Castro." Although Kennedy was unaware that the CIA was training an anti-Castro invasion force, when he came to the White House in January 1961 he gave the plan his enthusiastic support, even to the point of handing over complete control of the operation to the CIA. He undoubtedly saw the operation as an opportunity to show the nation and the world that he could be a tough leader, a president who would not hesitate to take action against communism.

The Bay of Pigs operation went badly from the start. American involvement was thinly disguised, and exposed almost immediately by the *New York Times*. The operation began on April 15 when six old B-26 bombers strafed and bombed three Cuban airfields. The land invasion began two days later and was an immediate fiasco. Forewarned, and even aware of the location of the landing, Castro had assembled several thousand troops and more than fifty Soviet-made tanks at the invasion site by the time the landing force consolidated on the ground. The plan was also doomed to failure because it was contingent upon a mass anti-Castro uprising, which never occurred.

The administration made several statements to the press, in the United Nations, and even to Khrushchev that the United States would not become involved in the action no matter what the consequences. Even though the aircraft carrier *Essex* stood nearby, Kennedy chose to do nothing as the situation at the landing site deteriorated and then finally collapsed. Sixty-eight of the invaders were killed; another twelve hundred were captured. Schlesinger wrote, "The vision of men shot down on the beaches or hauled off to Castro's prisons haunted [Kennedy] that week and many weeks and months to come."

The invasion made Castro even more popular in Cuba, while adding nationalistic sentiment to the growing support for his economic policies. It was only after the invasion that Castro declared his revolution to be "Marxist-Leninist," and he immediately moved closer to the Soviets.

BERLIN AND THE WALL

Berlin was the most obvious potential flashpoint in the Cold War. There, the U.S. and Soviet armies faced each other along a line through the middle of the city. It was a situation which, after World War II, was intended to be temporary, but fifteen years later West Berlin was still the primary American outpost inside the Communist bloc—and a major thorn in Khrushchev's side. In the summer of 1961, just after the Bay of Pigs, Kennedy agreed to meet Khrushchev in Vienna to discuss their differences, to "size each other up," as the press called it, and to discuss the situation in Berlin.

The topics at Vienna were more general than specific. Kennedy argued that the Soviets should agree to maintain the balance of power as it stood and stop putting pressure on areas such as Taiwan and Berlin. Khrushchev talked of the natural right of the world's people to revolt against the forces of imperialism and capitalism. But on Berlin, Khrushchev took a hard line, demanding that a settlement be reached within a year. Kennedy responded that the United States would neither surrender its rights in West Berlin, nor remove troops. Khrushchev responded with a threat: "I want peace," he told Kennedy, "but if you want war, that's your problem."

The exchange shook Kennedy. He believed he had been too meek, too intimidated by Khrushchev's harassment. Indeed, Khrushchev wrote in his memoirs that he had succeeded in pushing Kennedy to the brink on the issue. Kennedy "was a reasonable man," he wrote, who "knew he wouldn't be justified in starting a war over Berlin." In early July, Khrushchev upped the ante by announcing a one-third increase in the Soviet military budget and threatening to seal off West Berlin. "We shall . . . order our armed forces," Khrushchev said, "to administer a worthy rebuff to any aggressor if he dares to raise a hand against the Soviet Union or against our friends."

On July 25 Kennedy ratcheted up the exchange once more with an address to the nation. He called Berlin "the great testing place of Western courage and will, a focal point where our solemn commitments stretching back over the years since 1945, and Soviet ambitions now meet in basic confrontation." The United States, he added, would defend the city "at all costs. . . . We do not want to fight," he continued, "but we have fought before. And others in earlier times have made the same dangerous mistake of assuming that the West was too selfish and too soft and too divided to resist invasions of freedom in other lands." He requested from Congress a massive $3.2 billion boost in military spending and for the authority to expand the draft and mobilize two infantry divisions and forty-four air squadrons. He also requested funds for a comprehensive civil defense program. It was all a definite signal to Khrushchev that the United States was going on a war footing, and that a nuclear response was on the table.

For two weeks the world was tense. Khrushchev told an American diplomat in Moscow that Kennedy had declared war. A half-hearted attempt to set up a conference to discuss the problem failed. Finally, on August 13 Khrushchev responded with roadblocks, barbed wire, and finally the Wall. He sealed off the western sector of Berlin from the east, and the crisis subsided when Kennedy accepted the situation.

The Wall became the most enduring symbol of the Cold War. To the West, it was evidence of the Soviet Union's intentions to isolate itself and its people from the rest of the world, of its belligerence, and of its attempts to keep its citizens from seeing and experiencing Western successes in West Berlin. The Wall was that symbol. Few westerners realized that the Wall's construction brought an end to a serious military showdown.

It was Kennedy's July 25 speech that had, more than anything, escalated the Berlin crisis and made war a real possibility. By building the Wall, Khrushchev had been forced to back down, to choose a measure other than war. For Kennedy this was his first Cold War victory, and the incident forced Khrushchev to respect the new president, and that caused tensions to ease. Two years later Kennedy flew to Berlin to celebrate his triumph. Speaking to a tumultuous crowd from the balcony of Rathaus Schoenberg, the Berlin city hall, Kennedy said, "as a free man, I take pride in the words 'Ich bin ein Berliner'" ("I am a Berliner"). The crowd roared their support. It may well have been his finest hour.

THE CUBAN MISSILE CRISIS

Kennedy's victory in Berlin placed a great deal of pressure on Khrushchev. Just as Kennedy had to mollify his hardliners at home, so did Khrushchev have to

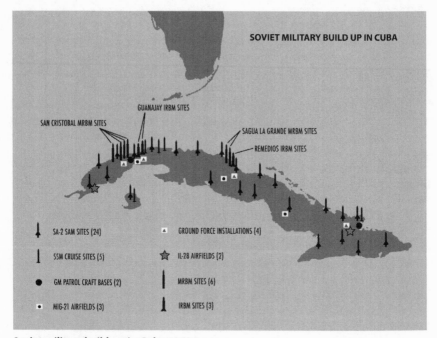

Soviet military build up in Cuba 1962.

answer to his own cold warriors at the Kremlin. By late 1961, Khrushchev was in desperate need of a strategic victory, or faced losing his job. At the same time, the Soviets had difficulty keeping pace with the Kennedy administration's massive arms buildup, and had, in fact, fallen far behind in the construction of ICBMs and Polaris-type missile submarines. To make the situation worse for Khrushchev, Kennedy frequently bragged about U.S. nuclear superiority—mostly to show the nation that he had kept his campaign promises. In 1961 he announced that the United States had attained a tremendous strategic advantage over the Soviets in weapons numbers, size, and delivery. A year later, Washington claimed a 16-to-1 advantage in long-range bombers, and a 6-to-1 lead in ICBMs. Khrushchev responded by renewing atmospheric nuclear testing and by increasing megatonnage, which culminated in a monstrous fifty-eight–megaton bomb, some three thousand times more powerful than the Hiroshima bomb and many times more powerful than anything exploded by the United States. In response, Kennedy authorized underground testing, and in April 1962 ordered atmospheric testing. The buildup on both sides was immense, and growing more dangerous all the time.

The situation in Cuba had not really cooled since the Bay of Pigs debacle, and over the next year Castro continued to fear a second U.S. invasion. Khrushchev responded by agreeing to deploy intermediate-range nuclear missiles to Cuba, ostensibly to protect the island. But most likely, Khrushchev intended to use the missiles as a bargaining chip: to agree to remove the Cuban-based missiles in exchange for U.S. concessions elsewhere—most likely in Turkey, where the United States had just deployed fifteen Jupiter intermediate-range ballistic missiles (IRBMs) that could reach most of the Soviet Union's western cities. In addition, if Castro remained in power with Soviet help, Khrushchev could point to Cuba as an example of his effective leadership and a Soviet success in the Western Hemisphere.

During July and August 1962, Soviet construction workers and troops began pouring into Cuba. CIA director John McCone and a few others feared that the Soviets might be attempting to establish an offensive capability, but surveillance operations refuted that possibility; and the Soviets assured the administration that no weapons would be placed in Cuba that could strike the United States. In fact, forty medium- and intermediate-range missiles were making their way to Cuba, with a capability of striking the farthest reaches of the United States. Suspecting the worst, Kennedy warned the Soviets in September that "very grave issues" would arise if they placed offensive weapons in Cuba. By September 16, six Soviet SS-4 and three SS-5 IRBMs had arrived in Cuba. Their strike range capability was something close to 2,500 miles.

Meanwhile, the 1962 congressional elections were approaching and the Republicans had made it clear that Cuba would be the main foreign policy issue. The party's right wing was gaining strength, and their principal campaign theme, as it had been since World War II, was that the Democrats were soft on communism. Senator Barry Goldwater (already the frontrunner for the 1964 Republican presidential nomination) had called Kennedy an appeaser and charged the president with a "do-nothing" policy toward Cuba. Kennedy fought back, attacking "those self-appointed generals and admirals who want to send someone else's sons to war."

On October 14, a U-2 reconnaissance plane photographed long-range missile sites under construction in Cuba, and for the next fourteen days the world's two superpowers faced each other in the first nuclear standoff in history. At no time has the world come closer to nuclear war.

The reconnaissance photographs indicated that there was no need to act quickly. It would be at least ten days before the missiles would be on their pads and operational. Kennedy took six days to discuss the situation with an internal group of top advisors, including his brother Robert, McGeorge Bundy, General Maxwell Taylor, McNamara, Rusk, John McCone, Adlai Stevenson, Theodore Sorensen, and others. This ad hoc group soon took the name "ExCom," or the Executive Committee of the National Security Council.

Kennedy's first instincts were to use force to remove the missiles. Led by generals Taylor and Curtis LeMay, the majority of ExCom favored an air attack against the missile sites as the most obvious solution. There was, however, a significant minority, including Robert Kennedy, Rusk, and McNamara, who thought a blockade might work as an alternative. It quickly became clear that the job of removing the sites could not be done completely by air strikes, that eventually a ground invasion of some sort would be necessary to complete the job. The ExCom members also began to consider such factors as U.S. prestige abroad, especially in Latin America, if the United States attacked Cuba. Quickly the consensus shifted from an air strike to a blockade, a belligerent act in itself, but one that would give Khrushchev an opportunity to back off rather than respond militarily. Since a blockade is deemed an act of war under international law, Kennedy chose the term "quarantine" instead.

At the same time, the president prepared for war. Missile crews were placed on maximum alert, B-52 bombers were loaded with nuclear weapons and sent aloft, the Atlantic fleet of 180 ships steamed toward the Caribbean, and the largest invasion force ever assembled in the United States began to form in Florida. Meanwhile, Allied commanders were briefed, NATO was placed on full alert, congressional leaders were asked to return to Washington, and plans were made to evacuate Guantanamo naval base in Cuba.

On October 22 the president went on television to explain the situation to the American people, complete with U-2 photographs of the missile sites. First he explained the quarantine and expressed hope that the Organization of American States (OAS) would support the action. Then he proposed to protect the entire Western Hemisphere from the Soviet threat: "It shall be the policy of this nation," he said, "to regard any nuclear missile launched from Cuba against any nation in the Western Hemisphere as an attack by the Soviet Union on the United States, requiring a full retaliatory response upon the Soviet Union." He also promised retaliation if the Soviets moved against U.S. allies anywhere else in the world, "including in particular the brave people of West Berlin." Then he called on Khrushchev to end "this clandestine, reckless, and provocative threat to world peace" and "to move the world back from the abyss of destruction" by withdrawing the missiles.

Kennedy's speech turned the threat against the United States into a threat against the Free World, and he had placed the United States in the position as its protector. The nation and much of the world rallied behind Kennedy. A Gal-

President Kennedy (center) confers with members of the Executive Committee of the National Security Council (ExCom) during the Cuban Missile Crisis in October 1962. *Source*: John F. Kennedy Presidential Library

lup poll showed that 84 percent of Americans approved of his actions. There was strong backing in the United Nations, the OAS, and among the Allied powers.

Moscow responded by calling the quarantine an act of "piracy" and "outright banditry." Khrushchev accused Kennedy of taking the world "to the abyss of a . . . missile nuclear war." Meanwhile, twenty-five Soviet ships carrying missiles and possibly warheads made their way across the Atlantic toward Cuba. The ships were being escorted by several submarines, and ExCom assumed they were armed with nuclear missiles. Khrushchev made his threats through William Knox, the president of Westinghouse Electric, who was in Moscow on business. If the U.S. ships stopped the Soviet vessels, Khrushchev told Knox, he would order the submarines to sink the ships.

On Wednesday, October 23, two Soviet ships, shadowed by a Soviet submarine, approached the quarantine zone, and then suddenly stopped dead in the water. After a few tense moments, they altered their course away from Cuba. "We were eyeball to eyeball," Rusk commented in his now famous statement, "and the other fellow just blinked." America sighed in relief. But the crisis was far from over. The construction of the launch sites continued in Cuba, and invasion was still the only plan Kennedy had for removing the missiles.

A break in the crisis came on October 26 when the Soviets offered to withdraw the missiles in return for a guarantee not to invade Cuba. The next day, the Soviets upped the ante by also insisting that the fifteen IRBMs be removed from Turkey. But while ExCom was considering the options, the crisis nearly flared up again. On October 27 a U-2 was shot down over Cuba by a Soviet surface-to-air missile. Several ExCom members insisted that the United States had to respond by knocking out the surface-to-air missile sites. Tensions were increased even further when a second U-2 flying near the North Pole strayed into Soviet airspace and jets from both sides scrambled to intercept. McNamara is said to have turned white and yelled, "This means war." But cooler heads prevailed and tensions eased when the U-2 was allowed to return to its base.

On that day, October 27, Kennedy resolved to end the crisis by accepting Moscow's first offer. In exchange for the removal of the missiles from Cuba, Kennedy would state publicly that the United States would not invade Cuba or try to overthrow Castro. The next day, Robert Kennedy informed the Soviet ambassador to the United States, Anatoly Dobrynin, that the United States would also accept the second demand and remove the Jupiter missiles from Turkey. Kennedy's only request was that the Soviets not make public the second offer in deference to the coming congressional elections. When Khrushchev agreed, the crisis ended.

For fourteen days, from the first U-2 sightings of the missile sites on October 14 until Khrushchev accepted the deal on October 28, the world had been on the verge of war. An important aspect of the event was that the American people knew it. Television followed the story closely. Network commentators constantly interrupted programming, pointing to maps of the Caribbean, showing the quarantine line around Cuba and, with little war-room-type toy boats, pointing out the location of Soviet freighters steaming toward Cuba. The American people were tense and frightened. With the exception of the behind-the-scenes aspects of the negotiations, they knew what was going on, and that mutual annihilation would be the cost of failed diplomacy. There was relief when the incident ended, but there was also a conviction that it should not happen again.

Kennedy emerged from the incident victorious. His popularity ratings soared, and world leaders congratulated him on his toughness. He had finally displayed the leadership qualities that he himself most prized. And because the deal to remove the Jupiter missiles from Turkey remained secret, it appeared that Khrushchev had lost a second showdown against Kennedy. Khrushchev would be ousted from power in two years, in part because he precipitated the Cuban Missile Crisis and then appeared to back down. In April 1963 the United States quietly removed the Jupiter missiles from Turkey.

One important result of the Cuban Missile Crisis was the signing of the Limited Test Ban Treaty in Moscow on August 5, 1963. Among other things, the treaty froze nuclear armament production. It was immensely popular in the United States, but Kennedy was widely criticized by the Republican Right for accepting a halt to nuclear development when U.S. capability was growing much faster than the Soviets'. The treaty also opened a dialogue between Washington and Moscow that eventually brought on a new rapprochement that eased tensions considerably.

JFK AND VIETNAM

South Vietnam was of no major strategic interest to the United States in the early 1960s. The primary reasons for American involvement can be found among the old foreign policy postulates, lessons, and myths of World War II and the immediate postwar era, all of which were strongly subscribed to by Kennedy and his advisors when they first came to Washington. First, the president believed that he could not accept the political repercussions of having "lost" South Vietnam to the forces of communism, as Truman had "lost" China in 1949. Second, if South Vietnam fell to the Communists, it was commonly believed that all of Southeast Asia would follow. Third, the appeasement of communism would bring on an expanded war. Fourth, communism must be contained. And fifth, American prestige abroad would be damaged irreparably if the United States withdrew from Southeast Asia and allowed a Communist victory. As Kennedy became more experienced, he saw a need to moderate his position on several of these points. But generally, these foreign policy principles pushed the Kennedy administration into Vietnam, along with the chauvinistic American attitude that a show of U.S. military might and money would dispose of the problem easily and quickly.

In his first months in office, Kennedy sent Vice President Johnson to Saigon to reassure the American-backed government of Ngo Dien Diem that the new administration in Washington supported his fight against communism. The vice president reported back with glowing praise for Diem, calling him "the Winston Churchill of Southeast Asia." "The battle against communism," Johnson told Kennedy, "must be joined in Southeast Asia with strength and determination to achieve success here." In the fall of 1961 Kennedy sent General Taylor and presidential aide Walt Rostow to Vietnam. Their report argued that the United States should continue aiding South Vietnam, and with significant military force, not just financial aid and advisors. In June 1962 McNamara reported to the president that "every quantitative measurement we have shows we're winning the war." At Diem's request, and with all his best advisors in agreement, Kennedy expanded the U.S. military involvement by sending in 100 more military advisors and 400 special forces troops on top of the 885 advisors left behind by the Eisenhower administration. A year later there were eleven thousand advisors and special forces units in South Vietnam, and U.S. pilots were providing transport and air cover for the South Vietnamese army. The escalations were small, but they were increasing in frequency.

At the same time, the Communists were able to match the U.S. escalations. In 1960 there were as few as 7,000 Viet Cong (Communist guerillas) in the South. By 1964 that number had reached 140,000. The American escalations were also matched by Chinese and Soviet assistance to North Vietnam; both Communist bloc nations were eager to see the United States bogged down in a land war in Asia. Of the two, the Soviets were the chief suppliers to the North Vietnamese, while the Chinese aided the North mostly with technical support and training. All this allowed the North Vietnamese to increase dramatically their infiltration of arms and supplies to the Viet Cong in the South. By 1963 there was enough materiel moving down the Ho Chi Minh Trail (the principal artery from the North into the South) to keep the growing Viet Cong army well armed and supplied.

Kennedy's biggest problem in South Vietnam was the Diem regime. Despite Johnson's glowing reports, Diem was unpopular among a vast majority of the Vietnamese people and often difficult to deal with. By the summer of 1963 the Kennedy administration believed he was on the verge of losing control in Saigon. His power base was weak and growing weaker, and he maintained his power only through the force of his army. On June 11 a Buddhist monk, Thich Quang Duc, burned himself to death in downtown Saigon to protest Diem's repressive regime. His self-immolation was followed by others. Several were shown on U.S. television, and for the first time the horrors of the Vietnam War came home to America. By the fall of 1963 it was clear to the American people that there was something deeply wrong with the U.S.-backed government in Saigon. To the Kennedy administration that problem was Diem.

By August a coup was being planned by some of the leading officers of the South Vietnamese army. The generals made their intentions known, and Kennedy sent word that the United States would support the new government, but that there would be no U.S. participation in the coup. Henry Cabot Lodge, the U.S. ambassador to South Vietnam, authorized some minor CIA assistance to the generals, and then cabled the president that the wheels were in motion: "We are launched on a course from which there is no respectable turning back: the overthrow of the Diem government." On November 1 the coup began. Diem's guards were immediately overwhelmed, and Diem surrendered. As Diem and his brother Ngo Dinh Nhu were being transported to the coup headquarters both were shot. Kennedy insisted that he was repulsed by the incident, but he certainly understood the consequences of such events.

There is some evidence that Kennedy intended to withdraw from Vietnam after the 1964 election. He told Senator Mike Mansfield early in 1963, "If I tried to pull out completely now, we would have another Joe McCarthy red scare on our hands, but I can do it after I'm re-elected." He apparently made similar statements to aide Michael Forrestal, Ken O'Donnell, and Senator Wayne Morse. But he made no such statements to Dean Rusk, and Robert Kennedy insisted that his brother did not discuss a withdrawal with him. Kennedy's last speeches in Dallas were filled with Cold War rhetoric: "Our assistance to these nations can be painful, risky, and costly, as in Southeast Asia today. But we dare not weary of the task." Had Kennedy lived and served two terms, it is more likely that the deteriorating conditions in South Vietnam would have forced him to respond to the lessons that had governed the nation's foreign policy since the end of World War II: containment, dominoes, the rejection of appeasement, the specter of a "lost" Vietnam, and the need to maintain American prestige abroad by combating Communist aggression. Lyndon Johnson was much less of a warrior than John Kennedy, but the forces of the Cold War and the situations that developed in Vietnam pushed him into escalation. Most likely, those same forces would have directed Kennedy's policies as well.

Within weeks of the Diem coup Kennedy himself was dead. By then the U.S. commitment in Vietnam had increased to sixteen thousand advisors and special forces troops. America was already at war, although few Americans realized it.

TRAGEDY IN DALLAS

Kennedy had barely carried Texas in the 1960 election, and as the 1964 campaign was about to kick off he was advised by Johnson that he needed to go to Texas to shore up his flanks there. Democrats in Texas were split between liberals and conservatives, and that division threatened to damage Kennedy's chances at winning Texas. So, taking his vice president's advice, he traveled to Dallas on November 21, 1963. At just after noon the next day, the president's motorcade was winding its way through the city. Riding with the president were his wife and Texas governor John Connally and his wife. Three shots were fired. One hit the president in the neck. A second struck the top of his head. He was fatally wounded and pronounced dead at Parkland Hospital at 1:00 P.M.

Americans would compare the personal impact of the assassination to Pearl Harbor, and later to the collapse of the World Trade Center in New York. Everyone would remember where they were when they heard the news. To some degree because no one understood what was happening, Lyndon Johnson took the oath of office in the safety of Air Force One, parked at Dallas' Love Field. In a solemn ceremony, Kennedy's body was moved from the White House to the Capitol in the same caisson that had carried the remains of Abraham Lincoln ninety-eight years earlier. In one of the most poignant images in the postwar era, a young John Kennedy Jr., age two, turned at his mother's urging and saluted his father's casket as it passed by.

The man arrested for the assassination was Lee Harvey Oswald, a twenty-four-year-old ex-Marine and avowed Marxist with ties to the Soviet Union and Cuba. Two days later, while Oswald was being transported from one jail to another, he was shot and killed by a Dallas nightclub owner named Jack Ruby. The oddity of these events, along with several other strange coincidences and assumptions, stirred an enormous interest in a possible conspiracy.

In an attempt to stop the rumors and accusations, Johnson named a com-

Lyndon Johnson takes the oath of office, November 22, 1963, aboard Air Force One (while parked at Love Field in Dallas). The oath is being administered by Judge Sarah T. Hughes. Johnson is flanked by his wife, Lady Bird, to his right, and Jacqueline Kennedy to his left. *Source*: Lyndon B. Johnson Library, photo by Cecil Storghton

mission of seven public figures to settle the matter and put the conspiracy theories to rest. Headed by Chief Justice Earl Warren, the Warren Commission conducted an exhaustive investigation and issued a report the next year that determined that Oswald was the lone gunman; there was, in fact, no conspiracy. But the bizarre nature of the events, along with the tremendous shock that accompanied it, caused the rumors of conspiracy to continue, and even grow. No credible evidence, however, has ever surfaced for any explanation for the events of November 22 except for the "lone gunman" theory. As late as 2007, independent investigators used digital technology to decipher police radio recordings that, they said, showed there were other shots fired on that fateful day. Perhaps all the questions will never be answered. Or perhaps there are those who will simply never accept anything but a conspiracy.

CONCLUSION

Kennedy actually accomplished little in his one thousand days in office. His domestic achievements were of minor significance, although many who study his administration would rightly applaud the Peace Corps and the Nuclear Test Ban Treaty. And in foreign affairs his need for victories over the Soviets caused a dangerous arms buildup that pushed the nation toward war. In addition, he escalated the war in Vietnam, and increased tensions by heightening the Cold War rhetoric. But there was something about Kennedy that seemed to give the nation hope for the future. His tragic death undoubtedly added to that speculation.

There was a feeling in 1961 that the nation was somehow on the verge of something new, that there would be a new beginning. For many Americans the Eisenhower administration never realized the promises and hopes that the end of World War II brought. Now, here, in 1961 many Americans seemed to believe that Kennedy would take the nation on that journey to realize all the potential the end of the war had promised. For many Americans it was a new dawn.

Kennedy, of course, was never able to attain those ideals and hopes, and for those who expected specific things from his administration he was generally a disappointment.

Reading: Lee Harvey Oswald

In the annals of America's most infamous figures, Lee Harvey Oswald stands alone, perhaps even above Charles Manson, Timothy McVeigh, and Mohamed Atta. He was the man who shot Kennedy, the man who, on November 22, 1963, took from America some of its innocence. It is an overused statement, but true: Everyone who was alive then remembers where they were when they heard President Kennedy had been shot.

For many Americans, Kennedy seemed to be more than just a president. He represented hope for the future of the nation, and his death seemed to bring an end to that hope. He was young. He had young children, and a wife who looked like a movie star. He was attractive and intelligent. Somehow his youth represented what the future might hold. For many of his followers he represented a reprieve from the sterility of the Eisenhower years, a man of the future, the person who would "get the nation moving again," as he had said over and over during the 1960 campaign. Whether that promise and hope was political rhetoric or a road map for the future of the nation mattered little. It was what he represented, what he might make of the future.

The murder of a president is the most heinous of crimes. Four American presidents have been killed while in office, but most Americans know only two, Lincoln and Kennedy, and perhaps their assassins, Booth and Oswald. In the case of Booth's assassination of Lincoln, a conspiracy was uncovered; the conspirators were captured, tried, and hanged. In the case of Oswald's assassination of Kennedy, no conspiracy was ever uncovered, no conspirators were ever captured, and Oswald was murdered before he could confess to or even explain his reasons for shooting Kennedy.

Because of the nature of the American political system, the assassination of a president is especially gut-wrenching. The president of the United States is more than just a national leader; he is an American among Americans, a representative of the people, their agent, their delegate. In campaigns, presidential candidates work to become as close to the people and as much like the people as possible. Many Americans took Kennedy's assassination personally, as if they had known the man. They mourned his death, felt sympathy for his wife and family, and came to despise his murderer.

Had Kennedy died for a cause, had he been killed by a gunman who hated his stand on an issue, Americans might well have accepted it, a martyred president who died for a noble cause at the hands of a fanatic. But Oswald was a nobody, an insignificant little man with no important background and no real future, and with convictions that were exclusive and individualistic. He apparently did not kill for a reason or a specific cause. Kennedy had done nothing to him. He was the quintessential lone gunman, the man who killed an important person just to absorb his importance—to be as important as the man he killed. As Jackie Kennedy told William Manchester, "He didn't even have the satisfaction of being killed for civil rights. It had to be some silly little Communist."

At least in part for that reason, conspiracy theories have flourished. As Manchester wrote, "[I]f you put the murdered President of the United States on one side of a scale and that wretched waif Oswald on the other side, it doesn't balance. You want to add something weightier to Oswald. It would invest the President's death with meaning, endow him with martyrdom. He would have died for something. . . . A conspiracy would, of course, do the job nicely." According to a 2003 poll, seven in ten Americans believe that Kennedy's assassination was a conspiracy and not the act of Oswald alone. About 50 percent of the nation believes that there was more than one shooter at Dealey Plaza in Dallas on November 22, 1963.

After the president's death, Jackie Kennedy told journalist Theodore White that Jack had loved the Broadway play *Camelot*, and that she saw her husband's administration in much the same light. "At night before we'd go to sleep," Jackie told White, "we had an old Victrola. Jack liked to play some records. . . . [A]nd the song he loved most came at the very end of this record, the last side of *Camelot*, sad *Camelot*. 'Don't let it be forgot,'" she recited the words from the last song of the play, " 'that once there was a spot, for one brief shining moment that was known as Camelot.'"

Oswald was born in New Orleans in 1939. By age sixteen he had attended twelve different schools and lived in twenty-two different residences. At age fourteen, while his mother was living in New York, he was diagnosed as schizophrenic with passive-aggressive tendencies. However, his mother moved back to New Orleans before he could receive treatment. At age fifteen, just as World War II was coming to an end, he introduced himself to Marxist ideology and made the effort to tell the Socialist Party of America that he was, in fact, a Marxist.

Oswald's Marxism did not, however, translate into anti-Americanism; in 1956 he joined the Marines and never expressed any contradiction in that choice. He was trained as a radar operator and served in Japan and other American bases in Asia. In 1959, after he had left the army, he renounced his American citizenship and emigrated to the Soviet Union. The Soviets, however, found him of no use and rejected his application for citizenship. Oswald reacted by attempting suicide. The incident apparently changed the mind of the Soviet government and they allowed Oswald to enter the Soviet Union. He was sent to Minsk to work in a factory, and quickly became disenchanted with the Soviet system.

In 1961 he married Marina Prusakova, a nineteen-year-old pharmacology student. In 1962 she gave birth to their first child, and about a year later Oswald returned to the United States with his family, settling in Dallas. He worked for a short time at a local welding company, but was almost immediately fired. Within only a few days (in April 1963), Oswald apparently attempted to murder General Edwin Walker, a notorious right-wing anti-Communist and segregationist. A few months following the Walker assassination attempt, Oswald ordered a Mannlicher-Carcano bolt-action rifle and began planning to send his wife and child back to Russia. In late April 1963, he returned to New Orleans, his place of birth. His job prospects there were poor, and he began contemplating a return to the Soviet Union.

But something, perhaps the Cuban Missile Crisis, caused Oswald to focus on Cuba, and he soon became an advocate for Castro and Cuban communism. In New Orleans, he often passed out fliers in support of Castro and Cuba, and he joined an organization called the Fair Play for Cuba Committee. In September, Oswald headed for Mexico and tried unsuccessfully to enter Cuba from there. He returned to Dallas, and through a friend found a job at the Texas School Book Depository.

President Kennedy traveled to Dallas on November 22, mostly at the insistence of Lyndon Johnson. Texas would be crucial in the coming 1964 presidential campaign, and Johnson wanted to make certain he could deliver his home state for the president. The Democratic Party in the state was warring between the conservative governor John Connally and the liberal senator Ralph Yarborough, and Johnson hoped that Kennedy's visit would go a long way toward patching the party's differences and unifying the Democrats as the election approached.

November 22 was a beautiful day, crisp and clear. The president and vice president were both relieved that there were no organized protests along the motorcade route. At about 12:30, the president's motorcade turned onto Elm Street off Houston. At least three shots rang out. The president was hit in the left shoulder and head. John Connally, riding with the president, was hit in the back. The president's car accelerated at high speed toward Parkland Hospital. Connally's wounds were severe but not life threatening. Kennedy, however, had a massive head wound. At 1:00 P.M. he was declared dead.

Witnesses at the scene said they heard shots from the sixth-floor window of the Texas School Book Depository building and from behind a wooden fence on a grassy knoll. Police investigated these claims and found a Mannlicher-Carcano rifle hidden among some boxes near a window on the sixth floor of the book depository. At about 1:15, while Oswald was apparently leaving the scene on foot, he was confronted by Dallas police officer J. D. Tippet. Oswald shot Tippet with a handgun, leaving him for dead. Oswald then headed to a local movie theater where he was arrested. His palm print was found on the Mann-licher-Carcano rifle. He was interrogated by Dallas police for two days. He denied being involved in the assassination, and at one point referred to himself as a "patsy," a word often used by the Italian Mafia to describe a person who is accused and convicted of a crime committed by others.

At about 11:20 (CST) on November 24, while being transferred to Dallas County Jail, Oswald was shot by Jack Ruby, a Dallas nightclub owner who claimed he was distraught over the assassination. Oswald was rushed to Park-land Hospital, where the president had died just two days earlier. He died there.

·6·

"We Shall Continue"

On November 22, 1963, Lyndon Johnson took the oath of office and stepped
onto the stage as President of the United States. He was undoubtedly qualified and prepared for the job, but Johnson was so different from John Kennedy
that the abrupt change was itself a jolt to the nation. Americans had become
attached to the glamour, the charisma, the vigor, and the myth that surrounded
John Kennedy. Now they were faced with Johnson: not young (he was only fifty-
five, but looked much older and had already had a serious heart attack), not
attractive, not athletic, a political insider, a southerner, a farmer who had pulled
himself up from modest beginnings. He had been educated at a small Texas college, and his wife (although she certainly had some special qualities) was not
glamorous. As a senator, Johnson had shown an uncanny ability to persuade others and to get things done, but to most Americans he exhibited about as much
charisma as one of his prize breeding bulls. He had always hovered outside the
Kennedy circle, treated mostly as a political necessity who did not fit the mold of
the young New Frontiersmen. In fact, he was quietly referred to by Kennedy
insiders as "Colonel Cornpone."

Americans were shocked at Kennedy's death, and they may have winced at
their new president, but Johnson was reassuring to most Americans. His sagging
face stared at Americans in their living rooms, and in a deep Texas drawl he said,
"Let us continue," a follow-up to Kennedy's "let us begin."

Perhaps the best way to view Johnson is through his own expectations. He
believed that he was the president who would carry out the promises that had
been unfulfilled since the end of World War II. He wanted to be a reformer, to
do what others said they would do but did not. He wanted to make use of the
wealth of the greatest economic power in history to help the nation's downtrodden, the minorities, the urban poor, the rural poor, and the elderly. He wanted
to be another Roosevelt, the man he had most admired in his youth, to be
remembered as the president who had helped the many, expanded the middle
class, and brought equality to America, both racial and economic.

The result was the Great Society, a domestic program that included at least

131

two hundred reform bills. It was a legislative offensive rivaled only by the Hundred Days of 1933, and it was aimed mostly at aiding the poor, those people Johnson believed needed assistance at some level. But by the end of the decade it was clear that the Great Society had fallen far short of its goals. The general failure of the Great Society contributed to the greater sense of failure attached to the entire decade of the 1960s.

Certainly, Johnson delivered much: three landmark civil rights bills, two important education bills, Medicare and Medicaid, the Food Stamp Act of 1964, the mammoth Housing Act of 1968, the Model Cities program—they all offered the hope of raising the standard of living for the nation's underprivileged. But there were few successes. Living conditions in the urban ghettos deteriorated during the 1960s; almost half of all African American families still earned less than $5,000 in 1970; three out of four Americans living below the poverty line never received any assistance at all; conditions in Appalachia did not improve significantly; and by the end of the decade most of the anti-poverty programs had become too expensive to be effective. By the 1970s and 1980s the Great Society had become a Republican Party whipping boy, an example of how big government and big spending cannot cure social ills and the prime example of the Democratic Party's "big spending" excesses. Liberals responded that the Great Society failed only because it was underfunded, and because Johnson simply tried to do too much.

One reason the Great Society did not reach its potential was that Johnson regularly promised more than he could deliver. He spoke to the American people in near-utopian terms, with grandiose rhetoric that promised to heal all the nation's ills almost immediately. "I want to be the president who educated young children . . . who helped to feed the hungry . . . who helped the poor find their own way," he told Congress in 1965. "God will not favor every thing we do . . . but I cannot help believing that He truly understands." "They came in darkness and they came in chains," Johnson spoke of African Americans when he signed the Civil Rights Act of 1964. "Today we strike away the last major shackle of those fierce and ancient bonds." The idea of the Great Society itself conjured up visions of a coming utopia, an America rebuilt. "We have the power to shape the civilization we want," he told the nation. Lyndon Johnson's promises, however, generally went unfulfilled.

Johnson's primary problem was Vietnam, a situation that was quickly growing into a major military conflict just as the Great Society legislation was making its way through Congress. There was not enough money, nor was there enough national will, to engage both of these monumental endeavors. Senator J. William Fulbright, an early supporter of both the Great Society and the war in Vietnam, came to oppose both. "Each war feeds on the other," he said, "and we are not winning either of them." It became all too clear to Johnson that those who supported his Great Society did not support the war, and those who supported the war detested the Great Society.

Certainly, both the war and the reform agenda suffered. Johnson was a brilliant consensus builder, and he worked feverishly to forge a congressional consensus, a coalition of liberals and moderates that would enact his social programs. However, he feared that any confrontation over Vietnam might destroy that coalition and stall his reform agenda. He later said that he was deeply concerned that a congressional debate on "that bitch of a war," as he called it, would destroy "the woman I really love—the Great Society." In 1966 he admitted: "Because of Vietnam, we cannot do all that we should, or all that we would like to do." For Johnson, there was a need to compromise in both areas to keep his fragile political coalition working in his favor. The result was that both the conduct of the war in Vietnam and the president's ambitious domestic reform program suffered from fiscal anemia.

LYNDON JOHNSON AND THE KENNEDY LEGACY

When Johnson became president he was fully prepared to take on the job. He was born in the Texas hill country into a relatively poor family of full-time farmers and part-time local politicians. In 1931 he worked his way from high school teacher to a legislative assistant for a Texas congressman, and made a fateful transition from the Texas Barrens to the staid columns of Washington. Johnson's father had been old friends with powerful Texas representative Sam Rayburn, and by courting that relationship, young Lyndon was named to head the New Deal's National Youth Administration in his home state. Succeeding there, and having developed a reputation as a Roosevelt supporter and a southern New Dealer, Johnson won a special election for a seat in the House of Representatives in 1937. Four years later, with Roosevelt's personal endorsement, Johnson ran for the Senate, but was narrowly defeated by a right-wing demagogic hillbilly singer named Pappy O'Daniel. In 1948 he ran again, defeating Coke Stevenson, a conservative Texas governor. Johnson's senatorial victory in 1948 was dubious at best (many suspected that he obtained his eighty-seven-vote margin of victory through fraud) giving him the Washington sobriquet of "Landslide Lyndon."

Johnson delighted in the Senate's power politics, its power structure, and its power relationships. His leadership qualities (based mostly on his ability to influence others and build coalitions) impressed power brokers like Senator Richard B. Russell of Georgia, and Johnson quickly became one of the most powerful men in Washington. In 1951, only three years into his first term in the Senate, he was elected Democratic whip; two years later he was elected minority leader, and when the Democrats won control of the Senate a year later, Johnson moved to majority leader. At the beginning of his second term he was, behind Speaker of the House Sam Rayburn, the second most powerful Democrat in Washington. It was only natural that when party operatives spoke of presidential timber, they spoke of Lyndon Johnson.

In the 1950s it was assumed that southerners could not become president, that the southern stance on race was simply too volatile and divisive for a southern politician to overcome in a national election. In order to avoid that dilemma, Johnson tried hard to present himself as a national figure (rather than the southerner that he was) and as a moderate on most issues. He rejected the hard-line southern attitudes toward race, and he even took the lead in the Senate's passage of the 1957 and 1960 civil rights bills. He also refused to sign the Southern Manifesto, a harsh statement signed by most southern congressmen against the Supreme Court's 1954 *Brown* decision. Southern pols like Rayburn and Russell understood Johnson's strategy and national ambitions, and often worked to protect him from other southerners who wanted Johnson to join them in their war against the civil rights movement.

Johnson hoped his legislative accomplishments would bring him the Democratic nomination in 1960, but he was quickly swamped by the Kennedy organization and the new presidential politics of winning state primaries. Big-city power brokers like Chicago's Mayor Richard Daley and Carmine DeSapio of New York liked the idea of attaching Johnson to the Democratic ticket headed by a young easterner, and lobbied hard to make Johnson the vice presidential candidate. The Kennedys, however, resisted. They saw Johnson as wedded to the old-time Democratic politics, a southern conservative, a leader of the wing in the party that had kept liberalism at bay since the late 1930s. He hardly represented the Kennedy image of youth and national rebirth. Johnson, however, finally got the nod because, as Robert Kennedy later recalled, "one of the major factors that persuaded [John Kennedy to accept Johnson on the ticket] was that he would be so mean as majority leader that it was much better having him as Vice President, where you could control him."

Seldom in the twentieth century has the vice presidential candidate actually made much of a difference in the general election. But in 1960 Johnson played a key role in holding Texas and a large portion of the South for the Kennedy ticket. Despite that significance, Johnson was forced to remain outside the loop throughout the Kennedy administration, unable to use his considerable talents as persuader and power broker. Another Texan, Roosevelt's first vice president, John Nance Garner, compared the vice presidency to a "bucket of warm spit." Johnson, less colorfully (but on the ticket for much the same reason as Garner in 1932) said of the job, "In the end, it is nothing. I detested every minute of it." But history took a turn on November 22, 1963.

Johnson found himself in the position of an unelected president at the head of an incomplete, but generally popular, agenda. His reaction was to work to fulfill his predecessor's promises, to give the American people what they had voted for in 1960. He put Congress on notice that he would press to enact all the legislation proposed by the Kennedy administration; and in his first State of the Union address, just six months after Kennedy's assassination, he made it clear that he expected early passage of the Kennedy tax cut and the civil rights bill. By then, Johnson, playing on the nation's sympathy for the martyred Kennedy and using his own power of legislative genius, had gained control of the apparatus of the federal government like no president since Roosevelt. He was well on his way to fulfilling Kennedy's promise of getting the nation moving again. Johnson immediately broke the legislative deadlock that had stalled Kennedy's legislative agenda and formed a coalition of Democrats and moderate Republicans. That coalition would keep his own programs moving through Congress at least until 1967, when it finally collapsed under the weight of the Vietnam War.

In the next congressional session, beginning in January 1964, Johnson pushed through at least twenty major reform measures, including the most important civil rights bill in American history, the Economic Opportunity Act that defined the embryonic War on Poverty, and the Kennedy administration's $10 billion tax cut (almost 10 percent of the appropriated tax budget for 1964). Congress complained, but Johnson effectively evoked the memory of John Kennedy to force Congress into action.

THE ELECTION OF 1964 AND THE LIBERAL MANDATE

Johnson's successes in his first year in office had as much to do with the Kennedy legacy as with Johnson's own legislative abilities. But like Truman, Johnson wanted his own mandate, his own election victory to legitimize his place as President of the United States—and to carry out his own agenda. As the 1964 election approached, the Democrats (who characteristically find themselves mired in intraparty turmoil, factional fighting, and pelted by the demands of interest groups) emerged reasonably united behind Johnson. The Republicans (who characteristically keep their dirty laundry hung behind closed doors and emerge into the open as a unified party prepared to attack the enemy in force) came up divided along ideological lines, bitter, and radical. It was a very uncharacteristic election.

The Republicans offered a candidate from the political right, Arizona senator Barry Goldwater. Goldwater and the GOP right had complained for years that the Republican Party had followed a me-too moderate course since 1940, and with the notable exception of Eisenhower, had gotten nowhere with the likes of Wendell Willkie, Tom Dewey, and Nixon. It was Robert Taft who had worn the mantle of the party's right wing through the forties and fifties, but whose dour personality (along with Ike's popularity) had kept him from winning his party's nomination. By the mid-sixties, the right in the Republican Party had reached a new peak of influence and power, and in 1964 Goldwater emerged as their leader.

The rise of the Republican Right occurred to a certain extent because the moderate wing of the Republican Party had lost its leadership. Eisenhower, by now the old man of the Republican moderates, refused to name any successors; Nixon had retired after losing his bid to become governor of California; and New York governor Nelson Rockefeller had gotten a divorce, which made him morally suspect in the minds of many Republican voters. Nearly by default, the conservative right floated to the top of the Republican Party power structure. Their agenda was simple and clear: They opposed big government and government intervention in the affairs of the American people, and they opposed high taxes to support social programs. They also pushed for individual economic freedom, and they maintained the basic Republican Party hard line against international and domestic communism.

The Democratic convention, held in Atlantic City in August, was to be little more than a party coronation of Johnson. He had delivered on most of Kennedy's legislative agenda, and a Gallup poll showed that he was now popular, well out front of Goldwater. The convention planners had even scheduled the final nominating vote for August 27, Johnson's fifty-sixth birthday.

The only drama at the convention came from the racially integrated Mississippi Freedom Democratic Party (MFDP). They insisted that they be seated as the true representatives of the people of Mississippi instead of the all-white Mississippi delegation, known as the Regulars. Hubert Humphrey struck a compromise between the two groups that defused the situation but satisfied neither delegation. For his efforts, however, Humphrey was given the number-two spot on the ticket. Johnson was nominated by acclamation. He seemed headed for an easy victory.

Hardly anyone noticed the campaign of Alabama governor George C. Wallace. Wallace was a classic southern demagogue who had risen to prominence by riding the crest of opposition to the Supreme Court's 1954 *Brown v. Board of Education* decision that brought an end to legal segregation in the South's public schools. In 1964 Wallace seemed only to dabble in the Democratic primaries, more or less unnoticed, with what most pundits believed was a distinctly southern message of opposition to the 1964 Civil Rights Act (then making its way through Congress), support of states' rights, and a call to anti-communism. But Wallace opened eyes when he did well in several working-class areas outside the South where he was able to get his message across. He took one-third of the votes in the Wisconsin primary, did well in working-class Gary, Indiana, and nearly won the Maryland primary by sweeping the working-class districts of east and south Baltimore. Within just a few years it would be clear that Wallace had, in 1964, just begun to scratch the surface of what would become, by 1968, a full-blown backlash against American liberalism and the excesses of the entire decade of the 1960s.

The election is interesting if only for the Democrats' campaign tactics. Goldwater was an amiable character. Political analyst Richard Rovere called him "the cheerful malcontent . . . about as abrasive as a jar of cold cream." But the Johnson campaign successfully portrayed him as a wild man, who, as George Will has written, "as president would delay incinerating the planet only until he had time to dismantle the government." One of Johnson's television campaign commercials showed a sweet, blond child (by some accounts the daughter of Johnson aide Bill Moyers) lazily counting the petals of a daisy, followed by a stern male voice counting down to zero, then a flash and a mushroom cloud. With no words spoken, the message was clear: Goldwater would provoke nuclear war. The commercial was shown on television only once, during a break in the popular *Saturday Night at the Movies*. But it was shown over and over again as part of the networks' coverage of the campaign.

At the same time, Johnson strove to contrast himself as cautious on international affairs. During the Tonkin Gulf Incident in August (discussed in more detail below) Johnson tried to show firmness against Communist aggression by destroying the North Vietnamese gunboat bases and their storage facilities, but without dragging the nation into a war over the incident. Congress agreed with Johnson's actions by passing the Tonkin Gulf Resolution. When Goldwater urged a tougher stance, Johnson replied with words that would haunt him later: "We're not about to send American boys nine or ten thousand miles from home to do what Asian boys ought to be doing for themselves."

The voters liked the domestic emphasis and the foreign policy restraint and gave Johnson the largest mandate since Roosevelt's victory in 1936. Goldwater won only in the Deep South, and he barely carried his home state of Arizona. Johnson's landslide brought in on his coattails thirty-seven new seats for the Democrats in the House and two in the Senate. It was truly a mandate to deal with foreign affairs (particularly in Vietnam) as he wished, and to move forward as the greatest reform president in the nation's history.

GREAT SOCIETY

In a speech at the University of Michigan in the spring of 1964, Johnson declared that "the Great Society rests on abundance and liberty for all. It demands an end to poverty and racial injustice, to which we are totally committed in our time." He had used the term "Great Society" several times before, but the press had missed the reference; they finally caught it here. Johnson's Great Society was an ambitious program to solve the nation's problems. It was big promises, supported by big ideas and big money. It promised to conduct a "war on poverty," to bring an end to racial discrimination, to provide aid to those who could not afford medical care, and to revitalize the cities, the environment, and the nation's schools.

One of the greatest achievements to come out of the Great Society (although the initiative was inherited from the Kennedy administration) was the legislative advances in civil rights. The most important of these was the Civil Rights Act of 1964. The bill had gotten bogged down during Kennedy's last months in office, but it was finally shaken loose by Johnson as a result of a coalition that he forged along with the Senate minority leader, conservative Republican Everett Dirksen of Illinois. It was, said Dirksen, "an idea whose time has come." The new law brought an end to discrimination in all places of public accommodation, and it banned prejudicial hiring practices in businesses employing more than twenty-five people. As an enforcement measure, the law created the Equal Employment Opportunity Commission to investigate complaints.

' Before Johnson left office in 1969 the administration passed two more land-mark civil rights bills. The first, the Voting Rights Act of 1965, went a long way toward guaranteeing the rights of African Americans to vote. The second bill, the Civil Rights Act of 1968, was designed to bring an end to racial discrimination practices in housing. To further his commitment to the movement, Johnson, in 1967, elevated NAACP attorney Thurgood Marshall from the Federal Circuit Court to a seat on the Supreme Court.

Another nagging problem was poverty. Despite America's economic successes since World War II, a full forty million Americans (20 percent of the population) still lived below the poverty line. Most lived in unproductive, isolated rural areas like Appalachia, or in urban slums and ghettos. The majority were unemployed or drastically underemployed. They had been mostly invisible until books like Harrington's *The Other America*, and large photo layouts in magazines such as *Life*, awakened Americans to these conditions. It was, however, television reports and extensive news programs that finally showed the nation the face of poverty. America could no longer look away. John Kennedy had made poverty a campaign issue in 1960; that was followed by promises, and finally the embryo of a program in the Kennedy administration. America was prepared to do something about the problem when Johnson became president.

In his first State of the Union address the new president told the nation that his administration "here and now declares an unconditional war on poverty in America. We shall not rest," he added, "until the war is won." The result was a whole series of antipoverty measures designed to aid the nation's poor, both urban and rural. In 1964 the Food Stamp Act was passed to make available to the poor the basic nutritional necessities at a lower cost. The program was placed under the control of the Department of Agriculture and included increased support payments to farmers. Also in 1964, Congress passed the Manpower Development and Training Act to provide money to train and retrain the unemployed.

The most wide-sweeping antipoverty program was the Economic Opportunity Act, also passed in 1964. Ten separate programs were established by the act, all to be administered by the Office of Economic Opportunity (OEO). To run the OEO, Johnson tapped Sargent Shriver, the head of the profoundly successful Peace Corps and a name associated with the Kennedy family. The OEO was innovative and controversial, and it received considerable attention as the center-piece for Johnson's Great Society and War on Poverty. The Community Action Program (CAP) received the most money and the most attention. CAP was designed to set up a whole series of programs at the local level in both rural and urban areas, including job training and vocational rehabilitation, small farm and business loans, legal counseling, community health programs, and a spectrum of educational programs. The most notable programs included Head Start, a program for underprivileged preschoolers; Upward Bound for underprivileged college students; Legal Services to provide legal advice to the poor; VISTA (Volunteers in Service to America), a sort of domestic Peace Corps that sent young people into poverty-stricken areas of the nation, both urban and rural; the Job Corps, which taught marketable skills to inner-city youth; and Neighborhood Health Services. An important focus of the program was to make use of the disadvantaged themselves whenever possible in developing and directing these projects.

Following Johnson's 1964 landslide victory, the volume on the War on Poverty was turned up even higher. In 1965 the passage of the Appalachian Regional Development Act provided $1.1 billion in subsidies for highway construction and resource centers throughout the economically depressed Appalachian region. That same year the Public Works and Economic Development Act pinpointed other depressed areas of the nation for similar federal aid.

Since the end of the war the Democratic Party had championed a federally sponsored medical program. Truman had fought the American Medical Association lobby over the issue in 1949 and lost the battle, and one sort of medical aid bill or another had been bottled up in Congress for nearly two decades. Johnson concluded that a bill providing universal health care was probably not possible, so he focused on providing medical insurance for the elderly. He called his plan Medicare. He was on firm ground here; polls showed that fully two-thirds of the nation agreed that some plan was necessary. But the AMA refused to be bowled over and countered with their own bill, and then the Republicans offered a compromise plan called "Bettercare."

Arkansas representative Wilber Mills, head of the powerful House Ways and Means Committee, had succeeded in stopping all medical aid bills from reaching the floor of the House for a vote. However, convinced by Johnson's mandate in the 1964 election and by polls that called for a breakthrough in the area, Mills allowed Johnson's Medicare bill a fair hearing and approved it out of committee in early March 1965. The final bill incorporated features of all three plans: the administration's plan, the AMA plan, and Bettercare. Medicare would be compulsory, funded through payroll taxes, and administered through the Social Security Administration. A supplementary plan was voluntary and was financed through monthly premiums deducted from Social Security retirement payments. Accompanying the bill was the Medicaid Act, a program that made federal funds available to states to help cover medical care for the underprivileged. Johnson signed the bill at the Harry S. Truman Library in Independence, Missouri, as the eighty-one-year-old Truman looked on.

Johnson often said that he wanted to be known as "the education president." To that end, he made aid to education the cornerstone of the Great Society and the War on Poverty. He saw education as the key to America's future, but not in the Eisenhower-Kennedy Cold War sense that the United States must upgrade its education system in order to win the race against the Soviets. Federal aid to education had been stalled in Congress at least since the war, and Johnson vowed to pass an education bill that would upgrade the entire national system. All other attempts to aid education had come up against two questions: (1) whether the federal government should provide aid to parochial schools; and (2) whether federal aid to education would undermine the South's control over its segregated school system. The second question had generally been answered by the civil rights movement. By the mid-1960s, old-style southern segregation had become nearly indefensible, and the old southern fire-eaters in Congress could no longer depend on the support of northern conservative Republicans to defeat civil rights legislation.

The administration dealt with the issue of religion by giving aid to individual students instead of to the schools they attended. To make the plan even more attractive, the administration tied the funds to the number of impoverished children in each state. The result was the Elementary and Secondary Education Act of 1965, the first law in U.S. history to provide federal funds for education. Johnson pushed the bill hard, insisting it be passed quickly, and "without a comma changed." Congress complained, but in just eighty-nine days the bill, virtually intact, was on the president's desk. "As President of the United States," Johnson said at the signing of the bill in the one-room schoolhouse he once attended in Stonewall, Texas, "I believe deeply that no law I have signed or will ever sign means more to the future of America." The bill provided over $1 billion to low-income school districts for textbooks, library materials, adult education programs, media centers, and research laboratories. Nearly 90 percent of the nation's school districts qualified for some federal funding. The bill went a long way toward equalizing educational funding in the nation.

Aid to colleges and universities came in the form of the Higher Education Act of 1965. That bill provided federal funds for such things as scholarships and grants to students from low-income backgrounds, money for library improvements and an expansion of the work-study program, federal funding for small struggling colleges, and low-interest student loans to just about anyone who wanted to attend college. These programs caused a surge in college enrollments that carried on into the next decade. Government grants and low-interest loans became the chief means of paying college expenses for middle-class Americans.

Another focus of the Great Society was the nation's decaying cities. Middle-class flight to the suburbs had left the nation's urban areas to a new underclass of poor—and with a weak tax base. The predictable result was increased crime, poor housing, poor schools, inadequate services, poor health care, and resulting despair. The Economic Opportunity Act and its Community Action Program provision set up a number of important programs. But Johnson wanted to go further. In 1965 he pushed Congress to pass the Housing and Urban Development Act, which provided federal funds for health and recreation centers, a rent supplement program, and money for low-income home improvements. A year later, Johnson orchestrated the passage of the Demonstration Cities and Metropolitan Area Redevelopment Act, better known as the Model Cities Act. The spin from the White House was that the plan would bring an end to substandard housing. It provided just over $1 billion to improve housing, health care, education, and recreation, and for job training, welfare benefits, and urban transportation. The act also provided for a vigorous slum clearance program by providing cities with up to 80 percent of the cost of demolition, followed by the reconstruction of what were called "model communities," which included not only housing, but also recreation and health care facilities and education projects. Unfortunately, the Model Cities Program operated under a haze of accusations of political favoritism and local mismanagement of federal funds. In addition, the designated "model communities" became little more than high-rise slums, clusters of poverty and crime, the new home of the urban underclass. Most Americans called them "projects."

In 1968, just as his liberal-moderate coalition was collapsing, Johnson was able to convince Congress to pass the most extensive public housing proposal in the nation's history. The bill called for the construction of twenty-six million new homes or apartments—nearly six hundred thousand low-income housing units annually. The emphasis was placed on privately owned homes, financed through government loans and government-insured loans up to $20,000. Prospective homeowners purchased their homes through private builders, which led to the construction of thousands of substandard houses and apartment buildings throughout the nation. For the most part, builders got rich, but the 1968 housing effort did little to help the nation's inner-city poor.

The Great Society also became involved in a number of areas outside the program's focus of aiding the underprivileged. One such area was the environment. Improving the nation's environment had long been a Democratic Party commitment, and Johnson wanted to lay the groundwork for a national program to improve the quality of the environment for the future. He pushed through Congress a number of important environmental acts, including the Federal Pollution Control Act, the Water Quality Control Act, the Water Resources Planning Act, the Air Quality Act of 1967, the Water Pollution Act of 1967, the Water Pollution Act of 1968, and the Wildlife Preservation Act.

Johnson also took an interest in consumer and safety legislation. He supported the passage of two important bills: the Highway Safety Act and the Traffic Safety Act of 1966. Both were a response to the publication of Ralph Nader's book *Unsafe at Any Speed* (1965), which documented the failures of the American automobile industry in general, and in particular described the hazards of driving the poorly conceived Chevrolet Corvair. The administration also initiated the Consumer Credit Protection Act of 1968, or the Truth in Lending Act, as it was called. The new law required lenders to give full and complete information to customers on interest rates.

Liberals looked to these massive programs as a key to America's future, a new New Deal that would solve the nation's most nagging problems: those associated with poverty, race, and inequality. These programs would produce the rising tide, as Kennedy had said, that would float all boats. Most Great Society programs, however, suffered the same fate: They were too expensive, under-funded, or both. The scattering of programs under the OEO received only $800 million in its first year. CAP received only a piddling $340 million its first year, and the Job Corps became the best example of a program that was simply too expensive to work. Between 1964 and 1967 the entire cost of the War on Poverty was only $6.2 billion. Compared to Roosevelt's $5 billion spent on relief pro-grams in 1935, it is no wonder that Johnson's War on Poverty could only barely scratch the surface of the nation's massive problems. In addition, very little of the money ever reached the hands of those who needed it. The real beneficiaries were the construction companies that built the highways into Appalachia, demolished urban ghetto neighborhoods, and built the high-rise housing projects. Urban renewal dislocated thousands of poor families, and ultimately it reduced the sup-ply of low-rent housing. Poverty in the central cities was not abated by Johnson's programs. In fact, middle-class flight to the suburbs continued, the cities deterio-rated at a quickening rate, and the underclass that was left behind grew larger, more violent, and even more alienated from American society.

Johnson and his supporters, both in and out of government, believed that the nation's social problems could be solved through a massive infusion of legisla-tion and money. Since 1945 Americans had come to believe that they had the power to solve these problems, but Congress stalemated under Truman, the nation lacked the will under Eisenhower, and Kennedy barely got started. It was up to Johnson, the president with the mandate and the money, to attack the problems as Roosevelt had done, and to solve those problems through legislation. The ideas, the money, the will, and even the support in Congress were all there for Johnson to put into place the greatest legislative achievement in American history. But the Great Society foundered, mostly for lack of funds, money sent to carry on the crusade in the Far East. It is no wonder that by 1968 the Great Society was in shambles, the war was lost, and America was disenchanted with liberalism and its hollow hopes and promises.

THE SECOND RECONSTRUCTION—CONTINUED

The March on Washington in August 1963 signaled the end of legal segregation in America. The march had begun as a lobbying campaign to push the Kennedy administration's civil rights bill through Congress. It instead turned into a momentous event, the high point of the civil rights movement. The bill itself, however, languished in Congress. President Johnson threw his full weight behind the bill, and with the united forces of liberal lawmakers, civil rights leaders, orga-nized labor, and various religious groups, an even stronger bill was finally passed—but only after the Senate shut down a filibuster of southern senators that lasted fifty-seven days. The new law, the Civil Rights Act of 1964, brought an end to legal segregation and provided specific mechanisms to enforce the new law.

The March on Washington and the Civil Rights Act did not bring an end to the civil rights movement. Those events were, however, a watershed that marked the coming of major changes and new objectives in the movement. It would now be directed toward removing prejudices and inequalities, with its focus directed toward legislative and political activity. And there were other changes in the movement. With the major objective of ending legal segregation in the South generally attained, the movement began to splinter, mostly along lines of age, but also by methods and objectives. Young black leaders, particularly in the North, were beginning to move away from King's nonviolent protest philosophy. They were simply not attuned to the southern-black-religious foundations of the movement; they began to look toward their own ideologies of black racial pride and black-only leadership, and away from an integrated movement. By 1964 the force of the movement began to shift north, to the urban ghettos, and simple race pride would soon be replaced by the more radical concept of black power. By the end of the decade the civil rights movement would change its

Dr. Martin Luther King Jr. waves to the crowd from the steps of the Lincoln Memorial on August 28, 1963, during the March on Washington. His "I Have a Dream" speech would be the highlight of the event. *Source*: Agence France Press/Hulton Archive/Getty Images

character beyond recognition. What had been a southern, religious, nonviolent, integrated movement would become primarily a northern, urban, mostly violent, anti-white separatist movement. By then a debilitating backlash had set in.

FREEDOM SUMMER

Many of the transformations in the movement can be traced to the Freedom Summer of 1964, a voting rights drive in Mississippi orchestrated by the Council of Federated Organizations (COFO), generally the combined forces of SNCC and CORE. The Freedom Summer had its origins in a mock election organized by COFO and held in Mississippi in the fall of 1963. The intent was to draw African Americans to the polling places to cast votes in protest of the mass disfranchisement of the black population in the state. It was also intended to show the nation that blacks wanted to vote, and that they indeed would vote. The strategy worked better than anyone imagined; seventy thousand black Mississippians showed up to vote in the mock election, and national media attention was diverted for a while to the abomination of southern racism and a democratic system that refused to give American citizens the basic right of the ballot.

One reason for the success of the mock election was the presence of about one hundred white students from Yale and Stanford who took two weeks off from school to work in Mississippi as volunteers for COFO. These students were idealistic, hard-working, and strong leaders; but most importantly, they brought increased press coverage and considerable FBI protection for all the workers on the project, blacks and whites alike. They also attracted essential financial and moral support from white liberals in the North. The members of the COFO leadership, particularly Robert Moses and Fannie Lou Hamer, were so impressed by the work of these white students that they struck on the idea of sending out a general invitation to northern college students to come to Mississippi during the next summer, the summer of 1964, to help conduct a voting rights drive. They dubbed the event the "Freedom Summer." The COFO leadership hoped the white students would bring additional press coverage to the movement.

The plan, however, divided the movement in Mississippi. A vocal minority inside COFO argued against the need for whites in a black movement. Moses, Hamer, and others, however, insisted that the movement must remain biracial. They prevailed, and in February 1964 COFO sent out invitations to northern white college students to join in the Freedom Summer.

The students were trained and prepared for their work in Mississippi by COFO at Miami University in Oxford, Ohio. During the orientation, word came that three civil rights workers had disappeared near Meridian, Mississippi. President Johnson responded by sending FBI agents on an exhaustive search for the three workers. Their bodies were found, and twenty-one Ku Klux Klan members from the vicinity of Philadelphia, Mississippi, were arrested for the crime.

Despite the incident and the accompanying show of force, Johnson (and FBI director J. Edgar Hoover) failed to aid the movement much further. Terrorists in Mississippi killed three more civil rights workers, shot another thirty, and burned thirty-five churches before the summer ended. Not surprisingly, civil rights workers, both black and white, began to wonder about the sincerity of the federal government in aiding the movement or even protecting the basic rights of the volunteers. Many of the white workers returned to the North disenchanted with the supposedly liberal White House and skeptical about the basic precepts of American justice.

Other problems developed. By the end of the summer tensions had grown between white and black civil rights workers. The African American workers began to resent the white students who would return to their safe suburbs and ivy-covered dormitories in the North, while they remained on in Mississippi to fight the real battles of southern racism. As the white students left Mississippi in the fall of 1964, the civil rights movement had begun to take on a wholly black appearance.

MISSISSIPPI FREEDOM DEMOCRATIC PARTY

In that same summer of 1964 the Democratic Party was preparing to nominate Lyndon Johnson to a second term. The leaders at SNCC saw this coming event as an opportunity to turn its success and publicity in Mississippi into a potent political force. In response to the Mississippi Democratic Party's exclusion of African Americans from the process of selecting delegates to the national convention, SNCC leaders formed the Mississippi Freedom Democratic Party (MFDP) and chose their own delegates to the convention. They pledged their support to Johnson and planned to attend the convention in Atlantic City.

Heading the MFDP was Fannie Lou Hamer, a staff member at SNCC and one of the leading organizers of the Freedom Summer. In an impassioned speech before the Democratic Party's credentials committee, Hamer told of her poverty-stricken existence on a cotton plantation near Winona, Mississippi, and how she tried desperately to register and vote. She explained that she was involuntarily sterilized; whipped, as she said, until her skin turned blue; and finally forced to move from the area. It was a passionate plea that was picked up by the press, and for a moment the plight of Fannie Lou Hamer caught the imagination of the American people—and threatened to turn the convention into a moral crusade for voter rights in the South.

Johnson, however, was determined not to allow that to happen. He did not want to alienate the white South, even though much of the South was about to desert him because of his support of the Civil Rights Act. But more importantly, he feared that by recognizing the MFDP he would anger the southern congressional delegation; without their support in Congress his Great Society reforms would certainly fail. Throughout the convention, however, Hamer and the other MFDP delegates continued to attract press coverage (during an otherwise uneventful convention), and that embarrassed Johnson.

The president, and candidate, forced a compromise. The MFDP would be awarded two "at-large" delegates while the remainder of the MFDP delegates would be designated "honored guests" with no voting privileges. The MFDP rejected the offer, insisting that it was no compromise. It effectively removed the MFDP from the process while allowing the entire Mississippi delegation to cast their votes. What was most disturbing to the rapidly growing radical faction within SNCC was that white liberals like Humphrey, Walter Mondale, Wayne Morse, and labor leader Walter Reuther backed the deal. Even King and Bayard Rustin, another prominent civil rights leader, agreed to go along.

The incident in Atlantic City was perhaps the most fractious event in the civil rights movement. Designed to defuse the issue, it satisfied no one. It drove a wedge between the moderate and radical factions within the movement, and then further between the general movement and the Johnson administration. It also damaged the relationship between Johnson and the South. For a growing number of young blacks, the liberal hopes represented by King and the white liberal establishment were quickly being replaced by a radical dogma that was feeding on disillusionment.

SELMA AND VOTING RIGHTS

The radical elements inside the civil rights movement continued to gain ground through 1964, but King, and the moderates who followed his lead, still defined the movement and its direction. In 1965 he took his newly acquired Nobel Peace Prize to Selma, Alabama, intent on showing the nation that Alabama continued to deny African Americans the right to vote. Only 335 out of nearly 15,000 eligible black voters in Dallas County (of which Selma was the county seat) were registered to vote. For King and his followers, Selma would be to voting rights what Birmingham had been to segregation just two years before.

But again the young radicals saw it all differently. A group of SNCC volunteers, led by Stokely Carmichael, had been engaged in a voter registration drive in Dallas and Lowndes counties for nearly two years, and they resented King's trespass on their project. They knew that King would grab all the glory (along with the fundraising potential) from a well-publicized, even spectacular, march on Selma.

King called the forces to battle in January 2 when he announced, "We are not asking, we are demanding the ballot." Two days later, in his State of the Union address, President Johnson promised to "eliminate every remaining obstacle to the right and opportunity to vote." On the opposite side of the battle line was Dallas County Sheriff James G. Clark. Clark, much like Birmingham's Bull Conner, had positioned himself before American television to do battle against forces that were far superior.

Through most of January, King led dozens of peaceful marches to the Dallas County courthouse, where blacks tried, mostly in vain, to register to vote. On February 1, Clark began arresting marchers—770 including King the first day, then 550 the next, and 330 the day after that. King was released on February 5 and immediately rushed to Washington to appeal to the president for voting rights legislation. Johnson agreed.

On February 18, one protester was shot and killed and another beaten to death in a nearby town. King planned a march from Selma to Montgomery for Sunday, March 7, to commemorate the murders, but at the last minute he called off the march, claiming a need to be with his congregation in Atlanta. Nevertheless, a large number of marchers began assembling at a small church near Selma, intent on making the march to Montgomery. Led by Hosea Williams of King's Southern Christian Leadership Conference (SCLC) and John Lewis of SNCC, over five hundred demonstrators marched out of town toward the Edmund Pettus Bridge on the road to Montgomery. Without warning, some five hundred Alabama state police fell on the marchers and crushed them with clubs, chains, C-4 tear gas, whips, and electric cattle prods. In fear for their lives, the marchers turned and ran back toward the city, only to be met by James Clark's advancing forces. "Bloody Sunday," one of the darkest days in the civil rights movement, was a brutal display of raw aggression that was seen by forty-eight million television viewers across the nation. King had wanted a Birmingham-like confrontation that would force Johnson's hand on voting rights legislation. Although he was absent, he got what he wanted at the Pettus Bridge outside of Selma.

On March 9, King intended to lead a march to Montgomery. But when it became clear that the result would be additional violence, Johnson intervened and asked King to call off the march. Despite his own words, "I would rather die on the highways of Alabama than make a butchery of my conscience," King relented. He led fifteen hundred marchers to the Pettus Bridge, where Alabama state police had again drawn up to meet the march. He asked the marchers to kneel, pray, and return to Selma. For the welfare of the marchers it was the right decision. But it further alienated the radical elements in SNCC, who continued to question King's leadership.

On March 15, President Johnson, in a televised address to a joint session of Congress, committed his administration to voting rights in the South. It was his finest hour. "Should we defeat every enemy," he told America, "and should we double our wealth and conquer the stars, and still be unequal to this issue, then we will have failed as a people and a nation." He added, "Every American citizen must have an equal right to vote. There is no reason which can excuse the denial of that right. . . . This cause must be our cause too. It is not just Negroes, but all of us, who must overcome the crippling legacy of bigotry in injustice. And," he concluded, "we *shall* overcome."

Johnson's bill, the Voting Rights Act of 1965, called for an end to literacy tests and authorized the attorney general to send federal registrars to states where patterns of voter exclusion were apparent. The president was on solid political footing. Gallup reported that a convincing 76 percent of the nation favored the bill. It moved through Congress with little opposition, even from southern congressmen whose overt racism was becoming less and less tenable.

On March 21, the march from Selma to Montgomery finally proceeded, this time under the protection of three thousand federalized Alabama guardsmen. Five days later, thirty thousand marchers entered the Alabama state capital. The prominent and well known joined the march on its last day. Rabbis, priests, and ministers, entertainers, political figures, and celebrities all joined, assuring massive media coverage. King spoke eloquently of the Promised Land and of going forward together. But the movement was badly divided, and the Promised Land was still far away.

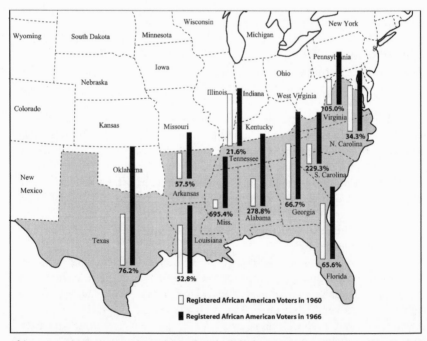

African American voter registration in the South before and after passage of the Voting Rights Act of 1965

LYNDON JOHNSON'S WAR

The war that Kennedy passed to Johnson in November 1963 was far expanded beyond the war that Kennedy had inherited from Eisenhower. Almost immediately after Johnson came to office it was clear that, if the United States did not intervene quickly, South Vietnam would fall to the Communists. And Johnson, wedded to the various foreign policy beliefs of the time, would not let that happen. "I'm not going to lose Vietnam," Johnson said within hours of moving into the Oval Office. "I am not going to be the president who saw Southeast Asia go the way China went." Johnson knew that if he could not stop the Communist threat in Vietnam, he would suffer the consequences—and those consequences would be political.

By the early months of 1964 it was clear that the November coup which had removed Diem (and then the government that had replaced him, led by Duong Van Minh) had not improved the situation in Vietnam. In January Minh was overthrown by Nguyen Khanh, who was even less effective than Minh. Secretary of Defense Robert McNamara, in a memo to the president in March 1964, wrote that South Vietnam was deteriorating rapidly, that "the situation has unquestionably been growing worse. . . . Large groups of the [U.S.] population are now showing signs of apathy and indifference, and there are some signs of frustration within the U.S. [military] contingent." He added that among ARVN (Army of the Republic of Vietnam) "desertion rates . . . are high and increasing. Draft dodging is high while the Viet Cong are recruiting energetically and effectively. . . . In the last 90 days the weakening of the government's position has been particularly noticeable. . . ." McNamara seemed to realize how untenable the situation was in Vietnam, that it was collapsing faster than the United States could shore it up. For Johnson, the only answer to the problem was to maintain the commitment, to stay the course. He responded by increasing the number of advisors from about sixteen thousand to twenty-three thousand over the next nine months, and by adding $50 million in economic aid. He also appointed General William Westmoreland to the American command in Saigon, and he approved destroyer patrols along the North Vietnam coast.

Through the summer of 1964 Johnson hoped to push a resolution through Congress that would give him greater leeway in dealing with the escalating events in Vietnam. A series of incidents in the first week of August gave the president just the excuse he needed to push his resolution and then escalate the conflict. On August 2 the destroyer USS *Maddox* was attacked by North Vietnamese torpedo boats in the Tonkin Gulf off North Vietnam's coast. Two days later, a second attack on a U.S. destroyer was reported but never corroborated (and by most accounts never occurred). Before receiving definitive confirmation of the second attack, Johnson informed the nation of the events and ordered air strikes against the North Vietnamese torpedo boat bases along the coast. He then pushed Congress to pass the Tonkin Gulf Resolution to deal with the growing situation in Vietnam, to "take all necessary measures to repel any armed attacks against the forces of the United States." The next day, August 5, the Senate voted 98 to 2 in favor of the resolution. The House vote the same day was unanimous. It was an extremely popular stance. Most Americans praised Johnson for taking decisive action in response to Communist aggression—and without dragging the nation into a war. His approval rating nearly doubled overnight. It was just three months before the election.

The Tonkin Gulf Resolution gave Johnson the authority to conduct the war in Vietnam for the next four years, as he pleased and without a declaration of war or any restraint or parameters from Congress. It would be the Johnson White House that ran the war, and it would be Johnson who would ultimately be blamed for the escalations, and finally the failure, of the entire adventure in Vietnam.

In Saigon the conditions had gone from bad to worse. General Khanh, using the Tonkin Gulf Incident, declared a military emergency on August 6 that made him dictator of South Vietnam. He was almost immediately ousted from power by street mobs. What followed was political chaos. Johnson began to fear that the extremely weak Saigon government might fall, or worse, that leaders in the government (or perhaps the military) might negotiate a separate agreement with the Communist leadership in Hanoi.

It was in this period, the mid-1960s, that the Chinese-Soviet relationship began to sour. These two Communist giants had developed a somewhat tenuous relationship through the 1950s (Communist China had been established in October 1949). The leaders of both nations spoke glowingly of the unification of the Communist world, but in fact the two cultures were so different, and their interpretations of international communism so conflicting, that by the mid-1960s they had come to blows along their common border regions in eastern Siberia. In addition, the Chinese leader, Mao Zedong, had concluded that his brand of communism should be exported from China to the rest of the world, a proposition that offended Moscow. Lyndon Johnson moved to exploit these differences, although not as aggressively as he might have. He seemed to understand that by moving closer to Moscow he might isolate China, then the primary supplier of materiel to the Communist troops in Vietnam. The Soviets hoped that they might ease the threat from China by moving closer to the United States. With nearly the same goal in mind (the isolation of China) but for different reasons, Washington and Moscow eased relations. They signed a nuclear nonproliferation treaty designed to stop the spread of nuclear weapons, and trade between the two nations improved. But nothing more came from the situation. With a common enemy, it might have been the right moment to end the Cold War. But the deep-rooted distrusts outweighed the common concern. Old cold warriors like Secretary of State Dean Rusk insisted that the Soviets would not and could not mellow. In addition, Johnson's military advisors were too wrapped up in events in

Vietnam to consider what could come from a Sino-Soviet split. It may have been a missed opportunity.

On February 6, 1965, the situation in Vietnam took a turn. Viet Cong soldiers attacked the U.S. base at Pleiku in the Central Highlands, killing eight soldiers and destroying five aircraft. Johnson immediately ordered reprisal strikes against the North, intent on disrupting the flow of supplies to the Viet Cong in the South. Johnson's primary objective here was not so much to stop North Vietnamese infiltration into the South (which was insignificant in February 1965) but to prop up the sagging Saigon government, which was quickly losing a civil war against the Viet Cong.

It was just a short step from reprisal bombing to sustained bombing. Within three weeks of the Pleiku attack, Johnson approved Operation Rolling Thunder, a massive sustained bombing operation against the North. In 1965 the U.S. Air Force flew twenty-five thousand sorties against the North. In March, ostensibly to protect the planes and their support personnel, Johnson sent in the first combat troops. Westmoreland had requested the support, and on March 8 two Marine landing teams went ashore to protect the U.S. airbase at Da Nang. It was the beginning of the Americanization of the war. During the summer, over one hundred thousand more American soldiers poured into Vietnam.

The bombing continued for seven years. In 1965 there were seventy-nine thousand bombing attacks of the North. By the end of 1966 the United States was sending in twelve thousand sorties a month. The massive bombing, however (more than all the bombs dropped by the United States during all of World War II), had little effect. Such bombing campaigns are most successful against fixed targets, such as industry. North Vietnam had little war industry (or industry of any sort) to destroy. To bomb North Vietnam back to the Stone Age, as Air Force General Curtis LeMay had advised, was to send the North Vietnamese not so very far back in time.

The sustained bombing had several effects, mostly negative. It caused Hanoi to look for more aid, particularly from China. Historically, China had been the enemy of Vietnam, and Ho Chi Minh distrusted Beijing. But China was suspicious of U.S. military involvement on their southern border and was eager to aid Hanoi in their fight against Beijing's old enemy. The bombings also served to send North Vietnamese troops into the South to counter the growing U.S. contingent there. Hanoi had kept its own regular forces out of the war thus far in an attempt to deter the United States from escalating its influence in the South. But now those restraints were removed. The result was, of course, an increased threat from the North and a significant escalation of the war that the Johnson administration felt a need to match. By 1966 there were eleven North Vietnamese regiments in the South to fight 200,000 Americans and 550,000 ARVN troops.

In Saigon the political situation worsened. In February, General Nguyen Van Thieu and flamboyant Air Vice Marshal Nguyen Cao Ky had overthrown the civilian government. ARVN desertions had increased to nearly 50 percent,

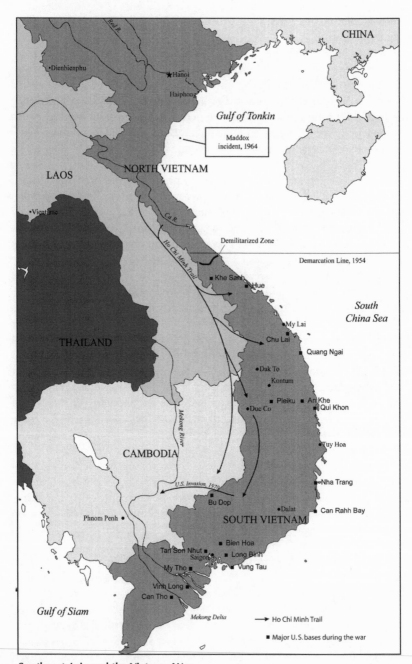

Southeast Asia and the Vietnam War

and it seemed certain that the South Vietnamese forces would soon topple easily under a full-scale offensive from the North.

In April 1965 Johnson relented to Westmoreland's demands and allowed U.S. soldiers to take an offensive role in the fighting. Later that month he agreed to send in more troops, bringing U.S. troop levels to 125,000. He also agreed that he would allow an additional escalation of 50,000 more soldiers later in the year, and he promised, privately, that he would send more troops as needed.

CONCLUSION

Lyndon Johnson was one of America's great tragic figures. It is often said that he tried to do too much. He wanted to solve the world's problems by fighting a war against communism in Vietnam, and he wanted to solve the nation's problems through his Great Society. Clearly the nation had neither the will nor the resources to win both wars at the same time. What emerged from all this was a Greek tragedy–type character flaw in Johnson. He would compromise, settle for half a loaf, as he often said. When General Westmoreland wanted 179,000 soldiers, Johnson gave 50,000. If Congress would not appropriate the funds necessary for a project, he would compromise and accept what he could get. Never mind that the underfunded project might not be able to reach its goals. Even as he dealt with civil rights, he felt that it was necessary to slow the advance of the movement, to keep it in line to avoid a backlash from conservatives. Johnson's compromises were an almost pathetic attempt to satisfy all sides, to keep everyone happy. In most cases, however, he simply alienated both sides. His compromising caused the war in Vietnam to escalate slowly, a pace easily met by the enemy. It left the Great Society programs weak and underfunded. And his manipulation of the civil rights movement undercut King and the moderates, and they began to appear to the movement's young radicals as the lackeys of the administration.

Johnson wanted to be like his hero Franklin Roosevelt, a man who dealt decisively with the nation's economic and social problems, and who won a war against a palpable evil. But Johnson was not Roosevelt, the Viet Cong were not the Nazis, and the nation's problems in the 1960s did not measure up to the Great Depression.

Johnson did not leave office disgraced, or even a failure. But he did fail to accomplish his goals. His presidency was a tragedy.

Reading: Lyndon Johnson, "Promises to Keep," Johns Hopkins University Speech, April 7, 1965

One month after sending the first U.S. combat troops into Vietnam, President Johnson, in a landmark speech at Johns Hopkins University, explained to the nation why he felt it was necessary for the nation to go to war. "Why," he asked, "must we take this painful road?" Johnson's speech is, unfortunately, remembered only for the president's reasons for escalation and not for his vision of a peaceful world order, or even for his simple concept that war is a manifestation of man's failures.

Tonight Americans and Asians are dying for a world where each people may choose its own path to change.

This is the principle for which our ancestors fought in the valleys of Pennsylvania. It is the principle for which our sons fight tonight in the jungles of Vietnam.

Vietnam is far away from this quiet campus. We have no territory there. Nor do we seek any. The war is dirty and brutal and difficult. And some too-young men, born into an America that is bursting with opportunity and promise, have ended their lives on Vietnam's steaming soil.

Why must we take this painful road?

Why must this nation hazard its ease, its interests, and its power for the sake of a people so far away? We fight because we must fight if we are to live in a world where every country can shape its own destiny, and only in such a world will our own freedom be fully secure.

This kind of world will never be built by bombs or bullets. Yet the infirmities of man are such that force must often precede reason, and the waste of the war [must often precede] the works of peace.

We wish that this were not so. But we must deal with the world as it is, if it is ever to be as we wish.

The world as it is in Asia is not a serene or peaceful place.

The first reality is that North Vietnam has attacked the independent nation of South Vietnam. Its object is total conquest.

Of course, some of the people of South Vietnam are participating in attacks on their own government. But trained men and supplies, orders and arms, flow in a constant stream from North to South.

This support is the heartbeat of the war. . . .

The confused nature of this conflict cannot mask the fact that it is the new face of an old enemy.

Over this war—and all of Asia—is another reality: the deepening shadow of Communist China. The rulers in Hanoi are urged on by Peking. This is a regime which has destroyed freedom in Tibet, which has attacked India and has been condemned by the United Nations for aggression in Korea. It is a nation which is helping the forces of violence in almost every continent. The contest in Vietnam is part of a wider pattern of aggressive purpose.

Why are these realities our concern? Why are we in Vietnam?

We are there because we have a promise to keep. Since 1954 every American president has offered support to the people of Vietnam. We have helped to build, and we have helped to defend. Thus, over many years, we have made a national pledge to help South Vietnam defend its independence.

And I intend to keep that promise.

To dishonor that pledge, to abandon this small and brave nation to its enemies, and to the terror that must follow, would be an unforgivable wrong.

We are also there to strengthen world order. Around the globe from Berlin to Thailand are people whose well-being rests in part on the belief that they can count on us if they are attacked. To leave Vietnam to its fate would shake the confidence of all these people in the value of an American commitment and in the value of America's word. The result would be increased unrest and instability, and even wider war.

We are also there because there are great stakes in the balance. Let no one think for a moment that retreat from Vietnam would bring an end to the conflict. The battle would be renewed in one country and then another. The central lesson of our time is that the appetite of aggression is never satisfied. To withdraw from one battlefield means only to prepare for the next. We must say in Southeast Asia—as we did in Europe—in the words of the Bible: "Hitherto shalt thou come, but no farther."

There are those who say that all our efforts there will be futile—that China's power is such that it is bound to dominate all of Southeast Asia. But there is no end to that argument until all of the nations of Asia are swallowed up. . . .

Our objective is the independence of South Vietnam and its freedom from attack. We want nothing for ourselves—only that the people of South Vietnam be allowed to guide their own country in their own way.

We will do everything necessary to reach that objective and we will do only what is absolutely necessary.

In recent months attacks on South Vietnam were stepped up. Thus, it became necessary for us to increase our response and to make attacks by air. This is not a change of purpose. It is a change in what we believe that purpose requires.

We do this in order to slow down the aggression.

We do this to increase the confidence of the brave people of South Vietnam who have bravely borne this brutal battle for so many years with so many casualties.

We do this to convince the leaders of North Vietnam—and all who seek to share their conquest—of a simple fact:

We will not be defeated.

We will not grow tired.

We will not withdraw, either openly or under the cloak of a meaningless agreement. . . .

We hope that peace will come swiftly. But that is in the hands of others besides ourselves. And we must be prepared for a long continued conflict. It will require patience as well as bravery—the will to endure as well as the will to resist. . . .

Such peace demands an independent South Vietnam securely guaranteed and able to shape its own relationships to all others, free from outside interference, tied to no alliance, a military base for no other country.

These are the essentials of any final settlement.

We will never be second in the search for such a peaceful settlement in Vietnam. . . .

The United Nations is already actively engaged in development in this area. As far back as 1961 I conferred with our authorities in Vietnam in connection with their work here. And I hope tonight that the secretary-general of the United Nations could use the prestige of his great office, and his deep knowledge of Asia to initiate, as soon as possible, with the countries of that area a plan for cooperation in increased development.

For our part, I will ask the Congress to join in a billion-dollar American investment in this effort as soon as it is underway. And I hope that all other industrialized countries, including the Soviet Union, will join in this effort to replace despair with hope, and terror with progress.

The task is nothing less than to enrich the hopes and the existence of more than 100 million people. And there is much to be done.

The vast Mekong River can provide food and water and power on a scale to dwarf even our own TVA. The wonders of modern medicine can be spread through villages where thousands die every year from a lack of care. Schools can be established to train people in the skills that are needed to manage the process of development.

And these objectives, and more, are within the reach of a cooperative and determined effort. . . .

Well, this can be their world yet. Man now has the knowledge—always before denied—to make this planet serve the real needs of the people who live on it.

I know this will not be easy. I know how difficult it is for reason to guide passion, and love to master hate. The complexities of this world do not bow easily to pure and consistent answers. But the simple truths are there just the same. We must try.

This generation of the world must choose: destroy or build, kill or aid, hate or understand. We can do all these things on a scale never dreamed of before.

Well, we will choose life. In doing so we will prevail over the enemies within man, and over the natural enemies of all mankind.

Source: Public Papers of the Presidents of the United States: Lyndon Johnson, 1965. Washington, DC: U.S. Government Printing Office, 1966.

· 7 ·

The Nation in the 1960s

The 1960s are usually perceived as a tumultuous decade, one of rebellion and change, of brutal war and a response at home that led to an almost naive quest for peace and equality. The decade is distinct in the nation's postwar history because it was a reaction to the conservative decade it followed; and the conservative movement that emerged in its wake is often seen as a reaction to it. If the events of the 1960s had a catalyst, it was most likely the civil rights movement, a fight for equality that many Americans saw as honorable and courageous in the face of brutality and hate. If the decade had a messenger it was television, the new medium that delivered into America's living rooms the horrors of Vietnam and Birmingham, and made it all too clear that something had to be done.

The impact of the 1960s will always be debated. Historians often see the decade as the end of the nation's postwar innocence, the end of the exuberance of the postwar years when Americans thought they could achieve anything, solve all problems, and live in harmony and prosperity. By the end of the decade, the nation was torn apart on many levels and over several issues. The nation's leadership role in the world was being questioned, its political system seemed weak and divided, and its economy was falling behind. It was a watershed decade; the nation had changed considerably when it was over.

YOUTH CULTURE: FROM BIRTH TO FAD

Certainly not all of the nation's youth became rebellious in the 1960s, but many did, and like rebels of other eras, the targets of their rebellion were not always uniform or clear. One common explanation was the need for these young rebels to break out of the patterns established by their parents, to look for goals and answers to life beyond the mere acquisition of wealth and personal status. The objectives of the previous decade, and the previous generation, had produced a society of conformists. The new generation of the 1960s intended to break from

157

that. Others simply rebelled against the war, oppressive government policy, and the status quo. Many of the decade's youth became hippies, social and cultural dropouts who adopted the lifestyle of the Beatniks and Bohemians of previous eras, including self-imposed poverty, a rejection of the monogamous family, and, of course, drugs.

By the mid-1960s, the nation seemed inundated with hippies, but in fact there were probably only a few thousand true hippies on each coast. The rest were look-alikes, wannabes, and weekend hippies, kids attracted to the style, the "look," and perhaps even some aspects of the hippie attitude toward life. By the later years of the decade, the hippie movement (if it can be called that) was mostly dead, killed by the gentrification of the style and a national press that sensational-ized hippie-ness into news stories about weird, drug-addled kids. By the late 1960s there were tour buses driving through the Haight-Ashbury district of San Francisco to see the hippies; American men of all ages were letting their hair grow and wearing psychedelic double-knit shirts and bell-bottom pants; and the hippie mantra of free love had turned into suburban wife-swapping. In addition, drug use became drug abuse for some, and the OD, or overdose, was a common problem for those who overindulged. By the end of the decade, the hippie mantra of "sex, drugs, and rock 'n' roll" had lost its luster.

The drug of choice for the hippies (and for those who wanted to be hippies) was marijuana, and its use was the ultimate rebellion against authority. Not only was it illegal, the laws against its use were nearly unenforceable, giving the added thrill of defying authority and indulging in forbidden fruit without much worry of prosecution. Aficionados spoke of its ethereal value, its ability to focus the senses and awaken the mind. In fact, it was a vehicle for getting high, and it was cheap, often free. By the late 1960s smoking pot was as commonplace in many circles as social drinking had been a decade earlier.

In other circles the primary drug was LSD (lysergic acid diethylamide), known universally as acid, a hallucinogen that took users well beyond a simple high to what was commonly called a psychedelic experience. Users insisted that LSD expanded the mind and piqued the senses. It was also billed as having the ability to bring love and understanding to its users and, ultimately, to all of man-kind. For many it was the road to personal peace and even spiritual awakening. The LSD guru was Timothy Leary, a one-time scientific researcher at Harvard who preached the use of LSD as a consciousness-expanding experience that could reach the soul. For some users, LSD did as advertised. For others it caused "bad trips," psychological problems, and flashbacks.

The drugs, the rebellion, the war—all seemed to converge in the 1960s. And pushing it all along was the music. More a function of the decade's rebellious attitude than even drug use, music in the 1960s created a genre, a style, and a sound—in fact, several sounds. By the beginning of the decade, the rock 'n' roll of Elvis and Buddy Holly had given way to the saccharine American pop music of the type it had supplanted about a decade earlier. Undoubtedly there were those who enjoyed the young Italian crooners, the twisters, and the girl groups, but the music had lost the raw energy of the hot rock 'n' rollers of the late 1950s. Today, it is easy to look back and see the nation's youth holding its breath, waiting for something new, something to push things forward again.

That happened in February 1964 when the Beatles landed at JFK Airport in New York. John, Paul, George, and Ringo, the "four lads from Liverpool," or the "Fab Four," as the American press insisted on calling them, brought from England what appeared to be a new sound. It was, in fact, basic rock 'n' roll, grounded solidly (as was all rock 'n' roll) in American blues, but with something undeniably fresh and new. The nation's cultural history turned. Not everyone saw it, of course. Jack Gould of the *New York Times* (who in 1956 wrote that Elvis had "no discernable singing ability") called the Beatles "a fine mass placebo." But the Beatles were irresistible to America's youth. Their appearance on the *Ed Sullivan Show* was a hallmark event that drew millions of viewers, and it became the real beginnings of the relationship between pop music and visual image. Certainly, Elvis opened that door with his TV appearances in the mid-1950s, but after the Beatles appeared on *Ed Sullivan* in 1964, any rock band wanting to succeed had to be seen on television and display some mass visual appeal.

The Beatles occupied the beachhead for the "British invasion" of Beatles-style bands from England. Some that followed, like the Rolling Stones and the Animals, were good, even innovative and cutting edge. Others, like Herman's Hermits and Freddie and the Dreamers seemed to do little more than play the role of the next-in-line longhaired British pop band. The good groups endured. The others did not.

The immense popularity of the Beatles and their music showed that there was a major demand among the nation's youth for music, all easily classified as rock 'n' roll, or just rock. And the varieties were wide ranging. Acid rock emerged in San Francisco, supposedly inspired by LSD and the psychedelic colors and images the drug produced in the mind. The great acid rock bands included the Grateful Dead, Jefferson Airplane, and Big Brother and the Holding Company fronted by the spectacular Janis Joplin. These groups and dozens of others often played at the Fillmore Auditorium in San Francisco to crowds of young people among pulsating strobe lights, abundant LSD, and random psychedelic images moving on the walls to the music's beat.

At the other end of the spectrum was folk rock. Folk music had always carried a message of liberal social conscience, and that was enough to force it underground during the McCarthy era. By the early 1960s the Kingston Trio led a revival, but they were quickly perceived by the nation's youth as much too clean-cut, and a reaction to their squeaky-clean image took folk in a new direction. Leading the way were Peter, Paul, and Mary, who sang about freedom and justice. They were followed quickly by Joan Baez with her protest lyrics and near-ethereal soprano voice. By 1963 Baez had begun introducing Bob Dylan to audiences. A singer-songwriter with a harsh nasal sound, Dylan seemed to awaken the world with his "The Times They Are a-Changin'," a clarion call for the remainder of the decade. In 1965 at the Newport Folk Festival, Dylan appeared before the folk music lovers wearing leather and playing an electric guitar. He was booed and finally ostracized by the folkies, but the much-celebrated event is usually identified as the origin of folk rock, the bridge between the two genres. Folk rock hit it big with such artists as James Taylor, John Denver, Simon and Garfunkel, and Carole King.

The diversification of musical styles expanded. The Beach Boys led a wave of what was called California surfer music, which was generally marked by a driving beat and a rapid-fire guitar technique first introduced by Dick Dale. The group's three-part harmonies and catchy lyrics turned them into chart-toppers, but by mid-decade, clean-cut surfer boys were pretty boring when compared to the emerging hard-pounding rockers. The surfer style finally morphed into a series of bad movies that always seemed to star Annette Funicello and Frankie Avalon.

Black America, on the cutting edge of American music since at least the turn of the twentieth century, produced two different types of music in the decade. In Detroit, Berry Gordy created the Motown label, one of the nation's great music business empires. Motown became associated with a distinct sound and style, punctuated mostly by bland lyrics and live performances that were famous for their synchronized dance moves. Led by the Supremes, the Temptations, and "Little" Stevie Wonder, the Motown sound was precise, smooth, and rhythmic. And then there was soul, perhaps the most aptly named of all musical styles. From the deepest depths of the Deep South, soul music had its origins in a black Baptist gospel sound, but with lyrics that often captured the essence of blackness. Aretha's "Respect" and James Brown's "Papa's Got a Brand New Bag" became the soul anthems of the age.

As the decade progressed, large groupings of bands played massive venues throughout the nation, drawing crowds that got progressively larger. By 1967 the events became huge festivals and were often held outside. In 1969 Woodstock took the rock festival to its logical conclusion. Some four hundred thousand young people gathered at a farm in upstate New York for three days of the greatest rock music ever brought together in one place. It was the defining moment for what became known as the Woodstock Generation. Despite all the fears, the rain, and the mud, the event transpired with few problems. In many ways, however, it seemed to be the last gasp of an exciting decade. After 1970, all that had been innovative and electrifying about the 1960s seemed to flit away, leaving behind a shadow of itself, a cheap copy of what had been. By then, several of rock's biggest stars had died of drug overdoses; Charles Manson's "family" of hippies had committed ritual murders in the name of peace and love; and at the Altamont Raceway outside of San Francisco the idea of the rock festival died when one person was knifed to death by a member of the Hell's Angels and three others died of drug overdoses.

Youth culture in the 1960s is often described as self-indulgent, self-absorbed, even narcissistic. But the decade's youth were doing what kids do. All the celebrated (and reviled) social and cultural weirdness of the decade was little more than the baby boomers growing up, looking for something new, finding themselves, and rebelling against those who had gone before them. They may have done it with more exuberance and less personal hygiene than earlier generations, but what transpired was not so very different.

THE AMERICANIZATION OF THE WAR

Quickly, the war came home. The economy was the first casualty. Inflation began to climb in the mid-1960s, and would remain a problem for over a decade. As consumer prices rose, and it became apparent that the war was the cause, the public began to relate the once-obscure war in far-off Asia to their own prosperity. It was just one of several reasons for many Americans to oppose the war.

The war also came home in the form of an antiwar movement that had its earliest stirrings in the mid-1960s and continued to grow almost in direct proportion to the escalation of the conflict. The antiwar movement was only part of a larger protest movement that engulfed the decade, but the war gave the larger movement a cause that brought growth, direction, and finally influence to what quickly became a mass movement of American counterculture.

The U.S. military entered the war with no real planned strategy for its prosecution. Consequently, the only viable solution to military setbacks was to turn up the heat, increase the American presence, and try to wear down the enemy. When Rolling Thunder was an obvious failure through 1965, Johnson and his advisors determined that the only solution was to escalate the bombing. When it became apparent that the Viet Cong and North Vietnamese ground forces were formidable, the only answer was to initiate a war of attrition, with the sole objective of killing as many enemy soldiers as possible—what Westmoreland called the "search and destroy" strategy of counterinsurgency. The objective was nothing more than to force the enemy to the bargaining table. When it became clear that the enemy would not negotiate, the only alternative was again to up the ante. Add to that the Johnson administration's perceived need to continue the war to avoid losing America's place as the leader of the "free world"—the defender of those opposing communism—and by 1967 the United States had placed itself in a very difficult situation. As Johnson's undersecretary of state George Ball said in his famous quote, "Once on the tiger's back we cannot be sure of picking the place to dismount."

The primary strategic difficulty for American planners in Vietnam was their inability to isolate the battlefield. Vietnam's western and northern borders with Cambodia and Laos were not secure, allowing for infiltration of men and materiel all along the Vietnamese border area. The result was no standard front, and the enemy could be supplied easily. The Viet Cong and North Vietnamese were also able to fight on their own terms. Because of the nature of the battlefield, they could engage American troops and then disengage almost at will. This allowed the enemy to choose their place for battle and then retreat into the countryside after inflicting sufficient damage on American soldiers—or if they believed they were about to be overpowered. They learned to avoid U.S. air power by hitting U.S. troops and then melting into the countryside before air support could arrive. Hiding places in local villages allowed the enemy to blend into the local landscape, hit, and then be gone. It was definitely a different type of war, fought to the enemy's advantage.

America's conduct of the war provided Hanoi with a propaganda weapon that was devastating to U.S. prestige abroad. To most of the world, Rolling Thunder was a brutal act of aggression, an unconscionable unleashing of American might against a small Third World nation fighting for its independence—and it ultimately placed much of the world in opposition to America's prosecution of the war. U Thant, the secretary-general of the United Nations, insisted that the United States work to find a peaceful solution to the war. American allies, particularly Britain, tried to bring Washington and Hanoi to some sort of negotiated settlement. Even Poland tried to intercede in 1966, and Soviet premier Alexi Kosygin also agreed to be a part of a settlement. But none of these proposals succeeded. To much of the world it was the United States that was intransigent, not Hanoi. By 1967 Secretary of Defense McNamara had concluded that U.S. status in the world had dropped considerably: "The picture of the world's greatest super power," he said, "killing or injuring a thousand noncombatants a week, while trying to pound a tiny backward nation into submission on an issue whose merits are hotly disputed, is not a pretty one." Much of the world, it seemed, agreed.

For the first time in U.S. history the American people could watch their nation at war. Into their living rooms, through their television sets, came much of the reality of Vietnam; and those who watched the news were made more aware of the war. At the same time, the arguments of antiwar activism were reported as a sort of counterpoint to the nation's involvement in the war. As a result the American people were generally well informed on the war after about 1965, at least as well informed as Walter Cronkite, David Brinkley, and Harry Reasoner could inform them on the network evening news. Add to that the print media coverage of the events, and the American people came to understand their war in Vietnam. And they began to ask questions: "Why are we there?" "What is the war strategy?" "What is the plan for withdrawal?" "When?" "On what conditions?" Often the answers were disconcerting.

By 1967 U.S. forces in Vietnam had increased to nearly four hundred thousand, and Westmoreland had asked for an additional forty-two thousand men by the end of the year. With the increased escalation in troop strength came the inevitable escalation in casualties. By the end of the year more than sixteen thousand soldiers had died in action, up from just four hundred two years before. With the dramatic rise in casualties came an escalation in the antiwar movement.

It seemed that the nation was on a spiral: As more troops were needed, the war escalated, casualties increased, and the antiwar movement intensified.

And the spiral of escalation was nearly impossible to stop. Once American troops were introduced into Vietnam, Johnson found it difficult to deny further requests to send support for those troops already in the field. At the same time, U.S. escalations and troop increases were always matched by the enemy, which in turn led to more American casualties and a need for more troops. Escalations, so it seemed, did little more than kill more American boys. The war developed into an unwinnable stalemate with no real honorable way out. "Unless the will of the enemy is broken or unless there is an unraveling of the VC infrastructure," Westmoreland told Johnson in the spring of 1967, "the war could go on for five [more] years." The frustrations mounted.

Toward the end of 1967, McNamara began a major policy shift in the administration when he sent a memo to the president stating that he believed the war was unwinnable. "Continuing our present course," he wrote, "will not bring us by the end of 1968 enough closer to success, in the eyes of the American pub-

This photo has always been given a great deal of meaning: the president, alone with the decisions of the war (while a bust of John Kennedy looks on from behind). In fact, Johnson is listening to a tape from his son-in-law, Captain Charles Robb, then serving in Vietnam. *Source*: Lyndon B. Johnson Library, photo by Jack Kightlinger

lic, to prevent the continued erosion of popular support for our involvement in Vietnam." He then suggested that the United States should try and keep northern troops out of the South, bring an end to the bombing, and look for a negotiated peace. McNamara's memo was devastating to Johnson, mainly because it raised "fundamental questions," as Johnson wrote in his memoirs, "of policy with reference to the conduct of the war. . . ." It was McNamara, more than anyone else, who had charted the course for U.S intervention in Vietnam. Now, with no warning, he had concluded that the war was unwinnable, too costly, destroying the administration, and dividing the nation. Johnson quietly fired McNamara and named Clark Clifford his new secretary of defense.

In the last months of 1967 there seemed to be a pulling back by the enemy, and that stimulated optimism among the war managers. "I am very encouraged," Westmoreland told the president. "We are making real progress. Everyone is encouraged." At just that moment, on January 31, 1968, the enemy launched the Tet Offensive, a surprise attack by Viet Cong and North Vietnamese troops. They attacked five of the six major cities in the South, thirty-six of the forty-four provincial capitals, and forty-four district capitals. In addition, munitions dumps, airfields, oil storage facilities, and minor U.S. and ARVN strongholds were hit. In the most dramatic of the attacks, nineteen Viet Cong commandos destroyed part of the U.S. embassy in Saigon and managed to hold the compound for nearly six hours before they were finally killed.

Whether or not Tet was a victory for the Viet Cong and North Vietnamese forces is a secondary question. In fact, they failed to hold any cities beyond a few days, except Hue, which they finally abandoned after three weeks of heavy fighting. They lost an estimated fifty-eight thousand men and the attack on the U.S. embassy was not a success. ARVN did not collapse, there was no general uprising, and the United States was not disposed to come to the peace table. The offensive, however, had a profound impact on the war. It began a major backlash in American public opinion against the war that continued until U.S. forces were withdrawn. As Clark Clifford later wrote, "The outcome of the Tet Offensive may remain in dispute, but there can be no question that it was a turning point in the war. Its size and scope made mockery of what the American military had told the public about the war, and devastated Administration credibility." On February 12 Westmoreland asked for more troops, 206,000 above the 1968 ceiling of 525,000. The Defense Department countered that such an increase would mean more U.S. casualties, a need for a tax increase, probably wage and price controls, an increase in the draft, and possibly a need to call up the reserves.

On March 10 a Gallup poll revealed the political effects of Tet. Fully half of the American public polled said they believed the United States should never have gotten into the war. And only 33 percent believed that the United States was making any headway against the enemy, a drop from 50 percent before Tet. Gallup also polled the self-described "hawks" and "doves." In February, the hawks outnumbered the doves 60 to 24 percent. In March, after Tet, they ran

South Vietnamese general Nguyen Ngoc Loan, Chief of the National Police, executes suspected Viet Cong officer Nguyen Van Lem on a Saigon street on February 1, 1968, at the beginning of the Tet Offensive. This photo, published widely in the American press, was instrumental in changing the American public's views on the war. It has become one of the most famous images in American journalism. *Source*: AP Photo/ Eddie Adams

about even. In addition, several polls showed that Johnson was losing popularity in free fall after Tet to a meager 35 percent. The discontent was growing, and an election was approaching.

Johnson's loss of popularity, along with the Democratic Party's disenchantment with the progress of the war, became apparent on March 12 when 42 percent of the Democrats in the New Hampshire Democratic primary spurned Johnson and voted for Minnesota Senator Eugene McCarthy. McCarthy had been leading a young people's movement to bring an end to the war, and his success in New Hampshire was widely perceived as a statement in opposition to the president's Vietnam policies.

McCarthy was not really a presidential contender, and his showing in New Hampshire prompted Robert Kennedy to enter the race for the Democratic nomination against the now-wounded Johnson. His name alone made him a much more formidable candidate than McCarthy, and he immediately sucked the wind from McCarthy's candidacy, along with most of McCarthy's supporters. That

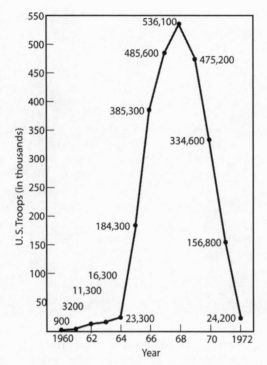

U.S. Troops in Vietnam, 1960–1972. Note the escalation of troops almost immediately after Johnson's presidential victory in 1964, and then the rapid de-escalation once he left office in 1968.

included several members of John Kennedy's old campaign and advisory team who had been working for McCarthy.

Of the four Kennedy sons, Bobby was probably the least likely to run for office. He lacked the charisma and charm of either Joe or John, and almost certainly Joe-the-father had no particular political aspirations for Bobby. At his best, Bobby was a talented behind-the-scenes powerbroker working John's will, the president's pit bull. When John died, however, the nation seemed to look to Bobby to succeed his brother, to carry on the mantle and what was perceived as the hope of a new generation—a role he shied away from, perhaps even feared. Bobby agreed to continue on as attorney general as Johnson had requested, which LBJ had done almost certainly because he believed he needed Bobby to keep the Kennedy mystique alive. But events turned the two into rivals. After nine months Bobby left the administration to run for a vacant Senate seat from New York. By then he had shown a growing liberalism that focused on opposition to the war and a developed sensitivity to the alienated young and the nation's poor. He promised to "end the bloodshed in Vietnam and in our cities . . . to close the gap

. . . between black and white, between rich and poor, between young and old, in this country and around the world." He went on to win important victories in several primaries. His successes severely undermined Johnson's Vietnam policies.

Johnson named Clifford to replace McNamara as secretary of defense on March 1. The post-Tet backlash was just beginning to set in, and Clifford was as much a target of the nation's complaints about the prosecution of the war as the president. In addition, the North Koreans had just seized an American intelligence ship, the USS *Pueblo*, and that frustrating incident threatened to spark another war against a Chinese military ally on the Asian mainland, something no one in Washington wanted.

Clifford had served as a senior advisor to Johnson since 1964, meeting with the president frequently and informally on Vietnam and other issues. He had pushed hard for Operation Rolling Thunder, and he opposed those who wanted to halt the bombing in order to open talks with the North. But when Clifford came to the Defense Department his attitude changed. He found no plan to end the war. He also found no good reason to increase troop strength in Vietnam—mainly because Westmoreland and the Joint Chiefs had made it clear several times that the additional 206,000 men they had requested could not bring victory. In view of the situation, Clifford quietly switched from hawk to dove. He also began leading others away from the administration's policy and toward a strategy to stop the bombing, end the war, and bring U.S. forces home. "As time went on," Clifford recalled, "my desire to get out of Vietnam went from opinion, to conviction, to passion. I was afraid that we were never going to get out. We were losing thousands of men and billions of dollars in an endless sinkhole. If I ever knew anything, I knew that: We had to get out." Clifford decided to try convincing the president.

In the last week of March, Johnson called a meeting of his top advisors on the war, a group famously known as the Wise Men. They included generals, justices, diplomats, and Wall Street lawyers, truly the exemplars of U.S. foreign policy. The biggest names were Truman's secretary of state Dean Acheson; generals Omar Bradley, Matthew Ridgway and Max Taylor; Supreme Court justice Abe Fortas; Averill Harriman; and Doug Dillon. In the past, the Wise Men had given support to Johnson's war policies, but they had begun to change their minds, to see the war as many Americans had come to see it: unwinnable. They told Johnson that the United States could not realize a classical military victory in Vietnam, that in fact the war could not be won. In a statement by Acheson that seemed to sum up the opinion of the group, he said, "We can no longer do the job we set out to do . . . and we must begin to take steps to disengage."

THE ANTIWAR MOVEMENT AND THE NEW LEFT

The war created a favorable climate for radical growth in the 1960s. Through 1965 and 1966 there were sit-ins, teach-ins, campus strikes, and marches throughout the nation. As the war progressed (and the military draft became a threat to the lifestyles of young middle-class men) the antiwar movement intensified. The masses of marchers in the streets of the nation's cities were mostly young people who opposed the war for any number of reasons. They may have seen the war as immoral, particularly the bombings; or they may have viewed the war as unwinnable; or they may have felt that it was too expensive when the nation needed economic assistance in other areas. Certainly, many believed that America's involvement in the war ran counter to the ideals of the United States, that the nation should not become entangled in another nation's legitimate independence movement. Young men of draft age often joined the ranks in opposition to the war because they simply did not want to fight in it. African Americans opposed the war for many of the same reasons, but with the added concern that (at least through 1966) African American men were being drafted into the military in greater numbers than whites, and that black soldiers in Vietnam were being killed more often than white soldiers.

The political radicalism that emerged at the beginning of the decade is usually touted as the New Left, a youth-driven movement more in tune with the equality of rights and opportunities than with Marxist revolution, the primary objective of the Old Left. The New Left had its origins on the nation's college campuses, and its activities and actions attracted a great deal of attention from the press through the decade. It is, however, a mistake to see 1960s campus radicalism as anything more than the actions and beliefs of a minority of engaged students. In 1960 there were 1.7 million college students in the nation; that number exploded to almost seven million by the end of the decade as the boomers came of age and college attendance became generally affordable because of the Johnson administration's policies. These students seldom wanted for much; they were mostly from the nation's affluent suburbs, so the object of their radicalism was not their own economic condition. Many had come to see the world as a troubling place, made that way by the actions of the previous generation; and they perceived the cold war and the bomb as direct and real threats. They insisted on the eradication of the nation's pockets of poverty, and saw a lack of equal rights and equal opportunity as inherent in that problem. Not unlike the old Progressives, these students and their supporters called for greater participation in the democratic process as a solution to many of the nation's ills.

The premier New Left organization was the Students for a Democratic Society (SDS). Founded in 1960 by a small group of students at the University of Michigan, the members of the SDS were initially inspired by the civil rights movement, claiming in their manifesto, "The Port Huron Statement," that one of the nation's most troubling problems was the "human degradation symbolized by the Southern struggle against racial bigotry. . . ." But by 1965 the SDS leadership had decided to take the lead in the antiwar movement. They organized the first big antiwar rally on April 17, a march on Washington that drew nearly twenty thousand young people to the Washington monument to protest the war.

The SDS continued its activities through the remainder of the decade by organizing antiwar groups on many of the nation's campuses. Late in the decade, however, the organization splintered between its moderate and radical wings and finally self-destructed.

"I WILL NOT ACCEPT": THE
TRAGEDY OF LYNDON JOHNSON

Johnson's policies in Vietnam had failed, and with much of the nation apparently turned against him, he planned to announce that he would not run for office in 1968. He hoped that without the political pressures of the campaign he could put all his efforts into ending the war before he left office and salvage the legacy of his presidency. On March 31 he surprised the nation: "So tonight, in the hopes that this action will lead to early talks, I am taking the first steps to de-escalate the conflict." He said he would halt the bombing north of the twentieth parallel, and he called on Ho Chi Minh to agree to peace talks. He then authorized the deployment of 13,500 troops over a five-month period, considerably less than the 206,000 that Westmoreland had requested. Then, with a short statement he took the nation by surprise: He looked into the camera and, with a stern face, said, "I have concluded that I should not permit the presidency to become involved in the partisan divisions that are developing this political year. . . . Accordingly, I shall not seek, and I will not accept, the nomination of my party for another term as your president." The announcement had not been included in the president's press release, and it surprised just about everyone. Johnson told Clifford afterward, "I never felt so right about any decision in my life."

Johnson was beleaguered and worn down by the war. He worried about his health. He also saw before him a bitter battle to win another term in the White House with his Vietnam policy at the center of the debate. He had gotten the nation deeply involved in a war it could not win. It was tragic, because Johnson had not wanted the war. Primarily a domestic politician, he had a glorious (though perhaps unattainable) vision for a nation that included the elimination of both poverty and racial discrimination.

Johnson, the domestic politician, was willing to sacrifice the effort in Vietnam for his domestic agenda. The consensus he had built in Congress to pass his domestic programs was extremely fragile. He feared that a national debate on Vietnam would split the coalition and wreck the congressional and public support he needed to enact his programs. Consequently, he refused to do anything that might bring his Vietnam policy into question. He escalated slowly; he refused to ask for the tax increases necessary to prosecute the war effectively; he refused to call up the reserves; and when possible, he kept the problems and horrors of the war away from the American people. The result was a slowly escalated war that was prosecuted without the necessary support from Washington or the people, a credibility gap between the president's policies and the portrayal of the war to the public.

Johnson prosecuted the war badly because it was his nature to compromise. Consensus building and compromise had always been the hallmarks of his successes as a politician. Fearing reprisals from liberals, he refused to do more than escalate the war slowly. At the same time, he feared attacks from conservatives if he did not continue to show success in Vietnam, or if he decided to withdraw altogether. He also refused to be the president who "lost" Vietnam, and that fear pushed him to grant Westmoreland's requests for more troops and to keep the pressure on Hanoi by escalating the bombing. Consequently, holding the middle of the road meant an escalation of the war. For Johnson, the war was unwinnable.

THE 1968 CAMPAIGN

Johnson had hoped that removing himself from the 1968 election process would allow him the freedom to put all his efforts into ending the war before his term ended. The Hanoi government agreed to begin talks in Paris, but the negotiations produced little. Then in May, the Viet Cong and North Vietnamese launched another offensive, quickly dubbed the "Mini-Tet Offensive" by the press.

The war had splintered the Democrats badly. The antiwar candidacy of Robert Kennedy gained momentum through the primaries, while the party regulars backed Vice President Humphrey, a renowned liberal but a loyal Johnson trooper and supporter of the president's war policies. As the primary campaigns wrapped up in California, it was Kennedy who had the momentum and, possibly, the votes to take the party's nomination in Chicago.

For most American liberals, Kennedy was the new light. Not only did he oppose what they perceived as an unjust war, he seemed to want to heal the divided country. He reached out to just about everyone, stressing a more inclusive nation. He spoke with Native Americans, Hispanics, African Americans, and labor. He even approached the new conservative groups like the suburban middle-class and working-class conservatives who were at the foundations of the rapidly growing backlash. He rejected the philosophical foundations of the old New Deal/Fair Deal/Great Society approach to social reform by criticizing welfare programs for creating a dependent underclass and by emphasizing the importance of local self-government and government-sponsored programs that kept all projects within the private sector and in local hands. Some historians have seen Bobby Kennedy as having a clear vision for the nation's future. Others have seen him as groping for a new way, looking for a new liberalism that was transcendent of the old reform paradigm of Cold War containment and Washington-directed social welfare reform. Either way, like his brothers, his was a vision unfulfilled.

Following the California Democratic primary in early June it appeared that Kennedy was moving toward taking the nomination from Humphrey. But shortly after issuing his victory speech at the Ambassador Hotel in Los Angeles, Kennedy was shot and killed by a Jordanian immigrant, Sirhan Sirhan.

In early August, the Republicans met in Miami and nominated Richard Nixon—for the second time in eight years. The events of the decade had given the impression that the nation was on the verge of some sort of breakdown, and that gave strength to the national conservative movement. The chief beneficiary was Nixon. Following his 1960 defeat by John Kennedy, Nixon made an ill-advised and unprepared run for governor of California in 1962, and lost. In his concession speech he blamed the press for his defeat, saying that "you won't have Nixon to kick around anymore." But instead of retiring from politics, he worked to build up his party credentials and reinvent himself, this time as a party power-house and a unifier of the party's two divergent wings. By 1968 he was able to bury his chief rivals and win the Republican nomination.

Three weeks following the Republican convention, the Democrats met in Chicago. It would be the political climax of the decade. As the Democratic convention approached, ten thousand antiwar protesters headed for Chicago. Most supported the antiwar campaign of Eugene McCarthy and opposed Humphrey and his support for Johnson's war policies. The Chicago police prepared to manage the crowds, but as the police and the protestors went head to head the inevitable occurred. In a series of clashes over three days, much of it caught on television, the helmeted police pushed their way into the crowds of protesters with tear gas and nightsticks. In one particular clash in front of the Conrad Hilton Hotel on Michigan Avenue, police pummeled protesters as the crowds chanted, "The whole world is watching." The entire incident was lighted by the floodlights of the nation's television camera crews.

Inside the Chicago Amphitheater, the convention was nearly as riotous. Delegates fought over the war, with antiwar supporters insisting that the party's platform include provisions to end the bombing and withdraw the troops. Humphrey's supporters relented to some degree by agreeing to a bombing halt and a de-escalation over time. These concessions won the convention's endorsement and ensured the vice president's nomination. Humphrey, however, refused to endorse those concessions and continued to stay the course with the president.

Throughout the campaign Humphrey was continually pressured by Johnson to hold the line on the administration's Vietnam policy. But Humphrey quickly fell behind Nixon in the polls. In addition, he failed to raise the money necessary to run an effective campaign, and he was continually heckled by antiwar protesters. As the election approached, Humphrey tried to distance himself from Johnson's increasingly unpopular Vietnam policies, and near the end of September he announced that he would support an end to the bombing of North Vietnam. Then on October 31, just five days before the election, Johnson announced an end to the bombing and a resumption of peace negotiations in Paris. Those two events rallied the antiwar activists to Humphrey's side and boosted his numbers considerably. The two candidates headed toward Election Day in a statistical dead heat.

In the meantime, Nixon realized that Johnson might spring an "October surprise" by announcing a de-escalation of the war, a surprise that might cost him the election. Nixon responded by persuading South Vietnamese President Nguyen Van Thieu to avoid the peace talks, promising him a better deal for South Vietnam under a Nixon presidency.

Nixon won the election. The popular vote was close, with Nixon taking 43.4 percent to Humphrey's 42.7 percent. In the Electoral College, however, Nixon won a commanding victory, 302 to 191. Humphrey won the industrial Northeast, along with Texas, Minnesota, Michigan, and Washington. Nixon was strongest in the Upper South, the Midwest, the Plains, and the Far West. George Wallace, running as an Independent, won 13.4 percent of the popular vote and took five states in the Deep South. Perhaps most important was the new Republican coalition that was forming. Nixon had pulled support from the West, the Midwest, and the South (the five states that Wallace took in the Deep South would almost certainly have gone Republican had Wallace not run). The new coalition, which now excluded the northeastern moderates, was much more conservative.

By 1968 the war had destroyed an administration and ended an era. The promises that Kennedy had brought with him to the White House in 1961, and then passed on to Lyndon Johnson in November 1963, had not been kept by 1968. They had been spent on a war that could not be won, in a far-off place that had, at best, limited strategic value for the United States. The war also did what Johnson feared it would do: It demolished the fragile coalition he had worked so hard to forge, the liberal-moderate consensus which had come together to pass the bills of the Great Society. Vietnam was the tragedy that haunted America in the 1960s, one of the decade's primary failures.

BLACK POWER AND THE RADICALIZATION
OF THE CIVIL RIGHTS MOVEMENT

It was almost a natural progression of events that King's leadership and his philosophy of nonviolence was challenged by a group of young black leaders who demanded more direct action, who were fed up with nonviolence as a strategy, and who no longer wanted to follow the lead of Washington liberals and white organizers. This new philosophy, best known as "black power," was more than just rebellious youth, more than a few hotheaded kids who wanted to lead with more flamboyance and dynamism than King. It was, in fact, a completely different approach, and a total rejection of King and his philosophy of nonviolence.

The first challenge to nonviolence came within SNCC. The leader was the

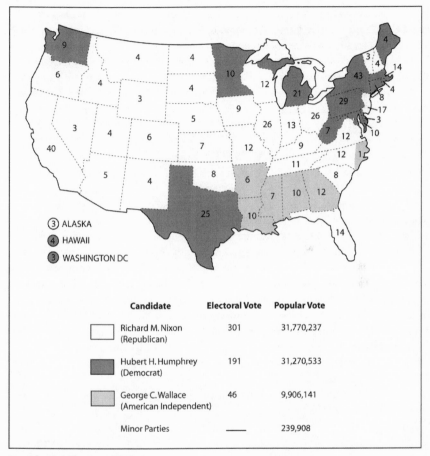

Candidate	Electoral Vote	Popular Vote
Richard M. Nixon (Republican)	301	31,770,237
Hubert H. Humphrey (Democrat)	191	31,270,533
George C. Wallace (American Independent)	46	9,906,141
Minor Parties	—	239,908

Presidential Election, 1968

charismatic Stokely Carmichael, an SNCC organizer and volunteer. Carmichael had opposed the MFDP effort in the summer of 1964, and had instead headed off to organize a voter rights drive in Alabama. He was the primary spokesman for those who resented white interference in the movement, arguing often that white liberals were insincere, could not be trusted, and should be expelled.

In May 1966 Carmichael, at age twenty-four, defeated John Lewis as chairman of SNCC and began pushing the organization away from King's philosophy of a biracial, nonviolent movement. At Carmichael's direction, white volunteers were expelled from SNCC and the organization issued a statement calling for "black Americans to begin building independent political, economic, and cultural institutions that they will control and use as instruments of social change in this country." CORE was experiencing a nearly parallel transformation. Led first by

black power advocate Floyd McKissick and then by the more radical black separatist Roy Innis, CORE formally repudiated nonviolence in 1966, denounced the
Vietnam War, and endorsed black power.

Black power was many things to many people. For some, it was little more
than black pride and a celebration of the African American heritage. To others,
it was control of the black community through the ballot box; for still others it
was the creation of a parallel African American society that rejected whites and
white institutions. For many black Americans—particularly young black Americans—compromise, gradualism, and a willingness to "overcome" inequality
"someday" simply was not enough. They also believed that relying on white liberals had damaged the civil rights movement—held it back by injecting a need to
compromise with the leaders in Washington. In fact, for many black power advocates it was King who was the real problem. As they saw it, he was the black
leader chosen by whites to lead the movement because he did not threaten the
white establishment. He was a moderate who would compromise with the white
leadership and who continually accepted the empty promises flowing from Washington. What King had come to represent, in the minds of these young radicals,
was failed liberalism, the promises and hopes for change that were a blatant lie.
The Civil Rights Act and Voting Rights Act, it seemed, had been the capstone
of the federal government's actions on civil rights, and Washington had no intention of pushing the nation any further forward toward racial equality. And King's
Promised Land suddenly seemed a long way off. The only alternative, these radicals had come to believe, was black nationalism, a closing of ranks, a total reliance
on blacks by blacks.

Carmichael had based his black nationalist beliefs on the ideas and teachings of Malcolm X, the primary spokesman for the Nation of Islam. By the time
Carmichael had risen to prominence in SNCC, Malcolm was dead, assassinated
in the early months of 1965 by his Nation of Islam enemies. He had, however,
touched Carmichael and many other young African Americans living in the
northern ghettos, principally through his *Autobiography of Malcolm X*, which
swept black America after his death. Malcolm called for black pride, pride in
black African roots, and pride in the ability of blacks to control their own destiny.
He called for a "revolt of the American Negro" as part of "a global rebellion of
the oppressed against the oppressor, the exploited against the exploiter." He often
mocked King, his nonviolent philosophy, and his "I-have-a-dream speeches." By
the time Malcolm died, his militant stance had awakened thousands of poor and
oppressed African Americans to his message of black nationalism.

Black power was denounced by the white liberal establishment and by the
black leaders of the nonviolent protest movement. At one point, King admitted
that "black power" was a gratifying slogan, but he called it nothing more than a
"nihilistic philosophy born out of the conviction that the Negro can't win." Roy
Wilkins of the NAACP said that black power was "the raging of race against race
on the irrelevant basis of skin color. It is the father of hatred and the mother

of violence." Bayard Rustin became the chief African American spokesman in opposition to black power, calling its leaders "racist demagogues." It was to many observers, however, a logical progression of the movement, a venting of anger and frustration over unfulfilled promises and a policy of slow-moving gradualism.

The black power movement also served to push white liberals out of the civil rights movement. As SNCC became increasingly militant, the once-ample funding from white liberals dried up. Carmichael moved away from SNCC and toward the Black Panthers, possibly the most radical of all the separatist organizations; and his successor as chairman of SNCC, H. Rap Brown, made Carmichael sound like a moderate with his calls to "burn, baby, burn!" By the end of the 1960s, SNCC was bankrupt and effectively dead. CORE quickly followed.

Undoubtedly the biggest blow to the civil rights movement was the murder of Martin Luther King Jr., struck down by an assassin's bullet on April 4, 1968, while standing on a balcony in Memphis. King had been a towering figure in the civil rights movement and in the nation's history. By 1968 he had moved to broaden his movement from civil rights for African Americans to an advocacy for the nation's poor. He had, in fact, been in Memphis to support a garbage workers' strike. Without his leadership, the civil rights movement began to wane, and his work against poverty never moved forward under other leaders.

URBAN RIOTS

The philosophy of black power had its greatest impact on the northern urban ghettos where African Americans were not denied the use of public accommodations or the right to vote, but where racial discrimination remained strong, systematic, and often as demeaning and violent as in the South. Ghetto housing was deplorable, city services such as police protection and education were almost always inadequate, and job discrimination left most blacks at the bottom of the social and economic structure. At the same time, northern urban blacks had, like all Americans, grasped at the promises and hopes of the postwar era: the promises to end poverty, put a stop to racial inequality, and bring peace and prosperity to the greatest nation on earth. But the promises had been empty and often politically motivated.

African Americans were not totally denied advancement in the postwar years; as the economy grew, so did the incomes of most African Americans. Black family income had increased from about $6,000 in 1964 to $8,000 by the end of the decade, and unemployment had dropped from 7.2 percent to 2.5 percent between 1962 and 1970. But the quality of life in the ghetto did not improve, and nonwhite youth unemployment increased dramatically during the decade. Perhaps more importantly, the civil rights movement in the South had stimulated rising black expectations, but the pace of that movement was slow and the objective was to remove the old Jim Crow racial barriers in the South, which had little to do with the problems facing blacks in northern cities. Black power grew to become the prevailing dogma in the ghettos. And between 1965 and 1970 urban riots, rather than marches and sit-ins, became the chief method of protest.

Riots first broke out in Harlem in the summer of 1964, and then spread to Rochester, Jersey City, and Philadelphia later that year. A year later, Watts, a sprawling black ghetto in central Los Angeles, erupted into a spectacular six-day riot that left thirty-four dead, over a thousand injured, and $40 million in property damage. It took fourteen thousand National Guardsmen and fifteen hundred policemen to bring the situation under control. The movement was changing dramatically.

The Watts riot began just five days after President Johnson signed the Voting Rights Act in August 1965, and the president (not unlike most Americans) was astonished by the events. While America watched Watts burn, another riot broke out in Chicago. At the beginning of the year, King had moved to Chicago in what seemed to be an attempt to get out in front of the movement's new direction, but his philosophy of nonviolence fell mostly on deaf ears.

The next summer, riots erupted in most major cities. National Guard troops patrolled the streets of Chicago, Milwaukee, San Francisco, Cleveland, and Dayton. Through the remainder of the decade, massive riots swept the nation. Almost every American city in the Northeast, Midwest, and California experienced racial unrest. The events were unparalleled in the nation's history. There were at least 250 deaths, 10,000 injuries, and 60,000 arrests. The largest and most destructive riot was in Detroit in 1967. For six long days, large sections of Detroit burned as fifteen thousand Michigan state police and National Guardsmen tried desperately to bring the city back to order. Forty-three people died and another two thousand were injured. Fourteen square miles of Detroit's inner city burned, leaving over five thousand African Americans homeless. Detroit's mayor compared the carnage to postwar Berlin.

The fury that led to the riots never quite resonated with white America. As they watched the chaos on their televisions, they asked why blacks would resort to burning their own neighborhoods, local businesses, even their own homes. The answers, at first, came in studies. The McCone Commission, headed by former CIA director John McCone, blamed the Watts riot on a few alienated youths. Other analyses insisted that most African Americans deplored the riots and were generally satisfied with the gradual liberal reforms emanating from Washington. President Johnson was not satisfied with that, however, and he appointed Illinois Governor Otto Kerner to lead a commission to investigate the riots. The Kerner Commission report pointed its finger directly at the consequences of white racism, calling it "essentially responsible for the explosive mixture which has been accumulating in our cities since the end of World War II." In its conclusion, the report noted that the nation is "moving toward two societies, one black, one white—separate and unequal." African Americans were angry. They had been promised first-class citizenship. They had been promised a shot at the American dream by liberal politicians in exchange for their votes. They had delivered, but the promises had gone unfulfilled.

By the late 1960s black power had entered the American vernacular, and at least in the minds of most Americans, civil rights had gone from a movement of social change to a movement of demands and violence in order to force change. Television images of burning cities, firemen being shot at, gun-wielding Black Panther "soldiers," and the anti-white tirades of Carmichael, Brown, Eldridge Cleaver, and Bobby Seale drove white America (whether once sympathetic to civil rights or not) away from the movement. The response was predictable. Whites began to call for law and order in the streets instead of sympathy for the protesters, punishment instead of understanding. At the insistence of white voters, funds were withdrawn from government-sponsored antipoverty programs and projects. Congress refused to pass legislation to help the inner cities; urban schools were left to decay; and ultimately whites continued their flight to the suburbs, leaving the decaying inner cities to a growing black underclass.

BACKLASH

Perhaps more than anything else, it was the 1964 Civil Rights Act which was the catalyst that brought on a severe national backlash against the civil rights movement, against liberalism and reform, and against the Johnson administration and the Democrats. It also widened a large divide within the Democratic Party between the northern liberals and the southern conservatives; finally, it served to accelerate the shift of white southerners into the Republican Party.

In late 1963 when Johnson became president, only 31 percent of the nation said the federal government was pushing civil rights too fast. Within five years, that number rose rapidly to over 50 percent, and it was clear that the backlash had moved out of the South and into the North, particularly into the northern suburbs. Whites feared that the new racial order would allow African Americans to move into white neighborhoods and into white schools. This fear was particularly prevalent in the white working-class neighborhoods in the North that frequently bordered black ghettos. To working-class whites, this situation translated into everything from high crime, to a loss of jobs and wages, to lower property values, to a weakening of the local school system.

All this seemed to breach the surface with George Wallace's barely noticed presidential run in 1964. The Alabama governor took his campaign into the North, into the northern working-class suburbs, where he found support among whites who feared for their jobs, their schools, and their property values. Wallace blamed it all on the 1964 Civil Rights Act. He dropped out of the race once the act was passed, but Republican candidate Barry Goldwater seemed to pick up the ball. "There is something to this . . . backlash," Goldwater said in a news conference. "The people . . . don't want their [own] property rights tampered with. The people feel they should have the right to say who lives near them." Over the next four years the backlash grew into a full-scale revolt that damaged many of the gains of the civil rights movement.

In the summer of 1968, Wallace, now running for president as an Independent, drew a crowd of seventy thousand for one speech in Boston, fifteen thousand in Pittsburgh, twelve thousand in San Francisco, and fifteen thousand in Detroit. The next month he packed Madison Square Garden in New York, the very heart of American liberalism. "We don't have riots in Alabama," he told his supporters in New York. "They start a riot down there, first of 'em to pick up a brick gets a bullet in the brain. That's all." The crowd erupted. The backlash had found its champion.

As the 1968 campaign progressed, polls showed that Wallace would have an impact on the election by taking most of the South, but it was also clear that he would take votes from the Republican candidate Richard Nixon in several other key industrial states in the Midwest. By September, Nixon came to realize that if he did not shore up his southern base he might lose the election. His response was to undercut Wallace's racism. In Charlotte, Nixon attacked school desegregation and court-ordered busing, calling both "counterproductive." Nixon beat Humphrey in 1968, but he lost the Deep South to Wallace—and nearly lost the election because of it. Nixon had learned the lesson well.

A CALL FOR SOCIAL CHANGE AND RECOGNITION

It was in the 1960s that television, really for the first time, was available throughout the nation. And for the first time the entire population could see the American dream and the affluent lifestyle enjoyed by the national majority. Not surprisingly, anyone who was denied that lifestyle wanted to be a part of it. More importantly, they understood that, as Americans, they had the right to rise to that level, that the laws of the nation declared that they could not be denied equal rights. Not surprisingly, Latinos living in the barrios and lettuce fields of California began to insist that they be given equal rights; the Native Americans living on the reservations of the West made the same demands. The stage had been set by the African American drive for civil rights. They had conceived of both the strategy and the tactics. Not surprisingly, others followed.

Latinos (the vast majority were Mexican-Americans in this period) were undoubtedly spurred on by the idealism, courage, and the successes of the civil rights movement. Their primary leader was César Chávez, an aggressive farm labor leader who took on the nearly impossible task of organizing the nation's five million Mexican-American migrant workers. He became to Latinos what Martin Luther King was to African Americans.

Farm workers were excluded from the National Labor Relations Act of 1935, which kept Latino farm workers from joining unions, and they were not covered by either minimum wage laws or Social Security laws. With no leadership and no real voting power, Latinos fell to the very bottom rung of American society. The result was predictable. They often lived in the worst kind of poverty, in barrios in large cities or in horrible living conditions provided by growers in the fields. Most of these workers were in the Southwest, but large groups of Latinos worked as migrant laborers through the Midwest, traveling between harvests of grains, tomatoes, and melons in central Indiana, and apples and cherries in Michigan.

The cycle was all too familiar. Latinos received the least education of all the minority groups, were paid the least, lived in the worst conditions, and consequently had fewer opportunities. There was almost no hope of escaping the debilitating poverty.

In 1962 Chávez formed the National Farm Workers Association (NFWA), and in 1965 he led a strike of California's grape-pickers. In a campaign that caught the imagination of the nation, the NFWA encouraged all Americans to boycott table grapes as a show of support for the workers in the fields. Possibly the most important result of the strike was the extensive national press coverage that revealed, on television, the poor living conditions of California migrant workers. That, in turn, put pressure on growers and politicians to deal with the problems and poverty that the migrant workers faced. Through the 1970s the United Farm Workers (changed from the NFWA) continued to organize strikes and boycotts, particularly against the California grape and lettuce growers.

Not unlike the civil rights movement for African Americas, the Latino civil rights movement splintered into radicalism. Pegged as the "brown power" movement, Latino radicals were led by Reies López Tijerina. Their primary cause was to demand the return of lands in New Mexico taken by European Americans despite various guarantees in the 1848 Treaty of Guadalupe Hidalgo. Tijerina's "Letter from the Santa Fe Jail" denounced white Americans as the "rich people from outside the state with their summer homes and ranches" and "all those who have robbed the people of their land and culture for 120 years."

Political activism among young Latinos was most prominent in Los Angeles. In March 1968, ten thousand Chicanos (a word often used to denote Latino race pride) stormed out of city high schools to protest poor education. The event led to the organization of the Brown Berets, an association of young Chicanos demanding better education opportunities and better treatment from L.A. police. By the end of the decade, many young Chicanos had rejected assimilation and began moving toward a celebration of their Latino cultural identity that included both race pride and community self-determination.

Not surprisingly, other groups demanded their rights as well. Native Americans demanded equal access to everything that American society offered. Nearly 70 percent of the nation's Native Americans lived on reservations, where unemployment and underemployment exceeded 50 percent. Large numbers of Native

United Farm Workers leader César Chávez pauses with supporters during a protest march through the agricultural valley of California in the summer of 1975. *Source*: AP Photo/Walter Zebowski

American families lived below the poverty line, and alcoholism was a severe problem among the population.

A demand for civil rights and cultural identity, however, turned to radical expression. In 1968 Native Americans in Minneapolis created the American Indian Movement (AIM) for the purpose of creating economic opportunity for Native Americans and to fight mistreatment by local police who had made a practice of harassing the Native American population.

In 1969, eighty members of AIM, chanting "Red Power," snatched control of Alcatraz Island, a notorious federal prison located off the coast of California near San Francisco. Their argument for occupying the island was that U.S.–American Indian treaties had included a provision that any land abandoned by the United States government became the property of the Native American population. They continued to occupy the island until 1971.

In 1973, AIM seized the town of Wounded Knee, South Dakota, the site of the 1890 Indian massacre. Their original intent was to force a change in the constitution of the Oglala Sioux that would restore the power of the tribal chiefs over the elected tribal elders. Despite the insignificance of the event to most Americans, U.S. marshals laid siege to the town, and following several gun fights two Native Americans died and several Native Americans and lawmen were injured. The standoff ended after seventy-one days.

The gay community felt as much oppressed as other minority groups. Many homosexuals hid their way of life, living an underground lifestyle that they knew was repugnant to most of general society. Others congregated in gay communities and frequented all-gay establishments. On July 28, 1969, the New York police raided the largest gay bar in Manhattan, the Stonewall Inn, located in the West Village. What followed was four nights of riots and fights outside the bar between the New York police and groups of gays and lesbians. The result was a catalyst for a nationwide gay rights/gay pride movement. The Gay Liberation Front was formed, annual gay pride days were organized on both coasts, and gays openly began to demand equality and equal rights on the same basis as other minority groups. Soon many of the age-old barriers began to break down. It would be a decade before the nation's gay communities would be decimated by AIDS.

Whether it was black power, brown power, gay power, or red power, civil rights movements all began with a basic desire for equal rights. But when those rights were not forthcoming, the movements quickly reached toward cultural pride and then into cultural separatism. It was almost a natural progression of events. The unifying factor was that these movements were efforts by the nation's minorities to define themselves through their own heritage and history, rather than through the mirror of white society. Not surprisingly, they questioned (and even rebelled against) the basic assumption that all Americans wanted to be part of the same homogeneous society.

THE NEW AMERICAN FEMINISM

The history of American women in the twentieth century is the history of setbacks. In the 1920s women seemed on the verge of breaking out of their role as second-class citizens. They had gotten the vote, and the new twenties lifestyle (for many women) was liberating. But the Depression seemed to end all that; the liberation of women took a backseat to other problems and needs in the family. The war put women in the workplace, mostly to replace soldiers who were fighting overseas. It was both patriotic and liberating, but when the war ended women were encouraged to give up their jobs to the returning soldiers and return to their kitchens. That was followed by the 1950s, an entire decade in which women were idealized as mothers and wives: the perfect hostess, the accomplished homemaker. The decade of the 1960s seemed to awaken women to a new era of change and liberation, much as it awakened other groups. Women were, of course, not a minority in America, but they acted and reacted much like a minority: oppressed by the majority and forced into a second-class citizenship. Not surprisingly, in the 1960s a significant minority of women began voicing their dissatisfaction with their domestic roles and rebelled against the status quo.

The call for change came from a new generation of women, the daughters of those who had aspired to be perfect homemakers. This new generation simply wanted more out of life than a clean house, and they saw the advances made toward equality by the nation's minority groups. Television (always a catalyst for change in the period) may well have shown young women that there was life beyond the suburbs. For whatever reason, large numbers of women in the mid-1960s stood up and insisted on being noticed and being given rights equal to men. Perhaps surprisingly, men did not put up much resistance.

The chief call of American feminists in the decade was a demand for equality in the job market. Job discrimination had relegated women to the lesser jobs of secretaries, telephone operators, nurses, and teachers. Beyond that, women were suppressed by the so-called glass ceiling, through which women could view the better jobs but not attain them. Beginning in the 1960s, activists battled to open all job categories to women. As women slowly made their way into the workplace, it became clear that their abilities at least matched those of their male counterparts.

A primary turning point in the decade's feminist movement was the publication of Betty Freidan's *The Feminine Mystique* in 1963. Freidan challenged the 1950s images of women as shallow, doting homemakers whose sole purpose in life was to service their family's needs. She called the suburban home "a comfortable concentration camp." And she wrote: "Each suburban housewife struggled with it alone. As she made the beds, shopped for groceries, matched slipcover material, ate peanut butter sandwiches with her children, chauffeured Cub Scouts and Brownies, lay beside her husband at night—she was afraid to ask of herself the silent question: 'Is this all?'" She gave eloquent voice to the movement.

One of the greatest victories for women and women's rights came directly from the 1964 Civil Rights Act, which included a provision to bar discrimination on the basis of sex as well as race. This Title VII was included in the final passage of the bill, but it was not immediately enforced by the Equal Employment Opportunity Commission (EEOC), the government agency responsible for enforcing the bill. In 1966 Freidan and other activists formed the National Organization for Women (NOW) as a pressure group to force the EEOC to enforce Title VII. And with that, the modern women's rights movement was born. NOW continued as the central focus of the movement, and within a decade NOW's membership ran to over sixty thousand. The movement called for equal pay for equal work, equal access to the job market, and an end to gender discrimination.

By the next decade, the movement for basic women's rights had evolved into women's liberation. Hardly radical (although there were certainly radical elements) the women's lib movement called for gender equality in all aspects of society, particularly in the workplace where women demanded "equal pay for equal work." In 1972 an Equal Rights Amendment (ERA) to the Constitution passed both houses of Congress, but failed to gain ratification by the states.

Betty Friedan, cofounder of the National Organization for Women (NOW), speaks to supporters in New York in August 1970. Friedan's book, *The Feminine Mystique*, was instrumental in launching the women's rights movement. *Source*: AP Photo

ON "THE PILL"

In 1960 the Food and Drug Administration launched the sexual revolution by approving the first birth control pill, marketed by G. D. Searle and Company. The pill released an explosion of sexual activity in the decade, notably among adolescents and young adults. There was a new tendency to celebrate uninhibited sexual activity, to experience sex to the fullest. With the pill, sex required no special preparation to interfere with spontaneity or sensation. Intercourse could mean nothing more than an expression of mutual physical pleasure, with no thought of the consequences of the reproductive process. By 1970 the Crosby, Stills, Nash, and Young song "Love the One You're With," actually had real meaning.

The pill, and the sexual revolution it spawned, shocked middle-aged and older Americans, always under the assumption that young women should maintain their virginity until marriage. Particularly shocking to the older generations was the pervasiveness of cohabitation, kids moving in together. The entire generation seemed to be turning their backs on the sanctity of marriage.

Most religions issued various statements in opposition to all the promiscuity. The Catholic Church insisted that artificial contraception distorted the nature and purpose of sex and reemphasized its traditional Catholic teachings on birth control in the 1968 papal encyclical *Humanae Vitae*. Historian Max Lerner wrote: "We're living in a Babylonian society that is perhaps more Babylonian than Babylon itself. . . . The emphasis in our society today is on the senses and the release of the sensual. All the old codes have been broken."

CONCLUSION

The decade of the 1960s was a giant lurch toward change—in fact in almost every aspect of life, from society to culture, from politics to science. Whether or not those changes were ever achieved, or to what degree they were achieved, is always a debatable issue. Certainly, a significant backlash emerged to challenge the changes, or at least the speed at which the changes were occurring. It might even be argued that the conservative backlash was itself stronger than the various movements, that the backlash ended the liberalism of the 1960s. In 1970 a Gallup poll showed that a full 70 percent of women opposed the feminist movement; a similar number of the general population a few years earlier agreed that the civil rights movement was moving too fast. The neoconservative movement (which would come to fruition with Ronald Reagan's election in 1980) seemed to be born at almost the moment the decade of the 1960s ended.

Historians will focus on the turmoil of the 1960s, the excitement, the movements, the *Fire in the Streets*, as Milton Viorst had depicted the decade. But in fact, the vast majority of Americans were not in the streets, did not march with King at Birmingham, did not burn their bras at Atlantic City. Most Americans lived their lives as Americans have always lived their lives: one day at a time, going to work, watching TV, visiting with friends and family. It was, nevertheless, a tumultuous decade, even a divisive one, and many Americans found themselves caught up in it, on one side of events or the other, with an opinion and ready to voice it. Sometimes Americans get excited; sometimes they calm down. In the 1960s, they were excited.

Reading: Space, the Final Frontier

The launching of the Soviet earth satellite *Sputnik* in 1957 awakened American scientists to the realities of the nation's technological inferiority. It was clear, despite Eisenhower's insistence to the contrary, that the Soviets were ahead in the space race, and by connection, in the arms race as well. Just as Americans were scratching their heads over the Soviet achievement, Soviet scientists launched another satellite, this one weighing over a thousand pounds and carrying a dog, Laika. American scientists rushed to meet the challenge, and on December 6 the navy attempted to launch a U.S. satellite from Cape Canaveral in Florida. As the nation watched on television, the Vanguard rocket rose about four feet off the launch pad, spewed rocket fuel in all directions, and exploded in a spectacular array of humiliation. Finally, American scientists perfected the Jupiter C rocket and in late January 1958 launched the first U.S. satellite into orbit, the *Explorer I*. The Eisenhower administration immediately sought to boost education with the National Defense Education Act, designed to expand and improve science education.

Americans seemed back in the race. Then in April 1961, the Soviets announced that they had succeeded in sending a man, Yuri Gagarin, into orbit. Again, American scientists scrambled. Less than a month later Navy Lieutenant Commander Alan Shepard was launched into a suborbital flight: a feat that did not measure up to Gagarin's orbital flight, but an answer to the Soviets nonetheless.

Three weeks later, America's space program changed its nature completely. President Kennedy, speaking to Congress, challenged the nation to win the space race, "to achiev[e] the goal before this decade is out of landing a man on the moon and returning him safely to earth." With that mandate, NASA (National Aeronautics and Space Administration) accelerated its programs. On February 20, 1962, Marine Corps Lieutenant Colonel John Glenn was launched into earth orbit. Four hours later, Glenn's spacecraft landed in the Atlantic after three orbits of the planet.

Americans were proud, but they were still behind. Just before Glenn's ride, the Soviets had sent Major Gherman Titov into space to orbit the earth eighteen times. Then just a year later, in August 1962, the Soviets launched two rockets into space at once. One orbited the earth forty-eight times, the other sixty-four times. It was an incredible feat. In May 1963, NASA sent Air Force Captain Gordon Cooper on an orbital flight that circled the earth twenty-two times.

Cooper's flight marked the end of the Mercury program. It was followed by Gemini, lasting two years and ten flights between 1965 and 1966. Gemini was marked by a general complacency by the American public toward the space program, while NASA worked out all the kinks and developed all the technology needed to send a spacecraft to the moon. Gemini was followed by the Apollo program that culminated in the July 1969 space flight of *Apollo 11* that put Neil Armstrong on the moon.

The Saturn V launched flawlessly from Cape Kennedy on July 16. Three days later, the command module *Columbia*, with its attached lunar module (the LM, or LeM), the *Eagle*, went into orbit around the moon. The next day, Armstrong and Edwin "Buzz" Aldrin guided the *Eagle* from *Columbia* and rode the small landing vehicle toward the moon's surface. Later that day, Armstrong maneuvered the lunar lander over the Sea of Tranquility on the dry lunar surface and set it down amidst a cloud of lunar dust. His report back to earth was, "Houston, Tranquility Base here. The *Eagle* has landed." Several hours later, as the world watched, Armstrong descended from the *Eagle* and made a short hop to the surface of the moon. His first words were, "One small step for man; one giant leap for mankind." (Armstrong later claimed he had actually said "One small step for a man; one giant leap for mankind," but that static garbled the transmission. The addition of the article *a* keeps the statement from being redundant.) Six hours later Aldrin joined Armstrong for a two-hour jaunt on the surface of the moon. Michael Collins, the voyage's third member, continued to orbit the moon in the *Columbia* spacecraft. The next morning, on July 21, the *Eagle* blasted off from the moon's surface and docked with the *Columbia*. Armstrong and Aldrin crawled into the *Columbia*, cast the *Eagle* adrift, and the three astronauts guided the *Columbia* back to earth. It was just twelve years after the launching of *Sputnik*.

The United States had not only achieved what Kennedy had hoped and promised, it had beaten the Soviets to the moon. It was a matter of extreme pride for the nation, an event that transcended politics, race, and social distinctions. While the nation seemed in turmoil, the moon was clearly a tranquil place.

Out of the 1960s and into the 1970s:
The Agony of Change

The end of the 1960s did not spawn a new era. As much as historians like to separate the twentieth century into decades, there is very little that is distinct about the next decade, the 1970s. There were few riots, no cultural or social revolution, no sexual revolution, no wars to divide the country and send the nation's youth into the streets. The 1970s was a time of calming, an interim period.

By the mid-1970s, the United States had lost the war in Vietnam, and this realization revealed that the nation had limits to its power and influence in the world. At the end of World War II, and for a couple decades after, Americans believed they were the strongest nation in the world and that they could work their will as they pleased and when they pleased. Americans also believed they were on the right side of history, that they were the leaders of the Free World against all that was evil. The war in Vietnam cast some doubt on that conviction. In addition, the Watergate scandal (coming at just about the same moment that the war in Vietnam was ending) convinced many Americans that their government was corrupt, or at least untrustworthy. Together, these two events dragged the nation down and caused many Americans to lose much of their pride, their patriotism, and even some of their hope for what the future might bring.

History has not treated Richard Nixon well. He is consistently placed at the bottom of any ranking of U.S. presidents, down in the cellar with Franklin Pierce and Rutherford B. Hayes, the presidents who achieved very little in office. Nixon is condemned for a different reason. He was the only president to resign from the office. In addition, he is harshly criticized for his prosecution of the war in Vietnam, a war he greatly expanded while promising to end it. Nixon did not, however, preside over a failed presidency. He had a number of foreign policy successes, and it could be argued that the world was a safer place in 1974 when he left office than when he came to Washington in 1969. And his domestic agenda, while certainly relegated to a secondary role behind foreign policy in his administration, was an Eisenhower-type middle-of-the-road program generally designed to be inclusive and to satisfy both liberals and conservatives.

NIXON IN THE WHITE HOUSE

Nixon's presidency suffered much the same as Johnson's. His agenda, both domestic and foreign, was mostly eaten up by the Vietnam War and his inability to extricate the nation from it. He wanted to return the United States to the calm of the Eisenhower years, when he was vice president, when the nation was generally strong, prosperous, and at peace—a time before Vietnam became a quagmire, before the antiwar protests, and before the conflicts and conflagrations of the 1960s dragged the nation into turmoil.

On the domestic front, Nixon hoped to build a consensus that would aid in his reelection in 1972. He signed several Great Society–type bills passed by the Democrats, including legislation that increased Social Security benefits (Ike had done the same), increased spending for subsidized housing, and increased food stamp funding. He also oversaw the creation of two programs that might be described as liberal, including the Environmental Protection Agency (EPA) and the Occupational Safety and Health Administration (OSHA). In addition, Nixon worked with the noted liberal Daniel Patrick Moynihan, then head of the Council on Urban Affairs, to draft the Family Assistance Plan, which proposed a guaranteed annual income of $1,600 in place of welfare benefits for poor families. That bill, however, died in Congress when liberals (who saw it as inadequate) joined forces with conservatives (who considered it excessive) to kill it.

At the same time, Nixon also believed (not unlike Eisenhower) that he could pull the conservative white South into a new Republican coalition. To that end, he pursued what has often been called his "southern strategy," an agenda designed to appeal to southern whites. That agenda, however, went beyond the states of the Old Confederacy. By the late 1960s and early 1970s it was no secret that northern conservatives, particularly northern suburbanites and ethnic groups in and around the North's major cities, maintained many of the same values as white southerners. Those groups were often associated with the white backlash and the presidential campaigns of George Wallace. Nixon also saw this white backlash rising in the Sunbelt, the most rapidly growing region of the country. To appeal to all these conservative groups, Nixon sought to constrain some aspects of the civil rights movement. In 1970 he tried to block congressional extension of the Voting Rights Act, forcing Congress to extend the act over his veto. He also delayed implementation of several court orders requiring the desegregation of public schools in the South. And he called for law and order, a phrase used often by Wallace and perceived by white conservatives as code for everything from keeping African Americans out of white communities to the aggressive prosecution of black criminals. Nixon also set out to appeal to these groups by claiming that the youth movements of the era were destroying America's values. "We live in a deeply troubled and profoundly unsettled time," he noted in a speech in the summer of 1969. "Drugs, crime, campus revolts, racial discord, draft resistance—on every hand we find old standards violated, old values discarded." And he promised to scale back the Great Society. "I say it is time to quit pouring billions of dollars into programs that have failed." Such statements endeared Nixon to the white middle class, who had grown tired of the turmoil of the 1960s and come to believe that their tax dollars were being wasted on what was being called the "undeserving poor." Nixon saw the future of American conservatism.

Perhaps the most divisive issue in the Nixon administration was the conflict over busing to achieve integration of the nation's schools. In the early 1970s, a series of court decisions found that de facto segregation of schools trampled the rights of minority students. As a remedy, the courts ordered the integration of school districts within individual cities, implementing busing if necessary to achieve racial integration and balance. The Nixon administration, however, worked to slow this process, arguing that students should attend neighborhood schools. In 1974, the Supreme Court ruled in *Milliken v. Bradley* that busing children across district lines was unconstitutional, limiting busing to achieve racial integration to individual metropolitan areas. This decision made suburbs attractive to those who wished to evade busing.

By most accounts, busing succeeded in integrating the nation's public schools. At no time before or since have more schools realized integrated student bodies and racial balance. But parents weighed that fact against long bus rides to substandard schools outside their neighborhoods, and they protested, complained, and voted. Through the 1980s busing was phased out as courts released districts from orders under old lawsuits. Busing was also a primary cause of white flight, which in turn left the nation's cities to largely poor African American populations. Along with that came a severely weakened urban tax base and the ultimate death of the nation's inner cities. But, in fact, whites left the cities (and were pulled out to the suburbs) for a multitude of reasons.

Nixon also took a hard line on crime and drug use. Many Americans saw crime and drugs as the two primary products of the turmoil of the 1960s, the nation's "liberal permissiveness," as Nixon described it. Congress responded by enacting a series of anticrime laws, which generally increased penalties for various federal crimes. Nixon also created the Office for Drug Abuse and Law Enforcement, mostly to combat heroin distribution and use. Although these initiatives failed to reduce crime or moderate drug use and abuse, Nixon reaped the political dividends. In the 1972 campaign he ran as the law-and-order candidate, the man who could point to problems being solved.

Nixon hoped to shape the Supreme Court during his presidency, and indeed he had the opportunity to name four judges to the high bench. In 1969 Chief Justice Earl Warren retired, and Nixon named Warren Burger to replace him. The Burger Court, however, proved to be anything but conservative. Usually regarded as independent and unpredictable, the Burger Court upheld busing, struck down the death penalty, and overturned several laws and practices that had led to gender-based discrimination in the workplace and the military.

Certainly the most controversial case decided by the Burger Court was *Roe v. Wade*, the 1973 decision in which the justices struck down state and federal laws restricting abortion. It was the most far-reaching case handed down by the court since the *Brown* decision just nine years earlier, and probably the most divisive court decision of the twentieth century. The court ruled that anti-abortion laws violated a woman's constitutional right to privacy under the Due Process Clause of the Fourteenth Amendment. The decision, written by another Nixon appointee, Justice Harry Blackmun, allowed women the absolute right to an abortion in the first trimester of pregnancy based on a medical consensus that a fetus is not considered "viable" during those weeks. In the second trimester, when viability is deemed uncertain, states could regulate (but not outlaw) abortions. Only in the third trimester could states pass laws outlawing the practice.

The decision prompted an immediate outcry from Catholics, but it was the Protestant religious Right that organized their forces and erupted into violent protests—insisting that abortion constituted murder of young children. Quickly, the *Roe* decision went from a volatile social issue to the political stage, and the religious Right placed it at the very foundations of their fight for traditional American values. The issue, perhaps more than any other, pulled the religious Right off the sidelines of politics and into the forefront of the national electoral process. For over forty years, a stand on abortion would be the litmus test for politicians seeking office from both the Left and the Right, with politicians from the Left supporting *Roe*, and those from the Right in opposition. Through that time, however, polls showed that Americans generally supported the right of a woman to have an abortion.

NIXON LOOKS AT THE WORLD

Presidents in the postwar era generally held foreign policy above domestic policy. Johnson was an exception to that rule. Nixon was not. He came to the presidency confident that he could allay world tensions, end the war in Vietnam, bring about better relations with the Soviets, and even open a dialogue with China.

At Nixon's side was his national security advisor, Henry Kissinger, the primary foreign policy voice throughout the Nixon administration. Nixon's secretary of state, William Rogers, was little more than a figurehead, and was generally excluded from the policy-making loop. Nixon believed that only the president could make foreign policy, and he had little use for foreign policy advisors beyond Kissinger. Kissinger was a noted Harvard professor who had worked in and out of government for at least twenty years. His 1957 book *Nuclear Weapons and Foreign Policy* argued for sustained strength against Soviet aggressions and the use of tactical nuclear weapons on the battlefield. Kissinger was a realist who sought to broker a stable and orderly balance of power in the world. He rejected the moralistic approach to U.S. foreign policy, the postwar view that a moral America would finally win over the world and end the Cold War. He hoped instead to negotiate a manageable relationship between the United States, the Soviet Union, and China.

Nixon generally shared this approach. His anti-communism had moderated through the 1960s and he had come to see a need for a working relationship with the Soviets. In July 1969, Nixon announced the Nixon Doctrine, a simple statement that was mostly a revocation of the Truman Doctrine. No longer would the United States assume responsibility for the defense of the world—against communism or any other order. Instead, he said, nations must accept responsibility for their own defense. The objective for the future would be America's carefully defined strategic interests, not its moralistic objectives.

When Nixon came to office there were 545,000 U.S. soldiers in Vietnam, and over 31,000 had already died there. He wanted to end the war quickly, at least in part because he saw what it had done to Johnson and the Democrats at a time when their policies were generally popular. In January 1969, just after he took office, Nixon told an aide: "I'm not going to end up like LBJ. . . . I'm going to stop that war. Fast." But Nixon, like Johnson and Kennedy, remained tied to the old Cold War foreign policy precepts that demanded standing firm against Communist aggressions. In the final analysis, his strategies prolonged the war and failed to save South Vietnam. He also provoked a violent domestic opposition and unleashed a harsh backlash against the "unpatriotic" advocates of withdrawal. This led to an angry division in the country that took decades to heal and poisoned his administration, leading to many of the excesses that finally destroyed his presidency.

Nixon had said in the 1968 campaign that he had a plan to win the war. His only strategy, however, was a faint hope that the Soviets would respond to his overtures and pressure Hanoi to the peace table. When that did not happen, Nixon tried to force the enemy to negotiate by expanding the war. In March 1969 he widened the war by attacking neutral Cambodia, where Viet Cong troops maintained sanctuaries. The bombings there simply sent the Viet Cong deeper into Cambodia with few results. Over fourteen months, nearly 2,750,000 tons of bombs were dropped on Cambodia, more than the total tonnage dropped by the Allies in all of World War II. A year later, a pro-American government led by Lon Nol staged a successful coup in Cambodia. Nixon sent in U.S. and ARVN troops to bolster Lon Nol, but the invasion did little more than add to the destabilization of Cambodia, which in turn pushed that nation into a holocaust in the mid- to late 1970s.

At home, Nixon hoped to calm tensions and undermine the antiwar movement by replacing the military draft with a lottery system, a plan intended to make the draft more equitable. Nineteen-year-olds whose birthdays were drawn (in the order of each day of the year) were eligible for the draft. Student deferments, however, remained in place for nearly everyone who stayed in college, and medical exemptions continued to be easy to get for white middle-class draft dodgers. The result was that the army in Vietnam remained disproportionately black, and from the poorest sectors of society. The lottery, somehow, seemed fairer, at least to those whose names were not drawn. No one whose number was higher than 195 (out of 365) was ever called.

The Nixon Doctrine in Vietnam manifested itself in Vietnamization, Nixon's plan to beef up ARVN with money and weapons until they could take over the brunt of the fighting from the American forces. The plan was to increase ARVN from 850,000 troops to over one million, and then begin withdrawing U.S. troops. Nixon ordered the immediate withdrawal of 25,000 U.S. soldiers and a phased withdrawal of another 140,000 troops over the next year. While this was under way, Nixon was further expanding the war into Cambodia, and even into parts of Laos. The entire plan was intended to bring what he called "peace with honor," the hope that the United States could pull out and leave South Vietnam intact and strong enough to repel the enemy.

In late 1969 the story of the My Lai massacre broke in the press, an event that would force much of the nation to confront the horrors of the war. In March 1968, a platoon of American soldiers led by Lieutenant William Calley slaughtered hundreds of Vietnamese civilians, primarily old men, women, and children, near the South Vietnamese town of My Lai. The crime seemed to show that the war had dehumanized the American soldier, while demonstrating just how far the United States had strayed from its ideals. Calley was convicted of murder and sentenced to life in prison, but Nixon had him released and confined to his quarters at Fort Benning, Georgia. In a final review of the case, Calley was sentenced to serve three and a half years under house arrest. In 1974 Nixon pardoned Calley.

The American people did not learn of Nixon's incursion into Cambodia until April 1970, a year after the bombings began—and then only after the *New York Times* broke the story. Nixon spoke to the American people in a televised address to explain the situation and the actions he had taken. His argument boiled down to the credibility of the American commitment. "When the chips are down," he told the nation in his most important war speech, "and the world's most powerful nation acts like a pitiful helpless giant, the forces of totalitarianism and anarchy will threaten free nations and free institutions throughout the world." And then he added, "I would rather be a one-term president and do what I believed was right than to be a two-term president at the cost of seeing America become a second-rate power."

For almost two years, the antiwar movement had been fairly quiet, but almost immediately riots broke out at several campuses, and then expanded over the next few weeks. At the most violent protest, at Kent State University in Ohio, four students were shot and killed by Ohio National Guardsmen; nine others were wounded. Across the nation, around thirty campus ROTC buildings were burned or bombed. Within weeks of Nixon's announcement, two million students at nearly 450 campuses were on strike, refusing to attend classes in protest.

President Nixon's revelation in 1970 of the U.S. invasion of Cambodia (and thus a significant widening of the war in Vietnam) caused students to protest on many college campuses. At Kent State University in Ohio, National Guard troops fired into a crowd of protesters, killing four. *Source*: Bettmann/CORBIS

By the end of 1970, U.S. troop strength had dropped to about 280,000. A year later the numbers had been drawn down to 140,000, with only half of those serving in combat.

It was evident that Nixon's plans to end the war had failed miserably. In fact, by invading Cambodia he had widened the war, Vietnamization had not worked, and by withdrawing U.S. forces he had diminished the American position at the peace talks with Hanoi. In late 1970 a National Security Council study concluded that the United States would be unable to push the Communists out of the South.

Although Nixon would continue to prosecute the war for three more agonizing years, by the end of 1970 America's involvement was essentially over. Nixon's plans for "peace with honor" had given a ray of hope to many Americans who wanted to believe that the United States could withdraw its troops and leave South Vietnam intact, a sort of "Koreanization" of the region. But by the end of 1970 even that hope was gone.

Following the 1970 student riots, the antiwar movement moderated. It is occasionally argued that an administration-ordered FBI surveillance and crackdown on the primary antiwar agitators contributed to the calming of the movement, but the movement was never well organized or leader-driven, and the primary agitators themselves were never very strong. Other causes, however, are more creditable. By 1970 the movement had splintered badly between the moderates and the radicals. In addition, the Vietnamization process had kept American soldiers generally out of harm's way, significantly reducing the number of soldiers killed in action. And Nixon's lottery draft may have mollified those who had joined the movement out of anger at the possibility of being drafted. Then, in 1972, Congress ended the draft.

In fact, the most significant phenomenon between 1970 and the end of the war was a strong backlash that developed in opposition to the antiwar protests, and more broadly, to the excesses of the entire 1960s decade. Public opinion polls showed that most Americans were more concerned with the urban riots and campus unrest than the war itself. A *Newsweek* poll determined that 58 percent of respondents blamed the students for the killings at Kent State, and 50 percent supported the invasion of Cambodia. These numbers might reflect Nixon's "silent majority" (conservatives who kept their conservatism to themselves), or they might simply show that middle America had finally grown tired of all the turmoil, rights movements, and cultural overindulgence that had marked the prior decade. Certainly, by the early 1970s all the fascination and curiosity toward the hippie culture had turned into outright hostility. And few Americans were sympathetic to the draft dodgers, who were clearly unpatriotic and selfish, while scores of young men had given their lives in the war—right or wrong.

Perhaps the most visible counterforce to the antiwar movement was the New York City Hardhat Riot on May 8, 1970, just four days after the Kent State shootings. About a thousand antiwar protesters were confronted and then attacked in New York's financial district by two hundred construction workers on lunch break from the World Trade Center construction site. As local police stood by, the construction workers pummeled the antiwar protesters, looted nearby Pace University, and then headed back to work after their lunch hour ended. A week later, the leader of the local union presented Nixon with an honorary hardhat at the White House, and later in the month over one hundred thousand construction workers marched in a traditional New York City tickertape parade in support of the war and the Nixon administration. The events received extensive press coverage and were depicted as the origins of a coordinated counterforce to the antiwar movement, and the beginnings of a shift by organized labor from the Democrats to the Republicans.

The war, however, was winding down on a number of fronts. Just before leaving office in 1968, Defense Secretary McNamara asked his aides to assemble a history of the war from Pentagon documents. The result was a mass of seven thousand pages of documents chronicling the decisions to enter, conduct, and escalate the war in Vietnam between 1945 and 1971. One of McNamara's aides, Daniel Ellsberg, leaked the papers to the *New York Times*, where selected documents were immediately published. The "Pentagon Papers" revealed a pattern of secrecy and dishonesty at the highest levels of government, designed to deceive the American public from the earliest days of the war. The papers revealed, among other things, that the government had deliberately expanded the war by conducting secret air strikes over Laos, raids along the coast of North Vietnam, and offensive ground and air campaigns well before the American public was told of the actions—and while President Johnson was promising not to further expand the war. The Pentagon Papers damaged the government's credibility and fed a growing suspicion of the federal government.

In the spring of 1972 the North Vietnamese army unexpectedly pushed hard into the northern provinces of South Vietnam, while Viet Cong troops invaded east from Cambodia. The two-pronged attack, known as the Easter Offensive, nearly split South Vietnam in half, while revealing the weakness of ARVN. When American generals warned of imminent defeat, Nixon responded by ordering a major air campaign, Operation Linebacker, and by mining North Vietnam's harbors. Just as the 1972 election approached, Kissinger announced that "peace is at hand." Just after the election, however, Nixon ordered a systematic bombing of North Vietnam, usually identified as the Christmas Bombings of 1972. It was the heaviest bombardment in history. American B-52s pounded targets in North Vietnam around the clock.

But the time had come to end the agony. Troop morale was low, Congress was no longer prepared to fund the effort, and polls showed that the nation did not support the war or Nixon's prosecution of it. Running out of options, the administration signed an agreement in Paris in January 1973 that allowed for the removal of all American troops. Kissinger often spoke of a "decent interval," a reference to the time following the agreement that would allow ARVN to build its strength to fend off a Communist attack without U.S. support. But to most Americans, Kissinger's "decent interval" came to mean the time between the U.S. withdrawal and the imminent collapse of South Vietnam. The Saigon government, headed by Nguyen Van Thieu, kept up the fight, but it was clear that time was running out.

THE LEGACY OF VIETNAM

The Vietnam War was more destructive to America than any event in the post–World War II era. Nearly sixty thousand Americans lost their lives; another three hundred thousand were wounded. An estimated two million Vietnamese died. The cost approached $170 billion, more than any other war in American history up to that time except World War II. And the excessive spending fueled a crushing inflation that would take years to contain.

In response to the events, Congress moved to curtail the president's power to make war, and in several instances over the next decades it balked at giving the president the carte blanche type of power it had given President Johnson in the Tonkin Gulf Resolution in 1964. In 1973 Congress passed the War Powers Act, a law severely restricting the president's ability to go to war without the express consent of Congress. The law allowed the president to send troops into combat for up to sixty days, but beyond that time limit any action required express congressional consent. The bill was intended to return to Congress its constitutional right to make war.

For at least a decade after the war ended, the United States seemed to lack its former confidence. The realization that there were, in fact, limits to U.S.

power caused Americans, for the first time, to question the validity of their Cold War mission of containing communism. The new attitude was described as "neo-isolationism," the general fear that there was little to be gained (and much to lose) by asserting power abroad. Every potential military endeavor, it seemed, begged the question, "Is this another Vietnam?" And the word "quagmire" entered the vernacular to describe a Vietnam-like situation that was all engulfing and seemingly endless.

Perhaps most importantly, the war divided the nation, and in many ways those divisions persist. The war bred cynicism, anxiety, and distrust—of the government, of the military, and of those who disagreed about the prosecution of the war. It would be some time before Americans would feel good about themselves, before they found themselves again on the right side of history.

There were many lessons to be learned from Vietnam. On the domestic front, it was clear that the American people had no stomach for a long, drawn-out conflict with no real objective and no clear plan for victory or withdrawal. The war also showed that American power, as great as it was, had limits, and that the United States did not always have the ability to enforce its vision of a world order.

The Vietnam soldier has been unfairly criticized. At first spurned by the nation as a pawn of the government in an immoral war, a victim of events in a losing cause, he (and she) was later represented by Hollywood as a crazed lunatic, either bitter or psychotic—but usually both. The titles could run on forever: *Coming Home* (1978), *The Deer Hunter* (1978), *First Blood* (1982), *Born on the Fourth of July* (1989), *Apocalypse Now* (1979), *Casualties of War* (1989), *Forrest Gump* (1994). Certainly, life after the war was difficult for many Vietnam War veterans. But the vast majority did their duty to their country and returned home to productive lives with no remorse, bitterness, or psychosis.

DÉTENTE

Nixon's focus on foreign policy led him to a new relationship with the Soviets that relaxed tensions and launched a new era in the U.S.-Soviet relations known as détente. Both Nixon and Kissinger realized that the world's balance had changed, that the old two-power conflict between Washington and Moscow was being replaced by a power structure that included Western Europe, China, and even Japan. In addition, Nixon and Kissinger pursued détente in hopes that improved relations with the Soviets might push Moscow to convince the North Vietnamese government to bring an end to the war. That never materialized, but détente led to a change in direction which avoided a nuclear arms race that threatened to grow into nuclear war—still an all-consuming fear in the late 1960s and early 1970s.

In 1969 Nixon signed a nonproliferation treaty with the Soviets, and then began negotiations on a strategic arms limitation treaty (SALT). In 1971, he signed an agreement to sell $136 million of wheat and a significant amount of equipment to the Soviets. That same year, the United States agreed to recognize East Germany as a legitimate state. In May 1972, Nixon went to Moscow and signed three important agreements. The first limited both nations' antiballistic missile sites and the number of ABM missiles. The second, SALT I, froze the number of strategic missiles for five years. And last, the "Basic Principles of U.S.-Soviet Relations" was an agreement that both sides would accept parity as the foundation for future arms control negotiations. None of the agreements limited the development of MIRVs (multiple independently targeted reentry vehicles), a multiple warhead system under development by both countries, but the agreements provided a degree of stability welcomed by both sides.

All of this went a long way toward stabilizing the arms race, while reducing the risk of nuclear war. Détente eased tensions.

NIXON AND CHINA

History may not have treated Nixon well. But he will always be credited with "opening" China, one of the greatest diplomatic coups of the postwar era.

When the Chinese Civil War ended in 1949, the Nationalist forces of Jiang Jieshi, defeated by Mao Zedong and the Chinese Communists, escaped the mainland to the offshore island of Formosa (Taiwan). On October 1, 1949, Mao proclaimed victory over the Nationalists and established the People's Republic of China with its capital at Beijing. The Truman administration refused to recognize Mao and his Communist government, instead recognizing Jiang and his government on Formosa as the only legitimate government of all the Chinese people. That decision was based, at least in part, on the hope (even the assumption) that Jiang would one day invade the mainland, drive out the Communists, and establish an anti-Communist government in Beijing. But by 1972 the situation had not changed: the Nationalists were on Taiwan; the Communists were in Beijing; and the United States, because of its long-term relations with the Nationalists, was cut out of the largest potential market in the world.

Nixon hoped to change all that. He also expected to alter the basic dynamic of the Cold War by allying the United States with China against the Soviet Union, or at least threatening such an alliance. Beijing and Moscow once had been strong Communist allies, but by the late 1960s that relationship had soured over ideological differences, and by the early 1970s the two were engaged in a series of intramural border skirmishes along the Ussuri River in eastern Siberia. Nixon intended to capitalize on that hostility.

The first break came in April 1971 when a U.S. ping-pong team on tour in

Japan was invited to visit China. The event may seem insignificant, but the doors had opened. Within two months, Kissinger was in Beijing laying the groundwork for Nixon's trip. The president arrived in the Chinese capital in February 1972 for a one-week visit. Nixon, the man who had made his name as a Communist hunter, was conferring with Mao, the Communist dictator and theoretician. The most significant diplomatic result of the event was the Shanghai Communiqué, mostly an agreement to disagree on most issues, although both nations resolved to work toward the normalization of relations. To that end, the United States conceded that Taiwan was not an independent nation, but, in fact, a province of China. Trade agreements and other contacts followed. The United States, however, did not establish a full diplomatic relationship with Beijing until 1979.

WATERGATE AND THE RESIGNATION OF A PRESIDENT

The Democrats headed into the 1972 campaign deeply divided and with no real frontrunner. Hubert Humphrey was making his second run, but Senator Edmund Muskie of Maine, Humphrey's vice presidential candidate in 1968, showed promise in the first months of the campaign. But the momentum was on the side of South Dakota Senator George McGovern, the darling of the New Left because of his call for an immediate end to the war. Other contenders included George Wallace, who had returned to the Democratic Party from his earlier run as an Independent, and Ted Kennedy, the last of the Kennedy brothers. Kennedy, however, could not overcome the infamous 1969 Chappaquiddick incident in which a young woman was killed in a car he was driving. George Wallace was shot during the campaign and severely injured by a would-be assassin and withdrew from the race.

In the New Hampshire primary, Muskie pulled a significant upset victory, but a letter planted in the New Hampshire Manchester *Union Leader* by some of Nixon's aides who specialized in dirty political tricks claimed that Muskie disliked the French Canadians in northern New Hampshire and that his wife was an alcoholic. Muskie's response during a press conference was meek and tearful, and the incident seemed to characterize him as weak and whining in the face of an attack on his wife. At a time when image carried the day, the incident destroyed his campaign.

That left Humphrey and McGovern in the fight for the Democratic nomination. Humphrey still suffered from his association with the Johnson administration and the failed war strategy, which he had continued to support through most of the 1968 campaign. McGovern seemed new and attractive, and he collected the party's antiwar wing, which was gaining strength as the situation in Vietnam both expanded and deteriorated. The party's convention in Miami was dominated by the Left, and McGovern took an easy victory.

But McGovern had no real chance to beat Nixon. A minority wing of the Democratic Party had rallied their forces to defeat the divided majority, in much the way that Goldwater had taken the Republican nomination in 1964 from the Republican moderates.

And Nixon was formidable. He had achieved détente with the Soviets, opened China, and wound down the war in Vietnam while bringing home most of the troops. In addition, the economy was strong and the antiwar activism and the urban riots had calmed. Nixon's appeal was to middle-class voters who had grown tired of all that was the 1960s: the hippies, the antiwar movement, the urban violence, busing, sexual permissiveness, welfare cheats, and drug users. Nixon said he stood foursquare against the liberalism, radicalism, and self-indulgence of the era's youth culture, and in favor of the middle-class values that the vast majority of Americans revered.

Despite his mammoth lead in the polls and his almost sure victory in November, Nixon maintained an obsessive paranoia, which often consumed him. Several of his special assistants concluded that the national interest required that Nixon win the election, and that just about any action justified that end. In June, several members of Nixon's Committee to Re-Elect the President organized a burglary of Democratic Party headquarters at the Watergate building in Washington. The plan was to install audio bugs in the office and to photograph sensitive campaign documents. The raids were led by G. Gordon Liddy, a White House official. Others involved included James McCord, a member of the Committee to Re-Elect the President; E. Howard Hunt, an ex-CIA operative; and several anti-Castro Cubans recruited for the job. Their initial objective was to find who, among Nixon's inner circle, was leaking information to the press; thus, as searchers for leaks, they were called "the plumbers." During the second burglary, the group was caught. Evidence at the scene connected the plumbers to Liddy and the Committee to Re-Elect.

The *Washington Post* broke the story and continued to investigate the events. The plumbers all pleaded guilty, but the judge in the case, John Sirica, continued to believe that the incident went deeper than the few men who were nabbed at the scene. Then in March 1973, McCord, in a letter to Sirica, charged that approval for the burglaries had come directly from the White House, and that the burglars had been coerced into silence with offers of hush money. McCord's letter prompted the Senate to set up a special Watergate committee to investigate further.

The case began to break open when John Dean, special counsel to the president, concluded that he was being marked as the administration's fall guy and agreed to turn over his version of the story to federal prosecutors. At about the same time, Jeb Magruder, the deputy chairman at the Committee to Re-elect, told the Watergate committee that orders for the break-ins had come directly from Attorney General John Mitchell.

In April 1973, Nixon went before the nation and explained that in dealing

with the nation's business he had failed to monitor properly his reelection campaign. He spoke of "overzealous subordinates," and announced the resignation of
two of his closest advisors, H. R. Haldeman and John Erlichman. He then
named a special prosecutor, Harvard Law Professor Archibald Cox, and promised him "complete independence" to investigate the incident.

The testimonies of Dean and Magruder before the Senate Watergate
Committee linked Nixon to the cover-up from the beginning, but Nixon continued to insist that there had been no cover-up. Then, on July 16, 1973, ex-
presidential aide Alexander Butterfield testified that recording equipment had
been installed in the Oval Office. Special Prosecutor Cox requested segments
of the tapes, but Nixon, citing executive privilege, refused to release the tapes.
When Cox protested, Nixon fired Cox. Two top officials in the Justice Department resigned in protest. Finally, in April 1974, Nixon agreed to hand over
transcripts of the tapes; then, under further pressure, he released edited segments of the tapes. Those tapes released, however, contained sizable gaps, era-
sures, and obvious omissions. In response, the new special prosecutor, Leon
Jaworski, indicted forty-one people in the case and named the president as an
"un-indicted co-conspirator."

In the House of Representatives, twenty-four Democrats and fourteen
Republicans worked together on articles of impeachment. On July 24, the
Supreme Court ordered the White House to turn over sixty-four tapes dealing
with the events of the summer of 1972. On that same day, the House Judiciary
Committee began a televised debate on impeachment. On August 5 Nixon
released the tapes. The tape of a conversation on June 23, 1972 (Nixon's first day
back in the White House after the Watergate break-ins), showed that Nixon had
been involved in the cover-up from nearly the beginning.

Republicans on the House Judiciary Committee switched their votes in
favor of impeachment. Several leading Republican senators, including Barry
Goldwater, approached Nixon and encouraged him to resign, insisting that he
would be removed from office if the impeachment proceedings were allowed to
play out. On August 9, 1974, President Richard Nixon became the first president
to resign from office. A month later, on September 8, President Gerald R. Ford
decided it would be in the best interest of the nation to end the agony of Watergate, and he pardoned Nixon.

Watergate was the most serious political scandal in American history. Government power had been used to subvert the political process, and then to initiate
a cover-up at the highest levels. For most Americans, the events were a reflection
of the nation's social and political environment, a consequence of the "imperial
presidency"—the tradition of presidential supremacy that had developed since
the end of World War II. It was also a result of an abuse of power that was rooted
in a Cold War mentality which justified any activity to overcome an enemy.

The long, drawn-out agony of Watergate (coming just as the United States
pulled out of Vietnam) dragged the nation into a deep national depression. For

the first time in the nation's history its military power came under question, and its government in Washington was under suspicion.

CONCLUSION

In the early 1960s Americans believed they had pinpointed their problems: poverty and racism. Promises were made to solve those problems, finally to do those things that the nation had wanted to do since the end of World War II, to see that the new abundance was shared by all. The vehicle of action would be Washington. Kennedy talked of promises to keep, of the equality of mankind, of ending poverty in our lifetime, and even of going to the moon. America, it seemed, could do anything it wanted. President Johnson made even loftier promises. The United States would end poverty, provide medical programs, build thousands of new low-income housing units, end racism, save the environment, save the inner city, improve education, save the world. Americans were ready, and in the 1964 election they gave Johnson the mandate to do it all. America had the will, it had the money, it had the ideas, and it had the leadership to do what it had wanted to do since 1945, to do what it had promised to do.

By 1970, however, it was all in shambles. The war in Vietnam had taken its toll on the decade. Johnson's Great Society was underfunded and largely unsuccessful. The cities were on fire, adding significantly to a growing backlash that threatened to turn back a number of reforms. Poverty was alive and well, and even getting worse. The grand promises had not been kept, and the nation sank into disenchantment, even despair. By 1972 America was defeated on the battlefield, suspicious of its government, discouraged, mad, and spent. The opportunity had passed.

Between 1968 and the early years of the next decade, what was left of the 1960s died a slow death. The hippie counterculture outgrew itself, lost its vitality, evolved into fad and fashion, and expired in a mass of bad drugs and psychedelic colors. Middle-class America wielded its powerful backlash against the decade and condemned the hippies' creed for having no intrinsic moral content. The hippies, of course, ignored the critics, but the critics were right.

The civil rights movement had reached its goals of ending legal segregation in the South, but it lost its leadership and changed its direction. For many white middle-class Americans the civil rights movement was moving too fast, demanding too much. The same backlash that attacked the other aspects of rapid social change in the decade hit hard at civil rights. By the mid-1970s the nation was beginning to make a right turn, away from all that the 1960s had been or intended to be.

Reading: A Golden Age: Sports from the Mid-1960s to the Mid-1970s

America has enjoyed some spectacular sports eras. One of those was the decade between the mid-1960s and the early to mid-1970s. The reason was television. Television had broadcast sports events before, certainly baseball, boxing, and even professional wrestling. But by the mid-1960s TV was able to capture more of the games, bring in other sports from the sidelines, and turn the big game into a spectacular event that everyone had to watch. Every game of the World Series was on TV. Pro football became a Sunday afternoon staple that included cookouts and family events. And the Olympics were live, all day for two weeks, every four years.

In 1960 Roone Arlidge became head of the sports division at ABC, and took sports to a new level—at least on Saturday and Sunday afternoons. He created *Wide World of Sports*, a weekend sports spectacular that covered all sorts of sporting events from skiing to gymnastics. Those who watched will recall the opening sequence, in which a hapless ski jumper is shown flying off the edge of a ski jump at spectacular speed, followed by the voice-over "the thrill of victory and the agony of defeat." Arlidge signed the first big contracts with college football, and in 1970 he created *Monday Night Football*, which took sports into prime time and made ABC the number one sports network.

The sport with the greatest growth in popularity was professional football. The NFL (National Football League) had existed since 1920 as little more than an outlet for a few college players to continue their careers. Even though college games continued to be an important part of the sports world, NFL games were rarely carried on early television. But in the late 1960s, NFL games began their regular stint on weekend TV, and the popularity of the sport exploded. In 1960 the growing popularity of pro football spawned the American Football League. The AFL players quickly gained the reputation of being less skilled than NFL players, and were often accused of trying to gain attention by wearing brightly colored uniforms to mask their lack of abilities on the field. In 1966 the two leagues agreed to merge, and they began playing an end-of-season championship game known then as the "World Championship of Professional Football." Still, the AFL was not considered much of a challenge for the NFL. But all that changed on January 12, 1969, when the AFL champs New York Jets, led by quarterback Joe Namath, beat the NFL champions Baltimore Colts, quarterbacked by the venerable Johnny Unitas, in the third annual championship game. The game was so spectacular it was called the "Super Bowl." Today it is considered, retroactively, "Super Bowl III." Never again would that sport be the same.

Baseball remained the nation's pastime, more a day at the park for most people than a sporting event. The game was always accused of being too slow, and in the 1960s football began to draw more viewers per game, both on TV and at the stadiums, than baseball. But even then, baseball set attendance records in the 1960s and 1970s as the nation watched the greats of the era, from Mickey

Mantle and Roger Maris (perceived as the true successors to Babe Ruth and Lou Gehrig) to Frank and Brooks Robinson and Bob Gibson. In an attempt to speed up the game to make it more exciting (and try to compete with football) the league lowered the height of the pitching mound to give the batter more of an advantage and made pitchers ride golf carts from the bullpens to speed up the agonizingly slow process of changing pitchers. A testament to the success of baseball in the era was its franchise expansions to Minneapolis, Atlanta, Houston, and Kansas City.

In 1969, the fall of the same year that Namath and the Jets beat Unitas and the Colts in January, the once-hapless New York Mets surprised the nation by winning the National League pennant and then going on to beat the powerhouse Baltimore Orioles in the World Series. The Mets had never had a winning season, and odds in Las Vegas gave them only a one-in-a-hundred chance of beating the Orioles. It was a good year for New York and a bad one for Baltimore.

Television did for professional basketball much of what it did for professional football. The NBA (National Basketball Association) had come into existence just after the war, and like football it existed mostly as an outlet for a few college players who wanted to continue their careers. In 1968 the American Basketball Association was formed and the sport expanded rapidly. By the late 1960s some marquis pro players boosted the sport's popularity. In Boston, the Celtics assembled one of the greatest teams, dominating the NBA through the 1960s. Wilt Chamberlain, undoubtedly one of the best players to ever play the game, controlled the boards for the Philadelphia 76ers (and later the Los Angeles Lakers) between 1965 and 1973. In 1976 the NBA absorbed four ABA teams and the leagues merged.

UCLA established a college basketball dynasty from the early 1960s to the mid-1970s that has never been equaled. Under coach John Wooden, the Bruins won seven consecutive national titles between 1967 and 1973. This was also one of the great eras in college football. In 1971, number one Nebraska met number two Oklahoma in what is still called The Game of the Century. Nebraska won the nail-biter 35–31, following a dramatic fourth-quarter drive. They went on to play undefeated Alabama in the Orange Bowl, a much-hyped game that turned out to be an anticlimax. Nebraska won easily, 38–6.

Golf had never been much of a spectator sport. Most aficionados had probably heard of Bobby Jones from the 1920s, or Ben Hogan from the early 1950s, or one or two others. But television brought golf into the nation's living rooms in the 1960s and 1970s and introduced the nation to the phenoms of the time, Jack Nicholas (the Golden Bear) and Arnold Palmer. Palmer was the first golfer to win $100,000 in a season; Nicholas was the first to win $200,000 (1971) and then $300,000 (1972). As a result of their play and television's coverage of the events, golf became a popular sport among the nation's suburbanites. Golf had once been a rich man's game, but by the mid-1960s golf courses were springing up in small towns and inside residential subdivisions all over the country. The golf green replaced the boardroom as the place where businessmen made their deals. Even women got into the game. For most who played golf, it was more about meeting friends at "the club" and enjoying a day outside than working on their handicap. In 1970 Alan Shepard used a six-iron to hit a golf ball off the surface of the moon.

In 1973, *Secretariat* won the Triple Crown of racing and entered history as one of the greatest racehorses of all time. At the Kentucky Derby he set the second-fastest time ever recorded at Churchill Downs, actually increasing his speed throughout the race. At the Preakness, he began the race in last place, and then pulled up on the outside to blow away the field. At Belmont, the "third jewel of the Triple Crown," he simply exploded, winning by an amazing thirty-one lengths and setting a world record for that distance that still stands.

The Olympics had been a source of rivalry between the United States and the USSR since the end of the war, a sort of metaphor for the Cold War itself. The United States, however, seldom did well against the Soviets. The excuse was always that Soviet athletes were allowed to train as "soldiers" at government expense, while American athletes were mostly on their own. But that began to change in the mid-1960s, at least in the summer events. In the 1964 summer games, the United States lost in the overall medal count to the Soviets (96–90) but took home more gold (36–30). At the winter games (held in the same year at that time) the Americans were humiliated, winning only six medals—only one gold—to the Soviet's impressive 25-medal victory. Four years later, in the high altitude at Mexico City, the pendulum began to swing. The United States took 107 medals to the Soviets' 91, with a 45–29 lead in gold medals. In the winter games, the United States was again trounced, winning only seven medals (and only one gold) to the Soviet's thirteen (and five golds). Despite the U.S.-Soviet rivalry, Norway was the overall medal winner that year. In the 1972 summer games at Munich, which were marked by the massacre of eleven Israeli athletes by Palestinian terrorists, the Soviets took ninety-nine medals to the Americans' ninety-four. The race for gold, however, gave the Soviets the advantage with a margin of 50–33. In the winter games at Sapporo, Japan, the Soviets won sixteen medals (the East Germans were second with fourteen), and the United States took home eight. Announcers and athletes alike insisted that the medal count did not matter, that the Olympic games were about camaraderie and international and individual competition. Television covered the events live, and they always kept up with the medal count.

Television changed the nation in so many ways. It made the 1960s and 1970s one of the greatest eras of sports in the twentieth century.

·9·

America in the 1970s:
The Post-Watergate Years

Postwar American history lends itself to a division by decades. The 1960s is a decade that is distinct on several levels: certainly culturally and socially, but also politically and even economically. It is difficult to deny that the 1960s deserves study as a unit. It would seem logical, then, to study the 1950s as the decade leading up to the 1960s. And then the decade of the 1980s is often studied as a distinct period because of the political and economic changes of the Reagan-Bush years, an era of a new conservatism and a new way of viewing the world. Of course, these lines of demarcation are not always valid. The Vietnam War, for instance, began in the mid-1960s and ended in the early 1970s. And whatever sexual revolution there was in the 1960s certainly did not end with the close of the decade. Decadal history, particularly in the few postwar decades, is one way of looking at things. There are others.

Thus, the decade of the 1970s might well be described as having no real distinction except that it is caught between two distinct periods. Peter Carroll wrote about the decade in his *It Seemed Like Nothing Happened*; Bruce Schulman, however, called the decade *The Great Shift in American Culture, Society and Politics*.

The decade of the 1970s began with something of a hangover. The 1960s had been raucous, even world-changing. The assassinations, the urban riots, the antiwar demonstrations, and the assertions and demands for equality from just about every minority group in the nation made Americans tired. By the end of the 1970s the nation was moving sharply to the right, both politically and culturally. For some, the 1970s was a reaction to the decades past; for others, it was the natural progression of things, a surging conservatism in a nation of conservatives.

TAKING STOCK: A STATISTICAL ANALYSIS

In 1970 the U.S. population was at 205 million. The median household income was $8,734, and gas cost about $0.34 per gallon. The decade saw the baby boom finally come to an end. It had peaked just after the war, in 1947, at over twenty-six births per thousand. By 1975 that number had dropped to just eighteen births. The end of the boom created a new problem—and anyone could see it coming. If the national population did not perpetuate itself in some way (more babies, more immigration), eventually the United States would become a nation of old people. That became even more probable with medical advances that allowed Americans to live well beyond seventy. In fact, by mid-decade the fastest-growing sector of the population was over seventy-five, and several of the next fastest-growing sectors were even older than that. Although it would be another thirty to forty years before the boomers would begin to retire, it was already clear that the younger generations would have difficulty maintaining the Social Security system and Medicare after about 2010. The question was just beginning to be asked: Who will take care of all these people when they get old?

The family itself underwent a number of significant changes in the 1970s. Perhaps the most apparent was the decline of the traditional nuclear family, the TV-type family with two parents and two young children. By the end of the 1970s, only one in five households (in which there were two parents) had a full-time stay-at-home mother. The trend was for both parents to work outside the home. The primary reason was to make ends meet and to achieve more economic freedom—although the reason most often given was for the wife to maintain equality and independence within the marriage. In addition, the divorce rate shot up, doubling between the mid-1950s (when it stood at about 25 percent) and the mid-1970s, when it hit 50 percent. That number has been fairly consistent since then. One disturbing result of that trend was that single mothers headed up more than one-third of all households living below the poverty level and children made up 40 percent of the nation's poor.

The American dream has been defined in many ways, but one has been that children live better lives than their parents. That was not necessarily the case for the baby boomer generation, at least not in their formative years. One reason may have been the persistently weak economy through the 1970s, which made it difficult for the boomers to get off the ground. During the decade, the economy grew at a paltry 1.6 percent per year and unemployment rates were higher than they had been since the Depression years of the 1930s.

THE ACCESSION OF GERALD FORD

The Watergate scandal had nearly destroyed the presidency. To many Americans, the office had lost much of its prestige, even its authority. The people were looking for leadership, someone to pull them out of the political and economic mess engulfing the nation. When Gerald Ford ascended to the presidency on August 9, 1974, he spoke to the nation, beginning his address with "I am a Ford, not a Lincoln." Some Americans undoubtedly found Ford's words corny. Others, however, saw them as reassuring. President Ford would not shake up the nation. He would bring an end to the tumult.

It would have been difficult in 1974 to have found anyone more representative of middle America than Gerald R. Ford. He was from Michigan, the child of divorced parents. His athletic career was extraordinary, particularly when placed up against his pratfall image as president. He played football at the University of Michigan, helping the Wolverines to two undefeated seasons in 1932 and 1933. Following graduation, he turned down offers to play for the Detroit Lions and the Green Bay Packers to take a coaching job at Yale, where he eventually attended law school. His first dip into politics was as a campaign worker for Wendell Willkie, the 1940 Republican presidential candidate.

The next year he returned to his hometown of Grand Rapids to practice law. He served in the navy during the war, and then returned to Grand Rapids and, by most accounts, would have been content to live happily there. But in 1948 he went to Congress. That same year he married Betty, a divorcee, model, and dancer. They waited until just before Election Day to tie the knot because Gerald was afraid conservative Michigan voters would disapprove of his divorcee-dancer bride.

Ford spent twenty-four years in the House. He called himself an internationalist, a moderate on domestic affairs, and a conservative on fiscal policy—making him something of an Eisenhower Republican. In 1965 he became minority leader, and earned the enmity of President Johnson (and the respect of Republican conservatives) by attacking the excesses of the Great Society and the president's managing of the war in Vietnam.

When Nixon's vice president, Spiro Agnew, resigned, party leaders pushed Nixon to name Ford. When Nixon resigned on August 9, 1974, Gerald Ford became president of the United States. He was the first president in U.S. history to become president without being elected to either of the two top executive offices.

Ford was, above all, a decent man who genuinely wanted to heal the nation's post-Watergate wounds. But for a lot of Americans, his presidential pardon of Nixon "for all offenses against the United States which . . . he has committed or may have committed," as the pardon stated, was an awful mistake. Critics immediately assumed that Ford had struck a deal: the office in exchange for a pardon. But that seems unlikely. Ford hoped that the pardon would begin the healing process and allow the nation to put the horrors of Watergate in the past and move ahead. To Ford, a long, drawn-out trial and then, most likely, a prison term for an ex-president, would have damaged the presidency and the nation even more. Ford probably had no idea of the bad feelings his decision would cause. His approval ratings plummeted immediately from a respectable 72 percent to 49 percent, and the pardon (and the suspected "deal") hung over the remainder of his presidency like a dark cloud. It also damaged his chances in the 1976 election.

During his twenty-four years in Congress, Ford had sponsored no bills. He had, in fact, made a name for himself by opposing Democratic legislation. As president, he continued with that agenda. In just two years he vetoed thirty-nine bills passed by the Democratic Congress, including the Freedom of Information Act, designed to open government files. The act reflected the nation's mood that the government was a secret, closed entity and that it needed to be open to the public. By vetoing the bill, Ford added fuel to the fire that he had made a deal with Nixon, a deal that was being covered up in government documents. Congress promptly overrode his veto.

POLITICS, WAR, AND THE OIL SHOCK

The United States had always been a major player in the world economy. Since the nation's founding, global commerce has been its economic lifeline. But not until the 1970s did the United States find itself held hostage by a global commodity that it could not control. And that was, of course, oil. Much of America's problems with oil in the 1970s resulted from the volatile politics of the Middle East.

The United States remained Israel's primary patron, supplying Israel with economic and military aid to ensure the survival of the Jewish state. At the same time, the United States relied on oil from the Arab states, especially Saudi Arabia. This tightrope walk placed the United States in a very bad situation. In addition, the Soviets had begun to court the Arab states, particularly Egypt, as a counter to U.S. influence in the region.

In the 1967 Six-Day War, Israel won a stunning victory over its Arab neighbors, seizing several Arab lands, including the Golan Heights (from Syria), the Gaza Strip and Sinai Peninsula (from Egypt), and the Old City of Jerusalem and the West Bank (from Jordan). In 1973, backed by Soviet arms, Egypt and Syria again attacked Israel. The United States airlifted the weapons and materiel Israel needed to push the Egyptian tanks and troops back across the Sinai. This Yom Kippur War (named because it began on the Jewish holiday) was a second humiliating defeat for Egypt and, by association, the other Arab states. The war ended when the Soviets threatened to aid Egypt if the United States did not force the Israelis to stop their advance.

For the oil-producing Arab states, however, it was U.S. aid that had turned the tide of the war against Egypt. Just days after the war ended, the Arab members of OPEC (Organization of Petroleum Exporting Countries) cut oil production by 5 percent, then announced that they would continue cuts until Israel returned the Arab lands taken in the 1967 war. Three days later, just after President Nixon said the United States would continue its aid to Israel, OPEC announced that it would cut off all oil shipments to the United States. The impact was disastrous to the U.S. economy. Crude oil prices jumped from a low of about $1.80 per barrel (which had been unchanged from 1961 until 1970) to $11 per barrel.

The average American was not aware that the nation had become so dependent on foreign oil. And certainly Americans had no understanding of the potential impact that such dependence might have on the economy. In 1950 the United States imported only about 8 percent of its oil. By 1970 that had increased to 21 percent. But within five years U.S. imports had jumped to almost 36 percent, making the United States vulnerable to commodity controls, cutbacks, and embargos.

In the 1950s, the United States controlled the world oil market as the producer of over half the world's total. In fact, in 1951 the United States flooded the market to control the impact of the nationalization of Iranian oil under Iranian Prime Minister Mohammad Mosaddeq. Years later, the United States continued to control prices by pouring oil onto the market to counter price pressures caused by other events, particularly the 1956 Suez Crisis and the Arab-Israeli War of 1967. But America's commanding role in the oil market ended in 1971 when rising world demand exceeded the excess capacity of U.S. crude. At that point, control of the market shifted to the Middle East, where most oil-producing nations had nationalized their oil industries and combined their interests into the oil cartel OPEC. Following the Yom Kippur War, these nations took their economic power onto the political stage in an attempt to strangle the United States into ending its support for Israel.

The OPEC nations had other motives. They also argued that their oil resources were finite, and that one day they would again be without resources in a world of commerce. In fact, they produced little else. At the same time, in the inflationary period of the early 1970s, the prices of manufactured goods were rising rapidly. Beyond punishing the United States for supporting Israel, the Arab states also believed strongly that the price of oil should rise. And the Americans were paying considerably less for gasoline than most of the rest of the world, particularly the Europeans.

The oil embargo lasted from October 1973 to March 1974 and triggered a horrible period of inflation that in turn produced the worst recession since the 1930s. Prices at the pump soared from $0.40 to $0.55 a gallon. Such prices seem preposterous when compared to later gas prices, but at the time these prices reflected a much greater percentage of the median family income than gas prices in later decades. But certainly more important than the price increases were the gas shortages. In an attempt to combat the rise in oil prices, the federal government instituted price controls on "old oil" (oil already discovered), while allowing the price of "new oil" to rise with the market. The intention was to spur oil exploration, and the new (thus unregulated) oil would increase the supply on the world market that would, in turn, push prices down. Instead, the plan led producers to shut down "old oil" production to avoid price controls, which led to an artificial scarcity of oil. Long lines at the pump were common, caused often by a near panic to obtain what little gasoline remained before the local pumps went dry. In an attempt to combat *that* problem, the federal government implemented a system in which those with license plates ending in odd numbers could buy gas on odd days of the month and those with even numbers, on even days. Anyone with any personal financial means would often complain that it was not the price of gas that was the problem; it was the availability.

The embargo damaged more sectors of the economy than commuters and vacation-goers. Farmers and truckers were hurt badly, and the rise in energy costs drove up the cost of just about everything produced and manufactured in the nation. The growing inflation rates finally caused the stock market to decline drastically. In addition, the cost of the war in Vietnam was beginning to damage the economy by increasing the federal deficit, which in turn put further pressure on the inflation rate. All this caused prices to rise. Food prices jumped by 20 percent in 1973 alone. The inflation rate after 1973 was between 5 and 10 percent per year. By 1979 the consumer price index had risen 13.4 percent.

By the time Gerald Ford took office in August 1974 the inflation rate had jumped to double digits—to 11 percent—and gas prices had doubled over the previous year. Of all the issues that needed attention, the economy was upper-

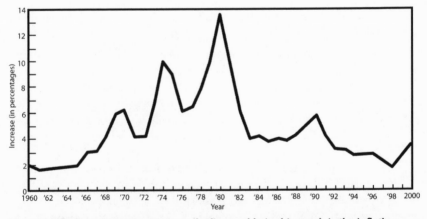

The U.S. inflation rate, 1960–2000. Easily discernable in this graph is the inflation brought on by the Vietnam War in the late 1960s, followed by the oil crisis of the early to mid-1970s, and then the debilitating inflation spike in 1980. The return to normal levels was a result of stringent polices by the Federal Reserve Board during the Reagan-Bush-Clinton years.

most in the American mind—specifically, inflation. Ford opposed wage and price controls, and settled on the thin thread of volunteerism. In the fall of 1974, he told the American people that the nation must "whip inflation now," and asked the American people to wear "WIN" (*Whip Inflation Now*) buttons as a symbol of their efforts. Americans made it clear that they were not interested in WIN buttons as a solution to the debilitating inflation problem (and Ford even admitted that the idea was only a gimmick). The oil crisis did end, however, and the inflation rate dropped to about 5 percent just as the 1976 presidential campaign got under way.

Inflation fed the recession in the mid-1970s, just as the recession fed inflation. Economists saw it as a dual problem that would be difficult to solve. Unemployment hit 8.3 percent, and the president, it seemed, had no response. Congress intervened by cutting taxes, which helped somewhat, but it caused the federal deficit to run to over $60 billion, which put even more pressure on inflation.

Attempts at energy conservation were largely symbolic. The president announced that the lights on the White House would be turned out in the evenings. A national highway speed limit of 55 miles per hour was imposed. And in 1974, all but a few states went to Daylight Savings Time. The federal government also imposed an average gas mileage restriction on new cars, and by 1980 the massive wide-track American ride of the early 1970s was a thing of the past. It was replaced by small, fuel-efficient, front-wheel-drive cars, generally with four-cylinder engines. These cars did little to satisfy the big-car appetites of the American consumer. To add to the pain, inflation caused the price of automobiles to jump 72 percent between 1972 and 1978.

The oil embargo ended as the result of a deal brokered by the Nixon administration. Nixon and Kissinger realized that the United States needed a significant presence in Middle Eastern affairs. For nearly two years, Kissinger jetted from one Middle Eastern capital to another, trying to mend fences between the Arabs and the Israelis and counter Soviet influence in the region. This "shuttle diplomacy," as it was called, did little to bring a lasting peace between the two warring groups, but Kissinger did persuade Israel to withdraw its troops from the Arab lands it had seized in the Yom Kippur War. And in exchange, OPEC agreed to raise its embargo. The oil crisis ended, but oil prices continued to rise. By 1983 crude prices had jumped to $35 per barrel, and gas prices at the pump averaged about $1.20.

Americans had come to depend on cheap energy. Access to cheap energy had, in fact, been an important contributor to the nation's economic growth since the war. Few realized the nation's vulnerability or even questioned U.S. energy consumption. The American standard of living was based on cheap energy, gas prices that seldom topped $0.35 a gallon, and home heating oil and natural gas that was even cheaper. The great American exodus to the South and Southwest had been, at least in part, fueled by the comforts of air conditioning that fed off cheap energy. Sprawling suburbs had sprung up all over the nation with no regard for the energy costs. Increasingly larger homes, bigger gas-guzzling cars, and longer commute times added to the problem that no one saw coming. To accommodate all that, the nation continued to build bigger and better highways. By the mid-1970s, cheap energy was one of the foundations of the nation's growth, and the American people had come to take it for granted.

Inflation can be an indicator of strong economic growth, particularly if wages and salaries keep up with the inflation rate. But the inflation of the 1970s was an economic indicator of a weak economy. The GNP dropped by 6 percent in 1974 and unemployment rates rose sharply, approaching double digits, the highest since the Great Depression of the 1930s.

Thus recovery came slowly, to a certain extent because the budget deficits kept the inflation rate above 5 percent for the remainder of the decade. The 1974 congressional tax cut led to a partial recovery by 1976, but the economy remained weak through the decade. Then in 1979, the Iranian Revolution and the overthrow of the shah threatened again to destabilize the Middle East. The result was another oil shock, sending crude oil prices to over $30 a barrel and prices at the pump to over $1 a gallon. Inflation rates pushed up again.

The nation's inflation woes of the 1970s damaged America's place in the global economy. Japan and the Western European democracies had, in fact, either moved ahead or gained significantly on the United States in most sectors of economic development. The auto industry suffered the worst. While Detroit tried to meet the consumer demand for smaller, more efficient cars, Japanese and German car manufacturers slowly and quietly moved into the American market. American automobile manufacturers were never good at being small and efficient, while Japan and several European nations understood the market, had produced nothing but small, efficient cars, and were ready to improve their products to meet the American demand. While Ford, Chrysler, American Motors, and General Motors spent over $70 billion in the 1970s trying to retool to meet the market for smaller cars, Japan and Germany were pumping small, efficient cars into the American market at a remarkable speed. Detroit also lost its creativity in the face of the challenge, delivering almost nothing substantially new through the decade. By 1977 imports were in control of one-fifth of the U.S. market, and in 1979 only a government bailout of Chrysler kept that company out of bankruptcy.

There were other parts of the manufacturing sector that were damaged by the 1970s "stagflation," as economists began calling the decade's economic woes. The steel industry, for instance, began a long decline. But just as it looked like the United States would weaken as a world economic power, the nation exhibited its economic might and resiliency. High-technology industries seemed to grow right out of the decaying flesh of the industrial manufacturing portions of the economy.

RISE OF THE COMPUTER

Computers had been around in one form or another since the war—massive, tube-laden machines called ENIACs (Electrical Numerical Integrator and Calculator). The ENIAC was developed in 1942 at the University of Pennsylvania and could calculate three hundred numbers per second, which was about a thousand times faster than any machine before it. The ENIAC used eighteen thousand vacuum tubes, took up about eighteen hundred square feet of storage space, and used about two hundred thousand watts of electrical power. It operated using punch cards to do agonizing calculations that usually took a human brain several days to complete.

Computing in the 1960s was generally directed at the production of computers for industrial use. By then, transistors had replaced the vacuum tube, making computers faster and smaller. But the nation was a long way from anything close to the affordable home computer. The IBM 1401, for instance, cost between $125,000 and $150,000 and was designed for use in big businesses and, occasionally, in university research. It had a capacity of four kilobytes of memory. Also in the 1960s programmable computer language was introduced, particularly FORTRAN and COBOL.

But by 1971 it was possible to see the nascence of the modern computer. In that year, IBM introduced its first mainframe computers, which included floppy discs as a removable storage device. Also that year, Intel announced the development of the first microprocessor, the Intel 4004, a four-bit processor. The next year, Intel doubled its memory capacity by introducing the eight-bit Intel 8008. In 1973 IBM introduced the first direct-access storage device (an external hard drive), the Winchester.

In 1975, the computer world (and perhaps the world in general) changed considerably when Bill Gates and Paul Allen founded Microsoft in Albuquerque, New Mexico, and began adapting and selling a small computer called the Altair PC. That same year Steve Jobs and Steve Wozniak produced the Apple I while working in Jobs's parents' garage in San Francisco. The Apple I was hardly a computer by any modern standards, but it was the origins of the modern home computer. It was hand built and encased in wood, with the word "Apple" carved out by hand on the back of the machine. It had no keyboard and no monitor. It was, in fact, little more than an assembled circuit board. The Apple II, however, was a different story. It had high-resolution graphics that could display pictures rather than just letters and numbers. Wozniak said later that he thought introducing high resolution was a waste of time and energy because he was certain no one would bother to use it. The Apple II also had a 5½-inch floppy drive for storage, a big advantage over other computers that still used cassette tapes. It was an immediate winner in the market, beating out the TRS-80 and Commodore PET. In 1980, Jobs and Wozniak took their business public and became instant millionaires. With Apple's success, Commodore and Tandy computer companies upgraded their systems and began to compete more aggressively in the market.

In 1979, Wordstar, the first modern word processor, was introduced, and secretaries everywhere were forced to give up their IBM Selectrics and learn the complications of Wordstar. Manual typing evolved into word processing.

In 1981 and 1982 the industry exploded. Commodore's VIC-200 home computer became the first real computer that the average American felt comfortable using at home. The system sold over one million units. IBM had been instrumental in most aspects of software development since the beginning of the computer age, but in 1981 it entered the personal computer market and immediately became the standard for the utility PC. Within twelve months, Compaq and Sun Microsystems had incorporated. Perhaps the most identifying event of 1982 was the introduction by Microsoft of the MS-DOS operating system. Within sixteen months, Microsoft had licensed MS-DOS to fifty microcomputer manufacturers. Within ten years, the computer had gone from a massive machine of tubes and magnetic tape wheels to something that resembles the modern computer. In 1982, *Time* named the computer its "Man of the Year."

FOREIGN AFFAIRS UNDER FORD

With only two years in office, it was difficult for Ford to place his stamp on the national economy. Much was the same in foreign policy. He did little more than work to achieve Nixon's foreign policy goals—while accepting the successes and failures of those goals. To ensure a smooth transition in foreign policy, Ford named Kissinger as his secretary of state.

It was during Ford's time in Washington that the last chapter on the Vietnam War was finally closed. Nixon's Vietnamization plan had brought an end to U.S. military involvement in Vietnam, but the war between the North and the South raged on.

A congressional ban had halted U.S. bombing on August 15, 1973. By the time Gerald Ford became president, South Vietnam was on the verge of internal collapse. A lack of U.S. aid and the Saigon government's own weak economy made a North Vietnamese victory almost certain. It was, in fact, only a matter of time before the South would fall—Kissinger's misinterpreted "decent interval." Nixon's resignation removed any possibility of U.S. military support as the end neared; only Nixon would have had a vested interest in making the fight in Congress to save the South.

South Vietnam's President Thieu, however, had come to believe that the United States would not turn its back on its old friend. In early 1975, North Vietnam prepared for the final blow. Military leaders there believed it would take about two years to take down the armies of the South; but as North Vietnamese troops began moving south, ARVN disintegrated quickly and fell back on the defensive network around Saigon.

As the North Vietnamese troops closed in on Saigon, Congress rejected Ford's request to send in military support. Congress would only approve $300 million to evacuate Americans from the city. Clearly, the United States had no stomach for further intervention in Vietnam. In April, Thieu resigned, blaming the United States for the entire mess. All that remained was for North Vietnamese tanks to enter the newly named Ho Chi Minh City and unite the nation of Vietnam. For the United States, the long nightmare was over.

The war carried on, however, along Vietnam's borders. In Laos, the communist Pathet Lao seized power and immediately cast their allegiance with Hanoi. In Cambodia, the response was genocide. Just before the Vietnam War ended, Nixon had bombed Cambodia in an attempt to destroy the Cambodian communists, known as the Khmer Rouge. The result was a social and political upheaval that eventually caused the collapse of the U.S.-backed government of Lon Nol. By April 1975, the Khmer Rouge, headed by Pol Pot, had launched a reign of terror and genocide throughout Cambodia that ended in the deaths of two million Cambodians, perhaps one in three of the nation's population. In January 1979, Vietnam invaded Cambodia to put an end to the killing. The Khmer Rouge had been supported by China, and within months Vietnam and China were at war along Vietnam's northern border. Thus, the United States found itself in the awkward position of supporting China's containment of Vietnam.

It was in this atmosphere that an American merchant vessel, the *Mayaguez*, and its crew were seized off the South Asian coast by the Cambodian government. Ford apparently wanted to show the world that the United States was not weak. He rejected all talks and sent in a detachment of Marines to rescue the crew. The Marines attacked an island where they believed the *Mayaguez* crew was being held. The crew, however, had already been released unharmed. Nevertheless, the Marines met stiff resistance from the Khmer Rouge soldiers defending the island. In the battle that followed, thirteen Marines and two Air Force personnel died in combat, while another twenty-three Air Force personnel died in a noncombat helicopter crash in Thailand. Another thirteen soldiers were declared missing and presumed dead when their helicopter was shot down over Cambodian air space.

Despite the events surrounding the *Mayaguez*, the fear of another Vietnam gripped the nation. In the West African nation of Angola an old Cold War scenario was playing out. In 1974, a civil war broke out among indigenous groups, and that attracted foreign powers. The United States and China supported one group; Moscow supported the other. When the Soviets began sending Cuban troops into the area, Kissinger approached Congress for the money to aid the U.S.-supported faction. Congress saw too many parallels to the Vietnam quagmire and rejected Kissinger's proposal.

Perhaps the most important foreign policy initiative Ford inherited from

Nixon was détente. Ford, however, did little to keep détente afloat. He met with Soviet Premier Brezhnev in Helsinki in 1975 to discuss a number of issues. The result was the Helsinki Final Act (better known as the Helsinki Accords), signed in August, which legitimized Soviet hegemony over Eastern Europe. In exchange, Brezhnev agreed that "participating States will respect human rights and fundamental freedoms, including freedom of thought, conscience, religion or belief, for all without distinction as to race, sex, language or religion." Not unlike the agreements made by Stalin at Yalta almost thirty years before, these agreements were never honored, with the result that a strong political opposition to the détente process began to grow in the United States.

It was in these years that the Soviet Union reached the peak of its political and strategic power in relation to the United States. The SALT I treaty, signed by Nixon in 1972, effectively established parity in nuclear weapons between the two nations. The Helsinki Treaty legitimized Soviet control of Eastern Europe, and the U.S. defeat in Vietnam, along with the Watergate scandal, had seriously weakened U.S. prestige abroad. In addition, it was in the 1970s that the Soviet Union, for the first time in its history, became a truly global naval power. The Soviets also had extended their influence into the Middle East, mostly at the expense of the United States. And in Africa, it had successfully intervened in the 1975 civil war in Angola and the 1977 civil war in Ethiopia. Détente had, however, quieted the rhetoric and kept the two superpowers from serious confrontation.

THE NEW ENVIRONMENTALISM

During the 1970s, new life was breathed into the environmental movement. It was undoubtedly a reaction to the oil shock and the understanding that humanity could not continue to drain the world of its nonrenewable resources, particularly oil. Others have argued that this new environmental awareness was caused by a series of photographs taken of earth by U.S. astronauts, which seemed to feed a realization that the world is fragile, even to the point of destruction by man's harmful behavior.

It was the oil shock, however, that seemed to wake up the nation to potential environmental problems. Carpooling, driving less, buying fuel-efficient cars, driving at a slower speed, adjusting the thermostat—Americans felt they had to do something to cut fuel emissions. Sometimes it was for themselves, to ease rising fuel costs; sometimes it was for the greater good, to save the population from itself, to save the planet. In addition, Americans pressured their representatives to act. In 1975 Congress passed the Energy Policy and Conservation Act, which established the Strategic Petroleum Reserve of up to one billion barrels of oil. The purpose was to end U.S. reliance on foreign oil, particularly during times of crisis. The law also set fuel economy standards for new cars. By 1981, new cars had to average 21.4 miles per gallon, up from about 15 miles per gallon in 1975.

The oil shock (along with the inundation of smog in the nation's biggest cities) sent environmentalists and consumers on a quest for alternative fuels and renewable energy. Solar energy generated the most excitement, but in the 1970s solar energy was not yet cost-effective. There were successes in the development of wind power, and that source of energy became a staple of power generation in some European countries. Americans, however, resisted the intrusion of giant windmills. Hydroelectric power (power generated by falling water, usually through a dam) was both clean and cheap, but it was not available in most areas of the nation and, because of the potential of drought, it could only be used in conjunction with other sources of more reliable generation. Coal, although plentiful and cheap, was determined to be much too dirty, which negated one of the primary purposes of environmentalism.

That left nuclear power, the cleanest of all the sources. In addition, the fuel source—uranium—is nearly inexhaustible. But nuclear energy gave environmentalists the jitters for a number of reasons. Nuclear plants produce large amounts of radioactive waste, which has to be discarded, stored, and disposed of. Environmentalists complained that any system of storage would eventually become hazardous to the environment by leaking into the groundwater.

Part of the general fear of nuclear energy might have been a by-product of the mid-1970s credibility gap. The U.S. government had said that nuclear energy production was safe. To a generation that had learned to distrust statements from the government, this was not terribly comforting. In addition, it was common knowledge that, under the right conditions, a plant could "melt down" if the cooling system failed. Containment of the core, in fact, was nearly impossible if it heated to its potential temperature.

Then, in March 1979, a partial meltdown occurred when the cooling system failed at the Three Mile Island (TMI) nuclear plant near Harrisburg, Pennsylvania. Though in the end the cooling system remained in place, there was no radiation exposure, and the reactor was stabilized, one hundred thousand people were forced to flee the Harrisburg area in anticipation of a radiation release.

The situation at TMI was made worse by the release of the movie *The China Syndrome* just days before the incident. This Hollywood blockbuster, starring Jane Fonda, Michael Douglas, and Jack Lemmon, dramatized just the type of accident that occurred at TMI. The fictitious plant in the movie had also stabilized at the last minute, but the cause of the near-disaster was shortcuts made by the contractors who built the plant and then covered up their shoddy work. *The China Syndrome*, in spite of being fiction, added a level of distrust to the nuclear power issue. The movie and the TMI incident together dealt a huge blow to the nuclear industry. In 1979 there were seventy-one nuclear plants in operation in the United States. After that date, no new plants began construction. By that time, it was no longer considered viable to build nuclear power plants in the

United States, partly because of government regulations and the overall cost, and partly because the American people had come to believe that the technology was unsafe.

Another environmental wakeup call in the 1970s was the discovery of a massive chemical waste dump at Love Canal, a residential area near Niagara Falls, New York. In the late 1940s, companies in the area began dumping chemical waste at the site. In the early 1950s, the site was covered by soil and finally sold to the city of Niagara Falls. The chemical companies warned the city that the site was unsafe. Nevertheless, the city built schools on the site, then residential neighborhoods. By the mid-1970s it was apparent that something was wrong. The residents of Love Canal had incurred high rates of cancer and birth defects. By 1978 Love Canal had become a media event, and that year the entire area was declared a "federal emergency." Eventually the federal government relocated over eight hundred families and reimbursed them for the loss of their homes. In response, Congress passed the Superfund Law (Comprehensive Environmental Response, Compensation, and Liability Act, passed by Congress in 1980) which, among other things, held industrial polluters accountable for the environmental damage they create.

ELECTION OF 1976

Ford was expected to take his party's nomination easily, but California governor Ronald Reagan put up a surprisingly stiff challenge. Reagan had become the preference of the Republican Right, a resurgent wing of the party that had been growing in popularity and numbers since Barry Goldwater's run in 1964. Reagan attacked Ford for not supporting the falling Saigon government and for "giving away" Eastern Europe in the Helsinki Accords. The primaries were particularly nasty and close, with Reagan scoring victories in most of the Sunbelt states and Ford showing strength in the industrial regions. At the convention in Kansas City, Ford grabbed a narrow victory among the delegates and clinched the nomination.

For the Democrats, the field was wide open. Thirteen Democratic candidates threw their hats into the ring. From that madding crowd emerged Georgia Governor James Earl Carter. He called himself "Jimmy." Carter's appeal was that he ran as the consummate outsider when the nation was fed up with the culture of Washington politics. He said he would restore the integrity of the government and the office of the presidency, and he asked the nation to trust him. He also counted himself a "born-again Christian," a phrase that had come to define deep religious convictions. His victories in the primaries showed he had appeal in both the North and the South. He went to the convention in New York with more than enough delegates to take the nomination on the first ballot.

Most of the fireworks were shot off in the primaries; the general campaign was generally uninspiring. Ford tried to run on his meager record. Carter carried on with the issues that had served him well in the primaries: namely, to separate himself from Washington and to promise a renewed integrity in government. Carter's victory was narrow, about forty-one million to Ford's thirty-nine million. He carried the South, where African American voters made the difference. He also took several northern industrial states, where he appealed to organized labor, more black voters, and traditional liberals. Ford won in the West, by now a bastion of the Republican Party.

Carter's victory can be viewed as a direct result of the nation's post-Watergate disillusionment and the country's revulsion for all things Washingtonian. Americans, it seemed, were willing to take a chance on someone with no foreign policy experience and minimal understanding of the workings of the nation's capital. Carter is almost always described as a good man, but his presidency is often lumped with Ford's two years as a sort of interregnum between two dynamic eras in postwar American history. To writer Tom Wolfe, Carter was "an unknown down-home piney woods footwashing testifying share-it-brother soft-shelled holy roller. . . ."

THE CARTER PRESIDENCY: THE DOMESTIC FRONT

The Carter presidency never seemed to reach fruition. His outsider role, which had worked effectively in the campaign, did not serve him well in office. Even though Democrats maintained majorities in both houses of Congress, Carter had difficulty getting support for his bills. He seemed to want to work outside the Washington system, above the political fray. Some analysts insisted that, as an outsider, he never really understood the workings of the federal legislative process, and his insistence on relying on advisors from Georgia may have added to that problem.

Carter inherited the nation's economic difficulties and did little more than Ford to solve the problems of inflation, recession, and spiraling fuel prices. In 1977, he pushed Congress for a tax cut in an attempt to halt the recession and get the economy back on track, but the stimulus just put more pressure on inflation. By 1978 inflation was moving up toward double digits again, and unemployment neared 7 percent. In October, Carter proposed a voluntary wage and price freeze to hold down inflation, but that plan broke down when businessmen refused to hold the line. Inflation immediately jumped to over 13 percent. Then, in an attempt to stop the inflation, the Federal Reserve Board raised the discount rate, causing interest rates to hit an all-time high. Large-ticket item purchases (houses, cars, products purchased on credit) dried up and the economy stagnated again. Carter was caught on a teeter-totter; when he pushed down on one side, the other side just came up. His attempt to solve one problem simply made the other one worse.

Carter did have some successes in the domestic arena, although those successes hardly carried the nation in any new directions. He created the Department of Education, separating it from the old Department of Health, Education, and Welfare. The intended purpose was to give more significance to education by the creation of a separate, and thus more powerful, department. He created the "Superfund" to clean up the nation's worst pollution sites. And he pardoned ten thousand Vietnam War draft resisters, most living in Canada.

Carter had promised to solve the nation's energy problems, and in April 1977, in a speech to the nation, he called his energy policy "the moral equivalent of war." He created the Department of Energy and, like Education, intended to give that department greater authority. His goal was a national energy policy that would guide the United States through the future. His plan was to force the nation into voluntary conservation by cutting price controls on energy and allowing energy prices to rise. To the average American, that meant little more than costly energy. Carter then intended to place a windfall profits tax on the oil companies to put an end to their rapidly growing profit margins. Conservatives applauded ending price controls, contending that it would encourage more exploration and drilling, but they opposed the windfall profits tax. Liberals favored stricter vehicle gas mileage standards, along with various types of incentives to reduce fuel consumption. The final bill incorporated a pick-and-choose from both sides. Price controls on the energy industry were lifted, and tax breaks were awarded to owners of fuel-efficient cars and homeowners who invested in solar power. The use of coal, still the cheapest and most abundant form of energy, was encouraged, particularly in new power plants. The bill hardly put a dent in the nation's energy crisis, but it went a long way toward establishing a new policy of giving incentives to those who would work to conserve energy.

The inadequacy of Carter's energy bill was felt almost immediately. In 1979 OPEC raised its prices again. Prices for crude jumped to over $30 a barrel, gas prices topped $1 a gallon, and long lines of angry motorists returned to the nation's gas stations. And again, the problem was primarily political. The civil war in Iran had produced an anti-American government in that country, which had combined its economic forces with other unfriendly OPEC states to pressure the oil cartel to raise prices. They intended to aid their own economic needs, but they also wanted to punish the United States for its continued aid to Israel. And, as in the early years of the decade, rising fuel prices caused a jump in the cost of nearly everything else. Americans complained bitterly, but much of their antipathy was aimed at the oil companies. The boom in domestic prices sent oil profits through the roof. In 1980, Exxon's first-quarter profits were $1.9 billion.*

Carter seemed befuddled by the economic mess. He responded by inviting 130 of the nation's leaders to Camp David for a series of meetings to deal with

---

*By comparison, Exxon-Mobil profits for the first quarter of 2007 were reported at $9.3 billion.

the problems. The result was an infamous speech delivered to the nation on July 15, 1979, in which the president chastised the American people for their "crisis in spirit" and told them that they had lost faith in themselves and abandoned their traditional values. The presentation was more reminiscent of a Protestant sermon than a presidential speech, and the American people did not take well to being told that their economic problems were a result of their own lack of character. The criticisms were immediate and harsh. Critics argued that the nation's problems stemmed more from a lack of presidential leadership than any character flaws in its people. Immediately following his speech, Carter set about cleaning house by firing several cabinet members. His critics chimed in again, accusing him of blaming others for his lack of leadership—first the American people, and now his cabinet. By the end of his term, his poll numbers had dropped to 26 percent, below even what Nixon had suffered at his lowest point. Carter never used the word "malaise" in his speech; the word was later used by one of his advisors, Patrick Caddell, to describe the speech, but the word stuck. It came to describe the entire Carter presidency and the economic problems that Carter could not solve.

THE CARTER PRESIDENCY: FOREIGN AFFAIRS

Carter had a minimal background in foreign affairs. He relied mostly on his idealism, his moralism, and his religious convictions to determine his foreign policy. To that end, he found his calling in human rights, and told the American people that human rights would be "the soul of [his administration's] foreign policy." Nixon and Kissinger had embraced a realism in foreign policy that had rejected the old Cold War shibboleth that America's moralism—a taking of the moral high ground in a war for the hearts and minds of the world—would and could win the competition with the Soviet Union. Carter wanted to return to the strategy that the United States was right, and that right would prevail. This philosophy fit well into his born-again religious beliefs. International human rights, however, proved easier to pursue than obtain.

Carter's greatest diplomatic success—in fact, the greatest success of his presidency—was the forging of a peace agreement between Israel and Egypt. Egyptian President Anwar Sadat initiated negotiations, first by saying that he would be willing to go to Jerusalem to meet with Israeli Prime Minister Menachem Begin, then by offering peace in exchange for the return of the Sinai Peninsula. In 1977, Begin invited Sadat to Jerusalem for talks. There, Sadat also insisted on an Israeli pull-back from the West Bank and the Golan Heights and a homeland for the Palestinian Arabs. Begin agreed to withdraw Israeli troops from the Sinai, but he refused to surrender the other regions. The result was an impasse. Carter then invited both Sadat and Begin to Camp David. For thirteen days, Carter goaded the two men into hammering out what was called a "framework" for peace in the Middle East. On March 26, Begin and Sadat signed a peace treaty that ended the state of war between the two nations. In addition, Egypt formally recognized Israel's right to exist and Israel returned the Sinai to Egypt. The Camp David Accords never became the foundation of a general peace in the Middle East as Carter and much of the world had hoped, mostly because the other Arab states in the region refused to follow Egypt's lead. Nevertheless, the agreement marked a rare success for the Carter administration.

Carter went a long way toward improving relations with Latin America by returning the Panama Canal to Panama. The treaty was ratified by the Senate in April 1978 and the Canal was turned over to the Panamanians through a gradual process that was completed in 2000. The U.S. Canal Zone was one of the last vestiges of U.S. colonialism and a source of long-time resentment by anti-American nationalists in Latin America. The United States, however, continued to maintain certain rights there. The treaty stipulated that the United States could intervene to keep the canal open and could require priority in times of international crisis.

Carter's inexperience in foreign affairs became most apparent in his dealings with the Soviet Union. One of his earliest objectives was to attain ratification of SALT II, the second phase of the U.S.–Soviet Strategic Arms Limitation Treaty. Carter and Brezhnev signed the treaty in Vienna in June 1979, but the Senate refused to ratify the agreement. Hardliners in both parties argued that Carter had given away too much by recognizing Soviet parity instead of demanding U.S. superiority. For critics like Senator Scoop Jackson, a fellow Democrat, Carter had done little more than affirm the decline of U.S. strategic power. Carter responded to the criticism by ramping up the nation's missile defense systems. He approved the multiple warhead MX Missile as a replacement for the older Minuteman ICBMs and authorized the construction of the Trident missile submarine, perhaps the most deadly war machine on earth. Amid all this escalation of weaponry, Carter withdrew the SALT II treaty from Senate consideration before it could be voted down. At just that moment, in December 1979, eighty-five thousand Soviet troops invaded Afghanistan. The event brought an end to détente; it also ended all hope of a strategic arms treaty and put U.S.-Soviet relations on edge.

DEBACLE IN THE MIDDLE EAST

Earlier in that year, in January, America's most dependable ally in the Middle East, Shah Reza Pahlavi of Iran, was overthrown by Islamic fundamentalists. Iran was America's stronghold in the Middle East, and it provided a predictable source of oil from the most unpredictable of regions. It was also America's primary defense post against Soviet influence in the Middle East. When Carter visited the shah at the beginning of his presidency, he called Iran "an island of stability in one of the most troubled areas in the world." The overthrow of the shah was a major blow to U.S. foreign policy.

The Iranian Revolution was led by Ayatollah Ruhollah Khomeini, a fundamentalist cleric living in exile in France. As the demonstrations in Iran against the shah's government increased, the shah fled into exile. The new government, led by Khomeini, turned Iran into a theocratic Islamic state, and the new leaders made it clear immediately that the United States, as the primary supporter of the shah's repressive government, was the enemy of the Iranian people.

In October, the deposed shah, suffering from cancer, asked to receive medical treatment in the United States. Carter granted the permission, considering it nothing more than a humanitarian gesture to an old friend. The response in Iran, however, was explosive. On November 4, a group of militants, often described as students, stormed the U.S. embassy in Tehran and took fifty-three embassy workers as hostages. In a display that disgusted Americans, the Iranians paraded the blindfolded hostages before world cameras. They insisted that the Americans would be tried as spies and executed if the United States did not hand over the shah.

Carter's diplomatic efforts to settle the crisis were ignored by the Khomeini government. Attempts at punishing Iran by freezing Iranian assets and sending Iranian students in the United States back to Iran also had no impact on the events. Carter's hands were tied as the crisis deepened into the fall, and he realized that he had no leverage over the situation. The nation, however, rallied behind their president, at least for a short time, and his approval ratings jumped up from a dismal 30 percent to over 60 percent. But soon, the patience of the American people began to grow short. The crisis was the lead story on every nightly news report, showing almost daily riots in Tehran that featured burnings of the American flag, effigy burnings, and a continuous parading of the hostages. The American people began demanding that something be done.

In December, the Soviets invaded Afghanistan, and although there was no connection between that event and the hostage crisis in Iran, Carter was stymied by both.

He responded by cancelling shipments of grain and high-tech equipment to the Soviet Union. Then he ordered a U.S. boycott of the 1980 Moscow Summer Olympic games. The acts seemed mostly empty. The grain boycott hurt American farmers probably more than it hurt the Russians, and hardly any other nations honored the Olympic boycott. In addition, most Americans did not see a Soviet invasion of Afghanistan as particularly significant in the greater scheme of world events.

The Soviets had entered Afghanistan to protect a friendly Marxist regime that was in danger of being overthrown by Islamic fundamentalists. The war finally turned into a Soviet bloodbath at the hands of the mujahideen, a group of anti-government and anti-Soviet fighters. Supplied by U.S. weaponry (particularly U.S. shoulder-mounted surface-to-air missiles that took a toll on Soviet helicopters), the mujahideen dragged the Soviets into an unwinnable quagmire that many called Russia's own Vietnam. The Saudi Arabian terrorist Osama bin Laden was a primary mujahideen financier and organizer. In 1989, mostly beaten and facing strong international criticism, the Soviets left Afghanistan.

The events in Iran and Afghanistan led Carter to proclaim a "Carter Doctrine" for the Middle East, warning that any "outside aggression" (meaning, of course, the Soviet Union) would be repelled with military force. Carter asked for an increase in defense spending and an upgrading of weapons systems, and, for the first time since the end of the Vietnam War, men were required to register for the draft. As the nation looked at the new decade, the Cold War was heating up, the United States had lost influence in the Middle East, and a presidential election was on the horizon.

The hostage crisis took on significance as a symbol of America's declining power and influence. Carter continued to work for a diplomatic solution to the crisis, but it was clear that the Tehran government and those who held the hostages were in no hurry to bring the crisis to an end. Carter allowed the crisis to consume him to the point that he had stopped seeing it as a diplomatic crisis and began taking it personally. "The release of the hostages," he later said, "had become almost an obsession with me." At one point, he announced that he would not leave the White House until the hostages were released.

Burdened by the pressure of the events, Carter ordered a secret military mission to free the hostages. The covert operation began on April 24, 1979, under the command of "Chargin' Charlie" Beckwith, a no-nonsense soldier's soldier. The results were disastrous. Three helicopters broke down in an Iranian dust storm; a fourth collided with a C-130 cargo plane, killing eight and injuring five more. The catastrophe only added to the frustration and humiliation of the entire event. Secretary of State Cyrus Vance, who had opposed the operation, resigned. The American people made no pretense. They blamed Carter.

PRESIDENTIAL CAMPAIGN OF 1980

Carter took almost nothing into the 1980 campaign. He had been unable to solve the economic crises that continued to cycle between recession and inflation. The situation in Iran seemed worse rather than better. His approval ratings had sunk again, to below 30 percent. He seemed isolated, holed up in the White House, refusing to campaign until the hostages were released.

Carter's weakness translated into vulnerability. In 1968, Robert Kennedy had smelled the blood of Lyndon Johnson's vulnerability over the Vietnam War and entered the campaign for the Democratic Party nomination. In 1979, Ted Kennedy, Robert's little brother, detected Carter's exposed position and announced that he would run against the president. In the annals of twentieth-century politics, however, it has proven impossible to take the nomination from a sitting president. Carter maintained control of the party's apparatus and was able to fend off the threat from Kennedy. He was aided by an obsession in the press with the Chappaquiddick incident and how that determined Kennedy's integrity and character.

Carter's failings, lack of leadership, and bad luck combined to open the door for the Republicans in 1980. Republican candidates jumped in from all angles, but it was apparent from the beginning that Ronald Reagan would be a clear choice. Only George H. W. Bush, the past director of the CIA, was able to give Reagan a decent run. Reagan won the nomination with ease and chose Bush as his running mate. It was a strong ticket.

Reagan's people controlled the platform at the convention, and for the first time America got a glimpse of the future. The 1980 Republican Party platform called for massive tax cuts, a balanced budget, and large increases in defense spending. During the campaign, Bush had called such mathematical improbabilities "voodoo economics." But Reagan insisted it could be done. The committee also launched the culture wars of the next decade by opposing the Equal Rights Amendment, calling for a constitutional amendment banning abortion, and for legislation (or a constitutional amendment, if necessary) to restore prayer in the public schools. These issues would, collectively, define the future of American conservatism.

Reagan hit Carter hard for his mishandling of both the economy and the hostage crisis. When Carter began to lose ground, he challenged Reagan to a debate. Reagan agreed, and the two met for one debate, on October 28, just a few days before the election. In perhaps one of the most memorable moments in U.S. debate history, Carter attacked Reagan for his record on Medicare. Reagan responded with the aplomb of the seasoned actor he was with the memorable quip, "There you go again"—meaning that Carter was misrepresenting facts. Then in his concluding remarks, Reagan leveled one last shot: "Are you better off than you were four years ago?" The answer for many Americans was a resounding no. The debate allowed Reagan to show that he was not, as Democrats had portrayed him, an old (at age sixty-nine, he was the oldest candidate in U.S. history from a major party), out-of-touch madman. He came across as both firm and warm.

The debate turned a close election into a landslide that surprised nearly everyone by its scale. Carter took only six states and the District of Columbia. Reagan wrapped up a decisive 489 electoral votes, giving him a strong showing in every region of the nation and among blue-collar voters, Catholics, Hispanics, southerners, ethnic voters, and middle-income voters. He even did well among Democrats. Republicans gained thirty-three seats in the House and twelve in the Senate, giving them control of that body for the first time since Eisenhower's first term. It was a rout.

Was this the birth of a new Republican majority? Or was it a referendum

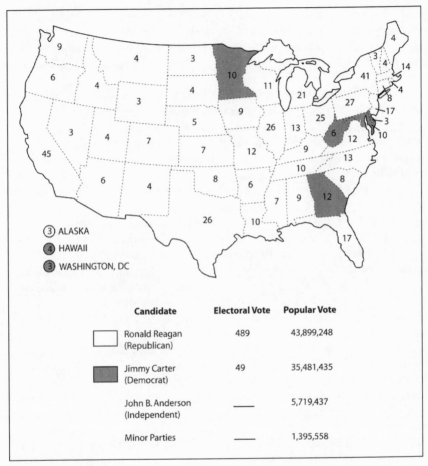

Candidate	Electoral Vote	Popular Vote
Ronald Reagan (Republican)	489	43,899,248
Jimmy Carter (Democrat)	49	35,481,435
John B. Anderson (Independent)	—	5,719,437
Minor Parties	—	1,395,558

Presidential Election, 1980

on Carter's ineffective leadership? Certainly, it was both. Reagan would go to Washington with new ideas, a new mandate, and a new coalition. That coalition would stay in place for at least twenty more years—in and out of power over that time. Carter had not been a successful president, and the American people were well aware of that as the campaign progressed. The nation wanted something new, and Reagan was that.

In the early fall of 1980 it appeared that the hostage crisis might take a turn and finally come to an end. In July the shah died, and in September Iran was invaded from the west by Iraq. With very little money (because of accounts frozen by the United States) or modern weapons, Iran was on the verge of being overrun by an Iraqi army intent on taking advantage of its neighbor's weaknesses. In

October, just before the election, Carter offered to release Iran's assets in exchange for the hostages. Khomeini desperately needed the money (about $8 billion), and his revolution now had a new cause in its war with Iraq. He no longer needed the hostages. Finally, on January 21, 1981, Carter's last day in office, and a few minutes after Reagan took the oath of office, the hostages were released—after 444 days in captivity.

CONCLUSION

Watergate and the end of the war in Vietnam brought on a malaise of a type never before seen in the United States. To most Americans, the government was barely trustworthy, and the nation's military was no longer formidable. The Helsinki Accords had given the Soviets hegemony in Eastern Europe, and the SALT agreements had given them parity in weapons deployment. There were times, since the end of World War II, that the United States may not have been the strongest nation in the world, but in the 1970s it was all too apparent that it was true. The United States had lost its supremacy. In addition, the American people were reticent, afraid to get involved in world affairs, intent on avoiding anything that looked or smelled like Vietnam. Add to all that a severely stagnant economy that showed no signs of improvement, and it was easy to see that the nation was in decline. Historians compared the United States in the 1970s to Spain in the nineteenth century, a has-been powerhouse that had lost its strength, its wealth, and its integrity abroad. It was, perhaps, one of the worst times in American history.

Reading: Jonestown

The events that occurred at Jonestown, in Guyana, in November 1978 were tragic. On the evening of November 18, just over nine hundred members of the Peoples Temple either committed suicide or were murdered. The first reports of the incident reached the United States early on the morning of Monday, November 20. Additional reports, including grisly photos of the bloated dead, trickled in over the next week.

The Peoples Temple was first established by Jim Jones in Indianapolis in the mid-1950s, but the Temple's successes there were limited. Following an affiliation with the Disciples of Christ, the Temple gained more members and a respectable reputation. By the mid-1960s, Jones had gathered up about one hundred members and moved the Temple to the Redwood Valley in Northern California, reportedly to avoid nuclear fallout from what Jones considered an impending nuclear attack on the United States.

Jones gained a reputation as a strong supporter of social causes, particularly social equality that focused on racial integration, the welfare of the elderly, and the rehabilitation of drug addicts and alcoholics. Consequently, his ministry attracted society's castoffs, the poor, and the downtrodden, particularly poor African Americans, the elderly, and rehabilitated addicts.

In 1972 Jones moved his congregation to San Francisco, where he ministered to that city's poor. But following a series of scandals and a growing investigation for tax evasion, Jones began planning to move his Temple out of the country. He finally settled on Guyana, a remote jungle nation in northeastern South America. In 1974 he leased a large plot of land from the Guyanese government and Temple members began moving into the region. By 1978 over nine hundred people had moved there, most in hopes of finding a better life.

The settlement—called Jonestown—can best be described as a large commune under Jones's dictatorial control. Members who were able to get out before the tragedy of November 1978 told stories of strict discipline administered through coercion, punishment, and fear, and that those who wanted to leave Jonestown were punished severely. There were rumors of some "defectors" being killed.

The events that led to the Jonestown tragedy began with a visit by Congressman Leo Ryan. In an attempt to follow up on a series of stories about the conditions at Jonestown, and at the behest of relatives of several Temple members, Ryan asked the House Foreign Affairs Committee for permission to investigate the Peoples Temple. On November 14, 1978, Ryan, with a team of journalists and relatives of Temple members, flew to Guyana. His specified purpose was to investigate allegations of human rights violations at Jonestown and to determine if individuals were being held there against their will.

On November 17, Ryan visited Jonestown and met with Jones. While surveying the commune, Ryan and other members of his group were given notes by Temple members asking to be rescued from the commune. Others stepped forward and asked to leave with the congressman. This situation angered Jones, who apparently saw such actions as a betrayal. He also seemed to believe that defectors from Jonestown would divulge the manner in which the commune was being run, with the result that he would ultimately be arrested or even killed.

In the late afternoon of November 18, Ryan and his party, including sixteen Temple defectors, left Jonestown for the airport at Port Kaituma, about six miles from Jonestown. There they were met by gunmen who opened fire on the group. Ryan, three journalists, and one of the Temple defectors were killed. Ten others were wounded, five seriously.

Back at Jonestown the mass suicide had already begun. A concoction of Kool-Aid laced with cyanide and tranquilizers was first given to babies through hypodermic syringes. Mothers were told to give the poison to their children and then to drink themselves. Families lay down together to die, often holding each other. Those who resisted were either forced to drink or were shot. Jones himself died of a gunshot wound to the head.

Over nine hundred members of the Peoples Temple committed mass suicide in November 1978, most by drinking cyanide-laced Kool-Aid. *Source*: AP Photo

Two signs hung from the ceiling above the open-air pavilion where the lethal drinks were administered. One said, "Love one another." The other quoted George Santayana: "Those who cannot remember history are condemned to repeat it." The final count was 909 dead. Only four survived, including a seventy-nine-year-old man who was too deaf to hear the late-night call to assemble.

The tragedy at Jonestown was the culmination of one man's fanaticism and his ability to prey on the weak, the elderly, and the dispossessed.

· *10* ·

The Reagan Years

R onald Reagan's election changed the national political landscape—in part
because of the new president's convictions and his dedication to conservative
principles, but also because he came to Washington with an agenda that was a
clear alternative to most established policies. The time became known as the
Reagan Revolution, and it was nothing less than that. Reagan proposed a drastic
transformation to the role of the federal government at home and a far-reaching
change in America's posture abroad. Few American presidents have truly altered
the condition of the nation and affected the way the people thought of it. Reagan
was one.

Reagan's inaugural address set the tone for his administration. He spoke of
the nation's battle with inflation, "the longest and worst sustained inflation in our
history." One of the primary problems, he continued, was high taxes that were
keeping the nation from achieving its full productivity; another was skyrocketing
federal deficits. We cannot continue to pile "deficit upon deficit, mortgaging our
future and our children's future for the temporary convenience of the present."
But for the new president, the real culprit, the point that he clearly intended as
the high mark of his speech, was the bloated bureaucracy. "In the present crisis"—his voice rose—"government is not the solution to our problem. Government *is* the problem." The crowd roared, and the nation took note. "In the days
ahead," he promised, "I will propose removing the roadblocks that have slowed
our economy and reduced productivity. It is time to reawaken this industrial
giant, to get government back within its means, and to lighten our punitive tax
burden." Then, he concluded, there would be no compromises on these objectives. This was Reagan's revolution.

In international affairs, Reagan seemed to understand that the nation was
unsure of itself, its power in certain situations, and its ability to influence world
affairs. Much of this reticence came from the experience in Vietnam, still fresh
in the national memory. Reagan knew the nation needed strong leadership in
foreign affairs. He told a reporter in 1980 that he was certain he would succeed
as president "for one simple reason. . . . The American people want somebody

in command." Reagan's strong leadership, however, often translated into a new, aggressive stance that threatened to bring an end to détente, open old Cold War wounds, and drag the world into another dangerous phase in the Cold War.

Reagan sounded the trumpet for his new conservatism in his inaugural address, but conservatives were not all in agreement. Conservatives in 1980 had rallied around Reagan's candidacy, but in January 1981, when Reagan came to Washington, they were a long way from an integrated, cohesive group. Beyond their devotion to their candidate, American conservatives shared only one real common characteristic: they all considered the last fifty years a time of insufferable creeping American liberalism. What parts of the liberal estate would be replaced, how it would be replaced, and what (if anything) would replace it were questions of great debate among conservatives. Many were prepared to attack what they called "forced busing"; others wanted to cut affirmative action programs that were intended to guarantee equality to minorities; anti-feminists opposed the Equal Rights Amendment; still other conservatives opposed any attempts to protect rights for gays and lesbians. Evangelical Christians pointed to a need to stress religion and the family. Some focused on what they saw as abuses at the Supreme Court, which had granted women the right to abortion and then outlawed school prayer. Then there were the liberal-sponsored welfare programs that most conservatives wanted cut, high taxes, rising deficits, and a federal government that was perceived as much too powerful. There was the John Birch Society, the National Rifle Association, National Association of Manufacturers, Southern states' righters, and a large number of big business leaders. It was truly a diverse coalition. Reagan was their messiah, and (in most cases) he was able to hold them together—with anti-liberalism as the adhesive. Not unlike Roosevelt's 1936 liberal coalition, the Reagan conservatives would argue over definitions and intentions, but they were kept together by the character and the agenda of their leader.

REAGAN THE MAN

Reagan was an interesting figure, a man who might well be described as having lived two complete lives in succession. He was born in Tampico, Illinois, in 1911 and raised in a series of northern Illinois river towns. He attended faith-based Eureka College and then went to work as a sports announcer for a small radio station in Des Moines, Iowa. In the first of a series of almost mythical life-altering events, Reagan was sent to Los Angeles to cover the 1937 Chicago Cubs training camp, where he more or less fell into an acting career. Despite his handsome good looks and an infectious grin, he never became an A-list star. As he would later recall, "It was always some other guy who got the girl." He did, however, have a successful career, making over fifty movies; a couple were memorable, particularly *King's Row* in 1941 and *The Knute Rockne Story*, in which he played Notre Dame football star George Gipp. His ever-memorable death scene and his character's last words to his coach—"win one for the Gipper"—would carry Reagan throughout his life.

By the end of the war, however, Reagan's career was on the wane, and through the next decade he became increasingly interested in politics while making a celebrated shift from Roosevelt liberal (he had backed Helen Gahagan Douglas against Richard Nixon in her 1950 Senate race) to right-wing conservative. Historians have almost desperately tried to chronicle this transition, but it really was not complicated. Reagan's conversion revolved mostly around his intense hatred of communism and his growing understanding and belief in the powers of the free market. This change of political heart was also influenced by his tenure as the president of the Screen Actors Guild. In that role, he led a fight in the late 1940s against a takeover by Hollywood Communists.

In the mid-1950s Reagan became a spokesman for General Electric. He served as host for a GE-sponsored television show called *Death Valley Days* and traveled the country promoting the company's interests. By 1960 his talks, by now much sought after in conservative circles, had evolved into attacks on centralization in Washington and world communism, along with a powerful defense of free market capitalism and individual responsibility. In 1964 Reagan supported Barry Goldwater's run for the presidency. At the very end of Goldwater's doomed campaign, Reagan went on national television to promote Goldwater's candidacy. The event became something of a turning point in the history of American conservatism.

Two years later, Reagan became governor of California by defeating the Democratic incumbent, Edmund "Pat" Brown. Brown had presided over a period of growth in California, but much of the middle class had become tired of the high taxes that liberals insisted were necessary to fund the expansion. In addition, the 1965 Watts riot, the antiwar demonstrations, and the Berkeley Free Speech Movement had alienated many Californians from Brown's liberal administration. Reagan was able to link Brown to everything from high taxes to welfare cheats, and won the election by more than a million votes. Reagan's star was on the rise.

In his two terms as governor, while talking of lowering taxes and cutting spending, Reagan actually approved the largest tax increase in California's history and doubled state spending. He also signed one of the nation's most liberal abortion bills.

In 1976, Reagan challenged President Gerald Ford for the Republican nomination. Ford had tried to make peace with the party's moderate wing by naming Nelson Rockefeller as his vice president, but the move only made Reagan and others on the Right angry. The party's right wing also opposed Kissinger's détente initiative with the Soviets, often calling it a policy of appeasement. Reagan lost the nomination, but it set him up as the uncontested leader of the

GOP Right (the successor to Taft and Goldwater) and the party's next presidential hopeful.

REAGANOMICS

Much of what would become Reagan's economic plan was spelled out fairly well in his inaugural speech in January 1981: lower taxes, less bureaucracy, a balanced budget. Added to that was a stronger military (thus a larger military budget). All of this translated into an economic philosophy known as "supply-side economics." Reagan's reputed whiz kid on this plan was David Stockman, a former Michigan congressman who saw the nation's economic future in the numbers. First and foremost, Reaganomics, as it was most commonly known, was a repudiation of the liberal-Keynesian economic philosophy that called for deficit spending and tax manipulation for the purpose of putting more money into peoples' pockets—which would, in turn, create aggregate demand. Greater demand would then fuel the economy from the bottom. This was, generally, the national economic policy that began with the big spenders in the Roosevelt era through the Carter administration. It was the economic policy and philosophy behind the New Deal, the New Frontier, and the Great Society. Even Eisenhower subscribed to it, or at least he accepted it.

Reagan and Stockman had been influenced by supply-siders like Arthur Laffer, an economist at the University of Southern California who had argued that significantly lower taxes would spur economic growth. In a now-renowned event among conservative economists, Laffer in 1974 sketched his economic theory (now known as the Laffer Curve) on a cocktail napkin at a Washington hotel bar to explain his idea to President Gerald Ford's chief assistant Dick Cheney and *Wall Street Journal* writer Jude Wanniski. To Wanniski this was "one of the most important economic events in the last half-century." Laffer argued that lowering taxes would spur economic growth, ultimately raise tax revenues, and finally allow for a balanced budget. It was not really a new idea. In fact, Laffer often credited John Maynard Keynes with the general principle. His innovation was that the point to which taxes could be reduced for revenues to rise was much lower than anything Keynes (or anyone else) had ever considered. To conservative economists, the idea was the economic equivalent of an epiphany.

At the heart of the administration's economic program were two bills: the Omnibus Budget Reconciliation Act and the Economic Recovery Tax Act. The budget bill was passed in May 1981 and included administration cuts of over $35 billion for the coming fiscal year and then another $130 billion over the next three years. The bill began to fade almost immediately, and the president's poll numbers began to slip when stories in the press focused on how the budget cuts would affect various lower-income groups.

But the bill was pushed through Congress, to some degree as a result of the president's popularity following an attempt on his life in late March. He emerged from the event strong in the polls, and the bill passed both houses with impressive numbers.

The Democrats, however, were not willing to allow the president's tax bill to go so easily. They mounted an attack, claiming that the bill was designed to help the wealthiest 5 percent of the population at the expense of the nation's poor. But on July 27, Reagan went before the American people (with economic charts and graphs in hand) and made all the arguments for his cuts, claiming, "You are entitled to the fruits of your labor." It was a basic concept, and the nation responded. Congress passed the tax cut bill with strong Democratic support in both houses. The law cut tax rates by 25 percent over three years. The Reagan Revolution was in place.

Reagan also sought to reduce federal regulation of the economy. The assumption was that relaxed regulations would allow business and industry to be more productive, and that the free market would be a fairer and more efficient regulator than the federal government. These ideas were hardly new, but they resonated with Americans.

Did it work? The immediate answer was no. Within a year the nation was stuck in the worst economic recession since the 1930s. Reagan's tax cuts, combined with his heavy military spending, had pushed the deficit to over $100 billion, the largest in history. The problem was that the tax cuts failed to stimulate business investments, and continued high interest rates kept consumer spending low. Unemployment skyrocketed, business bankruptcies rose to Depression-era levels, and the homeless on the streets of the nation's largest cities (particularly Washington) became the new poor. Over 15 percent of the population was living below the poverty line, the most since the Kennedy administration. In the 1982 mid-term elections, the Republicans lost additional seats in the House.

There was, however, a silver lining. The new economic policies did bring inflation under control; then in 1983 the economy began to recover. Within a year, housing starts and new car sales increased dramatically, consumer income finally began to rise, and the rate of inflation dropped even further. The economic rebound turned into an economic expansion that tripled growth in the stock market and continued well into the 1990s. But serious economic problems continued to plague the nation. Unemployment remained high, while lower taxes and massive military spending kept the federal deficit high. Perhaps the most apparent failing of the new economy was that the nation's poor remained in poverty.

THE NEW COLD WAR

On March 8, 1983, Ronald Reagan told the Annual Convention of the National Association of Evangelicals in Orlando, Florida, that the Soviet Union continued to act with the "aggressive impulses of an evil empire." He went on to argue that the United States should not enter into any nuclear freeze agreements with the Soviets, and that peace would be attained only through strength. Later that same month, Reagan spoke to the nation on much the same topic. He defended increases in the military budget, and then, near the end of his speech, explained his plan for a missile defense shield that would protect the United States from a nuclear attack. These two speeches set the tone for U.S.-Soviet relations for the next six years.

Reagan and his supporters in the Republican Party might best be described as nationalists. They generally opposed the idea of collective security; they distrusted most other nations; and they had little use for the United Nations, either as a peacekeeper or as a humanitarian organization. The idea that the United States would answer to other nations through the mechanisms of the United Nations was a nonstarter among Reagan conservatives. These nationalists also had misgivings about foreign aid, they shunned foreign entanglements that might commit U.S. troops, and they expected the American military to be second to none. At the same time, these Reagan Republicans were not true isolationists, although it might be argued that they came from that tradition and there were certainly Fortress America–type isolationists who were supporters of Reagan and even inside Reagan's circle. But Reagan saw the world much as Barry Goldwater had: The United States needed to be engaged in world events, and it needed to be a world leader. The United States needed to be powerful and, if necessary, aggressive. However, when Reagan acted, he acted unilaterally.

Reagan had spent most of his adult life fighting communism, and he would spend his two terms as president doing the same. His 1983 statement that he believed that the Soviet Union was an "evil empire" was not hyperbole. He believed it. In that same speech, he went on to insist that the United States must win the Cold War because it was a spiritual nation that "must terrify and ultimately triumph over those who would enslave their fellow man." Most Americans had grown complacent about détente and peaceful coexistence with the Soviet Union, but Reagan and those around him saw détente as a surrender to international communism, the appeasement of an aggressor. The Soviets, they argued, had used détente to build weapons systems to match or exceed NATO's firepower; to extend their power into areas such as Angola, South Yemen, and Afghanistan; and to build a huge navy that included missile-firing nuclear submarines. Reagan immediately began a new, harsh rhetoric that many Americans feared would bring on another dangerous period of renewed Cold War.

CENTRAL AMERICA

The nations of Central America had always been unstable and unpredictable. In fact, the only real stability in the region through most of the twentieth century had been right-wing dictators who, with support from the United States, kept communism at bay. The regime of Anastasio Samoza in Nicaragua is perhaps the best example. Even when the political left managed to gain power, as in the case of Jacabo Arbenz in Guatemala in 1953, the United States simply changed the government by force. In Cuba that strategy failed in 1961, and Cuba's periodic attempts to destabilize Latin America became a thorn in the side of every American president after Eisenhower. When Reagan came to office, El Salvador was engulfed in a civil war between the right and left. The political right included both the central government and the military, and they employed violent death squads in an attempt to suppress the left. In nearby Nicaragua, the leftists (known as the Sandinistas), led by Daniel Ortega, overthrew the Samoza regime and immediately established close relations with Cuba. The Sandinistas then began running supplies and weapons to the leftist rebels in El Salvador. The new Reagan administration immediately concluded that these events were a test of America's will in the region and a direct and aggressive expansion of Soviet communism within the American-dominated hemisphere. Within a year of coming to office, Reagan approved a CIA plan to destabilize Nicaragua by building up a strong anti-Sandinista military force in nearby Honduras and Costa Rica that Reagan called the Contras. The United States blockaded Nicaraguan ports to stop weapons supplies from the Communist bloc and continued to support the Contras. Not surprisingly, many Americans saw several comparisons between the escalating situation in Central America and the escalations in Vietnam in the early 1960s. Reagan called the Contras "the moral equivalent of our Founding Fathers."

Cuba's influence seemed to be everywhere in Central America and the Caribbean. On the small island of Grenada, a group of Marxist revolutionaries overthrew the government there in 1983 and immediately opened relations with Cuba. Nearly a thousand American medical students on the island were reported to be in harm's way, and several hundred Cuban construction workers were in the process of building a large landing strip on the island. Those two situations were enough for Reagan to order an invasion of the island. Seven thousand U.S. troops hit Grenada in a massive assault that was marked mostly by poor communication between units and a general lack of coordination. Nevertheless, the island was overwhelmed easily and quickly; the Cuban effort came to an end, and the students were rescued. The United States had to veto a resolution in the United Nations condemning the operation, and most of the world wondered why the American giant needed to overwhelm a little Caribbean island. But the Grenada invasion was important to the American psyche. It was a victory, clear-cut and on the side of right. There were no gray areas like in the jungles of Vietnam, where there was no discernable enemy, no clear objective, and no victory to be had. And there were no hostage-takers, as in Iran, tying American hands. In addition, the rescue of the American medical students added some glory to the event. America needed the glory. And America needed a victory, no matter how small or how insignificant.

REAGAN IN THE MIDDLE EAST—AND LEBANON

Despite the Camp David agreements, the situation in the Middle East remained volatile. The primary conflict (although there were many) was between the Arabs and the Israelis over control of Palestine. To the Reagan administration, however, the situation there had Cold War connotations, with Israel as the American-supported cornerstone in the region against Soviet expansion and influence with the Arab states. By the time Reagan took office, Israel was at peace with Egypt and Jordan, but the other Arab states continued to oppose Israel's existence. Chief among these was the Palestine Liberation Organization (PLO), an armed guard of exiled Palestinians housed in southern Lebanon on Israel's northern border.

Following a series of terrorist attacks, the Israeli army, in June 1982, attacked PLO strongholds in southern Lebanon, carrying the attack as far north as West Beirut. Reagan sent an envoy, Philip Habib, to negotiate a ceasefire that included a provision that the PLO would be allowed to evacuate Lebanon intact. The vacuum that remained was quickly filled by the Israeli army, which occupied parts of southern Lebanon and West Beirut. Syria, backed by the Soviets, moved in and occupied parts of eastern Lebanon, and Iranian militants began training and arming Shiite militias known as Hezbollah. In addition, Lebanese Christian militias (often allied with Israel) grew in strength. The resulting civil war turned Lebanon into a war zone.

Reagan sent in fifteen hundred U.S. Marines to restore order and force the Syrians and Israelis to withdraw their forces. This was undoubtedly a diplomatic stretch for Reagan, who had always decried the U.S. role as an international peacekeeper and generally opposed U.S. intervention for reasons other than protecting America's direct interests. On October 23, 1983, Hezbollah terrorists exploded a car bomb that killed 241 Marines at their compound near the Beirut airport. Reagan quickly decided to cut his losses and withdraw the troops. It was the worst U.S. military disaster since Vietnam. There were a number of consequences that resulted from these events, but perhaps the most important was that the United States was perceived in the Muslim world as the chief backer of Israeli interests and thus a prime target for terrorists in the future.

SDI AND U.S.-SOVIET RELATIONS

By about the mid-1950s, U.S. anti-Soviet rhetoric and Soviet anti-American rhetoric were usually considered a matter of course in the Cold War. American leaders needed to shore up hard-line support, just as Soviet leaders had to satisfy hardliners in the Kremlin. But Reagan's anti-Soviet rhetoric during the 1980 campaign and his first term in office disturbed the Soviet leadership. His "evil empire" statement in early 1983, along with his insistence that the United States would not be a part of any nuclear freeze agreements, and then his proposal for a missile defense shield, or Strategic Defense Initiative (SDI), set the Soviets back on their heels. In addition, Reagan's military budgets soared in his first administration. Soviet premier Yuri Andropov began calling Reagan "irresponsible" and even "insane." Tensions and fears began to rise.

SDI was truly a new chapter in the history of the Cold War. Called Star Wars (after the popular science fiction movie) by the press and the program's critics, SDI was a source of controversy throughout Reagan's terms in office. The plan did sound much like a science fiction movie: U.S. missiles would intercept and destroy enemy missiles before they could reach their targets in the United States. Billions of dollars were pumped into a number of programs that produced few results. The Soviets protested the plan, pointing out that it violated the ABM Treaty of 1972. But Reagan continued to push SDI, and Congress continued to go along with big appropriations.

Undoubtedly the most important aspect of SDI was not what it achieved, but that it contributed to the collapse of the Soviet economy. By the end of the decade, the Soviet economy was teetering badly, and their attempt to develop their own missile defense system undoubtedly led to that collapse.

CULTURE AND SOCIETY OF THE 1980s AND THE RISE OF THE RELIGIOUS RIGHT

American society in the 1980s revolved around the new conservative values that Reagan and his administration claimed to represent. President Reagan himself, along with those around him and his most ardent supporters, stressed family, religion, education (particularly the basics of elementary and secondary education), and cultural unity (as opposed to cultural diversity). All of this seemed to be a reaction to many of the cultural experiments and adventures of previous decades. In fact, many conservatives in the 1980s saw their values as a crusade against the scourges of the 1960s and 1970s. Weak family values, they argued, had led to a skyrocketing divorce rate. Casual drug use had led to drug and alcohol abuse in the 1980s. Casual sex had led to sexually transmitted diseases. And a lack of attention to religion had caused the general breakdown of the nation's moral character. A rise in conservative values, then, would bring the nation back to its moral roots, to its moral center.

A religious revival was at the foundation of cultural conservatism in the 1980s. The Christian Right, as they would be called through the next decades, had begun to surface in the mid-1970s. Just a decade before, only about one in four Americans identified themselves as having experienced salvation, or being "born again," as the Bible describes the experience. By the late 1970s that number had nearly doubled, and the born-again Christians had begun influencing society. A move into the political arena seemed like a natural progression. It was just another means of changing the moral face of the nation.

As mentioned above, the "born-again" movement was, in many ways, a general backlash against the extremes of the previous decades. But it had emerged and gained momentum in the mid-1970s in direct opposition to two specific Supreme Court decisions that conservative Christians believed interfered with biblical teachings and denied them their right to pray when and where they pleased. The first, the 1973 *Roe v. Wade* Supreme Court decision, which allowed abortions, was marked by the Christian Right as the legalization of genocide, and opposition to the *Roe* decision immediately became a litmus test for any political candidate hoping to win votes from this group. Religious groups also chafed at Court rulings in the early 1960s that outlawed prayer in public schools. The need, as the Supreme Court saw it, to keep the church and the state separate as required by the Constitution did not resonate with the Christian Right. The Reagan administration denounced both of these rulings (both coming before Reagan took office) and encouraged a whittling away at the decisions, but did little to overturn the court rulings.

Reagan and his Christian Right allies also opposed most Supreme Court cases and laws that furthered civil rights of African Americans and other minorities, although the administration vehemently denied that their stances on these issues were connected to race. In the early 1970s the courts had ruled that schools must desegregate, even if it meant transporting students by bus to different schools to achieve that goal. Reagan opposed busing, and even supported a constitutional amendment outlawing the practice for the purpose of racial desegregation. He also opposed all affirmative action laws, many of which dictated quotas for hiring minorities in the workplace and admitting minorities to universities. Such programs were intended to end segregation practices in hiring and admissions processes. Reagan, however, claimed that such laws gave minorities an unfair advantage, and that opportunities should be the same for all Americans. The president also worked to stop Congress from establishing a holiday in honor of Martin Luther King Jr. and tried (unsuccessfully) to stop Congress from renewing the Voting Rights Act of 1965.

It was Jimmy Carter, and not Reagan, who was the first to draw a relationship between religion and presidential politics. But Reagan pulled that movement into the Republican Party, and by the time he left office, the Christian Right was a strong core group within the GOP. The leaders of this social phenomenon were the televangelists, the TV preachers who promised salvation, old-time religion, and entertainment. Some were more outrageous than others. Most asked for money, mostly with good results. The big names were Oral Roberts, who broadcast from his church/university in Tulsa; Jimmy Swaggart, who broadcast from Baton Rouge; and Jim Bakker, who, with his wife Tammy Faye, ran a multimillion-dollar operation known as the PTL (Praise the Lord) Club from Charlotte, North Carolina. The message from most of these televangelists was clear: The accumulation and flaunting of wealth was not only acceptable, it was just another step toward salvation. With no apologies, the Bakkers owned six homes and an air-conditioned doghouse. And there were others. Pat Robertson, on his *700 Club*, often told his viewers of his conversations with God. He also regularly condemned communism—and any and all of America's enemies. And Jerry Falwell's Moral Majority became a significant political action group that focused on electing politicians who had found salvation while adhering to specific religious values.

By mid-decade, the televangelists had collected something close to $1 billion. Bakker and Swaggart, however, became fallen angels. Bakker was finally convicted on fraud and conspiracy charges and served eighteen months in prison. Swaggart was caught having a liaison with a prostitute in a seedy New Orleans hotel; he asked forgiveness from his viewers in a tearful spectacle during his Sunday-morning broadcast. Of course, not all televangelists were dishonest and insincere, or even flamboyant and materialistic. For example, Robert Schuller, whose "Hour of Power" broadcast from the massive Crystal Cathedral in Los Angeles, could boast the largest church membership in the nation in 1980. His program reached millions each week and is often cited as the antithesis of the most acquisitive and flashy of the Sunday morning preachers. And, of course, Billy Graham continued to preach at huge venues around the world through the 1980s and beyond. The televangelist movement attracted hundreds of thousands of viewers from the political right—as well as a great deal of scorn from the left.

Reagan himself was not much of a churchgoer, but he held strong religious convictions and often spoke of himself as a "born-again Christian." But perhaps more important, on almost every issue, he fell in on the side of the Christian Right. He opposed abortion and supported school prayer and the strength of the family. Almost as a trade-off, the Christian Right supported Reagan's foreign and domestic policies. They were a good match, and the Christian Right would remain a cornerstone of the Republican Party for decades to come.

WAR ON DRUGS

By the 1980s the nation had developed a drug problem. In the early years of the decade, only about 1 percent of Americans considered drugs a national problem. Within five years, that number had jumped to over 50 percent. The cause was "crack," an inexpensive cocaine derivative that swept through urban America (particularly low-income black communities) in the last half of the decade. The scourge continued on well into the 1990s before leveling off at about the turn of the century. Crack had the unique character of being both inexpensive and highly addictive. Users often turned to crime to support their habit, tearing apart families and neighborhoods. Crack addiction spawned everything from turf wars to child abuse, from murders to poverty. As the economy worsened for young inner-city black men, the production and sale of crack was one of the few ways of making money, of joining in the consumer culture. Crack became so lucrative that urban gangs formed to control its production and sale, and old-style gangland wars broke out in the nation's cities as the various gangs attempted to control turf.

To combat the problem, the Reagan administration launched an anti-drug campaign with the slogan "Just say no." This war on drugs, as it was called, focused mostly on ferreting out and arresting the drug dealers and suppliers, and did little to educate young people or rehabilitate users. By the end of the decade, the war on drugs had spent close to $15 billion on the program, with most of the money going to building new prisons and beefing up urban police forces. By the end of the century, crack use declined as its dangers became increasingly apparent. But not surprisingly, the end of one drug problem in America always seems to spawn another. Drug abusers turned to even cheaper highs with methamphetamines and easily acquired prescription painkillers like Oxycontin.

AIDS, "THE GAY EPIDEMIC"

Through most of the 1980s, an interstate billboard near a church in south Louisiana showed a scornful Christ on the cross. Below was written in large, bold letters, "AIDS," and then below that, "Consider Your Ways." The message was clear: There was a direct relationship between a lack of religion, sexual freedoms, homosexuality, and AIDS.

AIDS (an acronym for acquired immune deficiency syndrome) was first recognized in the United States in 1981 by the Centers for Disease Control and Prevention. The AIDS virus is transmitted sexually through the exchange of bodily fluids and, although it is most often associated with gay men, the disease can be transmitted through heterosexual contact as well. It is also prevalent among intravenous drug users through shared needles. AIDS was first encountered in the United States in the early 1980s with a rumor in the gay community of an unidentifiable "gay cancer." News of the disease began working its way into the press by mid-decade when the virus was finally identified and the methods of transmission had become clearer. But to most Americans, AIDS jumped to the forefront only when actor Rock Hudson died from the disease in October 1985. By 1988 there were over thirty thousand new AIDS cases reported in the United States. Within five years the disease had decimated the gay community; the number of AIDS deaths had jumped to almost 103,000, while another 1.5 million had tested positive for HIV, the virus that causes AIDS. The Reagan administration barely acknowledged the problem. The only significant response to the epidemic came from the public health community that encouraged "safe sex," a campaign that promoted the use of condoms, but also monogamy with a "safe" partner. Public health organizations nationwide also distributed clean needles to intravenous drug users in an attempt to stop needle-sharing.

EDUCATION IN THE REAGAN YEARS

While the Reagan administration, the religious right, and the new conservatism in America touted the family and the traditional values surrounding that institution, family life in the nation seemed to be deteriorating rapidly. In 1981 the divorce rate had jumped to an all-time high of 1.2 million annually, or about 41 percent of all marriages. At the same time, the number of births to unwed mothers also rose dramatically, causing an unprecedented increase in the number of single-parent families from about four million at the beginning of the decade to about ten million in 1990. By the end of the decade, one-fourth of the children born in the United States were born to a mother who had never married. It was the African-American family that suffered the most from this trend. By the end of the decade over 60 percent of all African American families were single-parent families. Predictably, that condition often led to poverty. By 1983, the Census Bureau reported that thirteen million children under the age of six were growing up in poverty.

Many on the religious and political right pointed their fingers at the failures of the nation's education system. The criticism came from the belief that the nation was pumping money into state and local school systems, encouraging what was perceived as "new age" educational philosophies, and producing little more than illiterates, graduates who could not function well in society because they lacked both the very basics of education and the technical skills needed to function. They blamed sex education, multiculturalism, permissive teachers, and a lack of attention to the basics, which usually included the "three R's" and the study of the nation's history.

The Reagan administration continued to repeat the right-wing argument that the government cannot throw money at a problem, when in fact the nation's schools were sorely underfunded and overcrowded, and teachers' pay scales were so low that the profession had stopped drawing qualified new recruits. The president responded with cuts to education, insisting that more discipline, rather than more money, was the answer. The situation was made worse as large numbers of middle-class white families began abandoning the public school systems for the stronger curriculums (paid for by high tuition) in private schools. In addition, many religious families began homeschooling their children to shelter them from what they saw as the evils of a secular education, including everything from a ban on school prayer to the teaching of evolution. Public school districts soon found themselves teaching what was left: the less motivated students, the poorest students, and often the inner-city black students. With busing no longer an available alternative for desegregating public schools, the result was a new segregation in many American cities, with inner-city schools remaining predominantly poor and black, while schools in the suburbs became increasingly white—either public or private. Education problems in the 1980s were not solved, despite all the talk, and as the system continued to deteriorate it caused the nation to take another large step toward increased racial polarization.

THE "ME" GENERATION AND
THE CULTURE OF NARCISSISM

Eras can often be captured in a statement or phrase, a saying or slogan. In 1985, phenomenally successful stockbroker Ivan Boesky told a crowd of enthusiastic college students at the University of California, the very hub of 1960s radicalism, that "greed is all right." That small statement of principle probably did not resonate with most Americans, but in 1987 Oliver Stone made *Wall Street*, a movie about an unscrupulous Wall Street trader named Gordon Gekko, played by Michael Douglas. Paraphrasing Boesky, Gekko told an audience, "Greed, for want of a better word, is good." (Both Boesky and the fictional Gekko went to prison for fraud and insider trading.) Reagan himself had said much the same thing: "What I want to see above all is that this country remains a country where someone can always get rich. That's the thing we have and that must be preserved." If the 1960s was punctuated by an idealism that responded to Kennedy's inaugural statement "Ask what you can do for your country," then it is these statements that mark the character of the 1980s. During these years, middle-class America found solace in the accumulation of wealth; they turned away from political idealism, cultural rebellion, and the notion of change, and turned their attention to making money. As Haynes Johnson wrote in *Sleepwalking through History*, "Not in decades, perhaps not in the century, had the accumulation and the flaunting of wealth been celebrated so publicly by so many." The nation's icons were Boesky, Donald Trump, Leona Helmsley, Carl Icahn, T. Boone Pickens, and Lee Iacocca, men and women who had accumulated great wealth and power and reveled in flaunting it. Many, like Boesky, Pickens, and Iacocca, had pulled themselves up from modest beginnings, and thus became heroic examples of what could be in a free-market economy.

It was not all flash and attitude. Growth rates averaged between 3 and 4 percent per annum, and many corporations enjoyed record profits. This was reflected in the stock market, with a bull market that continued upward throughout the decade. And with that, consumer spending increased and confidence in the economy rose. Perhaps the most telling statistic was that the number of households declaring annual incomes of over $1 million jumped from five thousand in 1980 to over thirty-five thousand in 1990, and the number of people claiming over $1 million in assets went from about 500,000 to 1.5 million in the same period.

There was, however, another side to the ledger. Amidst all the new money and visible affluence, the number of Americans living in poverty increased sharply during the decade, reaching nearly 15 percent—about where it had been in 1960. The average family income of the poorest fifth of the population had declined by over 6 percent, while family income for the top fifth had risen by over 11 percent in the same period. The average income of the top 20 percent of the population increased by about $34,000 during the decade; while those at the very top, the top hundredth percentile, saw their incomes jump by nearly $130,000 in the same period. At the same time, real wages continued to stagnate in many parts of the country, and nationally, take-home pay for wage-earning factory workers declined. It was clear that economic (and thus political) power was flowing steadily from the middle class to the very top of the economic scale.

It was, however, the grinding poverty that seemed to show (despite all the conspicuous consumption and affluence) that there were problems. In the decade and a half after the end of World War II, poverty was generally out of sight. But poverty in the 1980s was different. It was visible everywhere, particularly in the nation's cities where the poor walked the streets and openly begged for money. Americans described them accurately as the "homeless." Many of these homeless were unemployable young men who were pushed out of the shrinking job market because of everything from racism to low education to a general lack of skills. But others were mentally ill, drug or alcohol abusers, young runaways, AIDS victims, generally the people who had fallen through the cracks of the nation's social systems. Survival was difficult, and life was often dangerous. Most slept in public parks or back alleys or on subway heating vents. New York City seemed to grow an entire underground city of homeless in the tunnels below the city's streets. To the aboveground inhabitants they became a nearly mythical group known as the "moles." Another large group living on the edges of poverty was single mothers and their children. Perhaps not as visible as the homeless, they lived very hard lives. And when the Reagan administration cut funds to the Women-Infant-Children program (WIC), their plight became even worse. It seemed ironic that the nation was developing two very visible economic types: the conspicuously affluent and the conspicuously homeless.

Despite these extremely serious problems at the lowest income levels, the nation's economy continued to grow through the 1980s and well into the 1990s (with the exception of a brief recession in 1991–1992). In addition, the nation's economy grew at a much faster rate than its primary international competitors. By the turn of the century, the United States was the undisputed global economic leader.

REAGAN IN HIS SECOND ADMINISTRATION

In 1984 Reagan's campaign slogan struck a chord with the nation: "It's morning again in America." For a nation that had been dragged through Vietnam, Watergate, urban riots, the energy crisis, and the failed presidencies of Ford and Carter, Reagan seemed something of a ray of sunshine. He was confident, clearly a leader, and he seemed to want to take the nation back to a better time—or at least what Americans thought was a better time. Reagan's opponent in the 1984 presidential campaign was Walter Mondale, a traditional liberal Democrat in the mold of his mentor Hubert Humphrey. Mondale spoke often of new programs that he would implement as president. When pressed, he admitted that his programs would, indeed, require an increase in taxes. Right or wrong, it was not what Americans wanted to hear in 1984. Reagan won in a genuine landslide; he took every state except Mondale's home state of Minnesota.

By the early 1980s, it was becoming clear that the Soviets were falling behind, that their economy was weakening and might be heading toward collapse. Advisors close to Reagan pushed the president to put economic pressure on the Soviets in an attempt to weaken their economy further. That pressure came from Reagan's massive defense buildup. American defense spending jumped from $134 billion at the beginning of the Reagan administration to over $250 billion at the end of the decade, increasing defense spending to about 7 percent of the GDP. To keep up, the Soviets were forced to raise their defense spending to a debilitating 27 percent of their GDP. It was more than their economy could sustain.

The Soviets' economic situation worsened as the quagmire in Afghanistan deepened. The Reagan administration supported the Afghan mujahideen against the Soviets, sending them shoulder-fired surface-to-air Stinger missiles that decimated Soviet helicopters. The war cost the Soviets dearly in men and materiel, and finally contributed significantly to the eventual bankruptcy of the Soviet economy.

Perhaps one of the most important turning points in modern Soviet history was the death of Leonid Brezhnev in 1982. Truly the last of the Marxist-Leninist Soviet hardliners, Brezhnev had ruled Russia with an iron hand, suppressing dissidents and maintaining firm control over the Communist Party structure. At the same time, however, he allowed the Soviet economy to stagnate. By the time Brezhnev died, the Soviet Union was involved in a war it could not win in Afghanistan, and massive food shortages were becoming a problem throughout the USSR. Both of his two successors died almost immediately after coming to office and were followed in 1985 by Mikhail Gorbachev.

Gorbachev was not a Marxist-Leninist ideologue. He recognized the shortcomings of the Communist system, a system that was not keeping up with the West's productivity and its standard of living. And perhaps more importantly, all of that was becoming apparent to the Soviet people through the proliferation of telecommunications. Gorbachev's solution was perestroika, a plan to overhaul the Soviet economic system, and glasnost, a new openness that was intended to ease the old authoritarian suppression of Soviet society. Gorbachev then looked to better relations with the West.

Reagan and Gorbachev met in Geneva in 1985 and again in Reykjavik, Iceland, in 1986. At Reykjavik, Gorbachev surprised Reagan by offering to eliminate long-range missiles if Reagan agreed to abandon Star Wars, a program that the straining Soviet economy could not match. Reagan countered (with apparently no input from his foreign policy advisors) by agreeing to eliminate all nuclear weapons if Gorbachev would agree to accept Star Wars. Reagan most likely saw the future, when the greatest threat to the United States would not come from the Russians but from what were being called "rogue nations," belligerent states that might develop nuclear and delivery technologies. If the United States could successfully defend itself using a Star Wars system, it would not need nuclear weapons as a form of defense. Gorbachev, however, refused to accept any deal that included Star Wars and turned down Reagan's offer.

The Reykjavik summit is usually considered a failure, but Reagan and Gorbachev emerged from Reykjavik with a healthy mutual respect, and that was an important factor leading to the 1987 INF (Intermediate Nuclear Forces) treaty. That agreement, signed in Washington, removed all intermediate range missiles from Europe, including Soviet SSIs and U.S. Pershings and cruise missiles. A year later, Reagan went to Moscow, where he acknowledged that the Soviet Union was not quite as "evil" as he had proclaimed just five years before. Neither man knew it, but the Cold War was about to end, and they would both get much of the credit.

IRAN-CONTRA

By the mid-1980s, popular support was beginning to wane for the U.S.-backed Contra war against the Nicaraguan Sandinistas. The comparisons with Vietnam were simply too great. In 1982 Congress halted aid to the Contras for one year. Then in 1984, a ban on aid—known as the Boland Amendment—was passed by Congress, mostly over concerns about widespread human rights abuses by the Contras. In the 1986 congressional elections, the Democrats regained control of the Senate and increased their hold on the House, and immediately stopped the administration's direct intervention in Central America. Reagan sought to circumvent the Boland Amendment by turning to private interests and foreign nations to fund the Contras. Some $37 million was raised for the Contra cause in Central America.

To increase their funding, the Contras also engaged in cocaine trafficking, which turned out to be a much more lucrative and consistent source of funding than the Reagan administration. The cocaine was destined for U.S. consumption and largely fueled the American cocaine obsession in the latter years of the 1980s.

On the other side of the world, Iraq and Iran had gone to war in 1980 in what was little more than a drawn-out religious conflict. The ruling Sunnis in Iraq, led by strongman Saddam Hussein, were intent on stopping the Shiites in Iran from spreading their radical version of Islam throughout the Middle East. At the same time, Saddam hoped to emerge as the undisputed leader of the region with complete control over its vast oil resources. The war lasted eight years and the United States supported Saddam as a counter to Iran, Washington's sworn enemy since the rise of Ayatollah Khomeini and anti-American Shiite radicalism there.

In the early to mid-1980s, a wave of political kidnappings struck Beirut, a notorious breeding ground for Hezbollah and other Shiite radical anti-Israeli groups supported and influenced by Iran. In 1983 Hezbollah took thirty hostages, including six Americans. Members of the Reagan administration believed that if they could sell arms to Iran (which needed them desperately in their fight against Iraq), they could force Iran into pressuring the Hezbollah kidnappers to release the hostages. In August 1985, President Reagan authorized the sale of over five hundred TOW antitank missiles to Iran in exchange for the release of one hostage, Benjamin Weir. The United States continued to sell weapons to Iran, eventually selling over two thousand TOW missiles and eighteen HAWK antiaircraft missiles. Two additional hostages were released.

At the beginning of 1986, Lieutenant Colonel Oliver North, a Reagan administration National Security Council aide, concocted an idea that would connect America's interests in the Middle East with the Central American conflict. North concluded that the proceeds from the sale of the weapons could be used to fund the Contra war in Central America. He would later call his revelation "a neat idea." North's clever plan was initiated, and the proceeds went to the Contras. North and his cohorts, however, apparently did not inform Reagan of the plan, later citing "plausible deniability." That is, if the president had no knowledge of the actions, he could not be held liable for any wrongdoing in the affair.

By the end of that year the entire story had broken in the press, including the diversion of funds to the Contras in explicit violation of the congressional mandate. The affair unfolded as a shady, covert operation that had been designed from the beginning to circumvent Congress and even the will of the American people. Reagan called North "a national hero"—and then promptly fired him. Reagan's national security advisor, John Poindexter, then resigned.

A Senate investigative panel threw most of the blame on North, and cited Reagan for allowing such operations without close scrutiny. In the summer of 1987, Congress held televised hearings on the Iran-Contra scandal. North admitted lying under oath and destroying and falsifying documents to conceal the scheme. He insisted that his only concern was for the welfare of the nation. North quickly became a favorite of the political right.

In the final analysis, the congressional committee found no evidence of Reagan's direct wrongdoing or knowledge of criminal activity, but it did criticize the president for his lax management style and for tolerating an environment that allowed for such activity without his knowledge. North was indicted and finally found guilty of three minor counts, but the convictions were dismissed on appeal because he had been given immunity for his congressional testimony. Others in the scandal were indicted, tried, and convicted, but all either had charges dismissed or were pardoned. Reagan emerged from the affair fairly unscathed. His approval ratings suffered during the hearings, but they rebounded to previous levels once the scandal passed.

The incident divided the nation. Some Americans concluded that the federal government could deal with such matters as long as they are in the national interest and that the president should have unconditional authority to conduct foreign policy. The other side of the argument leaned toward constitutional principles, citing mostly the need for the president to adhere to laws passed by Congress even if those laws appear to interfere with foreign policy. The primary constitutional issue that arose from the Iran-Contra affair has, however, never been answered: Does Congress have the authority to oversee functions of the executive branch?

THE EIGHTIES CHARACTER

If the heroes of the decade were Ivan Boesky and T. Boone Pickens, then it would stand to reason that the celebrated character-type of the era would be those who aspired to such wealth and power, the upwardly mobile. Thus emerged the celebrators of greed, the Young Urban Professionals, the Yuppies. These were generally the boomers coming of age. The boomers had originated the counterculture, protested the war, smoked pot, and perhaps even flirted with radicalism. But by 1980 they were ready to drop back in, make money, and live well. They became entranced by affluence. The most visual icon of Yuppiedom was the movie *The Big Chill*. Here a group of hippies/radicals-turned-Yuppies reunite at a friend's funeral (who had died for their sins) and mourn their lost idealism while in pursuit of money, sex, and power. "What happened to us?" asks one character.

Socially, Yuppies retained much of their 1960s character: individual rights, human rights, abortion rights, minority rights, women's rights, and environmentalism. Politically, however, many had simply grown cynical about the political process and any possibility of changing what they saw as a corrupt system. Others had seen the light in Reagan's economic policies and made a shift to the right.

They were, after all, aspiring investment bankers. Saving the world had become passé.

This was, however, no re-hashing of the 1950s. There was no desire to fit in or be a part of the homogenous society. Yuppies wanted to stand out, to flaunt their conspicuous consumption. Their identifying mark was the BMW or Porsche; their drug was cocaine (they left marijuana behind); and their dress was "preppie," a style akin to prep school-type uniforms. They were fond of things identified as "designer," in everything from food to clothing, and they took up jogging. Fitness, in fact, seemed to replace something lost on the generation before. Perhaps the marathon run (a profoundly individualistic endeavor) had replaced the "love-in."

Not surprisingly, the media turned the Yuppies into caricatures. They were quickly made into single-minded money-grubbers like the celebrated characters in the prime-time soap operas *Dallas*, *Falcon Crest*, and *Knots Landing*. The character Alex in the sitcom *Family Ties* aspired to be a Yuppie and spoke glowingly of his personal greed and his near-worship of Ronald Reagan. To appeal directly to the Yuppies there was the television show *thirtysomething* about Yuppies trying to deal with life, their money, and their idealism; and *Moonlighting*, about two Yuppie private investigators in a love-hate relationship. The *Cosby Show*, perhaps the most popular show of the decade, introduced America to Buppies: the Black Urban Professionals.

By the end of the decade, the word Yuppie had become overused, used up, and finally turned into a pejorative; even those who fit the form perfectly avoided any association with it. But the character did not leave the stage—only the word.

If the Yuppies had their own music, it was something called "arena rock" or sometimes "anthem rock." Led by groups like Journey, Foreigner, Boston, Survivor, and Styx, the style was big hair, big voices, and really big guitars. Instead of the timeworn rock concert, these groups put on *shows*, giant productions at huge arenas throughout the world. Perhaps its greatest claim to fame was that it replaced disco.

If rock 'n' roll in the 1950s was distributed through the car radio, 1980s music was distributed by MTV. Although the format has since changed considerably since its inception, MTV was originally music videos, one after the other, around the clock, good ones and bad, often the same ones over and over. The distinction from other forms of media was obvious. Not only did consumers listen to their favorite group, they could now watch them sing the song. And that was mostly what MTV was in 1981 when it went on the air: bands singing. Soon, not surprisingly, the individual videos evolved into productions, even in some cases mini-movies like Michael Jackson's *Thriller*, released in 1983. Just as radio had made household names of Elvis and Chuck Berry, MTV made the careers of dozens of artists and groups, particularly Jackson, Madonna, Van Halen, The Cars, Eurythmics, Culture Club, and Bon Jovi. The magic of MTV could take a mediocre song like Peter Gabriel's *Sledgehammer* or Robert Palmer's *Addicted to*

Love, affix it to a clever video, and with almost nonstop showings on MTV, run it quickly to the top of the music charts.

Anyone could see that music tagged to television was probably a bad thing—that the quality of the music would give way to visual content. But MTV actually improved music quality. It quickly pushed aside disco (which received no benefit from being televised) and introduced several new music genres that might collectively be called pop.

For five years MTV avoided showing rap (hip hop) videos mostly because of their violent content and pepperings of expletives. Finally, in 1986 MTV began running the rap song *Walk This Way* by Aerosmith and Run DMC. Despite the song's lewd topic (high school girls having group sex), the song contained no expletives, which was enough for an MTV airing. With that, rap (which had strong influence in the black community) began moving into the mainstream of youth culture. Mirroring 1950s rock 'n' roll and 1960s rock, rap in the 1980s was almost universally hated by the white middle class. It was, nevertheless, exactly what music had been since the end of the war: the voice of hope and anger of a generation—and designed specifically to hurt parents' ears.

THE 1988 CAMPAIGN

Despite the embarrassments of Iran-Contra and a stock market nosedive in 1987, the Reagan administration ended its eight years in office with a significant reduction in Cold War tensions. And Americans saw that as an important accomplishment, brought on mostly by U.S. military strength. This newly acquired confidence allowed Reagan a luxury not given to many presidents: to designate a successor. And the nod went to his loyal vice president, George H. W. Bush. Despite Reagan's popularity, however, Bush was no shoo-in for the job.

The Democrats were glad to see Reagan ride off into the California sunset. He had been a hard man to beat, and his popularity had made it difficult to be a Democrat. The first two Democratic contenders were Colorado senator Gary Hart (Walter Mondale's adversary for the Democratic nomination four years earlier) and Jesse Jackson (the most prominent leader of the African American community in the late 1980s). Jackson, however, wanted to leave behind his role as black leader and appeal to the entire nation—to be a Democratic candidate, not a black candidate. Hart was an appealing figure, but when a reporter suggested that he was having an extramarital affair, Hart challenged the press to find proof. A reporter at the *Miami Herald* did just that: He caught Hart red-handed, and Hart dropped out of the race. With Hart gone and Jackson perceived as not strong enough to take on Bush, the door was left open for Massachusetts governor Michael Dukakis, the man credited with the "Massachusetts miracle." While many of the factories of the industrial East had turned to rust during the 1980s,

Dukakis had garnered credit for building a new economy in Massachusetts based mostly on high-tech industry—much of it from military contracts. He chose as his running mate Lloyd Bentson, senator from Texas.

The nomination for Bush was essentially in the bag. He had Reagan's support, plus a strong organization and important fund-raising strength. Nevertheless, Kansas senator Bob Dole put up a fight in the early campaign. In the New Hampshire primary, Bush ran several television commercials portraying Dole as a big spender and a tax-raiser. Bush won the primary, but an embittered Dole went on television to tell Bush to "stop lying about my record." Bush's campaign thundered on after that and he took the nomination at the convention in New Orleans. He chose Indiana senator Dan Quayle as his running mate, in part because Quayle had campaigned for the job. In his acceptance speech, Bush reiterated one of his campaign pledges, "no new taxes"—a pledge he would break.

Bush did well in the campaign by pointing to low inflation, new jobs, and a decrease in world tensions during the Reagan years. He also effectively courted the evangelical right, and kept most of Reagan's people in line. That alone probably would have been a winning strategy. But Bush attacked Dukakis with one of the most negative television campaigns in the history of American politics. The most notorious of these was the Willie Horton commercial. Horton, a frightening-looking black man with wild natural hair, committed rape and assault in Maryland while on a weekend furlough from a Massachusetts prison. The ad was designed to show that Dukakis was soft on crime, but it also exploited racial stereotypes and was clearly aimed at the most base of racial fears. The Willie Horton commercial was followed by the "revolving door" commercial in which criminals, mostly black, passed through a revolving turnstile, presumably in and out of jail.

Dukakis looked strong just after the convention, but his campaign quickly collapsed. He was a boring campaigner who focused mostly on his administrative abilities. In an attempt to punch up his foreign policy experience, which was lacking, he allowed himself to be filmed riding in a U.S. Army M1 Abrams tank. It was a public relations disaster. There was something about Dukakis, smiling, wearing a tank helmet that invited ridicule. The scene was played over and over again by the Bush people, and soon the phrase "Dukakis in a tank" came to mean a public relations fiasco.

In the final analysis, Bush won a respectable 54 percent of the popular vote to Dukakis's 45 percent. The Electoral College was a landslide at 426 to 111. Neither candidate sparked much excitement. Bush lacked eloquence when compared to Reagan, although his "no new taxes" pledge at the Republican convention kept the Republican faithful in line. He swept the South just as Reagan had done in 1984, but Bush did even better than Reagan, winning most of the Southern states by wide margins. He did unexpectedly well in the Northeast, in Dukakis's home turf. It was a big victory for Bush and the Republicans.

CONCLUSION

Most presidents claim to have a vision for the nation, but few do. Most presidents are, in fact, little more than crisis managers, dealing with problems as they come. Ronald Reagan was a true visionary. He disliked the direction the nation was moving and he came to Washington intent on changing that direction—and he succeeded. He directed the nation to the right: in fact, so far to the right on some issues that moderates like his successor, George H. W. Bush, found immediate opposition from those Reagan supporters who saw him as not conservative enough—not enough like Reagan. There have not been many presidents who truly have changed the direction of the nation. Reagan, like Franklin Roosevelt—the man Reagan looked up to all his life—was one.

Reading: Ronald Reagan's Farewell Address, January 11, 1989

It's been quite a journey this decade, and we held together through some stormy seas. And at the end, together, we are reaching our destination.

The fact is, from Grenada to the Washington and Moscow summits, from the recession of '81 to '82, to the expansion that began in late '82 and continues to this day, we've made a difference. The way I see it, there were two great triumphs, two things that I'm proudest of. One is the economic recovery, in which the people of America created—and filled—nineteen million new jobs. The other is the recovery of our morale. America is respected again in the world and looked to for leadership. . . .

Well, back in 1980, when I was running for president, it was all so different. Some pundits said our programs would result in catastrophe. Our views on foreign affairs would cause war. Our plans for the economy would cause inflation to soar and bring about economic collapse. I even remember one highly respected economist saying, back in 1982, that "The engines of economic growth have shut down here, and they're likely to stay that way for years to come." Well, he and the other opinion leaders were wrong. The fact is what they called "radical" was really "right." What they called "dangerous" was just "desperately needed."

And in all of that time I won a nickname, "The Great Communicator." But I never thought it was my style or the words I used that made a difference: It was the content. I wasn't a great communicator, but I communicated great things, and they didn't spring full bloom from my brow, they came from the heart of a great nation—from our experience, our wisdom, and our belief in the principles that have guided us for two centuries. They called it the Reagan Revolution. Well, I'll accept that, but for me it always seemed more like the great rediscovery, a rediscovery of our values and our common sense.

Common sense told us that when you put a big tax on something, the people will produce less of it. So, we cut the people's tax rates, and the people produced more than ever before. The economy bloomed like a plant that had been cut back and could now grow quicker and stronger. Our economic program brought about the longest peacetime expansion in our history: real family income up, the poverty rate down, entrepreneurship booming, and an explosion in research and new technology. We're exporting more than ever because American industry became more competitive and at the same time, we summoned the national will to knock down protectionist walls abroad instead of erecting them at home.

Common sense also told us that to preserve the peace, we'd have to become strong again after years of weakness and confusion. So, we rebuilt our defenses, and this New Year we toasted the new peacefulness around the globe. Not only have the superpowers actually begun to reduce their stockpiles of nuclear weapons—and hope for even more progress is bright—but the regional conflicts that rack the globe are also beginning to cease. The Persian Gulf is no longer a war zone. The Soviets are leaving Afghanistan. The Vietnamese are preparing to pull out of Cambodia, and an American-mediated accord will soon send fifty thousand Cuban troops home from Angola.

The lesson of all this was, of course, that because we're a great nation, our challenges seem complex. It will always be this way. But as long as we remember our first principles and believe in ourselves, the future will always be ours. And something else we learned: Once you begin a great movement, there's no telling where it will end. We meant to change a nation, and instead, we changed a world.

Countries across the globe are turning to free markets and free speech and turning away from the ideologies of the past. For them, the great rediscovery of the 1980s has been that, lo and behold, the moral way of government is the practical way of government: Democracy, the profoundly good, is also the profoundly productive. . . .

Ours was the first revolution in the history of mankind that truly reversed the course of government, and with three little words: "We the People." "We the People" tell the government what to do; it doesn't tell us. "We the People" are the driver; the government is the car. And we decide where it should go, and by what route, and how fast. Almost all the world's constitutions are documents in which governments tell the people what their privileges are. Our Constitution is a document in which "We the People" tell the government what it is allowed to do. "We the People" are free. This belief has been the underlying basis for everything I've tried to do these past eight years.

But back in the 1960s, when I began, it seemed to me that we'd begun reversing the order of things—that through more and more rules and regulations and confiscatory taxes, the government was taking more of our money, more of our options, and more of our freedom. I went into politics in part to put up my hand and say, "Stop." I was a citizen politician, and it seemed the right thing for a citizen to do.

I think we have stopped a lot of what needed stopping. And I hope we have once again reminded people that man is not free unless government is limited. There's a clear cause and effect here that is as neat and predictable as a law of physics: As government expands, liberty contracts.

Nothing is less free than pure communism—and yet we have, the past few years, forged a satisfying new closeness with the Soviet Union. I've been asked if this isn't a gamble, and my answer is no because we're basing our actions not on words but deeds. The détente of the 1970s was based not on actions but promises. They'd promise to treat their own people and the people of the world better. But the gulag was still the gulag, and the state was still expansionist, and they still waged proxy wars in Africa, Asia, and Latin America.

Well, this time, so far, it's different. President Gorbachev has brought about some internal democratic reforms and begun the withdrawal from Afghanistan. He has also freed prisoners whose names I've given him every time we've met. . . .

We must keep up our guard, but we must also continue to work together to lessen and eliminate tension and mistrust. My view is that President Gorbachev is different from previous Soviet leaders. I think he knows some of the things wrong with his society and is trying to fix them. We wish him well. And we'll continue to work to make sure that the Soviet Union that eventually emerges from this process is a less threatening one. What it all boils down to is this: I want the new closeness to continue. And it will, as long as we make it clear that we will continue to act in a certain way as long as they continue to act in a helpful manner. If and when they don't, at first pull your punches. If they persist, pull the plug. It's still trust but verify. It's still play, but cut the cards. It's still watch closely. And don't be afraid to see what you see. . . .

But now, we're about to enter the nineties, and some things have changed. Younger parents aren't sure that an unambivalent appreciation of America is the right thing to teach modern children. And as for those who create the popular culture, well-grounded patriotism is no longer the style. Our spirit is back, but we haven't reinstitutionalized it. We've got to do a better job of getting across that America is freedom—freedom of speech, freedom of religion, freedom of enterprise. And freedom is special and rare. It's fragile; it needs protection.

So, we've got to teach history based not on what's in fashion but what's important—why the Pilgrims came here, who Jimmy Doolittle was, and what those thirty seconds over Tokyo meant. You know, four years ago on the fortieth anniversary of D-Day, I read a letter from a young woman writing to her late father, who'd fought on Omaha Beach. Her name was Lisa Zanatta Henn, and she said, "We will always remember, we will never forget what the boys of Normandy did." Well, let's help her keep her word. If we forget what we did, we won't know who we are. I'm warning of an eradication of the American memory that could result, ultimately, in an erosion of the American spirit. Let's start with some basics: more attention to American history and a greater emphasis on civic ritual. . . .

And that's about all I have to say tonight, except for one thing. The past few days . . . I've thought a bit of the "shining city upon a hill." The phrase comes from John Winthrop, who wrote it to describe the America he imagined. What he imagined was important because he was an early Pilgrim, an early freedom man. He journeyed here on what today we'd call a little wooden boat; and like the other Pilgrims, he was looking for a home that would be free. I've spoken of the shining city all my political life, but I don't know if I ever quite communicated what I saw when I said it. But in my mind it was a tall, proud city built on rocks stronger than oceans, windswept, God-blessed, and teeming with people of all kinds living in harmony and peace; a city with free ports that hummed with commerce and creativity. And if there had to be city walls, the walls had doors and the doors were open to anyone with the will and the heart to get here. That's how I saw it, and see it still.

And how stands the city on this winter night? More prosperous, more secure, and happier than it was eight years ago. But more than that: After two hundred years, two centuries, she still stands strong and true on the granite ridge, and her glow has held steady no matter what storm. And she's still a beacon, still a magnet for all who must have freedom, for all the pilgrims from all the lost places who are hurtling through the darkness, toward home.

We've done our part. And as I walk off into the city streets, a final word to the men and women of the Reagan revolution, the men and women across America who for eight years did the work that brought America back. My friends: We did it. We weren't just marking time. We made a difference. We made the city stronger, we made the city freer, and we left her in good hands. All in all, not bad, not bad at all.

And so, goodbye, God bless you, and God bless the United States of America.

Source: Public Papers of the Presidents of the United States: Ronald Reagan, 1989. Washington, DC: U.S. Government Printing Office, 1991.

· *11* ·

The Kinder, Gentler Conservatism of George H. W. Bush

The four years between the presidencies of Ronald Reagan and Bill Clinton were important. By the end of that time the nation's politics had changed. For the Democrats, the liberalism of the New Deal era had passed, and the ideas, policies, and programs of that time no longer appealed to a majority of voters. By the end of the Reagan-Bush era, the Democrats had been out of the White House for twelve years, and they began looking for something new. For the Republicans, George H. W. Bush never quite filled Reagan's shoes. He lacked the charisma and the political abilities to pull together the various parts of his party. Despite Reagan's successes, despite the dynamic growth of American conservatism, the Republican ascendancy was beginning to wane.

American foreign policy also changed dramatically in those four years. The Soviet Union collapsed without as much as a whimper, and all of a sudden communism was no longer a threat. After forty-five years of attempting to manage the world order as a counterpoint of Soviet power and influence, the United States no longer had a force to push against. Most world conflicts, it seemed, had very little meaning. A conflict in, for example, Somalia or Kosovo did not necessarily mean a loss of world influence if the United States did not intervene. By 1992, the United States had to reevaluate completely its interests and its foreign policy. Also by that date, the United States had fought the Gulf War, and that event (as successful as it was) changed the relationship between the United States and the nations of the Middle East, which in several ways rearranged the world balance.

America was changing at home as well. There was a new diversity that the nation had not seen since the turn of the twentieth century nearly a hundred years before. Immigrants were sweeping onto the nation's shores again, this time primarily from Latin America and Asia, causing some parts of the nation to take on a new appearance. And as in past eras of high immigration, there was a reaction to it, mostly from those who refused to believe in the resilience of the American culture and economy.

THE FIRST PRESIDENT BUSH AND
THE MAKING OF AN AMERICAN DYNASTY

George H. W. Bush was elected president in 1988 primarily because of his association with Ronald Reagan. Reagan's time had been one of general peace and
prosperity, a record that is usually hard to beat on Election Day. Thus, Bush
came to office promising to carry on where Reagan had left off, to be the conservative that Reagan had been. But he promised to do it more humanely, with more
compassion than Reagan. He called for a "kinder, gentler" conservatism, a
"kinder, gentler" nation. Unlike Reagan, however, Bush had no particular vision
for the country or even for what his administration might accomplish in the
domestic arena. Consequently, he sponsored very few domestic initiatives, almost
nothing in health care, education, or environmental protection. If he had a style
in office it was crisis management, and as his presidency progressed it became
clear that Bush really had no plans to accomplish much. His most prolific impres-
sionist, Dana Carvey from *Saturday Night Live*, often mimicked Bush, a president forever confused by "the vision thing."

George Herbert Walker Bush was the son of Connecticut Senator Prescott
Bush, an Eisenhower Republican, a moderate who voted to censure Joseph
McCarthy in 1954. Immediately following his graduation from Phillips Academy, young George joined the U.S. Navy in the midst of World War II, becoming the youngest pilot, at age eighteen, in the history of naval aviation. His war
experience was significant. He flew fifty-eight combat missions, was shot down
once, and received the Distinguished Flying Cross and three air medals. After
the war, he got married and entered Yale. There he majored in economics, led
the Yale baseball team to the first college world series, and was tapped for membership in the "Skull and Bones" secret society, a Bush family tradition. George
H. W. Bush was the epitome of the New England elite. At the time, the Bushes,
not unlike the Kennedys, were destined to decide the fate of the nation.

Following college in 1948, Bush headed to Texas to become an oil man. In
1953 he and a few family friends created Zapata Oil, a conglomerate that began
in Midland, Texas, but soon moved its operations to Houston. In 1963, Zapata
merged with other oil companies to become Pennzoil. In 1964 Bush ran for the
Senate from his adopted state of Texas. His opponent, Ralph Yarborough, was
able to convince voters that Bush (who supported Barry Goldwater for the presidency that year) was a right-wing extremist, and Bush lost. Two years later, however, Bush was elected to the House of Representatives, and in 1968 he made
a modest and unsuccessful bid to be Nixon's running mate on the Republican
presidential ticket. In 1970, Bush made another run for the Senate and was again
defeated, this time by the Democrat Lloyd Bentsen.

During the Nixon administration, Bush served as ambassador to the United

Nations and chairman of the Republican National Committee during the Watergate days. In 1974 he was passed over as Gerald Ford's vice president. Ford considered Bush too conservative and chose instead Nelson Rockefeller. Bush was then sent to China where he was appointed chief liaison officer, at the time the highest-ranking U.S. official in China.

In 1976, Bush became director of the CIA, an organization he had been associated with since the mid-1950s. He is usually credited with restoring the agency's morale following a series of revelations that the CIA had been involved in illegal activities, including the assassination of foreign officials.

During the Carter administration, Bush returned to private life. In 1980 he ran for president and became Reagan's chief challenger for the Republican nomination. Following a fairly contentious campaign, Reagan won the nomination and chose Bush as his running mate. Reagan won the election and Bush became vice president. As the 1988 campaign approached, it looked at first as though Bush would be overshadowed by Senator Bob Dole. But the Bush organizational strength and fund-raising ability gave him the nomination.

BUSH AND THE WORLD

Like Nixon, Bush had a background in foreign affairs, and so it was that foreign affairs drove his presidency. At the same time, Bush did little to put his personal imprint on any aspect of U.S. foreign policy in the period.

Bush's foreign policy team was a combination of past and future Republican Party lights. The secretary of state, James Baker III, was a close friend. He had managed Bush's unsuccessful 1970 Senate campaign and served as Reagan's chief of staff and then as his secretary of the treasury in his second term. Bush's national security advisor, Brent Scowcroft, had served in that role in the Ford administration and, before that, as Nixon's military advisor. Bush's defense secretary was Dick Cheney, a conservative Wyoming congressman. General Colin Powell, Reagan's national security advisor, was named chairman of the Joint Chiefs of Staff. This group would have their hands full in Bush's packed four-year term.

The first test came in Panama. There, a one-time U.S. ally, Panamanian president Manuel Noriega, had become a problem by using his nation as a way station for the drug traffic from South America into the United States. The situation had become a growing embarrassment for the Reagan administration, and in December 1989 Bush felt compelled to act. He sent in twenty-five thousand troops to crush the Panamanian military and arrest Noriega. The event was hardly noteworthy. It was, however, another attempt—not unlike Reagan's invasion of Grenada in 1983—to raise U.S. esteem in the world, to show that the

United States was still a world power. And like Grenada, the Panamanian military put up little resistance.

THE COLLAPSE OF THE SOVIET UNION

The situation in the Soviet bloc was changing. In 1985 Mikhail Gorbachev came to power in Moscow and began a more conciliatory relationship with the United States and the West. The Soviet economy was growing weak following decades of poor planning and corruption. In response, Gorbachev announced the policies of *perestroika* (economic restructuring) and *glasnost* (openness). In addition, the Soviets had suffered a serious defeat in Afghanistan. Then, at the very end of 1989, Gorbachev announced that the people of Eastern Europe were free to determine their own destinies, that Moscow would no longer interfere in their affairs or decisions. It was a wakeup call for change; Communist regimes in Eastern Europe, propped up for decades by the repressive power of the Soviet Union, began to collapse like a house of cards. Presidents were elected in Poland (labor leader Lech Walesa) and in Czechoslovakia (playwright Vaclav Havel) without Soviet interference. Strikes and demonstrations broke out in Hungary, Poland, Czechoslovakia, Romania, and Bulgaria, and the old Communist regimes toppled. When there was no movement from Moscow to suppress these actions, local demonstrations quickly turned into mass celebrations in the streets. Romanian dictator Nicolai Ceausescu was hunted down and shot. In East Germany, the new leader, Egon Krenz, announced that East Germans could cross into the West, and on November 9 crowds gathered at the various checkpoints along the Berlin Wall and began flooding across. In the following spectacle that was beamed around the world, the Germans (both East and West) took sledgehammers and joined in a jubilant tearing down of the wall that had separated them since the 1960s. Then in October 1990 Germany was reunited under a single government for the first time since 1945. For most of the world, the event marked the end of the Cold War.

In the Soviet Union itself, Gorbachev had hoped to reform his nation by moving slowly toward a type of democratic socialism, but the forces he had unleashed in Eastern Europe now overwhelmed him. Nationalism seemed to break out everywhere. Between 1989 and 1991, the Baltic states—Latvia, Lithuania, and Estonia—declared their independence. Moscow made attempts to resist, but in 1991 all three were allowed to form governments and become independent. Several of the other Soviet republics declared their independence, and Gorbachev did not react.

The chaos and uncertainty damaged the Soviet economy even further. In August 1991, a group of Soviet military officers and Communist hardliners staged a coup and placed Gorbachev under arrest. Americans held their breath as one of the world's superpowers seemed about to descend into chaos. But the coup was quickly thwarted by the new president of the Russian Republic, Boris Yeltsin, who famously mounted a tank and demanded that the coup leaders back down and restore Gorbachev to power. When much of the Red Army and forty thousand citizens of Moscow threw their support to Yeltsin, the coup collapsed. Within two months, the Soviet republics split off one by one and claimed independence. On December 21, 1991, Yeltsin officially proclaimed an end to the Soviet Union, and the Soviet Communist Party collapsed. The successor to the old USSR was something called the Commonwealth of Independent States (CIS), made up of the eleven former republics, the three Baltic states, and an independent Georgia. At the 1992 Summer Olympics in Barcelona, the Soviet team had become the CIS, and for the first time in forty years there were no East German judges.

Americans were stunned as they watched the revolution expand. The statues of past Communist leaders were toppled amidst raucous celebrations. Throughout the world, Soviet embassies became Russian embassies and the red hammer and sickle flag was replaced by the old Russian tricolor. In May 1992, at Westminster College in Missouri, where Churchill had opened the Cold War by declaring that an "Iron Curtain" had descended over Europe, Gorbachev told the world that the Cold War was indeed over.

Any American born after World War II had not known a time when there was not a Soviet enemy, an enemy that might destroy the United States if given the opportunity. Somehow it seemed to leave a void. Some Americans began to see a utopia on the horizon of unarmed nations at peace, and a substantial "peace dividend," a cash amount sent to all Americans reflecting an end to massive defense spending. The reality was that the Cold War had suppressed regional, social, religious, nationalist, and ethnic differences throughout the world. It could be seen clearly in the breakup of Yugoslavia, the attempted secession of Chechnya from Russia, and the various Middle Eastern crises. There would be no "peace dividend" and no peaceful utopia. The United States and Russia immediately ended their mutually destructive ways, but the world continued to be a hostile place, perhaps even more hostile than before the collapse of the Soviet Union, and the United States continued to build its arsenals to maintain itself as the one and only superpower.

The end of the Cold War also brought an end to U.S. foreign policy as it had been constructed since the Truman administration. The fear of communism or of Communist expansion had been the glue that held all the analyses, interpretations, and strategies together. The result was a type of foundering without a plan or direction. The world situation lent itself well to George H. W. Bush's crisis management style; he simply reacted to events as they occurred. He was much criticized for it, but to devise a coherent foreign policy under such unusual and confusing situations was undoubtedly difficult.

The end of hostilities did allow the United States and Russia to move toward a significant reduction in nuclear warheads. In 1991, just before Gorbachev's fall from power, Bush and Gorbachev signed the START treaty, cutting each nation's warheads by 25 percent, to just under ten thousand. In late 1992, Boris Yeltsin, as the new president of the independent Russia, agreed to give up all land-based multi-warhead missiles, while the United States agreed to cut its missile-launching submarine fleet in half. The two also agreed to draw down the number of warheads to three thousand each—below the mid-1960s level. By 1990, the Warsaw Pact had disintegrated, and NATO announced a troop reduction of 50 percent.

The new Russian economy immediately stagnated, partly because of a lack of a basic understanding of the capitalist system. There were no commercial banks, no investment capital, and no free enterprise tradition of basic competitive strategy. Clearly it was in Washington's interest that the Russian economy be successful, but when Yeltsin asked for help, the Bush administration balked. Finally, with some prodding from Richard Nixon, Bush agreed to a $35 billion aid package. Several world leaders and economists complained that the aid was much too modest, arguing that the one primary lesson of the twentieth century is that radicalism and despotic rule will flourish in weak economic times.

The end of the Cold War changed the dynamic in several places throughout the world. In April 1989, just as Soviet control of Eastern Europe was in the throes of collapse, thousands of Chinese students rallied in Tiananmen Square in Beijing, first to mourn the death of a progressive Chinese leader, then to demand more democracy for the Chinese people. This pro-democracy movement mushroomed, spreading to China's major cities. Americans watched the events unfold on television and strongly supported the students and their allies. Analysts since George Kennan had insisted that communism carried the seeds of its own destruction, and here, in the summer of 1989, it seemed so. The Beijing government appeared uncertain on how to deal with the events; they were, in fact, gathering their forces and shoring up their political flanks. In the early morning hours of June 4, the Chinese Twenty-Seventh and Twenty-Eighth Armies moved tanks into Beijing and crushed the pro-democracy movement. Demonstrations in other cities were put down violently. The number killed ranged anywhere from one thousand to five thousand, depending on the source. President Bush condemned China but refused to take any concrete action, fearing he might damage the fragile U.S.-Chinese relationship.

In Central America, the end of the Cold War put a stop to Soviet support of all anti-American activity. In Cuba, Soviet aid ended. The old Soviet Union had propped up the weak Cuban economy since the 1960s with about $5 billion per year in aid. Without Soviet support, Castro was reduced to little more than a ranting anti-American dictator, a relic of the past. Soviet aid to the Sandinistas in Nicaragua dried up as well. Their response was to move away from guerilla warfare and toward political legitimacy. In early 1990, the Sandinista candidate, Daniel Ortega, was defeated by Violetta Chamorro in a nationwide presidential election. With no Soviet support, the Sandinistas handed over power peacefully.

At nearly the same moment, apartheid came to an end in South Africa. Although not really caused by the end of the Cold War, the collapse of all-white rule in South Africa was one of the most remarkable events of the late twentieth century. South Africa had been an abomination of racial separatism and ruthless suppression since the end of World War II. By the 1980s Americans had begun to demand that U.S. institutions (particularly colleges and universities) "divest," or sell their investments in South African enterprises and in American businesses that continued to do business in South Africa. In 1986, overriding a Reagan veto, Congress voted to end U.S. trade and corporate investment in South Africa. South African athletes, like golfer Gary Player and middle-distance runner Zola Budd, were excluded from international competition. This pressure finally forced the white South African government to begin modifying its overtly racist stance. In August 1989 F. W. de Klerk was elected prime minister of South Africa and almost immediately released Nelson Mandela, the head of the African National Conference (ANC), from prison. The ANC was the major black African political organization in South Africa. In 1991 de Klerk began dismantling apartheid, and President Bush agreed to lift all economic sanctions against South Africa. In April 1994, Mandela was elected president and apartheid ended.

A drought and famine hit parts of northeast Africa, particularly Somalia. The press covered the events there, daily sending back horrific shots for the evening news of starving children. In response, relief agencies sent in emergency supplies. When warring factions stole the supplies to sell on the black market, Bush, in December 1992, sent in thirty thousand troops to protect and deliver the aid. By then, Bush had been voted out of office, although he was still president until the president-elect, Bill Clinton, was inaugurated in January. It would be up to Clinton to deal with the growing chaos in Somalia.

THE FIRST GULF WAR

All wars have deep historical roots, and the 1991 Persian Gulf War was no exception. It might be argued that the war originated from the post–World War I drawing of boundaries by the British that kept the new nation of Iraq from having a usable port on the Persian Gulf. But for the United States, the events of the early 1990s originated with the overthrow of Iranian Prime Minister Mohammad Mosaddeq in 1953 by the Eisenhower administration. That event led to the U.S.-backed regime of Shah Reza Pahlavi. By the late 1970s, the shah's repressive government was hated by the vast majority of the Iranian people, and by association the United States was seen as the force behind the shah. In 1979 that led to the overthrow of the shah and the kidnapping of fifty-two U.S. Embassy workers in Tehran by Islamic Shiite fundamentalists. To the Iranians, America had become the enemy, the "Great Satan." At the same time, much of the Islamic world had come to see Israel's existence in Palestine as illegitimate, an affront to Islam, and American-supported.

In 1963 the Baath Party took control in Iraq following a bloody coup, and then again in 1968 after a brief ouster. A young Saddam Hussein worked as a torturer in this period at a Baath interrogation center in Baghdad, a little shop of horrors known as the "Palace of the End." He quickly rose to prominence as the head of the Baath secret police. By 1973 Saddam was in firm control of Iraq, and by 1978 he had taken the lead in the Arab world in punishing Egypt for making peace with Israel. Iraq became a sanctuary for the deadliest Palestinian terrorists, and the most boisterous anti-Israeli threats in this period came from Baghdad. It appeared that Iraq was about to become the leader of the Arab world, the position vacated by Anwar Sadat when he signed the peace treaty with Israel at Camp David in 1979. Through the 1980s the United States began to pull Iraq closer as a counterbalance to the radical Shiites who had taken over in Iran. As the situation in Iran hardened, Washington saw Iraqi strength as a way to neutralize the anti-American government of the Ayatollah Khomeini.

At the same time, Saddam was able to take advantage of the fear that the radical Shiite movement in Iran might spread to the rest of the Muslim Middle East. By moving to contain the radical Shiites, Saddam hoped to place himself into the role of leader of the Arab world. To that end, he launched a war against Iran in September 1980, a war that he intended to be quick and easy. Instead, Saddam found himself bogged down in an expensive no-win war against the revolutionary armies of radical Islam. The Reagan administration was willing to help Saddam in this war, but Kuwait and the rest of the Arab world refused—with either men or money. When the war ended in 1988, the outgoing Reagan administration and then George Bush continued to support Iraq with agricultural credits. But the U.S.-Iraq relationship soured when it was revealed that the United States had been secretly selling arms to Iran during the Iran-Iraq War and using the profits to support the anti-Sandinista rebels in Nicaragua. To Saddam this was a serious betrayal.

Saddam had come to believe that he had protected the Arab world from radical Islam. But he had destroyed his economy in the process, and he expected the Arab nations to come to his aid. Not only did they refuse, they continued to produce oil at record levels, driving oil prices down and damaging Iraq's economy even further. On August 2, after talks between Saddam and the leaders of the other Arab nations broke down, Iraq's Russian-made T-72 tanks blitzed into Kuwait and seized the nation in less than six hours. It appeared that Saudi Arabia (controlling close to 25 percent of the world's oil supply) would be next.

Bush responded by forming an international coalition under the auspices of the United Nations. The coalition deployed a force of 250,000 soldiers from the United States, Great Britain, France, and several of the Arab countries, including Saudi Arabia, Syria, Egypt, and the United Arab Emirates. The operation, under the command of U.S. General Norman Schwarzkopf, was known as Desert Shield.

Bush originally intended to protect Saudi Arabia from an Iraqi invasion and then force Saddam from Kuwait through economic sanctions over time. But he soon became convinced, mostly as a result of talks with British Prime Minister Margaret Thatcher, that boycotts and sanctions would not work. On November 29, 1990, the United Nations passed Resolution 629, setting January 15, 1991, as the deadline for Saddam's withdrawal from Kuwait. Bush began a buildup of 580,000 soldiers (from some twenty countries) in Saudi Arabia, south of Kuwait. On January 12, both houses of Congress enacted resolutions approving force against the Iraqi military and government.

The air assault began on January 16. About five weeks later, on the morning of February 24, Schwarzkopf sent an invasion force of over two hundred thousand coalition troops and twelve hundred tanks crashing into Kuwait. Desert Shield had become Desert Storm. A feint of a Marine column in the south forced Saddam to concentrate his efforts there, while the main body of Schwarzkopf's forces swung rapidly into Kuwait unnoticed from the west. Schwarzkopf called it his "left hook."

The war was over before it started. Within one hundred hours, Saddam's army was on the run, south toward Basra. General Colin Powell, head of the Joint Chiefs, decided to end the war quickly, fearing an international backlash or even a disintegration of the international coalition if the war turned into a slaughter. To pursue them further, he said, "would be un-American and un-chivalrous." He argued that the objective had been achieved: Saddam's troops were out of Kuwait.

Some complained that the war was ended too quickly, that the Iraqi army had not been destroyed. Others thought that Schwarzkopf should have marched to Baghdad, overthrown Saddam, and occupied Iraq. But Bush understood the ramifications of that, and decided instead to keep Saddam "in his box," to contain him, employ sanctions, and make certain that he did not again threaten his neighbors.

The Gulf War ended America's post-Vietnam reticence. The United States had shown its massive power to the world. It had organized and led an impressive coalition of the willing, including several Arab nations, to come to the aid of a weak nation that had been overwhelmed by a larger aggressor. Critics complained that the war had been about oil and who would control it in the future. But to most Americans, their country was again strong, and on the right side of history.

AMERICA AT HOME

Bush's domestic initiatives were minimal. His "no new taxes" pledge made it almost certain that he would not break any new ground in domestic affairs. In fact, in the first three years of his presidency he vetoed twenty-eight bills, killing just about every domestic initiative. He had promised during his campaign to be the "education president," but in fact he did almost nothing in the area of education, insisting that education should be left to the state and local governments.

He renewed Reagan's "war on drugs," but shifted the focus from ending U.S. demand for drugs ("just say no") to stopping the influx of drugs into the United States. He also pushed for drug-testing in the workplace and better enforcement of existing laws. The new laws and initiatives did little to curb the American appetite for drug use, particularly cocaine and crack.

By 1990 the federal deficit was rising rapidly, still reeling from the tax cuts and increased military spending of the 1980s. At the same time, entitlement programs were mushrooming. By the spring of 1991, Bush was under great pressure to reduce the federal deficit, by then approaching $300 billion, up from about half that in 1988. In addition, the national debt was headed toward $4 trillion. But Bush found himself caught: He felt unable to cut programs; at the same time, he was bound by his "no new taxes" pledge. To the consternation of Republican conservatives, he conceded to Democrats and agreed to a five-year deficit-reduction package that included a tax hike. The increase was mostly in the upper-income brackets, and it reduced the deficit by less than $50 billion. But party conservatives called it a betrayal and began to calculate the president's 1992 defeat almost as revenge. The event thrust conservative radio commentator Rush Limbaugh into the national limelight really for the first time, and it pushed Pat Buchanan to challenge Bush for the 1992 Republican nomination. The tax bill included significant budget cuts, but conservatives were never satisfied.

What followed was a fairly significant recession, the first in nearly a decade. Unemployment jumped to over 7 percent, housing starts and business investment dropped, and the median household income fell. The Federal Reserve cut interest rates, but the economy refused to respond. The GDP, which had soared to nearly 14 percent in the Reagan years, now dropped to a negligible 2.2 percent. Economists blamed the go-go 1980s, when Americans plunged into debt just to maintain their level of consumption. Now the bill was due. When asked how the administration would move to end the recession, Bush's chief of staff John Sununu replied that the administration would do nothing to end the recession.

THE CONTINUED AIDS CRISIS

AIDS in the 1980s was what polio had been in the earlier part of the century, what tuberculosis had been a hundred years before. It was a scourge that could not be cured, that took lives without warning. By 1993, AIDS had killed over two hundred thousand Americans. By 2008, the disease had killed twenty-five million worldwide, and approximately forty million continued to live with the disease. It destroyed societies and economies in large parts of the world, particularly parts of sub-Saharan Africa and southern Asia.

The parts of American society most vulnerable to the disease are gay men, and drug users who share needles. The virus was also spread through blood transfusions, until about 1990 when a process became available to screen the blood supply. The AIDS epidemic was so devastating that it invited all sorts of myths and accusations. Some saw it as God's punishment of homosexuals. Others believed it was a CIA conspiracy to decimate unwanted groups in society. Still others believed the disease could be passed on by casual contact. AIDS sufferers were ostracized, and many suffered alone. Homosexuals, who were just beginning to emerge from the closet to be accepted into mainstream society, were again shunned, even blamed for their condition.

But gay rights activists began to protest the situation, insisting that drug companies increase their budgets and research in an attempt to end the scourge by finding treatments or even a vaccine. High-profile figures who contracted the disease changed the landscape. Tennis great Arthur Ashe contracted AIDS through a blood transfusion and died in 1993, showing the nation that not all AIDS victims were gay drug abusers. Ryan White's death, also as a result of a transfusion, seemed to bring a great deal of sympathy for AIDS victims. Even the movie *Philadelphia* in 1993, starring Tom Hanks as a gay man fired by his law firm because they feared he had AIDS, was greatly sympathetic to AIDS sufferers and changed the nation's view of the disease. AIDS continued to be a concern into the next century, but the threat in the United States diminished considerably. Overseas, however (particularly in Africa and South Asia), the virus raged on, killing millions every year—including many children who contracted it from their mothers.

THE ENVIRONMENT AND GEORGE BUSH

George Bush compiled a strong environmental record. During the Bush presidency the Environmental Protection Agency flexed a great deal of muscle. It established ninety-three wildlife refuges, extended protection to millions of acres of wetlands, and pushed a bill that protected the Grand Canyon. The EPA also placed a ban on most uses of asbestos.

In 1989 the worst environmental catastrophe in U.S. history occurred when the supertanker *Exxon Valdez* went aground in Alaska's pristine Prince William Sound and spilled ten million gallons of crude oil. Over a thousand miles of coastline was poisoned by the black sludge. The operation to clean up the mess cost the Exxon Corporation an estimated $2.5 billion. Bush used the nation's outrage at the incident to push through the 1990 Clean Air Act, which built on the Clean Air acts of 1963, 1970, and 1977.

One aspect of the bill was to deal with acid rain, the emission of sulfur dioxide into the atmosphere, mostly by coal-fired power plants. It was a persistent environmental problem that had fouled water and foliage in parts of the Northeast and Canada. The act authorized emissions trading, which was designed to reduce emissions significantly over the next ten years. The act also set limits on pollutants emitted from automobiles and authorized tougher limits for ozone and carbon monoxide pollutants.

THE NEW COURT

Two retirements changed the face of the U.S. Supreme Court, which had maintained a fairly liberal stance since at least the ascension of Earl Warren in 1953. Many past decisions had been close, giving Bush the opportunity to shift the court to a conservative majority. In 1990 William Brennan retired, and a year later Thurgood Marshall left the court. Not surprisingly, Bush took the opportunity to make the court in his own image. His first appointment was David Souter who was easily confirmed by the Senate. Souter, somewhat surprisingly, slipped into the liberal wing of the court on most issues. In 1992 he joined the majority in *Planned Parenthood v. Casey* in upholding a Pennsylvania law requiring a twenty-four-hour waiting period before an abortion. More importantly, however, the decision upheld the 1973 *Roe v. Wade* decision giving a woman the constitutional right to have an abortion.

While Souter was uncontroversial, Bush's second appointee, Clarence Thomas, was about as controversial and polarizing as possible. Thomas, an African American and a conservative, was named to replace Thurgood Marshall, the venerable civil rights attorney who was instrumental in winning the *Brown v. Board of Education* decision in 1954. To African Americans, and to liberals as well, to replace Marshall with Thomas was contemptuous. In the early 1980s, Thomas had headed the Equal Employment Opportunity Commission, the agency charged with enforcing the Civil Rights Act of 1964. There he had opposed most doctrines that sought to end discrimination, including affirmative action. He had also criticized *Roe v. Wade*.

The Senate Judiciary Committee refused to recommend Thomas, sending the decision to the Senate floor for approval. During the Senate hearings, which were televised, Thomas evaded questions about abortion and other issues, much to the disgust of liberal senators. In the midst of the hearings, the media learned that Thomas had been charged with sexual harassment while head of the EEOC. His accuser was Anita Hill, an African American professor at the University of Oklahoma law school. She told the Senate, in a televised testimony, that Thomas had sexually harassed her while she worked as his aide in the early 1980s. While the nation watched, Hill recounted in sexually explicit detail Thomas's various attempts to interest her sexually. She spoke of pornographic movies, pubic hairs intentionally left on a Coke can, and larger-than-normal male sex organs. Thomas referred to the hearing as "a high-tech lynching." He was confirmed, with conservatives believing his testimony, that the events Hill described never happened, and with liberals believing her side of the story. Bush called Thomas's testimony "powerful" and "convincing."

Republicans who attacked Hill, particularly senators Orrin Hatch and Arlen Specter, argued that sexual harassment rules were unfair and too narrow, and that judges had a tendency to accept what they called the "feminist definition" of sexual harassment. They argued that the feminist definition was, in fact, little more than men being men, innocent courtship that should not be punished. The hearings opened a debate in the nation for the first time on the nature of sexual harassment in the workplace. Perhaps it was a response to the hearings that in the 1992 election women overwhelmingly voted Democratic.

THE NEW DIVERSITY

By 1990 the United States population stood at 240 million. During the Bush years, five million immigrants entered the nation, the highest rate since the turn of the century. Roughly 8 percent of the nation was foreign born, up from less than 5 percent just two decades earlier. Prior to 1965, when new laws liberalized immigration, the numbers were generally low; between 1931 and 1965 a total of only about five million legal immigrants came into the United States. But after that, the floodgates seemed to open. In the 1970s alone, 4.5 million immigrants came. In the next decade, that number jumped to 7.5 million. Of those, as many as 350,000 came in illegally each year. It is impossible to know how many of those stayed and how many returned to their homes.

In the 1992 presidential campaign, candidate Pat Buchanan complained that the rising immigration was tearing the nation apart. "Our own country is undergoing the greatest invasion in its history," he said, "a migration of millions of illegal aliens yearly from Mexico." He then added, "A nation that cannot control its own borders can scarcely call itself a state any longer." Of course, Buchanan did not stand alone on this. Environmentalists worried about population growth. Some educators complained about the costs of bilingual education. Wage-earners feared that foreigners would work cheaply and drive wages down. Another fear was that the United States was simply inviting in a new underclass, a mass of poor people with no health care, no skills, and no real prospects of success beyond migrant work, an underclass that would need support from the nation's taxpayers. There were, however, plenty of people who welcomed the influx, people who needed the work done and who might profit from the cheap labor. There were others who were simply not alarmed by the newcomers. After all, at least two other times in the nation's history a massive influx of immigrants did not change the national character. Between 1900 and 1910, the last big flood of foreigners, immigration had accounted for 40 percent of the nation's population growth, and the number of foreign-born in American society was almost 15 percent, the highest in the nation's history, and considerably higher than in 1990. And America did not change substantially; it maintained its multicultural roots and accommodated and assimilated the newcomers.

Hispanics poured into the American Southwest. In 1990 there were approximately twenty million Hispanics in the United States, double the 1970 total. They quickly became the fastest-growing minority in the nation, on the verge even then of replacing African Americans as the largest minority in the country. Some came legally, but most did not. In 1990 as many as twelve million Hispanics lived in the United States illegally. They came seeking a better life; they were willing to take jobs that most Americans did not want: as migrant workers in the fields of California, as domestic workers, yard workers, and service workers. Some took their earnings and returned home. Some were intent on staying, on becoming Americans.

Over 20 percent of the new immigrants lived below the poverty line. In 1986 a new immigration law sought to tighten border controls. Tougher laws were imposed on those who hired illegal aliens. That same year, California passed Proposition 63, establishing English as the official language of the state. Seventeen other states followed California's lead.

By 1990 the number of Asians coming to America had increased significantly. Much of that influx had to do with U.S. interests in Asia, particularly in Vietnam, the Philippines, and Korea. In addition, large numbers of Chinese began to head to the United States in the late 1980s and early 1990s, often intent on escaping the post-Tiananmen crackdown. Others came for the reasons immigrants have always come to the United States: They hoped to take advantage of the opportunities, to make a better life for themselves and their families.

The Chinese educational system was strong, but opportunities for college graduates in China were minimal. The United States had much to offer young, well-educated Chinese in the late 1980s and into the 1990s. By 1990, Asians made up 2.8 percent of the national population; within ten years, that number would jump to 4.2 percent, outpacing the growth of the national population. Chinese made up the majority of that growth.

Perhaps the most important aspect of this influx was the ability of Asians to succeed. The Asian emphasis on education was renowned. In addition, the Asians who came to America were highly motivated to succeed within the American system. The result was the highest rate of university attendance of any group in the United States, the highest rate of graduation, and thus, not surprisingly, some of the highest income rates of any group in the nation. Whatever the odds are against making it in America, the Asians seem to have beaten those odds.

A DIVIDED BLACK AMERICA

By 1990 most Americans had again fallen into the old trap of believing that race relations in America were at least stable, that racial reconciliation and mutual acceptance had become the standard. The urban riots had ended, radicalism seemed on the wane, and, perhaps most importantly to white Americans, there were large numbers of African Americans who had pushed their way into the middle class. This group was particularly visible to the rest of the nation. Their prosperity, however, masked the problems of the inner city that were not so visible. There, poverty remained; crime and drug use were both rising. And not surprisingly, with those problems came hopelessness, frustration, and anger.

By 1990 the black professional had become an American icon, the fictional Huxtables, an upper-middle-class, African American family enjoying good incomes, living in the best neighborhood, with a stable family life and several college degrees. In 1990, 12 percent of college students were black, a number that had doubled since the 1970s. In that same year, nearly 50 percent of African Americans in the labor force held white-collar jobs. In 1990 the median household income for blacks was roughly 60 percent of white household incomes. By 1995, however, the income for an African American married couple had jumped to about 87 percent of white couples. Stable black families, and black women in the workforce, did very well by the mid-1990s.

The other part of the African American community—perhaps as much as one third or more—was not doing so well. Nearly ten million African Americans lived in poverty in 1990, affecting almost 32 percent of all African Americans. An estimated nine million lived in crowded, poverty-stricken inner cities, where one in four black males between the ages of twenty and twenty-nine were either in jail, on parole, or on probation and the homicide rate for young black men was as much as ten times the rate for white males in the same age group. Unwed birth rates and divorce rates were at an all-time high. Nearly 70 percent of births to African American women were to single mothers, many of whom were too young to be responsible parents. High school dropout rates for African Americans in 1990 ran at about 13 percent nationally, compared to about 9 percent for whites. But in some inner-city schools the rate easily reached 50 percent. With no education, no training, and no jobs in the inner cities, these young people often found no alternative but life on the streets, where the only significant income came from the sale of drugs. It was, in fact, almost always the neighborhood drug salesman who "made it" in the ghetto, the only real role model, the only real standard of success. The life of the Huxtables might have been as inaccessible as life on the moon.

By 1990, America had become a segregated nation. Although it was still true that nearly half of all black families lived in racially mixed neighborhoods, the vast majority of African Americans lived in the black inner city or over the tracks in the black part of town, while the whites occupied the suburbs. And not unlike the segregated era of the first half of the century, the best schools were in the suburbs, along with the best police protection and the best city services. The amount spent on inner-city schools lagged behind spending for the white schools in the suburbs. The distinctions were clearest in test scores, with blacks and Latinos in the inner cities scoring well below the white kids in the suburbs. The testing gap between racial groups had narrowed substantially in the 1970s, but it began to widen again in the 1980s.

These years also saw an expanding drug culture, and by 1990 drug use in the inner city had begun to take its toll. Illegal drug use was found at all economic levels in the 1990s and crossed all racial lines, but among black youths in the nation's inner cities drug use reached epidemic proportions. The lucrative trade fostered the growth of gangs that often fought for geographical dominance. Gangs often franchised their names to other cities, and the drug culture grew. Murder rates jumped as gangs vied for control.

By 1990 it was clear that the nation was on the verge of establishing an underclass. Perhaps as much as one-third of the black population lived in these conditions; nearly two-thirds of all black children had been on welfare by the time they reached eighteen. Money was needed for programs, better schools, better housing, better training, more police on the streets, even more prisons. The cost of maintaining an underclass was enormous, and it soon became apparent to anyone in government that preventive solutions (like better education and training) were much less expensive than funding more welfare and building bigger prisons. Through the next two decades America would debate how to solve this growing inner-city problem.

These problems would, occasionally, produce bursts of violence. As was the case with many urban riots of the past decades, the riots of the late 1980s and early 1990s were triggered by police brutality—and perceived police brutality. In 1989 in Miami, the shootings of two black motorcyclists by a Miami police officer set off three days of riots and looting in the city's black neighborhoods. Six people were shot and four hundred were arrested. But it was the 1992 Compton riot that was the most serious. In March 1991, Los Angeles police tried to arrest Rodney King following a high-speed chase. The police, angry at King for trying to evade arrest, beat and kicked him for at least fifteen minutes. This event, disturbing as it was, might not have caused much consternation—except that the entire episode was caught on video by a bystander and shown over and over on national news reports.

The event, and the film, outraged the nation. Four policemen were indicted for use of excessive force, but the trial was moved out of multiracial Los Angeles to the predominantly white suburb of Simi Valley. In May 1992, a jury of ten whites, one Asian, and one Hispanic acquitted two of the policemen and convicted the third on a minor charge. Within minutes, South-Central Los Angeles erupted. Looting, fires, and beatings spread throughout parts of the city. The brutal beating of an innocent white truck driver was caught on tape from a heli-copter and became another news report shown repeatedly. In many areas the focus of the riots was on Korean-owned businesses, perhaps a symbol of success inside the failing black community. Many were burned. The root cause was the perception of racial injustice, but many participants took advantage of the chaos to loot and destroy. And when news reports showed Hispanics joining in the looting, there was a new outcry for more immigration restriction. When the smoke cleared after six days, fifty-three people had been killed, several gunned down at random. Federal troops and the National Guard were brought in to restore order, and in the end almost twelve thousand people were arrested, most for looting or receiving stolen property. Early the next year, two of the four offi-cers were found guilty in federal court in Los Angeles of violating Rodney King's civil rights.

1992 CAMPAIGN

As the 1992 campaign approached, Bush seemed unbeatable. His approval rat-ings at the end of the Gulf War made it fairly clear that he would win reelection. Several Democrats, in fact, considered the race unwinnable and decided to hold off until 1996 when, they surely thought, the field would be wide open. Among those who demurred were Governor Mario Cuomo of New York, House Major-ity Leader Dick Gephardt, and Senators Jay Rockefeller from West Virginia and Al Gore from Tennessee. Among those who chose to throw their hats into the ring were governors Bill Clinton from Arkansas and Jerry Brown from California, and senators Tom Harkin from Iowa and Bob Kerrey from Nebraska. There were at least six others.

Exploding onto the political scene was Texas billionaire businessman Ross Perot, who announced as a third-party candidate. Perot whaled against the national debt and played on the nation's continued distrust of professional politi-cians. He also insisted that, if elected, he would run the nation like a business, which seemed to make sense to a lot of Americans. In June (before the conven-tions) he led in the national polls with an approval rating of 39 percent. Bush trailed with 31 percent and Clinton with 25 percent.

Despite an early challenge from conservative journalist Pat Buchanan, George Bush and his 1988 running mate Dan Quayle took the Republican nomi-nation easily. The conservatives within the party, however, had forced Bush to take on a more conservative mantle than in 1988. When he broke his "no new taxes" pledge he had alienated conservatives, and large numbers began looking to Perot as an appealing alternative. To bring these conservatives back into the fold he was forced to embrace the far right: mostly evangelical groups who violently opposed abortion, favoritism for minorities, homosexuality, and pornography, and who spoke loudly for school prayer and what they called "family values." To that end, Bush agreed to allow Buchanan to deliver the keynote speech at the convention in Houston. Buchanan's speech, known as the "culture war" speech, alienated moderates. Buchanan said, "There is a religious war going on in this country for the soul of America. . . . The agenda [the Democrats] would impose on America—abortion on demand, a litmus test for the Supreme Court, homosexual rights, discrimination against religious schools, women in combat—that's all right. But it is not the kind of change America wants." Buchanan's speech placed Bush in the difficult position of walking lightly between the left and the right of his party, fearing that a shift one way would cause a defection from the other side. A charismatic Reagan could do it; Bush could not.

Bill Clinton was mostly unknown outside his home state of Arkansas. He called himself a centrist, a "New Democrat"—a phrase mostly assigned to fiscal responsibility. Clinton took on most of the liberal views of his generation, such as abortion rights and the right to health care, but he never really positioned himself on the left. He had been a fairly moderate governor of a conservative Southern state, and he was not at all associated with the failed liberal campaigns of Walter Mondale or Michael Dukakis. He said he wanted to bring middle-class voters back to the party, generally stayed away from labor unions, and was always reticent about being seen on a podium with Jesse Jackson. He called himself "born again," supported the death penalty, and said he would reform welfare, push for a tax cut, and cut the budget by half in four years.

Clinton made a strong showing in the New Hampshire primary, where he finished second behind Paul Tsongas, a one-time senator from neighboring Massachusetts and a self-avowed liberal. In the midst of the New Hampshire campaign, a woman named Gennifer Flowers accused Clinton of a twelve-year affair. Clinton headed for damage control by appearing on *60 Minutes* with his wife, Hillary. He generally talked around the issue, saying only that he had "caused pain in his marriage," while his wife sat stone-faced. By the time of the general election, Clinton had contained the issue, but it led some Republicans to look deeper into Clinton's past, certain that he was vulnerable on other issues. Following New Hampshire, Clinton won most of the "Super Tuesday" primaries and, with the exception of a flash-in-the-pan bid by Jerry Brown, easily took the nomination at the New York City convention. Clinton chose Tennessee senator Al Gore as his running mate.

Clinton won the election, taking 43.7 million votes and 370 electoral votes to Bush's 38 million votes and 168 electoral votes. Perot grabbed 19.2 million votes and no electoral votes. (Perot had decided to leave the campaign, then changed his mind and jumped back it. The entire ordeal hurt his credibility.)

The economy had damaged Bush's campaign badly. The nation's economic woes became the Democratic Party's behind-the-scenes slogan: "It's the economy, stupid." And, in fact, it was—even though the recession had ended before the election and had been fairly mild. On the other end, Bush's expertise in foreign policy, by 1992, did not seem quite as important as it had just a year earlier.

With the Soviet threat a memory, and with the Middle East now relatively calmed as a result of America's decisive victory in the Gulf War, voters in 1992 were not looking for the usual foreign policy expert in their president. And Bush really had little else to offer.

Clinton's election brought an end to the Republican Party's twelve-year domination of the White House. They had, in fact, controlled the White House for twenty of the previous twenty-four years.

CONCLUSION

By the early 1990s fights over a wide range of rights and social justice were beginning to polarize the nation: abortion rights, gun control, separation of church and state, immigration, school prayer, and "family values." These issues could divide families, start riots, end friendships. These few years even saw the birth of a new word (or at least an old word that became prominent): *polarizer*, a partisan whose attitudes and opinions were so strident as to provoke disdain from the opposition. By the mid-1990s, the nation was divided red and blue, liberal and conservative, and each group of ideologues considered the other foolish and uninformed. The old attitude from an earlier time seemed to have vanished, the belief that the other side had a legitimate argument—wrong, of course, but legitimate. Tolerance had been replaced by stridency.

There was also a great deal of economic pessimism. By the end of the 1980s the theme emphasized by most economists was one of decline. Economic growth, they argued, continued to be sluggish. The gap between the rich and the poor continued to widen, and nearly 13 percent of the population still lived below the poverty level, about what it was in 1960. The nation's education system remained below the standards in the rest of the developed world, and infant mortality was higher in the United States than in twenty-five other industrialized nations. The nation's urban areas were stagnating, even festering, developing into cesspools of poverty, crime, and bitterness. America's jobs were disappearing overseas, resulting in the demise of the nation's once-predominant manufacturing industry. The federal government was running a massive trade deficit. Real wages were not improving. Consumer debt was surging, diverting cash from productive investment. How could the nation survive such downward trends and such pessimism?

For those believers in the inevitability of economic cycles, the next decade would see a sharp upswing, beginning the longest period of growth in the nation's history. The growing economy would not solve all problems or float all boats, but life for most Americans would improve; the nation's economy would change its focus rather than simply decline.

Bill Clinton was the first baby boomer in the White House. He was the first president born after World War II, the first president of draft age during the

Vietnam War, and the first president to admit to smoking marijuana (although, he said famously, he did not inhale). Would it be a new era?

Reading: America's New Feminism

By 1990 the effort by women to assert themselves in the workplace had shown significant results. By then women comprised as much as 57 percent of the nation's workforce, up from 42 percent just twenty years earlier. Women often complained of "the glass ceiling," the metaphorical structure through which women could look to observe the highest rungs of business and society but, because of persistent discrimination, could not break and transcend. But in fact by 1990 women held as many as 40 percent of all executive and managerial positions in the United States. Those were encouraging statistics. But there were other statistics that proved more troublesome. By the late 1980s, one in four working women earned less than ten thousand dollars per year, below the poverty line for that time. At the same time, women with college degrees earned just about the same as men with the same amount of experience but *without* college degrees. And women earned only about seventy-four cents for every dollar earned by men.

Was the reason for these distinctions sexual discrimination in the workplace? By 1990, sociologists began to see other causes. The rising number of single-parent households may have been one cause. In 1970, 15 percent of households were single-parent households; twenty years later, that number jumped to 28 percent. For African Americans, 68 percent of households were single-parent households. As divorce rates skyrocketed, it was women who took on the child-rearing responsibilities, and such responsibilities inevitably interrupt careers. Consequently, women often found themselves near the bottom of the employment ladder—looking upward at the glass ceiling.

Thus, the primary discriminatory force against women was that society demands women make choices that men do not need to make. Seldom do men find themselves choosing between job and home life, a choice women must make all the time. With that came the question of the day: Can a woman have it all? Can a woman be a mother, a wife, and chairman of the board? In many ways that led to a refocusing of the woman's movement, with more concern for creating a more realistic balance that would accommodate both family and career. There was more emphasis placed on things like better child care (particularly child care in the workplace); extended pregnancy and postnatal leaves; and harsher penalties for "deadbeat dads," those divorced men who refused to pay child support.

Another refocus of the movement has often been described as an outgrowth of radical feminism. It makes the point that feminism should go beyond merely focusing on equal rights in the workplace (or, as one writer called it, "equal opportunity feminism") and accept the realization that men and women are distinctly different—and in that difference, women are superior. Innately, women are morally superior to men. They are more sensitive, nurturing, and compassionate. Men are competitive, aggressive, and less sensitive to the plight of individuals than women. Thus, women have an obligation to transform society by moving it away from competitive capitalism and the destructive culture of war and aggression, and by directing the nation (and presumably the world) toward a less aggressive, more compassionate and just social order.

Another direction for American woman might be seen as more traditional. At the beginning of the 1990s, women became less tolerant of sexual harassment, particularly sexual harassment in the workplace. The staunch stand came about, at least in part, because of the sexual harassment described by Anita Hill in her testimony against Supreme Court nominee Clarence Thomas in 1991. Besides the Hill-Thomas event, there were a number of high-profile incidents of sexual harassment and exploitation in business, the federal government, and in the military in the late 1980s and early 1990s. In addition, there were several movies that explored sexual harassment of women on the job. All of these factors helped establish boundaries. In addition, it became clear that women were more intent on reporting incidents of sexual harassment. At the same time, society was clearly more willing to judge it. On their own, businesses began enacting strict rules against any type of sexual harassment in the workplace. It went a long way toward leveling the playing field in many areas.

Women continued to call for an equal wage for equal work, and they continued to bump up against the glass ceiling, at least in many aspects of American business and industry. The relationship between men and women was beginning to change as the nation moved toward the new century.

· 12 ·

Bill Clinton's America

More than most presidents, William Jefferson Clinton obsessed about his place in history. Not unlike Lyndon Johnson, he admired Franklin Roosevelt; he wanted to follow in FDR's footsteps and be remembered as a great president with great vision and a great legacy. He also admired John Kennedy and took to heart JFK's promises of a better nation. Many Democrats saw something Kennedyesque in Clinton and believed that he might fulfill those promises and perhaps be the first truly liberal president in the White House since Kennedy. In a now-famous photograph taken in 1961, Clinton, not yet fifteen, is shown shaking hands with Kennedy while visiting Washington with an Arkansas youth group. For American liberals, the photo was akin to the finger of God giving life to Adam. In Clinton's inaugural address, however, he chose to quote Roosevelt: "Let us resolve to make our government a place for what Franklin Roosevelt called 'bold, persistent experimentation.'"

Clinton was certainly an interesting president. He was, first of all, both intelligent and articulate, and he had an unusual command of information. He had amazing energy; he was constantly on the move and he campaigned nonstop. In fact, to those around him, he seemed to lack the ability to *not* campaign. Collectively, these characteristics made for a good politician, and Clinton made the most of his abilities in the political arena. Joe Klein titled his biography of Clinton *The Natural*.

Perhaps Clinton's best characteristic, the one that kept his numbers up through most of his two terms, was that he was optimistic. He was also enthusiastic, and that gave the impression of an active presidency. It has been argued that Clinton adopted those characteristics from Reagan. But in fact it was Clinton's nature—as it was Reagan's. He was optimistic, enthusiastic, and eternally active.

He was, however, not without his warts. By most accounts, Clinton, as president, had an almost desperate need to please others, to be liked. Lyndon Johnson always looked for a consensus, drawing on all sorts of opinions before he made a decision. Clinton would try to please all sides, even to the point of contradicting himself to say what others wanted to hear. The modus operandi may have been

1992 Democratic presidential candidate Bill Clinton and his running mate, Al Gore, enjoy a rally in Carthage, Tennessee, Gore's hometown. *Source*: Bettmann/CORBIS

different, but the image to the American people was much the same: indecisive and unpredictable, words that have been used to describe both Clinton and Johnson. Clinton was also a careless administrator, even sloppy. He lacked discipline and restraint. He was notoriously late, often overbearing, and he had a temper that occasionally frightened underlings. He was also self-absorbed, even narcissistic by some accounts. His only objective seemed to be the advancement of his own political standing—often to the detriment of others. Those closest to him insisted that he always had a great deal to say, but seldom listened. "Mr. President," Treasury Secretary Lloyd Bentsen told Clinton, "I've sat beside you when somebody else is talking at one of these meetings, and I watch your eyes just fog over." And his dalliances with women, placing his family relationships in jeopardy, were notorious.

Despite all the missteps, Clinton left office in January 2001 with an unusually high job performance rating for an outgoing president. He did not approach Roosevelt's accomplishments, nor did he offer the hope and ideas of John Kennedy, but he served two terms during a period of general peace and prosperity. Since the end of World War II, only Eisenhower and Reagan could make that claim.

Clinton came to Washington with a majority in both houses of Congress, but he had carried the nation by only 43 percent in the election. At the same time, changing demographic trends favored the Republicans. A majority of Americans now lived in suburban areas, and the number continued to rise. Since the 1950s it had been clear that suburbanites associated more with the haves than the have-nots, and they intensely disliked paying taxes to support social programs. By the 1990s, the suburbs had also become the national focal point of the family and what Republicans had been calling "family values." These "values" were conservative, with a focus on religion and patriotism, and there was a strong faith in self-reliance and individual freedom. The suburbs were also mostly white. From a political standpoint, a nation divided between the conservative white suburbs and the mostly black inner city did not bode well for the Democrats. If there was any message that was clear to Clinton when he took office, it was that he would have to reach out—mostly to the nation's moderates, both Democrat and Republican.

PARTISANSHIP REBORN

In the 1990s party divisions developed into a particularly vile type of partisan rancor generally unseen since the war—in fact, more divisive and vicious even than during the Vietnam War or Watergate. Clinton seemed to evoke a special loathing among many conservatives. Although he said he wanted to govern from the center, he often took on the trappings of a liberal, even an extreme liberal. He associated famously with the Hollywood glitterati, many of whom gave lavishly to the most liberal of causes. His wife, Hillary, was frequently a focused

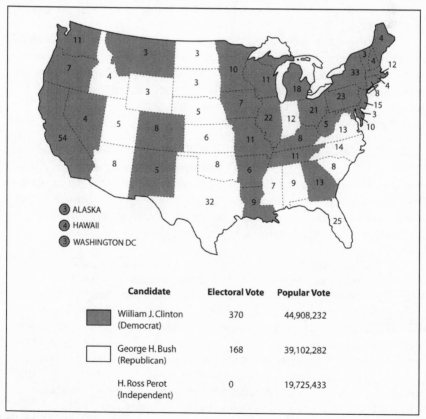

Candidate	Electoral Vote	Popular Vote
William J. Clinton (Democrat)	370	44,908,232
George H. Bush (Republican)	168	39,102,282
H. Ross Perot (Independent)	0	19,725,433

Presidential Election, 1992

target of the GOP Right. She was outspoken, clearly independent, and obviously intelligent, all of which translated into an unflattering feminism that repulsed many conservatives. But perhaps most importantly, Hillary refused to play the traditional role of adoring First Lady. In fact, she insisted on being a part of the administration, an open and active advisor to the president. Candidate Clinton said during the campaign that if he won the election, voters would "get two for the price of one." At another point in the campaign, Hillary infuriated country-western music fans and traditional women alike when she said (regarding her husband's apparent affair with another woman), "I'm not some little woman, standing by my man, like Tammy Wynette."

Much of this animosity toward the Clintons found a voice on the new phenomenon of conservative talk radio. By far the most popular of these talk show hosts was Rush Limbaugh, whose "talent on loan from God," as he said in his introductions, attracted as many as twenty million listeners (or "ditto-heads") daily. Through most of the decade, Limbaugh (and dozens of lesser talents like him) attacked the Clintons, liberals, feminists ("femi-nazis"), environmentalists ("wackos"), and even Republican moderates who refused to follow the dogma of the GOP Right.

The partisanship then spilled over into television news. In 1996, Reagan advisor Roger Ailes became the first chairman and CEO of Fox News, a twenty-four-hour cable news network patterned after CNN (Cable News Network). By most accounts, Fox was designed to report the news from the viewpoint of the political right. The station vigorously rejected that claim, however, insisting that its reporting was "fair and balanced"—a phrase that stuck in the craw of most liberals. Conservatives have complained at least since the mid-1960s that national news has had a liberal agenda, and that the new cable news channels, particularly CNN, has had an openly liberal agenda. By the end of the Clinton administration, liberals insisted that Fox spouted the Republican Party line and conservatives believed that CNN followed the Democrats. Whether it was absolutely true or not, Americans came to believe that they had two different news sources, making the nation even more partisan. Liberals watched CNN; conservatives watched Fox.

To feed the growing fire, liberal and conservative writers ground out books that, just by their titles, were designed to breathe fire into the partisan conflict. Al Franken wrote *Rush Limbaugh Is a Big Fat Idiot*; Democratic Party insider James Carville wrote *Had Enough? A Handbook for Fighting Back*; and conservative Ann Coulter wrote *Treason: Liberal Treachery from the Cold War to the War on Terrorism*. These were followed by dozens of other provocative books that touted one side or the other, all with the objective, it seemed, to be sensational enough to get on news interview programs to argue with someone from the other side. At just about any given time, the cable news channels carried programs pitting opposing talking heads in an always-volatile argument over the topics of the day. The space for compromise and bipartisan agreements seemed to shrink rapidly. By the 2000 election, the nation spoke often of its own divisions, of blue states (Democrat) and red states (Republican). The nation was equally divided, and increasingly less tolerant of the other side.

AN ECONOMIC FOCUS OUT OF THE BOX

Clinton came to office with his eye on the economy and the intention of stemming the tide of income inequality, which had been on the rise since the 1970s. Liberals insisted that this debilitating inequality could be blamed on Reagan's tax cuts which had, they argued, made the rich richer and the poor poorer. A new tax bill reversed many of the inequalities of the prior decade by increasing taxes on the very wealthy. This direction, along with a push to make the United States more competitive abroad, brought the new president the label of neoliberal.

Clinton had been successful in dealing with economic issues as governor of Arkansas, and he intended to be successful in the White House. Almost immediately he signed the Family and Medical Leave Act, a bill vetoed twice by George H. W. Bush. The new law permitted workers up to twelve weeks of unpaid leave to care for a spouse, parent, or child. This was considered a significant gain for women, many of whom (making use of computers and the Internet) could work at least part-time at home. Clinton also improved college student-aid programs by allowing more students to received federal loans.

In 1993 Congress passed the North American Free Trade Agreement (NAFTA), a treaty between the United States, Canada, and Mexico. The agreement ended the majority of tariffs on products traded between the three countries and gradually phased out other tariffs over the next fifteen years. The agreement was initially pursued by George H. W. Bush and was finalized in December 1992 just as Bush was leaving office. Clinton kept the basics of the original agreement, but added provisions dealing with the environment and labor. The treaty passed through Congress and became law in November 1993.

The effects of NAFTA have been questionable. Trade has increased dramatically between the three signatories and poverty rates in Mexico have fallen. However, trade has increased at about the same rate between the United States and non-NAFTA trade partners, and poverty rates in Mexico remain high. For those who originally believed NAFTA would be the magic bullet that would pull Mexico out of poverty and end illegal immigration into the United States, NAFTA has not been a great success.

HEALTH CARE

Clinton's first major setback was the failure of one of his campaign promises: comprehensive health care insurance. Perhaps his biggest mistake was to appoint his wife to head a high-profile task force to initiate health care reform. Many Americans refused to accept the First Lady in such a role. Her part seemed to set the entire plan off on the wrong foot, or at least make it vulnerable to criticism from those who believed that the role of the First Lady should be passive support for the president. The plan that emerged (explained in a massive tome of over thirteen hundred pages of regulations) required that employers pay 80 percent of workers' health care costs. The plan also proposed containing costs through health care cooperatives, a national board to monitor costs, and caps on health insurance premiums. A portion of the plan was to be paid for through an increase in the tobacco tax. The American Medical Association fought the plan with an extensive TV commercial campaign, and lobbyists for the insurance and the tobacco industries worked hard behind the scenes to undermine the plan. By the fall of 1994 health care reform had stalled. Americans wanted better access to health care, but they balked at paying for it with higher taxes or by rationing health care.

THE "NEW CLINTON"

When Clinton began looking at the 1994 midterm elections and on toward the 1996 presidential campaign, he saw the growing power of the conservative Right. His response was to call on his moderate side and distance himself from his party's left. Polls showed that anytime he appeared in public with Jesse Jackson his numbers dropped, and he took such information to heart.

In an attempt to steal some of the Republicans' thunder, Clinton pushed through Congress a $30 million crime bill that provided funds for more prisons, put one hundred thousand new policemen on the nation's streets, and banned assault weapons. It also included a "three strikes and you're out" penalty for federal crimes. Clinton intended to undermine the Republicans further by supporting a welfare reform bill. Although the bill at first failed to pass, it allowed Clinton to appeal to moderates and keep his distance from the left. The bill would finally pass in 1996. Its provisions are discussed later in this chapter.

By 1994 Clinton's poll numbers had begun to sag for a number of reasons. Out front was the failure of health care reform, which appeared to many Americans to be little more than the old tax-and-spend solutions of the New Deal/Fair Deal/Great Society eras. But there also appeared to be a lack of decisiveness in the White House, and Americans refuse to abide an indecisive president. Although Clinton definitely had a vision for the nation, his promises of more jobs and a stronger economy were not issues that generally translated into direct tangibles for the vast majority of Americans. Even as the economy improved, Clinton had difficulty convincing the nation that his policies were responsible for the expansion. He was also losing the culture wars. The Republican Right had succeeded in depicting the First Lady as a radical feminist and the president as a philanderer—in effect, a couple with a "modern marriage," well outside the norms of how conservatives viewed marriage. The Clintons also made some bad appointments, nuzzled up a bit too much to Hollywood types, and allowed themselves to be cast as the symbol of what was wrong with the American family. The result was that voters turned against the administration in the 1994 midterm election.

REPUBLICAN ASCENSION

For most of the 1994 campaign year, the Republicans in Congress were led by Georgia representative Newt Gingrich. Gingrich called for a highly visible Contract with America, a Republican agenda for the future in a Republican-led government. Gingrich succeeded in getting 367 Republican House candidates to endorse the Contract. Its preamble proclaimed that the coming election "offers the chance . . . to bring to the House a new majority that will transform the way Congress works. That historic change would be the end of government that is too big, too intrusive, and too easy with the public's money. It can be the beginning of a Congress that respects the values and shares the faith of the American family." In addition, conservative organizations coalesced and rallied their forces against the administration. Groups from the National Rifle Association to the Christian Coalition campaigned for conservatives. Conservative hosts saturated radio talk shows with calls for lower taxes, less government regulation, reduced welfare, and an additional shift of power from Washington to the state governments. They also hit hard at the liberal elite, radical feminism, and a Democratic Party that supported gay rights, abortion rights, sex education, and gun control, opposed school prayer, and lacked traditional family values.

In November, the conservative swing gave Republicans control of both houses of Congress for the first time since the Eisenhower administration. It also increased the number of Republican governors. Although the turnout was very small, Republican leaders hailed the victory as not only a right-wing shift, but a continuation of the conservative resurgence that began with the nomination of Barry Goldwater in 1964 and reached fruition when Ronald Reagan was elected sixteen years later.

The new Congress immediately set about enacting the Contract with America. The House passed a constitutional amendment requiring a balanced budget, but it was defeated in the Senate. The Republican House also passed the Communications Decency Act, which gave the federal government the power to censor what was perceived as pornography. In 1997 the law was struck down by the Supreme Court. House Republicans also tried to intimidate National Public Radio for its supposed liberal bias and cut funds to the National Endowment for the Arts for what some saw as offensive projects.

The biggest success for the Republicans came from their welfare reform bill;

they had no intention of allowing Clinton to undermine them on this issue. The Republicans argued that welfare costs were skyrocketing. With over fourteen million women and children on the welfare rolls, the cost had jumped to nearly $125 billion by 1994. Democrats argued that welfare costs were minimal compared to the government benefits enjoyed by the rest of America, including Social Security, farm subsidies, and Medicare. But the Republicans insisted that the problem was more than just economic. Welfare, they argued, was no longer merely temporary assistance for those who needed help; it had instead become an entitlement that encouraged a lifelong, even multigenerational, cycle of dependence. Along with that came a revolving door of irresponsible behavior, abject poverty, and crime.

At first, Clinton proposed federally funded child care and job training programs as a means to push welfare recipients back into the workforce. Congressional Republicans, however, wanted welfare reform to be focused on private enterprise and the states. Clinton vetoed two Republican-sponsored bills, but as the 1996 election approached he signed the Welfare Reform Act, reversing nearly sixty years of U.S. welfare policy and programs. Welfare reform is discussed further below.

THE GO-GO 1990s

The Clinton years began a period of sustained economic expansion that continued well into the next decade. Between 1992 and 2000, unemployment dropped from 7.2 percent to 4 percent. American businesses created twelve million new jobs in just those eight years. And the stock market soared; both blue chip and technology stocks took huge leaps, swelling retirement accounts, pension funds, and personal portfolios. The strong economy allowed interest rates to drop steadily, fueling a housing boom and leading to a dramatic rise in home ownership for the first time in fifteen years. And the gross domestic product (GDP) rose nearly 80 percent in the decade.

One result of the growth was increased federal tax revenues. Perennial federal deficits turned into surpluses for three successive years after 1998. Less borrowing by the U.S. Treasury led to lower interest rates, which in turn further fueled corporate expansion and dramatically increased consumer spending. Low inflation and increased international trade helped sustain the boom.

Clinton took credit for the growth, but the cause was never really clear. It may have been a result of the painful business restructurings that led to huge layoffs in the two prior decades. Or the expansion may have been caused by the efficiency and improved communications brought on by the ubiquity of personal computers. For whatever the reason, the growth was strong and sustained.

As with most periods of economic growth, the benefits were not always evenly distributed. Through the 1980s economic policy had allowed the rich to get richer and caused the poor to get poorer, and that trend continued into the late 1990s. From 1980 through 1996, the amount of income going to the wealthiest 20 percent of the population increased by 13 percent. Adjusted for inflation, the average worker's buying power did not increase much during the 1990s. In addition, many of the celebrated twelve million jobs created were in the low-paying service sector. A job at McDonald's was good work for an eighteen-year-old high school student, but not for a middle-aged single mother trying to raise a family.

America continued to lose ground in several areas. Because of poverty, drug abuse, and a lack of adequate prenatal care in low-income areas, infant mortality continued to be higher in the United States than in most of the industrialized world. The poor distribution of wealth had allowed for the development of a massive underclass with huge pockets of poverty in which people struggled to stay afloat in the new economy, and often drew on some aspect of public assistance. The cost to the American taxpayer had grown to enormous levels.

One of the wake-up calls of the 1990s boom was the realization that job training held the key to competing in the new job market. Those entering the workforce with no training or skills often found themselves in the lowliest of jobs, making minimum wage and with no union protection. All too often, those workers were African Americans or Hispanics, whose unemployment rates continued to rise well above that of whites. Unskilled jobs, truly the backbone of the American labor force over the previous hundred years, were readily being outsourced and sent overseas to China, Thailand, or Malaysia, where the work could be done cheaper while still meeting American quality standards. Clearly, the American economy was changing, and American workers would suffer the consequences if they did not adapt quickly.

FOREIGN POLICY IN THE CLINTON ADMINISTRATION

Governors-as-presidents usually find foreign policy challenging. Clinton was no exception; it became clear early that he had a short attention span when it came to international issues. After Clinton spoke to the United Nations in October 1993, the *Economist* noted, "[S]omehow the fire is not in Mr. Clinton's belly when he speaks on foreign policy. It will probably be events, not speeches, that will define American foreign policy more clearly."

At the same time, the Republicans mostly ignored foreign policy issues as well, pushing a decidedly go-it-alone, even isolationist, view of America's role in the world. They criticized America's foreign aid programs and denounced the United Nations. North Carolina Senator Jesse Helms, the new chairman of the Senate Foreign Relations Committee, condemned the UN's initiatives, particularly its environmental programs and its peacekeeping efforts. Congressional Republicans also withheld UN dues, amounting to over $1 billion. Despite Clinton's lack of interest and the Republicans' disdain for foreign entanglements, the United States would find that it could not turn its back on the world.

During the Cold War, decisions to intervene in world affairs were generally simple: The United States would send aid to help its allies against Communist incursions. In addition, much of the Third World had strategic importance, if for no other reason than that it was essential for the United States to eclipse Soviet influence in those areas. When the Cold War ended, the Third World necessarily lost its significance, and Washington no longer felt a need to aid poverty-stricken nations when their plight did not involve vital American interests. Several times the lack of a traditional Cold War threat made it difficult for Clinton to decide when the national interest required intervention. Consequently, military intervention in the Clinton years often turned U.S. soldiers into little more than world policemen—and the American people tired of that role quickly. So, the question was asked over and over: Is intervention in America's interest? And does intervention make the United States more secure?

One such case was Somalia, a nation located on the Horn of Africa that, during the Cold War, would have been vital to controlling the western Indian Ocean and the southern reaches of the Middle East. But in the 1990s, its strategic significance was minimal and, without Western aid, it fell into a labyrinth of ethnic and religious hatred. Clinton inherited the situation in Somalia, and he followed George H. W. Bush's lead in sending in twenty-five thousand peacekeeping troops in an attempt to deal with a widening civil war that had left thousands of Somalis dead and starving. The original objective of the intervention was humanitarian, to protect food supplies intended for famine victims. Increasingly, however, U.S. troops were drawn further into the internal conflicts, and humanitarian assistance quickly shifted to restoring order. As the nation was dragged deeper into the conflict, pundits fell back on the Vietnam-era word "quagmire," and political cartoonists began drawing Somalia in the shape of Vietnam. America's involvement continued to grow until October 1993, when a botched attempt to capture a local warlord in Mogadishu resulted in the death of eighteen U.S. soldiers. When photos appeared in the press of dead U.S servicemen being dragged through the streets of the city, Congress demanded that the troops be pulled out. Clinton quietly withdrew.

The event itself was terrible enough, but perhaps the most tragic aspect of it was the reasonable assumption that the soldiers had died because the commanders on the ground had not been given the tanks and air support they had requested. That failure seemed to make the new president gun-shy and indecisive. Clinton responded by pushing out his secretary of defense, Les Aspin, at least in part because he was perceived as indecisive in a variety of military issues, including Somalia.

Just ten days after the mess in Mogadishu, events in Haiti made the United States again look weak and indecisive. In 1991 a coup had driven the democratically elected Jean-Bertrand Aristide into exile, resulting in chaos in the capital at

Port-au-Prince. Clinton intended to send in two hundred noncombat soldiers to help and train the Haitian police force and ultimately restore Aristide to the presidency. But as the soldiers prepared to disembark, a mob chanting "Somalia, Somalia" formed near the proposed landing site. Clinton blinked, and ordered the troops to return to the United States. In 1994 former president Jimmy Carter worked out a compromise that allowed twenty thousand troops to land in Haiti unopposed. Aristide was restored to power in October of that year. But within two years, Clinton withdrew the forces and violence and corruption again returned to Haiti.

All this apprehension and indecision became most apparent when catastrophic ethnic violence broke out in 1994 in the central African country of Rwanda. For over three months, extremist Hutus slaughtered their Tutsi neighbors, mostly with machetes. As many as eight hundred thousand people died, perhaps 70 percent of the Tutsi population. The United States made the entire situation worse by taking the lead in discouraging Western intervention and insisting that the UN peacekeepers be withdrawn. Rwanda's fate resulted from its lack of strategic or economic interest to the West, and the world stood by as the carnage continued. Clinton later admitted that his lack of response was a mistake.

Meanwhile, in 1993, Russia's economy began to spiral downward into hyperinflation and low productivity. As an anxious America stood by, right-wing nationalists and former Communists in the Russian parliament attempted to overthrow President Boris Yeltsin. Unable to affect events, Washington feared the worst: a dictator rising out of the chaos, or a renewal of communism and a new, more volatile, Cold War. Finally, in October, Yeltsin crushed the coup attempt, and in an election later that year he consolidated his power and brought stability back to Russia. Washington breathed a sigh of relief.

Perhaps Clinton's greatest challenge came in the Balkans. The 1990 Soviet collapse had left a power vacuum in Eastern Europe, where Soviet control had dictated nearly all aspects of politics, economics, and society since the end of World War II. When the long arm of Moscow could no longer be felt in Yugoslavia, that nation began to disintegrate, breaking up into its various ethnic entities. In 1991 Bosnian Serbs attempted to dominate the region by launching a campaign of mass murder—euphemistically called "ethnic cleansing"—against Muslims and Croats in Bosnia; as many as two hundred thousand were killed and 3.5 million refugees required aid. Serbian president Slobodan Milosevic encouraged the Bosnian Serbs in this genocide. Clinton had criticized Bush for standing by and not intervening in these events, but he too balked at sending U.S. troops into the region. In fact, he seemed more interested in staying out of the conflict and keeping the war contained inside the old Yugoslavia than helping the Bosnian Muslims. The alternative—a few thousand UN troops—had no impact. In 1995, Clinton finally committed U.S. troops to a NATO peacekeeping force in Bosnia in an attempt to force the Serbs to stop the killing. But the war continued. In

December, Assistant Secretary of State Richard Holbrooke brokered a ceasefire that included sending in sixty thousand NATO peacekeepers to enforce the agreement.

Clinton reflected the nation's apprehensions. Polls showed that the American people had no interest in such interventions, or for getting involved in areas of the world where the nation's interests were not directly at stake. At the same time, Clinton did not get high marks for dealing with foreign affairs. Americans may have been skittish about their country's post–Cold War military involvements, but neither did they want a president who appeared apprehensive and indecisive at nearly every turn.

TERRORISM, FOREIGN AND DOMESTIC

Of course Americans did not realize it, but the February 1993 bombing of the World Trade Center in New York was a portent for the future. Five people were killed and scores were injured in the attack. The small group responsible was associated with Osama bin Laden and his terrorist organization, al-Qaeda. In 1995 a Shiite sheik and four of his associates were convicted of the crime. On August 7, 1998, bin Laden struck again when two powerful car bombs destroyed U.S. embassies in Nairobi, Kenya, and Dar es Salaam in Tanzania, killing 225. In October 2000 the USS *Cole* was attacked while anchored in the Yemeni port of Aden, killing seventeen U.S. sailors. Several al-Qaeda operatives were captured and convicted of the attack.

In the 1990s, however, foreign terrorism seemed peripheral to the terrorism that was growing up at home. In that decade a number of extremist groups emerged that believed, for various reasons, that the American system had destroyed their personal freedoms. These paramilitary groups, often called "militias," grew up and trained in several states to defend themselves against what they believed would be encroachment by the federal government. Some of these groups were religious, others were anti-government, and still others only wanted to be left alone. The militia movement seemed to quicken following a shootout at Ruby Ridge in northern Idaho, near the small town of Naples. There, federal law enforcement officials attempted to arrest Christian survivalist Randy Weaver for the sale of illegal firearms, and in two different firefights they killed Weaver's wife and son.

Just a few months later, in February 1993, federal officials in Waco, Texas, tried to arrest David Koresh, a charismatic religious leader of a congregation known as the Branch Davidians. The charges against Koresh included dealing in illegal weapons. The arrest attempt resulted in a shootout in which four federal agents and several Davidians were killed. Following a fifty-one-day siege, the Davidian compound caught fire, killing eighty-two of the inhabitants, including Koresh and twenty children. The tragedy led extremist groups throughout the nation to conclude that the federal government was conspiring to deny traditional American liberties and confiscate the firearms of law-abiding citizens. As many as 150 militia units sprang up in thirty-three states. Almost all found connections through religion, a loss of individual rights, and opposition to gun control, minority rights, and abortion rights. The paramilitary training activities of these militia groups, particularly a high-profile organization in Michigan, became a popular topic of television news reports.

Two years later, on the second anniversary of the Waco tragedy, Timothy McVeigh set off a powerful homemade bomb in a rented truck in front of the Alfred P. Murrah Federal Building in Oklahoma City. The massive explosion destroyed the building, killing 169 men, women, and children. Although McVeigh never spoke of his motives or who his accomplices were, it was clear that he shared the viewpoint of the militia movement. McVeigh was executed for the crime in 2001.

By the end of the decade the militia movement had gone dormant, perhaps because those involved saw the horror of the Oklahoma City bombing as a culmination of their association. Membership numbers dropped and most groups went into decline—including the infamous Michigan Militia.

If Americans had difficulty understanding the militia movement, they were even more perplexed by a series of school shootings. Between 1997 and 1999 there were deadly shootings in Pearl, Mississippi; Edinboro, Pennsylvania; Paducah, Kentucky; Jonesboro, Arkansas; and Springfield, Oregon. It was the incident at Columbine High School in Littleton, Colorado, however, that was the most frightening. On April 19, 1999, two troubled students, Eric Harris and Dylan Klebold, entered Columbine armed with automatic weapons and shotguns and killed twelve students and injured another twenty-four before killing themselves. The incident sent shockwaves across the nation. Many Americans blamed heavy metal music and violent video games and movies, particularly *The Basketball Diaries* in which the star, Leonardo DiCaprio (wearing a black trench coat like those worn by Harris and Klebold), fantasizes about shooting teachers and fellow students. Others saw problems emanating from patterns of school bullying and exclusionary cliques. The killers had obtained the guns with frightening ease, encouraging calls for tighter gun control. Both boys' parents had overlooked clear signs of psychological problems, prompting a call for parents to be more engaged in their children's lives. Perhaps the most lasting result was a nationwide emphasis on school security.

THE 1996 CAMPAIGN AND MORE MODERATION

In April 1995, Clinton's job performance rating hovered just below 40 percent. Gingrich commented in a press interview that the president was no longer "relevant." In some ways it seemed so. Then in November 1995 the Republican resurgence lost much of its steam when House Republicans allowed the government to be shut down rather than compromise over the budget. For three weeks Washington sat silent while eight hundred thousand federal employees went unpaid. Finally, the Republicans gave in when they realized that much of the nation was blaming them for the partisan bickering that led to the shutdown. Democrats smelled blood and hit back. They depicted Gingrich and his allies as hardhearted extremists who would resort to crippling the government to meet their agenda. The Republicans emerged from the event badly wounded. The shutdown led directly to Clinton's political resurrection and reelection in 1996.

Republican Party leaders tend to nominate the candidate who has paid his dues to the party, or even the candidate who is considered next in line for the nomination. In 1996 that was Kansas senator Bob Dole, certainly a capable politician, but his campaign style hardly resonated with voters. At seventy-three, Dole was the oldest first-time candidate in U.S. history to pursue the presidency, but because of Reagan's age when he ran, Dole's age was not much of an issue. By the end of the campaign, however, Dole was clearly worn out.

Dole was also not an inspiring campaigner or a compelling speaker, and interest in his campaign seemed to wane progressively as the election approached. His call for a 15 percent tax cut along with a promise to balance the budget and increase defense spending seemed contrived, little more than a parroting of Reagan's promises that he had never really achieved. Feeling the heat from conservatives, Dole accepted his party's anti-abortion plank and tilted to the right on most other issues. By the end of the campaign he seemed to be on cruise control and occasionally annoyed with the entire process. Those around him insisted it was just fatigue; others speculated that (like Barry Goldwater in 1964) he was just mad that he had been persuaded to give up his beloved seat in the Senate to run for the presidency.

Clinton intended to paint himself as a moderate. His 1996 State of the Union message made that perfectly clear when he antagonized party liberals by announcing, "The era of big government is over." And one of the primary themes of his campaign was the preservation of "family values." Much of the burden, he said often, should be on the shoulders of parents, who must take on the responsibility of parenting, while working to stop youth gang violence and reduce teen pregnancy. Late in the campaign he supported the Defense of Marriage Act that defined marriage as a union between a man and a woman.

Clinton also honored his pledge to reform welfare. His bill had failed to pass in the first Congressional session of his administration, and here in 1996 he vetoed two Republican welfare reform bills that he considered too harsh. But he did sign the Personal Responsibility and Work Opportunity Reconciliation Act (most commonly known as the Welfare Reform Act), which shifted the responsibility for the nation's poor from the federal government to the states. Under the new bill, the states would receive federal block grants and orchestrate their own welfare plans and programs. The bill also required able-bodied heads of households to find work or face the loss of aid after two years, and it cut out legal non-citizen immigrants from aid such as food stamps and Medicaid. Liberals insisted that the bill would do little more than force women off welfare and into low-paying, dead-end jobs. Conservatives argued that it would end the federal subsidy of welfare moms and sever the lifetime welfare cycle that kept poor Americans poor. Aided by the rapid economic growth through the remainder of the decade and a rising minimum wage, the program succeeded in moving welfare recipients into jobs. By 2001, the number of Americans on public assistance dropped from over 12 million to 5.3 million, and the number of unmarried mothers off welfare and in the workforce jumped from 48 percent to nearly 65 percent within only a few years.

The welfare bill had, as Clinton had promised, "ended welfare as we know it." And it allowed him to move to the center and expand his voting base. He widened his lead over Dole, mostly because of the general health of the economy and his appeals to the center. In November he won easily. Perhaps the most important aspect of the election was that no one really bothered to show up. Fewer voted in 1996 than in any presidential election since 1948. Those who analyzed the election insisted that the apathy was directly related to the national aversion to political gridlock—which was about to get worse.

Clinton seemed prepared to head into a triumphant second term. But his own character flaws overshadowed his successes and damaged his legacy.

KOSOVO

Events in the Balkans continued to dominate Clinton's foreign policy concerns. In 1999, Milosevic unleashed a new round of "ethnic cleansing" in the Balkans, this time against ethnic Albanians in Kosovo, a Yugoslav province inhabited by 1.8 million ethnic Albanians. When Milosevic revoked Kosovar autonomy within the Yugoslav state, the Kosovar Albanians formed their own breakaway state. Led by the Kosovar Liberation Army (KLA), the Kosovars insisted on independence from the Yugoslav federation and eventually political union with Albania. KLA militiamen attacked Serbian soldiers and policemen inside Kosovo, which escalated into a full-scale rebellion. Milosevic responded by attacking the Kosovar Albanians, forcing as many as eight hundred thousand to flee into neighboring states. Clinton and the heads of other NATO countries ordered the bombing of Serbia in March 1999 in an effort to force Milosevic to end the persecution of the Kosovars. Milosevic responded by stepping up his ethnic cleansing in Kosovo. Within weeks, the entire situation turned into a disaster. Thousands of Kosovar Albanians were slaughtered; another hundred thousand remain unaccounted for and presumed dead.

Finally, after seventy-eight days of bombing, Milosevic relented and signed a ceasefire. By then, however, he had achieved his goals of consolidating his power in Serbia and pushing the Albanians out of Kosovo. NATO troops were sent in as peacekeepers and to aid the Albanians in their return home. The KLA continued to operate, demanding independence for Kosovo, but that was never a part of any agreement. Milosevic was voted out of office, then captured and arrested. He died in 2006 while standing trial for war crimes before the United Nations International War Crimes Tribunal in The Hague, Netherlands.

SCANDAL AND "MONICAGATE"

Clinton was no stranger to accusations of adultery. During the 1992 campaign he was able to deflect Gennifer Flowers's accusations of adultery by denying any relationship. In 1994 Paula Jones filed a sexual harassment suit against the president, alleging sexual harassment while Clinton was the governor of Arkansas. Both revelations were fodder for the tabloids. Meanwhile, the attorney general had appointed an independent counsel to investigate some allegedly shady Arkansas real estate deals the Clintons had engaged in decades before. The independent counsel found nothing on the Clintons that was indictable, and in August 1994 he resigned to be replaced by Kenneth Starr, a judge on the U.S. Court of Appeals. Starr and his aides found little more on the Clintons than the first independent counsel. With no place else to turn, Starr began in 1998 to delve into Clinton's sex life. Critics would later charge that these investigations were outside Starr's purview, with no connection to his original authority. Starr's pursuit of Clinton was relentless. A Clinton friend once said that "Javert's pursuit of Jean Valjean in *Les Miserables* pales by comparison."

In January 1998 prosecutors called Clinton to testify during the Jones case, intending to show that the president maintained a pattern of womanizing, adultery, and sexual harassment. It was during this testimony that Jones's lawyers asked Clinton about his relationship with Monica Lewinsky, a young White House intern. Clinton flatly denied any relationship, as did Lewinsky. Rumors immediately began to fly, while Clinton continued to deny everything.

In fact, as evidence would later show, Lewinsky began a sexual liaison with Clinton sometime in late 1995. The affair went as far as oral sex, but never intercourse. In April 1996 a White House official had Lewinsky transferred out of the White House, and she was reassigned to the Pentagon. Finally, in March 1997, Clinton ended the relationship, but Lewinsky continued to see Clinton and pushed him to find her a better job. Clinton tried to find her a position at the United Nations. When that failed, he asked his friend Vernon Jordan to find her a job. Later, when these facts became public, critics claimed that Clinton was trying to buy Lewinsky's silence with a high-paying job.

Any attempt to keep the affair quiet failed miserably. Linda Tripp, one of Lewinsky's friends at the Pentagon, recorded telephone conversations she had with Lewinsky detailing the hot affair with the president. In January 1998 Tripp gave the tapes to Kenneth Starr, who then convinced the FBI to fit Tripp with a recording device to obtain more information from Lewinsky.

After spending approximately $30 million in public funds, Starr had reached a humiliating dead-end in his investigations of the Clintons' Arkansas land deals. He immediately shifted his attention to the Lewinsky affair. It was the tawdry liaison that kept America's interests piqued. But from a legal stand-point, the real issue was whether Clinton had lied about the affair while under oath in the Jones case and whether he had persuaded Lewinsky to lie. In August 1998, Lewinsky admitted the affair before Starr's grand jury. Clinton also admitted inappropriate activity with Lewinsky but insisted, under a narrow definition of the phrase, that their affair did not include sexual relations.

In September, Starr produced a report that recounted the Clinton-Lewinsky affair in explicit detail. It was informative, titillating, and disgusting all at the same time, and it became necessary Internet reading for anyone remotely interested in the events. The press reported the explicit details of the affair, and the tabloid press and popular news programs went into a feeding frenzy over the story. The affair became fodder for the late-night comedy shows, and horribly grotesque Monica Lewinsky and Linda Tripp impersonators were featured on *Saturday Night Live.*

To those who disliked Clinton, these events confirmed their arguments that he was an unprincipled lout. But even his closest supporters thought his actions were irresponsible and reckless. The very idea that the president of the United States would have an extramarital sexual liaison in the White House with some-one half his age was impossible to defend. In an attempt at his own defense, Clinton tried to explain in his memoirs that what he had done was "immoral and foolish," and that since his youth he had lived what he called a dual life, in which he had too often allowed his weaker self to take control of his personality. In the end, it seemed he had gotten involved with Monica Lewinsky merely because he could.

Starr's report recommended impeachment on the grounds that Clinton had lied under oath in the Paula Jones case, and had obstructed justice by persuading Lewinsky and possibly others to lie under oath. Republicans who opposed impeachment attempted to substitute a bill of censure for impeachment, but that move failed when partisan Republicans forced the dissenters into line. The House Judiciary Committee, on a strict party-line vote, handed down four articles of impeachment to the full House. In another partisan vote, House Republicans sent to the Senate two articles of impeachment: perjury and obstruction of justice. The president was, thus, impeached.

The American people did not agree. By an overwhelming majority, they did not believe that a U.S. president should be removed from office for a failing that did not involve major public policy. And apparently the nation was willing to overlook his personal failings. In the November 1998 midterm elections, Democrats gained five seats in the House and the Republicans barely held onto the majority.

In January 1999 the trial in the Senate began, even though Senate Republicans held only fifty-five seats; they would need a two-thirds majority to remove the president from office. As the trial progressed, Clinton's approval ratings soared. He seemed to go from lout to victim, a target of Republican right-wing zealots. On February 12, the Senate rejected the impeachment charges and the nation seemed to issue a collective sigh of relief.

Clinton may have escaped the Republican ax, the nation apparently having stood behind him. But the incident damaged his presidency irreparably. The American people may not have been willing to remove a sitting president for a sexual dalliance (or even for lying about it), but that did not mean they approved of what he did. In fact, most Americans considered the whole sordid affair distasteful, even demeaning to the office and the nation.

Clinton continued on with his last two years in office. He worked to resolve the Israeli-Palestinian dispute and he intervened in Kosovo. But his presidency was damaged badly. The Republicans were also hurt because they received the blame for the harsh partisanship, the gridlock, and all the political backbiting that led up to the impeachment. Americans were clearly fed up with it all.

BUSH VERSUS GORE: ELECTION OF 2000

As the 2000 presidential campaign approached, the Democrats seemed poised to extend their tenure. The economic boom of the 1990s had erased the federal budget deficit and brought prosperity to the nation. The biggest question for the Democrats seemed to be whether Clinton's personal failings had damaged the party's chances in the election.

New Jersey Senator Bill Bradley made an early run for the Democratic nomination, but his candidacy failed to garner much enthusiasm and he was eliminated early. With no further surprises, the Democrats chose Al Gore, Clinton's vice president for eight years. Gore was a party insider; he had spent the last eighteen years in Washington as a congressman, a senator, and vice president. He had been close to Clinton, and he could take some of the credit for the economic expansion. But Gore feared being associated with Clinton and the Lewinsky affair, and as the campaign progressed he began to put more and more distance between himself and the president. Gore seemed to discount Clinton's general popularity, his vote-getting appeal, and his ability to raise money. In the end, Gore's disassociation from Clinton was probably a mistake.

The Republicans embarked on a primary contest to choose their candidate. The early frontrunner was George W. Bush, the oldest son of the former president. "W," as his friends called him, had served two terms as governor of Texas, and before that had been part owner of the Texas Rangers baseball team. He called himself a moderate, but his greatest appeal was to the Far Right, the Christian Right, and the Republican Party leadership—and donations from those sectors bulged Bush's campaign chests. His chief opponent was John McCain, senator from Arizona. McCain was a war hero; his plane had been shot down over Hanoi during the Vietnam War, and he had been held in the infamous "Hanoi Hilton" for five years. McCain lamented the power of big money in the campaign and called for finance reform, as the Bush camp outspent him over and over in every primary campaign. McCain's issue of campaign finance reform seemed to resonate with the nation's voters, but McCain could not overcome the strength of the Bush coffers and the political power of the mainstream Republicans who supported his campaign. By the early spring, McCain was out.

The Democrats had to worry about a liberal spoiler. Ralph Nader, the celebrated 1960s consumer advocate, was running on the Green Party ticket and touting an environmentalist platform. Nader's candidacy threatened to take votes from Gore, and his critics argued that his only impact would be to assure Bush's victory, resulting in perhaps the most environmentally insensitive government since the war. Nader, however, soldiered on.

Since at least the 1970s, the primary elections had become increasingly important in deciding party nominations. Not surprisingly, the party conventions progressively lost their significance. That transformation became apparent in the 2000 campaign, when both conventions turned into cheerleading affairs for the candidates already chosen in the primaries. The only real drama was the choices for running mates. Gore chose Connecticut senator Joseph Lieberman, a surprise to most party insiders. But Gore hoped to separate himself from the Lewinsky scandal as much as possible, and Lieberman had gone out of his way to criticize Clinton for his transgressions. Some also thought that Lieberman, an Orthodox Jew, would attract Jewish votes in Florida, a state that promised to be close. Bush tapped Richard Cheney, his father's secretary of defense. Cheney appealed to the party's most conservative wing, and he had been one of the primary figures in the Gulf War. He was also intended to shore up Bush's inexperience in foreign affairs.

Perhaps the most notable aspect of the campaign was that it was the most expensive in the nation's history. Together, the two parties solicited, and then spent, well over $1 billion. Both men ran fairly cautious races, with the only real issue being how they would spend the windfall budget surplus. As the campaign moved down to the wire, polls showed a close race—but no one knew just how close. When the dust settled, Gore had won the popular vote: 50.99 million to Bush's 50.45 million, a difference of .5 percent of the total. In the Electoral College (not counting Florida) Gore led 266 to 249. He needed only four electoral votes to make the 270 votes to win. Bush needed 11. So it was Florida that would decide.

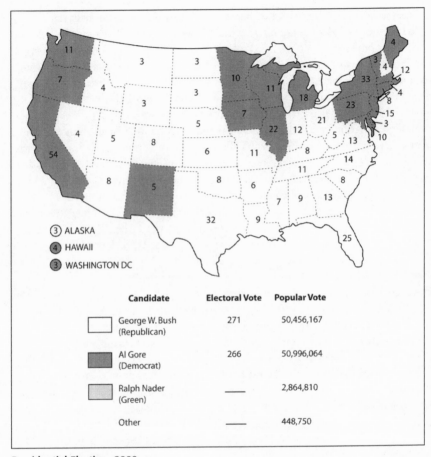

Candidate	Electoral Vote	Popular Vote
George W. Bush (Republican)	271	50,456,167
Al Gore (Democrat)	266	50,996,064
Ralph Nader (Green)	—	2,864,810
Other	—	448,750

Presidential Election, 2000

But the decision in Florida was too close to call. Following a mandatory recount over the next two days, Bush led by fewer than three hundred votes. Immediately, accusations began to fly from several directions. African Americans charged that crowds of black voters had been systematically kept from voting in several north Florida counties. At the same time, the state's antiquated voting machines came into question when it became apparent that large groups of voters in Palm Beach County had been confused by the "butterfly" ballot and may have voted incorrectly. Professional "counters" were brought in to determine the validity of certain ballots in which the chad (the bit of cardboard punched from the hole on the ballot) was not punched all the way through. Americans became aware of the difference between a "dimpled chad," a "pregnant chad," and a "hanging chad." As the recount progressed and Bush began to pull up in the numbers, Gore called for a hand recount of punch-card ballots in those counties where irregularities had been reported. In turn, the Republicans argued against any recount, and Florida Governor Jeb Bush, the candidate's brother, called a halt to the recount. Following that, the Florida Supreme Court, in a unanimous decision, ruled that the recount should continue and that the state of Florida should accept the results. The recounts proceeded, but in Dade County the local election board abruptly called off the recount.

In the meantime, the Bush campaign appealed to the Supreme Court to stop the recounts. On December 12, the Supreme Court, in a 5–4 vote along the justices' traditional voting pattern, overturned the unanimous decision of the Florida Supreme Court and stopped the ballot count. Their justification was that the evaluation of the punch-card ballots could not withstand constitutional scrutiny. It was perhaps the court's most controversial and unusual decision in its history. In a strongly worded dissenting opinion, Justice Stephen Breyer wrote that the Court's decision "runs the risk of undermining the public's confidence in the Court itself." With no recount option, the Court decided the election.

It was the closest election in U.S. history, and when it was over many Americans wondered if the final count would ever be known. Some Democrats also pointed their fingers at Nader, who polled 2.86 million votes, easily enough to put Gore over the top in a few states.

CONCLUSION

For the most part, the Clinton era was good for the nation. The 1990s saw a strong surge in the economy. It was, in fact, the longest period of economic growth in the nation's history. At the end of the decade, the unemployment rate was down to 4.1 percent, the lowest since the mid-1960s, while inflation remained under 2 percent. The prosperity increased income, which in turn increased tax revenues without raising taxes. In 1999, the president announced a budget surplus, the first since the late 1960s. Clinton went on to predict that the federal surplus would grow to nearly $2 trillion by the first decade of the new millennium. Images of tax relief danced in the heads of conservatives, while liberals thought of anti-poverty programs and universal health insurance.

Nationally, violent crime was down, perhaps because the national prosperity brought regions and groups out of poverty with jobs. Democrats often pointed to the one hundred thousand cops placed on the street and the after-school programs funded by the Clinton administration. For whatever reason, by the end of the century, violent crime had declined by 20 percent from the early 1990s.

The United States ended the twentieth century much as it began: looking to be a world leader while making the nation a better place to live.

Reading: O. J.

It was the trial of the century—or at least one of several.

O. J. Simpson was an example of an American celebrity. He was a spectacular running back for the University of Southern California, where he led the nation in rushing. In 1968 he won the Heisman Trophy with the highest vote margin in history. In the NFL he was the star running back for the Buffalo Bills and became the first player in NFL history to run for 2,000 yards in one season. Following his athletic career he parlayed his good looks and infectious smile into a career on the screen that began with several memorable commercials for Hertz, and then as a mediocre character actor in several not-so-great movies. He was, however, instantly recognizable as O. J.

In 1985 O. J. married Nicole Brown. But after a rocky marriage that included alleged wife-beatings and several police interventions, the two were divorced in 1992. On June 12, 1994, police found the bodies of Nicole Brown and an apparent companion, Ron Goldman, near the front of Brown's apartment in Los Angeles. They had been beaten and slashed with a knife. Police went to Simpson's home, where they found compelling evidence that Simpson had committed the murders. Simpson had left L.A. for Chicago. Once he was informed of the incident, he immediately returned to Los Angeles.

Most of America first became familiar with the case on June 27 when Simpson, now charged with the murders and having failed to turn himself in, took off in his Ford Bronco down Interstate 405, pursued by L.A. police and followed by TV helicopters in a low-speed chase. By the time the local feed was picked up by national news services, nearly 95 million Americans were tuned in to the drama.

The evidence against O. J. was strong. His blood was found at the scene, along with carpet fibers from his car and some of his own hair. There was dried blood on his car. One bloody glove at the crime scene matched another found at his house. In addition, Simpson could not account for his whereabouts at the time of the murders, and he had a past history of violence against Nicole Brown.

This incident would have been little more than tabloid fodder had it not been for the racial connotations that emerged from it. Black America began to see Simpson as a symbol of white oppression of black America through history, a black man persecuted and condemned by whites for having a white wife. Much of black America also came to believe that the LAPD (those who had beaten Rodney King in 1991) had set up O. J. and framed him. The trial divided the nation.

The prosecuting attorneys combined ineptitude with overconfidence. The "Dream Team" defense attorneys, led by the irascible Johnny Cochran, succeeded in convincing the jury that the LAPD was a bunch of rabid racists intent on punishing a black celebrity for having a beautiful white wife. He (and several of his high-profile associates) argued that they had planted the bloody glove at the crime scene and had tampered with and bungled the crime scene investigation. Cochran and his associates were even able to cast doubt on DNA evidence.

After only two hours of deliberations, the jury (made up of mostly black women) pronounced O. J. "not guilty." Black America cheered a victory over the white system. White Americans shook their heads in disbelief.

There were a number of repercussions. First, the nation's legal justice system was badly damaged. Outside the issue of race, many Americans (those who believed that O. J. was guilty) concluded that the justice system was flawed because, with enough money, a guilty person could hire the talent necessary to win acquittal. Thus the system was not equal, and did not treat Americans equally. The verdict also damaged race relations in the United States; perhaps more importantly, it revealed that black and white Americans saw things quite differently and were divided by their separate views of the world—certainly more than most Americans had thought.

In civil trials, Simpson was found responsible for the deaths of Brown and Goldman, and the courts ordered Simpson to pay $33 million to the Brown and Goldman families. Simpson has continued to claim his innocence and has refused to pay restitution. In 2006 Simpson attempted to publish a book entitled *If I Did It*, supposedly explaining how he would have committed the crime if he had been, in fact, the murderer. A judge awarded any proceeds from the book to the Goldman family. The book was not published.

In 2007, Simpson was arrested in Las Vegas and charged with twelve counts of felony kidnapping, armed robbery, and assault with a deadly weapon for allegedly stealing items at gunpoint from two sports memorabilia dealers. Simpson argued that the items belonged to him. The result was another O. J. trial, and another media circus. In late 2008, he was sentenced to prison for the offense.

· 13 ·

America After the New Millennium

As the nation entered the new millennium it was the world's uncontested military power. Americans felt much as they had between the end of World War II (when their enemies were vanquished and most of Europe lay in ruin) and 1949, when the Soviets got the bomb. For those four short years, the United States was the only nuclear power and the only real economic power in a world reeling from the horrendous impact of the war.

By 2000, American muscle was apparent, but the nation's culture was even more dominant. All things American had spread throughout the world, everything from television programs to movies, from clothing styles to music, from the American character to its food. McDonald's and Starbucks had become symbols of America's cultural proliferation. Much of the world lamented the imposition of American culture onto their local customs, but American companies recorded record profits in overseas sales. The first McDonald's in Beijing saw forty thousand customers on its first day. By 2011 there were 1,100 McDonald's restaurants in 120 cities in China.

Much of this Americanization of the world was a result of high-tech telecommunications systems that, for the first time in history, brought the world together in instantaneous communications. Americans were a part of an ever-expanding global village through websites, email accounts, and satellite hookups. An amazing amount of information and rapid communications were at the fingertips of anyone who was attached to the grid. Despite the ever-present glitches, the computerized nation (and the world it was attached to) ran smoother and ever more quickly, and it fostered the growth and development of all sorts of new industries and businesses that helped fuel the national economy well into the new millennium.

America may have been preeminent, but the problems the nation struggled with at home were many of the same problems it had been struggling with since at least the beginning of the twentieth century. Economic disparity was probably the most apparent. Despite the nation's wealth and growth, the gap between the rich and the poor in the United States was wider than it had been since the war, a trend that began in the early 1980s and continued to widen into the next century. By the turn of the twenty-first century, the nation's richest 20 percent had accumulated nearly half of the nation's income, while the poorest 20 percent took in only about 4 percent. At the very top, the upper 5 percent of the nation's wealthiest households saw their share of the national income grow from about 15 percent to 22 percent by the first years of the new millennium.

At the same time, Americans were no longer the world's wealthiest people—as they had been in the years between the end of World War II and about 1980. There were several nations, mostly in northern Europe, that could boast higher per capita incomes and a higher standard of living. On average, however, Americans did well. Despite the soaring economy of the 1990s, the median family income had declined by the turn of the century but had rebounded in the following years to a respectable $42,400. Even those Americans who fell below the official poverty level of $18,850 for a family of four enjoyed a living standard well above most of the rest of the world.

One of the nation's biggest problems remained health care. Soaring medical costs caused a spike in medical insurance costs, which in turn took a huge chunk out of wages and salaries. In 2011, almost 60 million Americans (26 percent) did not have health insurance. At the same time, over $8,000 was spent on health care for every man, woman, and child in the United States—the most, by far, of any nation.

And the poverty rate continued to increase. Although the poverty rate had dropped just before the turn of the new century, falling to about 11 percent (the lowest since 1975), the rate jumped back up to nearly 15.5 percent by 2011, leaving 47.8 million Americans living below the poverty line. It seemed like a problem that would not go away.

AFRICAN AMERICANS IN THE NEW CENTURY

At the beginning of the new millennium America's agonizing race problems remained alive and contentious. One problem was that the African American community had itself divided. The black middle class was thriving, moving into the mainstream of American society, enjoying the advantages of middle-class life. At the other end of the spectrum, African Americans in the inner cities were suffering, as they always had, with few job opportunities, high dropout rates, and the burdens of violent crime.

By 2011, the black unemployment rate stood at 15.3 percent, twice the national rate. But more importantly, that number jumped to a full 50 percent for young African American men between the ages of twenty-two and thirty. For African American men who did not complete high school, the number hit 72 percent. The result of that was almost certainly a high crime rate, and thus a high incarceration rate. In 2009, there were almost five thousand African Americans behind bars for every one hundred thousand in the population—compared to less than eight hundred for whites.

For those black women living in the inner city, the situation was often worse. In 1965, 25 percent of black children were born to unwed mothers, a statistic that was then considered frightening. By 2010, however, that number had jumped to 72 percent. Many of the mothers were teenage girls and young women with almost no prospects for employment or education. Clearly, these people were being left behind. With no political or economic power, this underclass was being ignored.

Affluent Americans shook their heads at the poverty, the drug use, and the crime, but often ignored the enormous cost of maintaining an underclass in welfare payments and medical costs, along with the growing costs of inner-city crime prevention and incarceration. In the first decades of the twenty-first century America was quickly becoming two nations: one thriving and intact; and one struggling, broken, and more often than not African American.

While African Americans in the inner city languished, a new black middle class was emerging that seemed to hold hope for the future. By 2004, the African American median family income had risen to over $40,000, nearly 14 percent above the 1990 figures. (That, however, remained well below the average income for white families at nearly $65,000.) In addition, college-educated African Americans enjoyed significantly higher earnings, and as many as 57 percent of black high school graduates went on to college. The number of black-owned businesses reached 1.2 million.

This new affluence sent many African Americans on the move—as far away as possible from the problems of the inner city. Many moved to better lives in the suburbs, where they found all the advantages of the American dream that whites had been looking for since the 1950s. There was also something of a reverse Great Migration, a trend of blacks moving back to the South. Since the beginnings of the twentieth century, African Americans had fled the racist South for good-paying jobs in northern industry. The mass movement altered the nation's political and social balance for nearly fifty years. But at the start of the new millennium, African Americans seemed to be pulled back home, to their family homesteads, to the places of their origin. Many felt more comfortable in the urban South, causing a mushrooming of the black populations in and around cities like Atlanta, Birmingham, and Jacksonville.

AFFIRMATIVE ACTION

One question that continued to haunt the nation was affirmative action. In 1978 the Supreme Court ruled in *Regents of the University of California v. Bakke* that rigid racial quotas could not be used to determine admission to colleges and universities. But the decision also said that race could continue to be used as one of several factors in determining admission. For those who opposed any and all aspects of affirmative action, this left a wide loophole in the process which continued to allow the admission of students to the nation's universities who were less qualified than majority whites. In several cases in the late 1990s it appeared that the Supreme Court might close that loophole and bring an end to all aspects of affirmative action.

In 1996, California voters approved Proposition 209, ending all affirmative action programs in state employment and in public education. Immediately, the enrollment of African Americans and Latinos at the Berkeley campus of the University of California dropped. Conservatives saw the result as proof that affirmative action programs had, in fact, lowered admission standards. Liberals argued that a diverse nation needs diverse leadership, and that the University of California admissions policy excluded minority groups while denying all students the educational benefits of a diverse student body.

In a landmark 2003 case involving the University of Michigan's affirmative action admissions policies, the Supreme Court (split 5–4) ruled that the university's admissions policy (with its formulaic point system that rated students and awarded additional points to minority applicants) had to be abolished, or at least modified. In addition, however, the Court ruled again that race may remain one of many factors in a university's admission process because it furthers "a compelling interest in obtaining the educational benefits that flow from a diverse student body." The Court added that, although affirmative action was no longer justified as a way of redressing past oppression and injustice, it did promote a "compelling state interest" in diversity at all levels of society. Justice Sandra Day O'Connor wrote for the majority: "In order to cultivate a set of leaders with legitimacy in the eyes of the citizenry, it is necessary that the path to leadership be visibly open to talented and qualified individuals of every race and ethnicity." The decision confirmed that affirmative action could continue. The 5–4 split, however, seemed to indicate that the question would again be raised.

IMMIGRATION AND MULTICULTURALISM

In 1986 the United States allowed about eight hundred thousand immigrants into the country. After about 2000, close to one million immigrants entered the United States legally each year. Between 2000 and 2010 nearly four million immigrants came to the United States. Not since the beginning of the twentieth century has the United States been asked to absorb so many new residents.

Illegal immigration is, however, a completely different matter to Americans. In 2009 there were as many as twelve million illegal immigrants in the United States, most from Mexico and other Latin American nations. These "illegals" often worked as day laborers, farm workers, and domestics. It was often argued that they took the low-paying jobs that American workers refused. Others insisted that the willingness of illegal workers to accept low-paying jobs outside the legal system kept wages from rising. Illegal immigration also took a toll on the nation's medical system, educational system, and social services. By 2006 there was a move in Congress to put a stop to illegal immigration, particularly from Mexico and the rest of Latin America. Congress and the president fought over a bill that would criminalize illegal immigration, build barriers along the two-thousand-mile border between the United States and Mexico, and create a new guest worker program. Through most of 2006 Washington and the nation were immersed in a debate about these proposals, with few results. In that year the U.S. allowed more immigrants through its borders than the next nine countries combine. By 2010 only the construction of a partial border fence had been approved.

Not surprisingly, it was California that saw the most dramatic increases. In 1973, 80 percent of the state was non-Hispanic white. By 2010 that number had fallen to about 40 percent. In about that same time, the percentage of Asians in Los Angeles had jumped from just 1 percent to 12 percent. L.A. and California had, in fact, become to modern immigration what New York City and parts of the East Coast had been about a hundred years earlier. An Arizona law, which went into effect in 2010, allowed law enforcement officers to question a person's immigration status. A similar law enacted a year later in Alabama caused a temporary exodus of aliens (legal and illegal) from the state.

America had always assimilated its ethnic populations. Some groups took longer than others, but just about all eventually became "Americans," whether they liked it or not. The ability of America to accomplish that had been celebrated in many circles. It is, in fact, one of the characteristics that has made the United States unique. But by the mid-1970s, the old idea of the melting pot was being challenged by a new metaphor: the "fruit salad," a rejection of assimilation and integration in favor of what was being called "multiculturalism." The idea was at least in part inspired by black nationalism, the idea that African Americans should embrace their ethnically distinct institutions as a conscious means of avoiding assimilation into the white culture. Portions of the Hispanic community followed, and the idea itself lost much of the radicalism it originally carried when espoused by black nationalists. Many Hispanics worked to maintain their heritage, their language, and their cultural identity within the American culture. Other groups followed, and all tried to win political support for their ethnic identities and their ethnically distinct institutions.

Criticism of multiculturalism came mostly from the political and social right. Conservative commentators and editorialists often complained that multiculturalism amounted to little more than separatist schemes that threatened the nation's social structure. The nation had succeeded, they argued, because past immigrants had willingly left behind their Old World ways and become "Americans." They called for English to be designated as the national language, and they opposed the use of languages other than English in classrooms. They also argued for a Eurocentric focus to history education in public schools and universities.

Perhaps the greatest victory for those who opposed multiculturalism was

California Proposition 227, passed in 1998, requiring the administration of the California English Language Development Test to be given to all public school students in California whose first language was not English. Students had to meet a certain level to continue toward graduation. Interestingly, the results of the exam, first administered in 2002, were distributed in both English and Spanish.

THE ABORTION DEBATE

By the mid-1990s, the right to an abortion had become one of several divisive issues that split the nation down the middle, right and left, liberal and conservative, red and blue. Those who supported the right to an abortion described themselves as "pro-choice." Their opponents, those who opposed the right to an abortion, called themselves "pro-life." This set the stage for a litmus test for all politicians, political appointees, judges, and just about anyone else in a leadership position.

Pro-lifers approached the debate from the standpoint of the fetus, arguing that an unborn child has the right to life, the same right as any other American. Beginning in the 1990s, and continuing into the next decades, pro-life advocates mounted protests outside abortion clinics, often accosting those who entered. Pro-life extremists even threatened to kill clinic workers and the doctors who performed abortions. Abortion doctors were murdered in New York and Florida. In Massachusetts, in 1994, a clinic worker was killed and five others were wounded; and in Kansas in 2009 an abortion doctor was gunned down while attending church.

Pro-choice advocates approached the debate from the standpoint of the woman, arguing that the right to a safe and legal abortion was crucial to a woman's control of her life and her body. The rallying cries were "It's my body; it's my choice" and "Keep your laws off my body." Moderates in the pro-choice camp often argued that abortion might in fact be wrong, but that it was a woman's decision to make, not that of politicians in Washington or in local statehouses.

Pro-life interest groups pressed state legislatures to restrict abortions in what pro-choice advocates insisted was an attempt to chip away slowly at the right to have an abortion. These laws, which varied depending on the state, required underage girls to obtain parental consent, denied public funds for abortions, and mandated elaborate counseling and waiting periods prior to an abortion. In *Webster v. Reproductive Health Services* (1989) and *Planned Parenthood of Southeastern Pennsylvania v. Casey* (1992), the Supreme Court ruled that most of these state restrictions were constitutional. But the courts continued to uphold the basic framework of *Roe v. Wade*, and the basic right of a woman to have an abortion.

GAY RIGHTS

Abortion was probably the most divisive issue as the nation moved into the next millennium. A close second, however, was gay rights. In the 1992 presidential campaign, Bill Clinton promised gay groups that, if elected, he would support gay rights, particularly the right of gays to serve in the military as equals. Gay rights advocates believed that acceptance into the military would go a long way toward acceptance into general society. However, when Clinton came to office there was strong pressure from the military against such a policy. Ultimately, Clinton backed off from his promise, finally agreeing to a "don't ask, don't tell" policy that satisfied no one—and homosexuals, if uncovered, continued to be discharged from the military. The gay community insisted that Clinton had broken his promise; conservatives believed he had opened the door to homosexuality in the military. Hillary Clinton repudiated "don't ask, don't tell" in her 2008 presidential campaign. In December 2010, President Barak Obama signed a law repealing "don't ask, don't tell." The law was finally implemented in September 2011.

Through the later decades of the twentieth century the gay community continued to organize and push the political system for equal rights under the law. One strategy in that fight was to have themselves designated a minority group before the law, giving them various protections and privileges in housing, education, and public accommodations. The public was never quite settled on the issue, but by the turn of the century most states had passed laws banning discrimination on the basis of sexual orientation.

The gay community, however, continued to make demands, particularly for legal rights for same-sex couples. At first, gay couples focused their demands on workplace health care coverage, insisting that gay couples should receive health care benefits on the same basis as heterosexual couples. From that, many in the gay community pressed on, demanding that their partnerships be recognized by law as legal marriages.

Immediately, the nation split over the issue of gay marriage. Those who favored it argued only that such unions hurt no one. Those standing in opposition insisted that the institution of marriage was sacred, a religious union between a man and a woman. Bumper stickers read: "A marriage is between Adam and Eve, not Adam and Steve." In the late 1990s, congressional conservatives moved toward a constitutional amendment outlawing same-sex marriage, but in 1998 Congress instead passed the Defense of Marriage Act, which prohibited the federal government from recognizing same-sex marriage, and allowed states to refuse to recognize gay marriages performed in other states. As of 2012, same sex marriage was allowed in six states and the District of Columbia, and prohibited by constitutional amendments in thirty-one states. Polls have shown that the general population favors same sex marriage by over 50 percent.

STEM CELL RESEARCH, INTELLIGENT
DESIGN, AND TERRY SCHIAVO

Another social division emerged over the question of stem cell research. Stem cells are grown from a human embryo. These cells, which continue to divide if given growth factors, have significant medical potential in finding cures for a variety of diseases from diabetes to Parkinson's disease. To create a line, however, a human embryo must be destroyed. Those who argue in favor of growing stem cells point out that embryos not used in an *in vitro* fertilization process are normally discarded anyway. By 2007 there were only twenty-two stem cell lines in the world.

Opponents contend that stem cell research is a slippery slope to reproductive cloning, and not too far from the sci-fi manufacturing of a human being. Pro-lifers contend that a human embryo is a human life and thus entitled to protection.

Twice, President George W. Bush vetoed legislation that would have eased restraints on federally funded embryonic stem cell research. This controversy gave Bush's critics the ammunition they needed to accuse the president of being anti-science. They would find other examples.

All this controversy, combined with the promise of new treatments for diseases, sent scientists on a quest to find new ways of establishing stem cell lines without destroying human embryos. In June 2007, a group of researchers reported that they were able to "reprogram" normal skin cells in mice to an embryonic state.

The debate over the relationship between science and religion raged on. By the turn of the twenty-first century, Christian fundamentalists had developed a new explanation for world creation that they called "intelligent design." This idea (which opponents criticized as little more than a backdoor explanation for creationism) claimed that the world, and all in it, is best explained by an intelligent objective, not by an undirected process such as natural selection. Proponents went on to contend that intelligent design reaches the level of a legitimate scientific theory and that it deserves equal billing beside evolutionary science. Thus, they argued, schools and universities should redefine science to accept a supernatural explanation for all things.

In 2005 a federal court ruled in *Kitzmiller v. Dover* that intelligent design cannot be introduced alongside evolution in public schools. And that year a Harris poll showed that only 10 percent of the American public accepted intelligent design as an explanation for creation. Later in the year, President Bush weighed in on the controversy, telling a group of Texas journalists, "Both sides ought to be properly taught . . . so people can understand what the debate is all about."

Of all these conflicts over the right to life and the place of religion in society, the case of Terri Schiavo was certainly the saddest. In 1990, Schiavo, a resident of St. Petersburg, Florida, fell into a vegetative state for reasons that are still unclear. By most accounts she had a severe heart attack or a stroke relating to excessive dieting. After eight years in such a condition, and having been diagnosed as being in a persistent vegetative state, her husband, Michael, determined that there was no hope of her rehabilitation and ordered her feeding tube removed. Terri's parents, Robert and Mary Schindler, opposed this decision, insisting that their daughter was, in fact, conscious and capable of interaction. To complicate matters, Michael Schiavo was romantically involved with another woman but, in order to maintain control of her care, refused to divorce Terri.

The case was heard in Florida courts some twenty times, and each time the courts ruled that Terri's husband had the right to make the decisions determining his wife's care. Terri's parents refused to accept the verdicts, and continued to show the press videos of what appeared to be an alert Terri. Detractors, however, insisted that the footage simply gave the appearance of a smiling Terri when, in reality, she had no ability to respond to stimulation of any kind.

On October 15, 2003, Terri's feeding tube was removed. Almost immediately, the Florida legislature passed "Terri's Law," giving Florida governor Jeb Bush, the president's brother, the power to intervene in the case. He immediately ordered the feeding tube reinserted. The Florida Supreme Court intervened to declare "Terri's Law" unconstitutional.

With that, Republicans in Congress took the situation to its lowest point when they subpoenaed Terri Schiavo to testify before Congress. The purpose of the subpoena was to postpone the removal of the feeding tube. (Congress has the power to hold anyone in contempt who prevents or discourages witnesses from testifying before Congress.) Thus, anyone ordering the removal of the feeding tube could be held in contempt. Leading this charge were Senator Rick Santorum, Senate Majority Leader Bill Frist, and House Majority Leader Tom DeLay. They threatened Florida judges with contempt of Congress if they ordered the feeding tube removed.

On March 21, 2005, Congress passed a bill allowing the federal courts to intervene. President Bush, on vacation at his ranch in Texas, rushed back to Washington to sign the bill. The federal courts, however, denied all petitions and appeals.

The press went into a feeding frenzy over these events. Every aspect of the situation was reported endlessly. In addition, protesters agitated for Terri's right to life, and dozens of people were arrested trying to "rescue" Terri from her hospice in St. Petersburg.

Following the exhaustion of all appeals, Terri Schiavo was allowed to die on March 24, 2005. An autopsy revealed extensive brain damage.

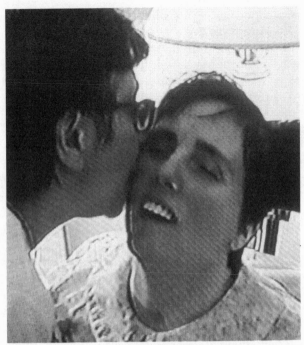

Terri Schiavo in hospice with her mother on August 11, 2001. *Source*: AP Photo/ Schindler Family Video

THE GRAYING OF AMERICA

As the population aged, there was a great deal of pressure placed on many of the nation's systems. Part of the problem came from the fact that Americans were simply living longer. One hundred years ago, Americans lived, on average, only about fifty years. By 2012, that number had jumped to seventy-eight years. And longer lives meant more older people. In 2000, one American in eight was over sixty-five, with projections that by 2050 one in every five would live to be that age. It was, however, the oldest group that was growing even faster: those over eighty-five grew by 38 percent during the 1990s. The good news was that life for the aged was much better than during prior decades. In 1960 nearly one in four of those over sixty-five lived in poverty. By 2010, fewer than one in ten suffered that fate.

The graying of the population placed great stress on the Social Security and Medicare systems, and there was much talk in Washington about reform. At the beginning of his second term, President Bush began pushing hard for a plan that would allow for the partial privatization of Social Security. This plan would have given recipients the option of placing some of their Social Security assets into private investment accounts. Opposition to the plan came mostly from liberals, but also from anyone who did not want to chance their retirement to the whims of the stock market. There was also a fear that the Republicans were conspiring to destroy the system altogether, a promise they had made many times since the program's inception in 1935. Bush mounted a national speaking tour in an attempt to rally public support for his plan, but the support was not there, and he dropped the proposal.

As the economy worsened after 2008 and the new president Barak Obama took the nation into a deep debt in an attempt to revive the economy, Medicare, Social Security and Medicaid reform became the targets of budget cuts needed to bring the national budget back into balance. Conservatives pushed hard for the cuts; liberals continued to protect their long-time entitlement programs. The year 2012 promised to hinge (at least in part) on that conservative-liberal conflict.

By the mid-1990s, drug costs in the United States had begun to skyrocket, in many cases beyond the reach of low-income Americans and the nation's elderly, particularly those living on a fixed income. Drug costs in Canada and Mexico were much lower, and the press often reported on "drug junkets," in which buses would transport elderly passengers over the borders to Canadian or Mexican pharmacies to get the prescription drugs they needed at a lower price. In 2003, under great pressure to regulate drug costs, the Republican Congress decided instead to expand Medicare to cover some prescription drug costs for the elderly. The bill, written under the watchful eye of the pharmaceutical industry, benefited the drug companies by allowing drug costs to climb even higher—now with the cost picked up by the federal government—and with no fear that Congress might step in and regulate prices.

The new plan, however, did nothing to solve the budgetary problem of rising Medicare costs. In 2010, Medicare expenditures rose to $519 billion, about 12 percent of the federal budget. The program covered about forty-seven million Americans, mostly elderly. That number was expected to rise rapidly as more and more baby boomers approached retirement age. By 2020, Medicare spending could rise to nearly $930 billion.

Medicaid, the government's health insurance program for the poor, added another $300 billion in federal health care expenditures. As medical costs continued to soar, the cost of those two programs threatened to take the national budget deficit to unsustainable heights.

THE ENVIRONMENT AND GLOBAL WARMING

By the turn of the century Americans had come to see that there was a real need to treat the environment with respect. If nothing else, a series of environmental disasters caused a demand for better regulation of industries and events that might, under certain circumstances, cause an environmental calamity. The situation at Love Canal, the near meltdown of the Three Mile Island nuclear plant in Pennsylvania, and the giant oil spill by the *Exxon Valdez* in Alaska, all made it clear that environmental disasters could ruin lives and even worlds. In Russia, the nuclear disaster at Chernobyl showed what could happen in the worst case. In 1984 in Bhopal, India, a U.S.-owned plant spewed a deadly chemical that killed hundreds. And the British Petroleum (BP) oil spill in the summer of 2010 fouled beaches and damaged the economies of much of the Gulf Coast from central Louisiana to the Florida Panhandle. These events awakened Americans to the damage that could be done as a result of carelessness and a lack of oversight.

It also became abundantly clear that the nation was too dependent on a finite supply of oil. With only 5 percent of the world's population, the United States managed to consume 25 percent of the world's energy resources. The situation threatened to leave the United States high and dry. One problem was that the rest of the world was beginning to drive cars the way Americans had been driving cars since the 1950s. The oil consumption of China and India began to siphon off reserves from the rest of the world. And to make matters worse, the United States could not keep up with its own demand for oil; its refinery industry was out of date and operating to full capacity with no plans in sight to build new facilities. The entire system was fragile and vulnerable. A storm in the Gulf or a fire at a refinery in California could cause gas prices to spike. In addition, the United States had developed a huge dependency on foreign oil, making it extremely vulnerable in times of world crises. The result produced many of the same ideas and attitudes of the 1970s and 1980s oil shocks.

The new technology in the quest for environmental correctness was the hybrid automobile, a complicated engine system that allowed a car to shift between internal combustion and an electric engine as needed. As gas prices climbed to over $4 per gallon in the summer of 2008 and then in the spring of 2012, there was again talk of alternative fuels, particularly wind power and slurry coal. But most Americans just bit the bullet and paid the price. The sale of gas-guzzling SUVs and pickup trucks declined as gas prices increased; hybrids sold well but did not really turn the market; and most Americans complained bitterly when it was suggested that new refineries or large windmills might be erected near their homes. In 2006 a group of the nation's best-known liberals fought tooth and nail to stop construction of a windmill "farm" off Martha's Vineyard in Massachusetts. The old acronym from the early 1980s, NIMBY (Not In My Back Yard), found meaning again.

Since the Industrial Revolution, technological advances have brought spectacular benefits to mankind. But the benefits have always come at great cost, ranging from poor working conditions to abysmal pollution. By the beginning of the twenty-first century, it had become abundantly clear that the earth was warming; to most scientists, the cause was mankind's continued abuse of the environment.

By the beginning of the twenty-first century it had become apparent that global warming was real. The most obvious statistic was that the twentieth century's ten hottest years all came after 1985, with 2005 recorded as the hottest year on record. Scientists concluded that global warming was most likely caused by the release of carbon dioxide and other emissions into the earth's atmosphere—the by-product of industrialization. These greenhouse gasses blanket the earth, preventing solar heat from escaping. Beginning about 1950, carbon dioxide levels began to jump. Through much of recorded history, carbon dioxide levels have maintained a point below about 300 parts per million. Since 1980 the release of these gasses into the atmosphere has increased enormously. In the United States alone, carbon dioxide emissions increased from 4.7 to 5.8 million metric tons. And by 2005 the carbon dioxide levels had reached 380 parts per million. Scientists predicted another 40 percent increase in carbon dioxide emissions by 2020. That would cause higher temperatures, a rapid melting of the polar ice caps, and a dramatic rise in sea levels.

In fact, the process may have already begun. British scientists in 2006 reported that Antarctica's ice cap has lost as much as 13,000 square kilometers in the last fifty years. If that trend continues, the world's sea level could rise by as much as thirty inches within the next hundred years. Satellite photos have shown that since 1995 three massive ice shelves have separated from Antarctica. The first, in 1995, was 1,600 square kilometers; the second, in 1998, was 1,100 square kilometers; and the third, by far the largest, the Larsen B Ice Shelf, measured 13,500 square kilometers. That massive ice sheet, the size of Connecticut, broke away in 2002.

Not surprisingly, these events elevated public concern which, in turn, led to a predictable political response. National public interest may have developed from a couple of dramatic movies and a documentary. In 1995, *Waterworld* presented a planet covered with water as a result of global warming. *The Day after Tomorrow*, released in 2004, depicted a world hit by bizarre weather events caused by a rapid melting of the polar ice caps. But perhaps the most important (certainly the most informative) was Al Gore's *An Inconvenient Truth*, released in 2006. This dramatic documentary explained global warming in an entertaining way with plenty of film footage and easily understood facts and figures. The documentary was not, however, without its detractors. A number of scientists complained that Gore had turned science into drama; a few others insisted he had played fast and loose with some of the statistics. But the documentary brought the problem of global warming to the attention of millions of Americans.

There remains, however, a credible opposing view to the causes of global warming. A number of scientists have argued that the warming planet might be nothing more than the natural cycle of warming and cooling, and not an affliction brought on by mankind's irresponsibility. This view was accepted by the Bush administration. When Bush came to office in 2001, he immediately stopped all efforts by the Environmental Protection Agency (EPA) to reduce carbon dioxide emissions from the nation's power plants. In 2002, when the EPA presented the administration with data supporting a growing scientific consensus on global warming, the president dismissed the evidence as a bureaucratic fabrication. Then in 2005, a Bush aide was accused of editing government reports to downplay the link between greenhouse gasses and global warming.

In 1997 the United Nations sponsored a conference on global warming in Kyoto, Japan. The result was an agreement that the world's industrialized nations would cut greenhouse gas emissions by 5.2 percent. President Clinton, then in office, had a hand in constructing the treaty, and he signed it. He did not, however, present it to the Senate for ratification. George Bush, when he came to office in 2001, immediately repudiated the Kyoto agreement, insisting that it would jeopardize the national economy. Later that year, representatives from 180 nations met in Bonn, Germany, to address the Bush administration's objections. The president rejected the revised treaty. In 2005 the Kyoto Protocol, as it was known, went into effect without U.S. participation. The treaty is set to expire in 2012.

Kyoto was only one aspect of the Bush administration's environmental policy that was based on deregulation and voluntary compliance. The Bush team cut or reduced federal regulations on protection for the nation's wetlands, arsenic in drinking water, and pollution controls and regulations required of electric utilities.

THE NEW ECONOMY

At the beginning of the twentieth century the nation moved from the country to the city. It was also deep into the process of making a remarkable transition from an agricultural economy to an industrial one. By 1900 the nation was the world leader in steel production and railroad mileage, two key indicators of industrial development at that time. Throughout the twentieth century the United States led much of the world in factory production and became a key economic player in the military victories in two world wars as a result of that industrial might. Somewhere in the mid-1960s, the nation's industrial economy began to give way to a professional and service-based economy. By 2010, 65 percent of the nation's workforce held white-collar jobs, while only 23 percent worked in construction, manufacturing, and farming—jobs that had dominated the nation's workforce as recently as the 1960s.

Much of this phenomenon resulted from globalization, or, more specifically, the globalization of the job market. Goods produced overseas at lower costs found a strong market in the United States, leading to a decline of American manufacturing. Perhaps the best example was the American automobile industry, the very heart of the nation's industrial might through the twentieth century. As foreign competitors like Toyota, Volkswagen, and Honda produced cars that were smaller, cheaper, and ultimately more efficient than American cars, American manufacturers began to fall behind. The problems began for the Big Three (Ford, General Motors, and Chrysler) as early as the mid-1970s, but by 2000 the numbers showed a rapidly reducing market share for American car manufacturers. In that year, Ford held on to about 25 percent of the market share; just five years later, that number had dropped to 17 percent. Ford immediately closed fourteen factories and cut thirty thousand jobs. Chrysler faced similar problems, and found itself vulnerable to a merger with Daimler-Benz, a relationship that ended in 2007 after only ten years. In 2005, General Motors announced layoffs of 113,000 factory workers; and in 2007 Toyota surpassed GM as the world's largest seller of cars, ending General Motors' seventy-four-year reign. Foreign auto manufacturers were quick to point out that they are major employers in the United States. In fact, in 2007 and 2008, Toyota alone employed as many as forty thousand Americans at its nine manufacturing plants in the United States.

One result of globalization—and the competition it produced for American goods—was outsourcing, the production of American goods overseas. This approach allowed American manufacturers to take advantage of cheap overseas labor, escape most U.S. taxes, avoid strict U.S. government regulations, and circumvent troublesome labor unions. The result was dramatically lower prices for consumers. Outsourcing, of course, sent American jobs overseas. It was a common refrain that China had become America's factory—and indeed, just about everything used by Americans was made in China, and if not there, in Mexico, India, or South Asia.

Outsourcing has had its advantages as well as its problems for the American economy and society. Goods produced overseas were, of course, cheaper. But outsourcing took jobs from American workers. That would seem to be damaging to the national economy, but over the last decades the situation pushed the American workforce to adjust, to find new sources of work in the United States, or to retrain and find jobs in growing sectors of the economy such as information technology or health services. But there have been disadvantages and problems. As Americans snapped up products made overseas, particularly those made in China, the U.S. trade deficit soared. By 2012 the U.S. trade deficit with China had jumped to $295 billion. Outsourcing affected the nation's textile industry probably more than any other. American textile manufacturers pushed the Bush administration to impose manufacturing quotas on textiles imported from China in hopes of breathing new life into the American industry. But Wal-Mart and other big-box discount clothing chains convinced Bush to abandon the plan.

Another problem was that the quality of outsourced goods could not always be monitored and did not always meet U.S. standards. The way the outsource system works in China is that goods are made for the American market in Chinese factories, with Chinese labor, to American factory standards. Such a system makes it difficult to monitor quality. The predictable results were that, in 2007, several poor-quality products were produced in China, including toothpaste laced with radiator fluid, children's train sets painted with lead-based paint, infant formula that contained toxic chemicals, and automobile tires that lost their treads.

The American companies and the Chinese government all promised better quality control in the future.

One casualty of outsourcing has been organized labor. Already in decline, labor unions were dragged down further by the impact of outsourcing, globalization, and the growth of nonunion industry in the United States. In the salad days of organized labor, the 1950s, workers fought to get into unions. It meant better pay, better working conditions, and at least a modicum of job security. In 1955, one in three of all nonfarm workers was organized. In 2010, that number had fallen below 9 percent. It was often argued that labor unions were no longer needed in the United States, that the era of menial wages and poor working conditions had passed. But as unions grew weaker, workers had less bargaining power to resist wage cuts and other concessions demanded by management. Large employers like Wal-Mart continued to fight union organization while paying low wages to their employees and denying them health care and other benefits.

If the old economy had passed, what was the new economy? As mentioned above, by 2012, 65 percent of all workers held white-collar jobs. These were professionals and technical workers, managers, officials, clerks, and salespeople; they were business and financial managers, doctors, lawyers, teachers, engineers, computer programmers, and office workers. Another 16 percent or so worked in lower-paid service jobs such as health care and food services.

Low interest rates pushed the economy upward by 4.2 percent in 2004 and 3.5 percent the next year. But the distribution was poor. While the real income for the nation's richest 1 percent jumped by 12 percent in those two years, the real income for the remainder of the population increased by a paltry 1.5 percent. At the same time, job growth remained weak.

The American economy had gone from Thomas Jefferson's agricultural mecca, to an industrial giant, to a service–high tech economy in just about one hundred years. It was a remarkable economic transformation, despite the occasional bumpy ride.

THE ORIGINS OF THE INTERNET
AND THE COMPUTER CULTURE

If the modern Internet had an identifiable point of birth, it was probably the Soviet launching of *Sputnik* in 1957. One result of that was a perceived need to link the radar systems throughout the United States. It was from that link that the Internet eventually developed. J. C. R. Licklider was selected to head the project. His team went live with the first packet-switched network at UCLA on October 29, 1969. By 1978, that network had been expanded to include Western Europe, then later Canada, and finally the Far East. In 1985 the network was opened to commercial use, which turned a useful tool into a potential profit-making enterprise. Other networks came on line, greatly expanding the system.

One in particularly, Telnet (which later became Sprintnet), came on line in the 1970s. That was a large, privately funded network that serviced several U.S. cities with free dial-up access. In the early 1990s, Sprintnet merged with several others, creating TCP/IP, which became the dominant system. By that time, the term "Internet" became ubiquitous in the English language to describe a single global internet network.

In the late 1980s, British scientist Tim Berners-Lee created HTML, HTTP, and the first few web pages. In 1993 the National Center for Supercomputing Applications at the University of Illinois released Mosaic, the first practical web browser. During the 1990s the Internet grew by 100 percent per year, with periods of even greater growth in the last years of the decade.

In 2008, it was estimated that over a billion people worldwide made use of the Internet, in some way, on a daily basis. By 2011 that number had doubled. One result has been the rapid growth of a global civilization, even a homogenization of civilization. The population of much of the world has at its fingertips a massive amount of information. That alone has changed the nature of the world and how information is processed and used. If nothing else, the new information technology has brought an end to closed societies and governments that attempt to control information for their own purposes.

The information age took another giant leap with the advent of social networking sites that managed to bring the world even closer together. MySpace was launched in the summer of 2003, followed quickly in early 2004 by Facebook. Facebook was founded by Mark Zuckerberg and a few of his Harvard buddies. By the summer of 2012, there were over 900 million active Facebook users. Twitter, a third popular social networking site, was founded in March 2006. After about 2010, antigovernment and mass actions worldwide were often orchestrated through social networking sites and services.

MEDICAL SCIENCE: THE HUMAN GENOME PROJECT

In the late 1980s geneticists set out to map the human genome. A genome is the entire DNA in an organism, including its genes. It is the genes that carry the information needed to make the proteins required by all organisms. These proteins determine everything about an organism. By mapping the genome (that is, identifying all the approximately twenty to twenty-five thousand genes in human DNA) scientists can open the doors to revolutionary new ways to diagnose, test, and perhaps someday prevent thousands of diseases and disorders. The knowledge may also aid in solving problems in agriculture, energy production, and the environment.

The project was initiated in a 1986 report funded by the U.S. Department of Energy, but the project was formally founded in 1990 and funded by a $3 billion grant from the Department of Energy and National Institutes of Health.

The project was expected to take fifteen years. Geneticists from the United Kingdom, China, France, Germany, and Japan also worked on the project.

By 2000 (five years earlier than expected) much of the work was completed. In April 2003 it was announced that the project was "essentially complete." And in May 2006 the sequence of the last chromosome was published in the journal *Nature*.

Scientists hope to use the genome data to determine if a person has a predisposition to certain illnesses, including breast cancer, cystic fibrosis, liver diseases, Alzheimer's disease, and many others, leading to advances in treatment. In addition, secrets might be unlocked to determine why certain ethnic groups are vulnerable to certain diseases.

CONCLUSION

America had changed again. It had—again—become a nation of immigrants, a role it had accepted at the turn of the last century but generally abandoned after about the 1930s. For many of those who came of age after World War II, the new wave of immigration seemed intrusive, even threatening. Their nation was always English-speaking and white. The influx of the new immigrants brought new languages, new religions, and new outlooks on life. These were the same fears and concerns that Americans felt at the beginning of the twentieth century. American society and culture has always absorbed and assimilated its immigrants; it undoubtedly would do so again.

The twentieth century was America's century, as publisher Henry Luce called it. This seemed to imply that, as the century ended, the United States would decline and the twenty-first century would belong to someone else, perhaps China or the new Russia. But as the new century dawned, the United States was still at the top of its game, perhaps tarnished a bit on the world stage, but still an economic leader and (maybe even more importantly for the future) a cultural leader.

America still had its problems, in fact many of the same problems it had a century earlier: race relations, poverty, and an uneven distribution of the world's greatest wealth. But at the beginning of the new century it had to add the new problems of energy, the environment, and a need for better and affordable health care.

Will the new age give the nation and the world as much as the past? Will there be as much anguish? As much advancement? As much change?

Reading: Bill Gates

There are few people in the world who have had more impact on the last half of the twentieth century than Bill Gates. And it is safe to say that his impact on the first half of the twenty-first century will be equally important.

Gates's job might best be described as cofounder, chairman, and chief architect of Microsoft, the most successful software company in the world. There are as many as ninety thousand Microsoft employees worldwide, and just about every computer in the world makes use of at least some software applications developed and manufactured by Microsoft. Consequently, Gates is the richest man in the world, a designation he has held since 1995. In 2006 his wealth was marked at about $57 billion; in the early years of the decade, however, that number may have exceeded $100 billion. That is about the GDP of Peru.

In 2000 Gates and his wife Melinda founded the Bill and Melinda Gates Foundation, which has provided grants for college scholarships for under-represented minorities, programs for the prevention of AIDS and other diseases in Africa, and other causes. The foundation has also pledged $1 billion to the United Negro College Fund. By some accounts, Gates, through his foundation, has given away $30 billion since 2000.

Gates was born in Seattle. His father was a successful lawyer; his mother was a schoolteacher and a board member for the United Way. He attended an exclusive secondary school in Seattle where he became interested in computers and computer programming at a young age.

In 1973, he entered Harvard with a major in pre-law. There he and his friend Paul Allen wrote a new version of BASIC programming language for the first personal computer, the Altair 8800. Micro Instrumentation and Telemetry Systems (MITS), which owned the Altair name, licensed the software to Gates and Allen. The result was the formation of Micro-soft in November 1975. Within a year they dropped the hyphen, and Gates dropped out of Harvard.

In 1980 Microsoft was approached by IBM to develop an operating system for their new personal computer, the IBM PC. Microsoft delivered PC-DOS, which later became the MS-DOS operating system. MS-DOS was then licensed to other computer manufacturers to become the leading software vendor in the home computer industry.

In 1983, Microsoft announced the development and sale of its Windows operating system, which promised more advanced graphics, easier usage, and more versatility. By the early 1990s Windows 3.0 succeeded in pushing most other operating systems out of the market. It sold ten million copies in its first two years. As Microsoft's stock soared, Gates became a billionaire in his early thirties.

Building on its success, Microsoft introduced Windows 95, followed by Windows 98, 2000, and Windows XP with its several versions. Each new edition gave Microsoft more market share, making Gates increasingly wealthy.

In 1998, Gates gave up his position as CEO at Microsoft to become more involved in the development of new technologies and products. In 2006, he announced that he would spend more time working with his philanthropic projects and less time at Microsoft, leaving the day-to-day operations to others.

Bill Gates's email address is posted periodically on various websites. He received four million emails in 2006, most of them spam.

· *14* ·

The Second Bush and Obama: From the War on Terrorism to the Audacity of Hope

Not unlike his father, George W. Bush had no real vision for the nation, no real plan of action that would push the country in any particular direction. Reaction to crises would define his presidency, and those crises would come; first in the September 11 attacks, and then in the wars on terror in Afghanistan and Iraq. Americans would follow him into battle, throwing their support to his initiatives against the terrorists. But many Americans quickly grew tired. They questioned the initial reasoning for going to war and the manner in which the wars were being fought. Then they asked the all-important questions: what is the strategy for withdrawing, and when? Bush's answers were unsatisfying, and Americans found themselves in two wars, fought in far-off parts of the world, while soldiers and civilians died in alarming numbers. Even the most critical of observers tried to avoid comparisons with Vietnam, because there were certainly important differences—but there were also obvious parallels. If it was true that George Bush, the father, had seen the ghosts of Vietnam when he fought Saddam Hussein in the early 1990s, George Bush, the son, was not similarly haunted. He found himself propping up an unstable government and fighting an irregular army on a battlefield that was not defined, and for reasons that were not entirely clear to the American people. In a 2007 speech, the president stepped back into the Vietnam quagmire by insisting that the United States should not have left Vietnam, that had the nation stayed the course in that war, it would have won. *Newsweek* called the remark "an abuse of historical fact."

There were a number of events in the Bush administration that showed that the United States was not invulnerable, that despite its great power, it could still be attacked, could still get bogged down in an expensive war, and could fall out of favor with the world and even diminish its leadership role. It was a frustrating time. Polls reflected a lack of confidence in the government. In 2007, over 70 percent of those polled said they did not like the direction the nation was headed—an amazing number, considering the strength of the economy and relative security at home. The president's approval ratings occasionally dipped below 30 percent; approval ratings for Congress often dropped below 20 percent. Both political parties began asking themselves: What do the people want? As the 2008 campaign approached, both presidential candidates, senators Barack Obama and John McCain, focused their campaigns on the issue of change.

GEORGE W. BUSH

George W. Bush was the son of a president and the grandson of a U.S. senator. Like his father, he attended Phillips Andover Academy in Massachusetts, and then Yale. During the Vietnam War he served in the Texas Air National Guard. Through the 1970s he lacked focus, a time he has called his "nomadic years." In response to questions about drug use in these times, Bush only answered that he would be able to pass a background check going back to at least 1974. In 1972 he entered Harvard Business School and earned an MBA. Following his father, he went into the oil business near Midland, Texas, and, although a drop in oil prices through the late 1970s and into the 1980s put him out of business, he generally did well financially. In 1977 he married Laura Welch, a former teacher and librarian. A year later he ran for Congress and lost. In 1986, he famously quit drinking and became more religious. A year later he worked on his father's presidential campaign, and then moved back to Texas where he joined a business conglomerate that bought the Texas Rangers baseball team. In 1998 he sold his share in the team for $15 million. In 1994 he ran for governor, defeating the incumbent Ann Richards. Four years later he was reelected. His popularity in Texas, and his victories over Democrats in the face of Bill Clinton's victories over Republicans during those years, made Bush a popular choice for the Republican nomination in 2000.

Bush's appointments are important in understanding his presidency. Because he went to Washington from a state governorship, it was assumed that he knew little about the workings of the federal government, making his appointments all the more important. He was also perceived as something of a lightweight, someone who would need strong and knowledgeable people around him. Bush did not accept any such analyses, but he nevertheless surrounded himself with some distinguished figures, people who could act as consultants on most any issue. His vice president, Dick Cheney, had been secretary of defense under his father and the leading figure representing the White House during the Gulf War. Cheney had suffered several heart attacks and was never considered physically capable of succeeding to the presidency when Bush left office. That, Cheney often said, made him more likely to serve as an effective vice president rather than positioning himself for a future presidential run. As secretary of state, the president named the well-regarded Colin Powell, another veteran of his father's presidency and of the Gulf War. Bush named Condoleezza Rice as his national security advisor. Rice was an administrator and foreign policy professor at Stanford. She received her PhD from the University of Denver, where she studied under Josef Korbel, the father of Madeline Albright, Bill Clinton's secretary of state. At defense, Bush appointed Donald Rumsfeld, who had held that position in the Ford administration. His attorney general was John Ashcroft, a Missouri conservative who had lost his Senate seat in the 2000 election. Cheney, Rumsfeld, and Ashcroft were best described as conservatives; Rice and Powell were generally perceived as moderates.

THE WAR ON TERROR

On September 11, 2001, America's innocence ended, along with its long era of impregnable national security. On that morning, nineteen Islamic suicide terrorists hijacked four U.S. airliners and used them as weapons to slam into targets in New York and Washington. Two jets, filled with passengers and a full load of jet fuel, were flown into the twin towers of New York City's World Trade Center. The first plane hit the north tower just before 9:00 a.m. As the nation watched in horror, the second plane hit the south tower about twenty minutes later. Within two hours, both towers had collapsed, carrying to their deaths nearly 3,000 workers trapped in the towers and about 350 firefighters and other rescue workers who were trying to save them. The terrorists flew a third plane into the Pentagon, destroying one wing of the building and killing another 245 people. Terrorists on a fourth plane, hijacked from the Newark airport, had turned the plane toward Washington when several passengers (apparently aware of the events in New York) fought to regain control of the plane. The passengers' efforts were obviously heroic. What actually occurred, however, is still unclear. The plane crashed in a field in southern Pennsylvania, killing all on board.

The events stunned the nation. Americans immediately saw the attacks as personal, against the people of the nation, against innocents who had played no part (or did not even understand) the terrorists' motives or cause. Not unlike Pearl Harbor, the event pulled the nation together. Political divisions faded, and the nation bloomed with flags as the people struggled to express their sorrow. The world seemed to feel America's pain. The headline in *Le Monde*, the French newspaper of record, read on September 12, "We Are All Americans."

The evening of the next day, President Bush spoke to the nation and called the attacks an act of war against the United States. On September 14, Congress passed a joint resolution authorizing the president to use "all necessary and appropriate force against the nations, organizations, or persons he determined planned, authorized, committed, or aided the terrorist attacks that occurred on September 11, 2001." Then on September 20 a somber President Bush addressed a joint session of Congress and pointed his finger directly at the terrorist network

Hijacked United Airlines Flight 175 from Boston crashes into the south tower of the World Trade Center at 9:03 A.M. on September 11, 2001. The collapse of both towers killed close to 2,800 people. *Source*: Spencer Platt/Getty Images News/Getty Images

known as al-Qaeda, headed by Osama bin Laden. He ordered the Taliban government in Afghanistan, where the terrorists trained and were protected, to turn over all members of al-Qaeda, including bin Laden, or face military attack. He then added that any state that harbored terrorists could expect to suffer the same consequences.

Bin Laden was a familiar name to most Americans. He had supported the Mujahidin in the Afghan war against the Soviet Union in the 1980s (ironically supported by the United States) and had come to hate the United States because of its war against Iraq in the early 1990s and its continued support for Israel. The United States had been trying to capture bin Laden for at least a decade. In 1998 he was linked to the attack on U.S. embassies in Africa, and in 2000 to the attack on the USS *Cole* in Yemen. In a December 2001 videotape, bin Laden claimed responsibility for the September 11 attacks.

The horror of the September 11 attacks put the entire nation on edge. Then, in the days and weeks that followed, there was a continuation of terrorism that drew out the anxiety. Journalists at NBC received packages and letters containing anthrax spores, a potentially deadly bacterium. In October, an editor at the *National Enquirer* died from anthrax exposure. When two Congressmen received letters containing anthrax, Capitol police closed down the Senate office building for decontamination. Four others died of anthrax contamination, and several more became seriously ill. After months of investigation, federal authorities were never able to find the perpetrator of the acts, although much of the evidence seemed to point to domestic terrorists rather than Islamic radicals of the type who masterminded the September 11 attack. Finally, in the summer of 2008, the FBI was about to charge a U.S. bio-defense researcher with the crime when he unexpectedly committed suicide. The FBI declared the case closed.

Washington's immediate response was to assume that the nation was under attack and to tighten its grip on just about everything. Airports were guarded by army reservists in full combat gear and automatic weapons. Airline passengers were subjected to long delays, endless lines, and rigorous screening procedures. Federal agents rounded up well over a thousand terrorist suspects, held them without charge, without evidence, and without legal counsel. Most were of Middle Eastern descent.

The September 11 attacks, followed by the anthrax mailings, made the nation jittery and fearful of further attacks. Then on November 12 an American Airlines plane crashed in Queens, New York, killing everyone on board. When it was determined that the accident was due to engine failure, the nation seemed relieved (despite the death of 246 people). On December 22 an al-Qaeda sympathizer named Richard Reid, on a flight from Paris to New York, tried to ignite some plastic explosives hidden in his running shoe. He was captured, but the event seemed to show that al-Qaeda would use any means at its disposal to kill Americans. It was a frightening time.

In late October, Congress passed the Patriot Act, giving federal authorities substantial powers to conduct criminal investigations. The act combined several U.S. agencies under the Department of Homeland Security, including the Immigration and Naturalization Service, Customs Service, Coast Guard, Secret Service, Transportation Safety Administration, and several others. The Patriot Act extended the government's authority to monitor telephone and computer communications, along with library patrons' Internet searches. A month later, Bush signed an executive order allowing for the use of secret tribunals to try suspected terrorists. The order, issued without the consent of Congress, stirred widespread criticism and began a lengthy debate about the cost of civil liberties as the price of maintaining national security.

As the situation settled somewhat into the next year, the nation began to look for blame. The news media reported that as early as the mid-1990s, William Cohen, secretary of defense in the Clinton administration, had been sounding the alarm about escalating terrorism around the world. In February 2001, the U.S. Commission on National Security had included detailed warnings of a growing terrorism threat. The new Bush administration, however, ignored the warnings. In August 2001, just a month before the attacks, the FBI disregarded a warning from a Minnesota flight school that several suspicious men had tried to enroll in flight training. Administration officials also conceded that in the months prior to the September attacks, the president's daily security briefings had included warnings of an attempt by al-Qaeda to hijack U.S. airliners. Despite what seemed to be conclusive evidence of negligence, most Americans accepted the administration's explanation that it is often overwhelmed with a vast flood of information that flows through its law enforcement and intelligence agencies, and that it is easier to pick out pieces of crucial information after the fact than before.

In the months following the September 11 attacks, the U.S. military focused on Afghanistan, a nation that few Americans knew much about or understood. Afghanistan had been torn by civil war since the Soviet invasion in 1979. In 1994 the Taliban emerged from the civil war and seized power. Both politically and socially repressive, the Taliban government became an immediate international pariah. By at least 2000, the Taliban had begun harboring al-Qaeda and its leader, Osama bin Laden.

In October 2001, the United States began bombing Afghanistan in an attempt to force the Taliban government to hand over bin Laden. By December, several anti-Taliban forces, known as the Northern Alliance, along with U.S. air and ground support, threw the Taliban out of power. Bin Laden, however, was able to escape to the mountainous regions of southwestern Pakistan. Rumors of his life and death continued to circulate for years. The al-Qaeda network (along with associated organizations and sympathetic individuals) continued to exist, and the United States and its allies persisted in their vigil of combating Middle Eastern terrorism.

On January 29, 2002, in his second State of the Union address, President Bush laid down a new American foreign policy. He repeated his promise to punish those responsible for the terrorist attacks, and then he singled out three nations: Iraq, Iran, and North Korea, which he identified as an "axis of evil." These nations, he said, not only harbored terrorists, but had the potential to produce chemical, biological, or nuclear weapons—weapons of mass destruction. Almost immediately, the administration began focusing its attentions on Iraq, and using euphemistic phrases like "regime change."

Following the Gulf War of 1990 and 1991, Iraq's dictator Saddam Hussein had agreed to accept UN weapons inspections, but he gradually made that process difficult, then impossible. The administration of George W. Bush concluded that Saddam was producing weapons of mass destruction, and the president made the removal of Saddam's regime the focus of his foreign policy. The president, Vice President Cheney, Defense Secretary Rumsfeld, and National Security Advisor Rice accused Saddam of complicity in the September 11 attacks and of stockpiling weapons of mass destruction.

Through the spring and summer of 2002 the Bush administration continued to threaten unilateral intervention in Iraq, and began preparations for an invasion. Saddam, in response to the threats, remained characteristically recalcitrant, giving Bush just about all the argument he needed to launch an invasion. On October 10, Congress authorized military action.

The decision was not without controversy. Many Americans felt that a preemptive war went against basic American principles and could offend Arab sensibilities and involve the United States in the Middle East for many years. Democrats in Congress found themselves up against Bush's strong approval ratings at the time, and a general fear in the public that if the United States did not act, terrorists would strike again. In the November 2002 midterm elections, Republicans regained control of the Senate and increased their House majority.

In early November, mostly as a reaction to pressure from Russia, Germany, and France, the United Nations adopted a compromise that gave Iraq one hundred days to allow for inspections. Baghdad agreed and UN inspectors returned, but they found nothing. When U.S. and British forces began to assemble in the Gulf region the inspectors withdrew. Then in February 2003, Secretary of State Powell, in a speech before the United Nations, told the world that Saddam was developing weapons of mass destruction. Privately, CIA director George Tenet had told the president that the case for finding weapons of mass destruction in Iraq was a "slam dunk." On March 17, 2003, Bush cut off all diplomatic relations with Baghdad. Two days later the United States led a full-scale invasion of Iraq. Cruise missiles rained down on Baghdad, followed by a land invasion by U.S. and British forces on March 21. Saddam's army melted as the invaders moved north toward the capital. Their greatest challenge came from sporadic guerrilla resistance. By early April, U.S. troops were in Baghdad, and Saddam had fled. On May 1, on the carrier *Abraham Lincoln*, President Bush declared an end to major combat operations under a huge banner that declared "Mission Accomplished." It appeared to be so. In fact, the mission in Iraq had barely begun.

One immediate problem was that a systematic search of Iraq produced no weapons of mass destruction, refuting the primary justification for the war. In addition, U.S. troops were immediately viewed by the Iraqis as invaders and not liberators. Iraq's Sunni population, now forced out of power by the invasion, resisted the invasion. Radical Muslims from around the Middle East began infiltrating into Iraq to join in the fight against the Americans. A large group of Sunni resistance fighters consolidated around Jordanian Abu Musab al-Zarqawi. Iraqi Shiites, who also opposed the Sunnis, rallied around Moqtada al-Sadr, a fiery young cleric who was popular with the Shiite poor in central Baghdad. By 2005 the Sunnis and Shiites were locked in their own civil war, while U.S. troops were caught in the middle in a seemingly futile attempt to keep order.

THE END OF THE BOOM ECONOMY

Fulfilling his campaign promise, Bush continued his push for the Republican goal of cutting taxes. He hoped to win over enough conservative Southern Dem-

President George W. Bush gives a "thumbs up" signaling the end of the Iraq War. The event took place aboard the USS *Abraham Lincoln* off the California coast on May 1, 2003. Problems in Iraq were just beginning. *Source*: AP Photo/J. Scott Applewhite

ocrats in Congress to compensate for those Republicans who believed that cutting taxes would cause high deficits. Bush won the fight, and in May 2001 Congress passed a bill that cut taxes by $1.35 trillion over a ten-year period, and then added immediate rebates of up to $600 for couples and $300 for individuals. To those in his own party who continued to demand a balanced budget, Bush argued that economic growth spurred by the tax cuts would bring in increased tax revenue that would, in turn, end the deficits. The Democrats (as they had argued in 1981 when Reagan cut taxes) insisted that the cuts favored only the rich, and they warned against huge budget deficits and a debilitating income disparity between the rich and the poor in the nation.

In March 2001, the U.S. stock market dropped 6 percent, the largest drop since 1989. The NASDAQ, an indicator of technology stocks, was hit particularly hard. Some 250 Silicon Valley businesses collapsed quickly and fortunes were lost as fast as they had been made. The crash turned into a recession; industrial production dropped and job growth came to a halt. Workers at the lowest end of the economic scale were hit the hardest, particularly unskilled workers and service sector employees, with as many as 2.6 million losing their jobs by 2003. The go-go nineties had come to an abrupt end. President Bush, having inherited a budget surplus from the Clinton administration, now talked of projected deficits, and his massive tax cuts added to those deficits. To combat the decline, the Federal Reserve Board cut interest rates eleven times, driving rates to a forty-year low. The economy rebounded to some degree, but deficits continued to mount, and the September 11 terrorist attacks shocked the economy and led to a further decline. In 2002 the economy seemed on the verge of recovery, but as the threat of a war in Iraq grew, the economy again slipped. In the face of a costly war, a weak economy, and massive budget deficits, the Republican-led Congress added another $320 billion in tax cuts in 2003 and then $95 billion in 2005. The new cuts were billed as temporary, and accompanied a promise to balance the budget by 2010. Critics charged that the cost of the tax cuts could surpass $1 trillion.

Bush came to office with a federal budget surplus of about $284 billion, but the war in Iraq, a recession, and the costs of hurricane recovery in 2005 spent that down fairly quickly. In 2002 the federal budget deficit jumped to $158 billion. The next year it went up to $378 billion, and then to $412 billion in 2004—the largest federal budget deficit in U.S. history. In 2005 Bush was able to pull the deficit back to about $318 billion, and then in 2006 to $296 billion. In 2007 he succeeded in cutting the deficit even further, insisting that he would cut even more before he left office. Despite the promises, the thought of such massive budget deficits was more than many budget-minded conservatives could take. But Bush supporters often noted that as the nation's GDP increased through those years, the deficit as a percent of the GDP was actually fairly small, smaller than most budget deficits (as a percent of the GDP) over the past twenty-five years. Some economists, however, continued to insist that the Bush tax cuts would drive the budget deficit back up—to over $500 billion by 2015.

One aspect of the economic downturn during Bush's first term was the dramatic collapse of several high-profile corporations that had based their economic growth on little more than an expanding economy and creative accounting practices. The poster child for this business meltdown was Houston's Enron Corporation. In 2000, Enron ranked seventh among the Fortune 500 companies, with

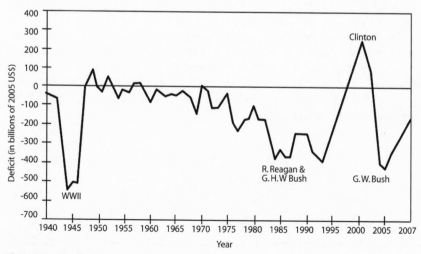

The Federal Budget Deficit and Surplus, 1940–2007

revenues of around $101 billion. It had risen to prominence as an energy broker and expanded its horizons to include telecommunications and utilities. In late 2001, Enron filed for bankruptcy and admitted to fraudulent accounting practices, including artificially inflating profits and creating private partnerships designed to hide company losses. Enron's shareholders lost over $50 billion, and five thousand Enron workers lost both their jobs and their investments. To make the situation even more ghastly, Enron's top officials had dumped their stock for big profits just before the collapse. In 2006, a Houston jury convicted Enron founder Kenneth Lay and former Enron CEO Jeffrey Skilling on multiple counts of fraud and conspiracy. Within months, Lay had died of a heart attack. Skilling was sentenced to twenty-four years in prison. Another casualty of the Enron scandal was the prestigious accounting firm of Arthur Andersen. Andersen had certified Enron's books, and after the Enron indictment, the company surrendered its license to practice as a Certified Public Accountants firm.

In 2002 WorldCom, Inc., a major telecommunications company, became the largest corporation in U.S. history to declare bankruptcy. Charged with inflating revenues and underreporting costs, WorldCom CEO Bernard Ebbers was sentenced to twenty-five years in prison. In 2005 two officers of Tyco, Inc., a large electronics firm, were convicted of bilking over $600 million from investors and sentenced to prison terms. In 2002 the head of Adelphia Corporations, a large cable company, was arrested, tried, and convicted of fraud that cost shareholders $2.5 billion. In New York, several Wall Street investment firms, including Merrill Lynch, received heavy fines for promoting stocks to potential investors at inflated prices.

The primary problem with such scandals was that it sent a message to the average investor that American business is intrinsically corrupt and that insider knowledge is the only way to advance in the market. To address just that problem, President Bush, in a July 2002 speech, spoke of dependable business morality as a necessity for confidence in the market. Congress followed up with regulations that enforced stricter accounting and reporting practices.

Despite these problems and distractions, the economy reacted to the low interest rates and grew by 4.2 percent in 2004, just before the coming election. The growth, however, was unevenly distributed, continuing a trend that had begun twenty years before.

THE 2004 ELECTION

Bush emerged from the rubble of September 11 a political superhero; his approval rating jumped to an amazing 90 percent. The American people clearly saw him as a solid leader in a time of deep crisis. But as the situation in Iraq soured and the nation moved toward the 2004 election, the president's numbers began to move back toward a more realistic 50 percent. Not unlike his father, he seemed to have won the war but not the peace. This was particularly true when a scouring of Iraq revealed only poverty and despair and no weapons of mass destruction. As questions on the topic increased, the administration began to isolate itself from the press and the public, and to dig itself more deeply into a "stay the course" response as its only answer to the growing problems in Iraq. The administration also lashed out at its critics, often referring to them simply as "elitists."

One critic, a retired diplomat named Joseph Wilson, challenged the administration's claim that Saddam was attempting to import uranium from Niger, in Africa. White House operatives retaliated by leaking to the press that Wilson's wife, Valerie Plame, was a CIA agent. Such disclosures are a breach of national security law. The case led to an investigation by a special prosecutor, and eventually to the trial and conviction of Lewis "Scooter" Libby, Vice President Dick Cheney's chief of staff. Immediately, the president commuted Libby's sentence.

Then in April 2004, disturbing photographs emerged in the press that showed American soldiers humiliating Iraqi prisoners (some in the press used the word "torture" to describe the scenes) at Baghdad's Abu Ghraib prison. The general in command was demoted, several of the participants were court-martialed, and one particularly visible soldier was given a ten-year prison term. Bush was generally able to deflect the incident by insisting that it was not the policy of the United States to be involved in such behavior, and that he would personally see that such events did not occur again. The prison, a symbol of U.S. oppressions in Baghdad, was torn down. However, later that year, the Red Cross described interrogation methods at the U.S. holding prison at the U.S. base at Guantanamo in Cuba as "tantamount to torture." A year later, Amnesty International followed up with a similar analysis.

Bush seemed to score the most points with voters when he spoke of achieving the goal of liberating Iraq from Saddam and of bringing democracy to the Iraqi people. But even that could not stand up against the realities of the war. As Iraq sunk deeper and deeper into chaos, and as more American men and women died, Bush no longer appeared unbeatable in November.

The Democrats, however, were in an even worse position. At that stage of the war, vocal opposition appeared unpatriotic and a pullout seemed to be an impossible solution. The only other viable option was to criticize the president's handling of the war, and that barely awakened voters. In addition, most Senate Democrats had voted for the war. Any attempt to repudiate their vote made them appear weak, and willing to change with the prevailing winds. So, the Democrats chose the only road they could. They would embrace the war and criticize the administration's conduct of it.

The party's early frontrunner was Vermont governor Howard Dean, an opponent of the war. But following his unexpected defeat in the Iowa Caucus and then his defeats in New Hampshire and Wisconsin, Dean left the campaign. That opened the door for Massachusetts Senator John Kerry, something of a

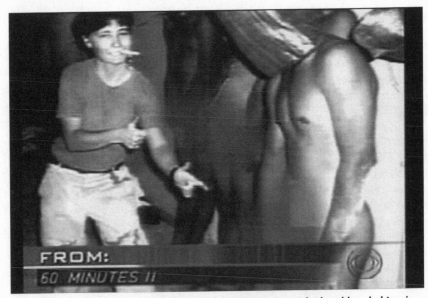

Abu Ghraib, Iraq. This photo of a U.S. soldier pointing to a naked and hooded Iraqi prisoner was captured from Al-Arabiya television broadcasting from the U.S. news program *60 Minutes*. The photo, and dozens like it, went a long way toward souring American attitudes toward the war. *Source*: AFP/Getty Images

Kennedyesque figure whose best feature was that he was a genuine Vietnam War hero, twice wounded and decorated for bravery in action. He had served in the war as the commander of a Swift boat, an aluminum shallow-draft river patrol boat. By contrast, George Bush had spent the Vietnam War years in the Texas Air National Guard, and even that service was questionable and spotty. Kerry's weakness, however, was all too apparent: He was not an engaging campaigner, reflected in his losses in most of the early primaries. The Democrats, however, saw Kerry as electable—at least the most electable of the field of candidates.

The Democratic convention was awash with patriotism: flags, retired generals, and (perhaps most notable) Kerry's Vietnam Swift boat crewmen. Kerry arrived on stage with a snappy salute: "Reporting for duty," he told the convention. The Republicans made certain that the patriotism at their convention was at least a notch above the Democrats'.

The campaign itself was saturated with attack ads, claims, and counterclaims. Independent organizations such as MoveOn.org and the Swift Boat Veterans for Truth ran parallel campaigns that worked as attack dogs for the candidates. In the final analysis, the Republicans were more effective in rallying their base: primarily evangelicals, suburban and rural conservatives, and those in the upper-income brackets who funded much of the campaign. Kerry and the

Democrats foundered; they never successfully identified their base much beyond the black community and traditional liberals.

In an amazing turn, the Democrats attempted to attack Bush for his less-than-stellar war record. Republicans countered through the Swift Boat Veterans, charging that Kerry's war record was fabricated. The accusations clung to Kerry, and the word "swiftboating" entered the American vernacular as meaning a successful smear campaign. At the same time, Kerry's voting record in the Senate carried some inconsistencies that came back to haunt his campaign. He could not explain why he had voted against, before he had voted for, an Iraqi funding bill. And the more he tried to explain it, the more ridiculous it sounded. The Republicans hooked onto the point and clamped down hard, calling Kerry a "flip-flopper." The name stuck and Kerry dragged it with him for the entire campaign. Bush stayed on the offensive, insisting that the war in Iraq was necessary, despite the hardship, and that the nation needed to "stay the course." Democrats hoped that the debates would give Kerry an advantage, but Bush held firm.

On Election Day, the nation showed up to vote. Over 68 percent of eligible voters went to the polls, the most since 1968. The popular vote was about 62 million for Bush to 59 million for Kerry, with Bush taking 51 percent to Kerry's 48 percent. In the Electoral College, Bush received 286 to Kerry's 252. It all came down to Ohio, which went for President Bush.

Bush had finally climbed out of the shadow of his contested first election. Although his victory was slim, it was a clear victory. The election map was decidedly red. He took everything except the Northeast, the three continental Pacific Coast states, and a few states in the upper Midwest. In his victory speech he said, "I earned capital in this campaign, and now I intend to spend it."

George Bush's approval ratings had been in a steady freefall since the September 11 attacks. The only real spike in his ratings had come at the very end of 2003 when Saddam Hussein was captured. At his reelection his approval rating stood at about 50 percent. But by 2006 his numbers had dipped to as low as 31 percent; by mid-2007 he was looking at a dismal 28 percent approval rating in a *Newsweek* poll. It was certainly some comfort that President Harry Truman had wallowed near those numbers at the middle of his second term, and history had approved his legacy. But Ronald Reagan and Bill Clinton had both enjoyed 60 percent approval ratings at that stage of their presidencies.

THE GROWING PROBLEMS IN IRAQ

The problem was, of course, the president's prosecution of the war. It was certainly so, as many claimed, that the nation had grown tired of the war, that the war had dragged on for four agonizing years and had claimed the lives of four thousand soldiers with an additional twenty-four thousand wounded. But in fact many Americans were discouraged that the president had not conveyed any specific plan to end the war, and had really not explained the war beyond a need to "stay the course" to avoid the chaos that would surely envelop Iraq if the American soldiers left.

Meanwhile, the conflict dragged on, with daily reports of suicide bombings, IEDs (improvised explosive devices), assassinations, death squads, and kidnappings. Most of the coalition forces packed up and went home, leaving the war to the Americans in Baghdad and the British in and around Basra in the south. In January 2005 an election in Iraq to choose a National Assembly went well, although most Sunnis refused to participate. The assembly chose as its prime minister Ibrahim al-Jaafari, a Shiite religious party leader with ties to radical cleric Moqtada al-Sadr. It was al-Sadr's private militias that had attacked Sunnis and U.S. soldiers. Out of power for the first time since the formation of Iraq in 1932, the Iraqi Sunnis began a campaign of organized disruption that eventually evolved into what was called "sectarian violence" against the Shiites. But by mid-2005 the American press had fallen back on the phrase "civil war" to describe the situation in Iraq. To most Americans, U.S. soldiers were caught between the Sunni-Shiite conflict. Suicide bombings at two Shiite holy shrines, one in Karbala and one in Samarrah, triggered reprisal attacks. Through 2006, thousands of Iraqis died in the sectarian violence. In April 2006, another Shiite, Nouri al-Maliki, replaced al-Jaafari as prime minister. Maliki promised to bring the two sides together, but the sectarian violence continued.

In November 2006, in the midterm elections, the Democrats took back con-

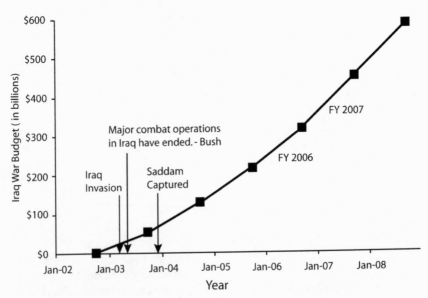

Budget Authority for Iraq War

trol of both houses of Congress—albeit by miniscule margins. The Democratic leadership considered the vote a referendum on the war, that they should end the war quickly. It may have been that. It may also have been a simple referendum on the administration's conduct of the war. Nevertheless, the Democrats forged ahead with a proposal to end the war by passing a bill in early 2007 that would allow funding for the war, but would include a timetable for withdrawal. The president not only vetoed the bill, he countered with a plan to increase U.S. involvement in Iraq by sending in more troops—as many as twenty-five thousand more. The word used to describe the strategy was "surge," intended to bring an end to the sectarian violence and establish peace in Iraq so that the fledgling democracy could take hold. He also appointed General David Petraeus to conduct the war. Petraeus said that he would report to Congress in September 2007 on the conduct of the war and reevaluate the situation then. As most Americans saw it by late 2007, the administration's argument had gone from "What will happen if we don't act?" to "What will happen if we leave?" In the summer of 2007, a *New York Times* poll revealed that 76 percent of the American people disapproved of the president's handling of the war, and 72 percent said the nation was on the wrong track.

By most accounts the surge worked. The surge, together with the willingness of the Sunnis to end their civil war with the Shiites, brought a relative calm to Iraq by the summer of 2008, and the Bush administration responded by announcing a slow troop drawdown. It seemed, however, that just as events in Iraq moderated, the war in Afghanistan began to heat up.

THE NEW NUCLEAR THREAT

One of Bush's planned initiatives was to revive President Reagan's "Star Wars" initiative. Clinton had mostly killed the plan, but Bush believed that a modest ground-based missile defense system would protect the United States from what was being called "rogue states" like North Korea, which might launch a small nuclear warhead at the American West Coast. The plan violated the 1972 ABM (Anti-Ballistic Missile) treaty with Russia. That treaty, however, ended in 2002. Bush and Soviet president Vladimir Putin immediately met to sign a new treaty that reduced nuclear weapons by two-thirds over ten years, and gave Russia an associate relationship with NATO, although not full membership. In 2007 Bush announced that the United States would expand its ground-based missile defense system to NATO nations in Eastern Europe. Putin complained bitterly, even threatening to change the "aim" of his own missiles toward Europe if Bush did not pull back his plans. The press spoke of old-style Cold War rhetoric, and perhaps even a new Cold War. Bush reconciled by inviting Putin to his family home in Maine, where the two smoothed each other's feathers. Neither could afford to alienate the other. They announced that they would "take a global approach" to missile defense and work together.

But in the summer of 2008 U.S.-Russian relations deteriorated significantly when Russian tanks rolled into Georgia (a staunch American ally) on Russia's southern border. Again, it seemed, Russia had taken on its old expansionist role, and George Bush hurled a litany of protests and threats. For most foreign policy experts, however, the events were little more than Russia exercising its power on its border, in a region where it had historically held influence.

Bush's inclusion of Iran and North Korea in his 2002 "axis of evil" speech seemed to induce both countries to enter the international nuclear club by developing their own weapons as defense. As they both moved forward in their production of nuclear weapons, Bush threatened that the United States would not allow either nation to obtain nuclear capability. But as the United States became more deeply involved in Iraq, its ability to stop such nuclear proliferation became increasingly limited.

North Korea was ruled by Kim Jong-Il, an eccentric Stalinist-style dictator who was often described as paranoid and even unstable. He was ruthless and oppressive, and his nation was notoriously impoverished in contrast to the prosperity in South Korea. He made no attempt to hide his nation's attempts to acquire nuclear capability. In fact, he made demands of the world in exchange for bringing an end to his nuclear quests. In 2003 he withdrew from the Nuclear Non-Proliferation Treaty and demanded massive economic aid, talks with the United States, a U.S. pledge not to attack, and further assistance with its program to produce nuclear power stations. Most of the world believed that China, North Korea's neighbor and historic ally, should take the lead in negotiations with North Korea, but the six-power talks led by China went nowhere. In July 2006, North Korea attempted a long-range missile test that failed, and then in October Pyongyang claimed to have conducted an underground explosion of a nuclear device. The Russians, monitoring the blast, said they were "100 percent certain" that the test was successful. The Americans, however, were never certain. Kim Jong Il died in 2011. He was succeeded by his son, Kin Jong-Un, but very little changed in North Korea as a result of the power transfer.

In 2002, Iran revealed that they had developed several uranium-enrichment laboratories that could be used for either nuclear power plants or for the development of nuclear weapons. The Iranians agreed to suspend their nuclear program in 2004. But two years later, following the election of Mahmoud Ahmadinejad, it resumed the enrichment of uranium. Ahmadinejad was an outspoken Islamic fundamentalist and fiery Iranian nationalist who came into the world's line of sight by insisting that Israel "should be wiped off the map." He continued to claim that Iran did not desire nuclear weapons, but insisted on his nation's right to develop them.

The end of the Cold War brought security from the horrors of global nuclear destruction, but the technology did not go away. Not unlike the various devastating weapons of the past, nuclear weapons may well proliferate. The question is, of course, who will police that proliferation, and will the United States alone have the power and the will to take on that challenge?

DISASTER AT HOME

As the United States worried about its open-ended commitments in the Middle East, it received a devastating reminder of its vulnerability at home. On August 29, 2005, Hurricane Katrina hit the Gulf Coast, pushing a massive storm surge of up to twenty-five feet of water over the levees into New Orleans and onto the Gulf coastal beaches of southern Mississippi. The storm itself was not catastrophic, perhaps only a Category 3, but the storm surge broke through the levees in several parts of New Orleans, flooding large parts of the city and killing close to fifteen hundred people. Over one hundred thousand residents of the city, unable to evacuate, huddled in the Superdome and the city's Convention Center waiting to be rescued. The slowness and inadequacy of the emergency response raised questions about the effectiveness of the Department of Homeland Security and the sincerity of the administration in sending aid. FEMA (Federal Emergency Management Agency) was not up to the task. Headed by Michael Brown, who had no experience in emergency management, FEMA foundered as New Orleans sank below the waterline. He quickly resigned, despite praise from the president: "You're doing a heck of a job, Brownie." In addition, FEMA spent $900 million on twenty-six thousand "FEMA trailers" (small, temporary mobile homes), that were never delivered to Katrina victims. At Bush's request, Congress appropriated $62 billion for recovery, and FEMA eventually provided housing for seven hundred thousand people from New Orleans and the Gulf Coast.

The incidents of late August and early September in New Orleans exposed some of the nation's worst poverty, which previously had been largely hidden from view. It became all too clear that segregation, inequality, and abject poverty in New Orleans still went hand-in-hand in the city that care forgot. By 2011, six years after the storm, the population of New Orleans was still over 100,000 below its pre-Katrina level, and major parts of the city were still abandoned with little hope of recovery.

Beyond tax cuts, there was very little in George Bush's two administrations that can be identified as domestic policy. Perhaps the president's greatest victory was the No Child Left Behind Act, signed into law in January 2002. The law was designed to increase standards and accountability in the nation's schools by requiring states to give annual performance tests in reading and math to all elementary school students. In an effective nod to bipartisanship, the president reached out to Democratic Party leaders, particularly Massachusetts senator Ted Kennedy, to forge a bipartisan consensus on the bill. The bill also increased federal aid to education by $4 billion.

The September 11 attacks will be seen as the defining moment in the early years of the twentieth century and in the administration of George W. Bush. When that horrific event occurred, the nation (and even the world) rallied around the president. It was a common refrain at the time that his presidency would be judged on how he spent that currency, both at home and abroad. The war in Iraq was universally unpopular. America's allies, except for the United Kingdom, backed away from the invasion. Although the president could tout a "coalition" on the ground in Iraq, the invasion and subsequent occupation was generally a unilateral affair, reflecting a longtime Republican outlook that has rejected collective security and embraced a go-it-alone strategy.

In 1985, Ronald Reagan, speaking at the Conservative Political Action Conference (CPAC) in Washington, said, "The tide of history is moving irresistibly in our direction. Why? Because the other side is virtually bankrupt of ideas. It has nothing more to say, nothing to add to the debate. It has spent its intellectual capital." He was, of course, correct. The nation's Democrats were still resting on their laurals of the New Deal and the party's successes at aiding the disadvantaged, the disenfranchised, and the working poor. By the mid-1980s the old solutions no longer worked—either that or they had worked so well that they were no longer needed. By 2008, it was the Republicans whose ideas were no longer new, no longer working, and the party had become top-heavy with interest groups and one-issue factions that needed to be placated and satisfied to keep them in the boat. In 1986, at the CPAC that year, Reagan spoke of the fear that the Republican Party might wind up as a huge diverse group that could damage the party's ideals. To make his point, he went to a Yogi Berra truism: "Nobody eats at that restaurant anymore; it's too crowded." Not unlike the Democrats and their splits over civil rights and states' rights, the Republicans, as the Bush administration came to a close, found themselves split over the war, abortion, immigration, and stem cell research. Republicans, however, insisted that they would pull together in 2008 and elect one of their own.

A STATISTICIAN'S VIEW

By 2007, household income was up over 1999 levels, but according to census reports that rosy picture can be traced to an increase in households in which a second adult had joined the work force. In reality, earnings for individual full-time workers fell. In 2005 and 2006, the median family income (adjusted for inflation) rose by 1.1 percent to about $47,000. At the same time, gains were substantially greater for high-income households than for those at the bottom of the income scale. The richest 20 percent of households enjoyed a gain in income of more than $3,000 to an average of $159,583, while the poorest 20 percent saw an average gain of $68, to a total of $10,655. For African Americans, the median income was around $30,000. While significantly lower than the median income for white Americans, it was 14 percent higher than in 1990.

The poverty rate in 2009 continued to climb, set at 14.3 percent, continuing a trend that began in 2000. At the same time, nearly thirty-seven million people lived below the poverty line (set by the federal government at $19,800 for a family of four), ninety thousand fewer than in 2004.

Perhaps the most telling statistic for the future of the nation's health, 52 million Americans were without health insurance in 2011, up by 4 million from 2008. In addition, the number of employees insured by their employers shrank in 2006, and government programs were not adequate to pick up the slack. In 2010 there were more than 8 million uninsured children, and that number was expected to rise considerably in the following years.

THE NEW POLITICS

The 2008 presidential election campaign began in earnest as early as 2006. It would be a wide-open campaign, the first since 1952 (when Dwight Eisenhower ran against Adlai Stevenson) in which neither of the two major party candidates was an incumbent or a sitting vice president. Even from the campaign's beginning, the nation seemed to anticipate the start of a new era.

It was, in fact, the Reagan Era that had run its course. Born as a backlash against the liberal reforms, the overindulgences and the excesses of the 1960s, and then reaching fruition with Reagan's election in 1980, the Reagan Era had changed the nation with its emphasis on lower taxes, smaller government, regulatory rollbacks, balanced budgets, and a more aggressive unilateral foreign policy. Whether or not those objectives were ever achieved was not nearly as important as the Reagan ideal of conservatism that became the underpinning of American politics for well beyond the next two decades. Even the administration of Bill Clinton, touted by some as liberal, sought to do little more than put a humane face on Reaganism and Reaganomics. (Clinton even famously acknowledged an end to the era of Big Government.) President George W. Bush often channeled Reagan as his spiritual guide, but he either misunderstood Reagan conservatism or found himself incapable of implementing those old ideas in a changing world. To most observers, the 2008 campaign would close the door on the Reagan Era. Almost certainly what would follow would introduce the dawning of something new.

Arizona senator John McCain won the Republican nomination following a bitter battle in the primaries. He defeated party rivals Mitt Romney, the former governor of Massachusetts; former New York City mayor Rudy Giuliani; and Mike Huckabee, the former governor of Arkansas. McCain made a dramatic comeback in the summer of 2007 from a fiscally anemic and internally divisive campaign to overwhelm his opponents and sew up his party's nomination in the spring of 2008.

At least nine Democrats jumped into the race, but quickly it became a two-person contest between New York senator Hillary Clinton and a newcomer, Illinois senator Barack Obama. Obama had raised the eyebrows and hopes of Democrats when, in 2004, he delivered the keynote address at the Democratic National Convention in Boston. He was an attractive candidate: clearly charismatic, the product of a mixed marriage, a Harvard graduate, a constitutional law professor, a state senator from Illinois, and a well-respected community organizer. Unabashedly, the press loved him and he was almost immediately transformed from (what *Newsweek* called) "a skinny, scholarly man with big ears into a sex symbol." It was a hard road; in March, for example, inflammatory remarks by Obama's pastor forced the candidate to deliver a major address on race in America (a speech that many in the media called a stunning success). But on June 3, 2008, following the longest primary season in U.S. political history, Obama secured enough delegates to claim the Democratic nomination.

John McCain had earned a renowned reputation as a centrist, a notorious straight talker who would buck his own party just as easily as he would stick it to the Democrats. But as the general campaign unfolded, he abandoned his centrist-rebel image and began to pander to the Republican right, to George Bush's political base, the group that had put Bush in the White House in two elections. To that end, he named Alaska governor Sarah Palin as his running mate.

By naming Palin, McCain had clearly hoped to win over women—the Hillary vote, now thought to be cast adrift by Obama's Democratic Party nomination. Palin described herself as a "hockey mom," an apparent reference to the "soccer moms" who flocked to Bill Clinton in the 1990s. For a brief moment, she fed new life into McCain's campaign and energized the party's social conservatives. But just as quickly she fell from favor following a series of interviews that revealed her as uninformed and detached; then she became a *Saturday Night Live* parody at the hands of lookalike Tina Fey. There were rumors that Palin was not working well with McCain's people; then a story broke that she had spent an inordinate amount of Republican National Committee funds—close to $150,000—on clothes. McCain's numbers fell.

THE GREAT RECESSION

By 2007 the economy began to slow. That was followed by a severe crash in the housing market that sent jitters through Wall Street. By 2008 several of the nation's largest investment firms were on the verge of collapse, and the federal government jumped in to take over the ailing mortgage consolidators Freddie Mac (Federal Home Loan Mortgage Corporation) and Fannie Mae (Federal National Mortgage Association). Fannie and Freddie are private (but government-sponsored) enterprises that purchase mortgages from approved lenders and sell them to investors. Then in late September, Washington, in a surprise move, bailed out the insurance giant AIG (American International

Group)—all in an attempt to keep the economy stable. The U.S. stock market and foreign markets, however, took a frightening nosedive in the latter months of 2008. Investors were desperately looking for the ground floor.

American stock markets began falling precipitously after the collapse of Lehman Brothers, a 158-year-old investment bank, on September 15, 2008. On September 29, the market took a plunge that sent newsmen scrambling for old photos and film of the Great Depression. Breadlines did not form, but the market dropped nearly 800 points in one day, followed by an eight-day losing streak of 2,400 points, or 22.1 percent. In October 1929, the market had lost about 25 percent in two days.

As in 1929, the 2008 market drop was a result, not a cause. During the summer, home prices began a rapid decline, dragging Fannie Mae and Freddie Mac toward bankruptcy. Thousands of "toxic," subprime home loans, often bundled and sold to financial institutions, headed toward mass foreclosure, and the institutions that owned the loans felt the pinch—along with the insurance companies that had guaranteed them. The market responded with a dramatic roller-coaster ride that caused economists to fear the worst.

These events led to a drastic loss of confidence in the system, and credit ground to a halt. The government responded with a whopping $700 billion emergency plan designed to cut the nation's banks' troubled mortgage-related assets. As several more financial institutions sped toward bankruptcy, the government stepped in and took equity stakes in a number of the weakened banks. The American people balked at the price tag, and many in Congress registered complaints and even apologized to their constituents. But Congress passed the bill, and on October 27 President Bush signed it—touting its necessity to save the economy from collapse.

Spiking gas prices in the summer of 2008, along with the slowing economy, caused automobile sales to nosedive. By the late fall, General Motors' stock had dropped to pre–World War II levels and the giant automaker warned of a catastrophic bankruptcy if the government did not step in with a bailout.

By mid-November, the federal government had agreed to assist homeowners who were having difficulty paying their mortgages, but then dramatically shifted course and announced it would buy huge blocks of stock in the nation's banks in an effort to increase the banks' capital and give the government the clout it needed to persuade the banks to lend more money. Understandably, the American people wondered where the growing federal bailout would finally end.

All of this greatly impacted the presidential election. Both candidates, McCain and Obama, were caught off guard by the economic debacle, and neither offered many specific answers. McCain, however, appeared decidedly out of touch when, on September 16, he told the nation that the "economy is fundamentally sound." It did not take a historian to recall Herbert Hoover's similar words in 1929 as the collapsing market dragged the nation into the disaster of the Great Depression. Almost immediately, polls showed that the nation trusted

Obama more than McCain on economic issues; and it was economic issues that would decide the election.

On election night it became increasingly apparent that Barack Obama would be the next president. Media analysts, however, refused to commit, fearing a last-minute surprise surge and a McCain upset. Election Day was, in itself, a spectacle. Americans turned out in droves, waiting hours to cast their votes. In the final analysis, Obama received 365 electoral votes to McCain's 162. In the popular vote, the Democrat received 52.7 percent to McCain's 46 percent. McCain's concession speech from Phoenix was universally acclaimed as gallant; Obama delivered his victory speech before a throng of nearly a quarter million enthusiastic supporters (including Jesse Jackson and a crying Oprah Winfrey) at Grant Park in Chicago.

In the final analysis, the election had hinged on the economy, dissatisfaction with the conduct of the Bush administration (one news analyst listed his top three causes for the Republican defeat as "Bush, Bush, and Bush"), and, some said, Palin's poor showing as McCain's running mate. McCain also stumbled strategically. By most accounts, he had tried to attract votes from his party's right

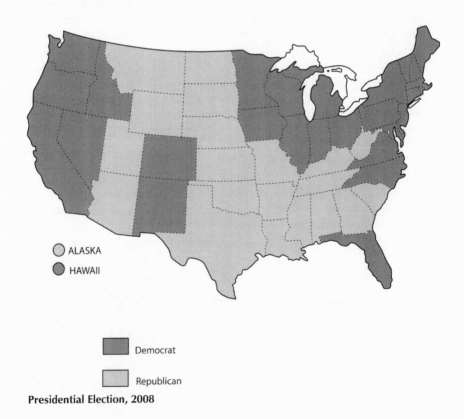

Presidential Election, 2008

wing, while hoping that the center would hold. That strategy had been a winner for President Bush in 2000 and again in 2004. Obama, however, succeeded in holding the center in a campaign that was decidedly centrist in its outcome.

Obama's winning coalition included the usual Democratic Party factions, but he added large numbers of Hispanics and made significant inroads into the Republican Party bastion of the white suburbs. He also took several so-called battleground states that were suffering from the growing economic problems, particularly Indiana, Ohio, Michigan, and Pennsylvania. Perhaps most importantly, Obama succeeded in presenting to his supporters a favorable image of change and hope, the harbinger of a defining moment in a new era in the nation's history.

OBAMA IN OFFICE

Although the Democrats controlled both houses of Congress following the 2008 election, Democratic legislative initiatives ran into strong Republican opposition. Perhaps the most contentious debate was over health care reform. Holding closely to a campaign promise, President Obama pushed through Congress the Patient Protection and Affordable Care Act, known disparagingly as "Obamacare." At the same time, the failing economy continued to rock Washington. Obama attempted to help the nation recover from an ever-deepening recession by signing a $787 billion economic stimulus package known as the American Recover and Reinvestment Act, and the Frank-Dodd Wall Street Reform and Consumer Protection Act. His administration also took steps to rescue the weakening auto industry, including a direct bailout of Chrysler and General Motors, and the "cash for clunkers" program, which temporarily boosted national car sales.

In the 2010 midterm elections, the Republicans gained control of the House of Representatives and made significant gains in the Senate. These victories seemed to jumpstart the "Tea Party," a decidedly far right movement that touted lower taxes, less government spending, and a smaller government footprint. The movement's leaders included the 2008 vice presidential candidate Sarah Palin, Minnesota congresswoman Michele Bachmann, Texas governor Rick Perry, and others inside and outside the Republican Party. In the summer of 2011, following a particularly bitter partisan fight, Congress passed the Budget Control Act, which, among other things, established a procedure to increase the debt limit, preventing an unprecedented U.S. government default on its financial obligations.

On October 21, 2011, President Obama kept one of his most important campaign promises from the 2008 campaign and announced that the war in Iraq would come to an end. U.S. troops, he said, would be home by the end of the year. The toll for the ten-year conflict was surprisingly high. The cost to the

American economy has been estimated at $3 trillion. Nearly 5,000 American soldiers lost their lives in the war, with nearly ten times that number having suffered severe injuries. In early May 2011, an American special forces operation killed Osama bin Laden in Pakistan. The war in Iraq had begun to wind down. The war in Afghanistan raged on, with no real end in sight.

CONCLUSION

It is difficult to say that the United States is no longer at the top of its game. It has, however, become a common refrain. It is true that the World Economic Forum (WEF) has ranked the United States fifth in global competitiveness behind Sweden, Singapore, Finland, and Switzerland. The Information Technology and Innovation Foundation has placed the U.S. even lower, behind the likes of South Korea, Japan, and again, Sweden. In the areas of science and math education, the WEF has knocked the United States clear down to 51st place. Other statistics have hurt even worse. The nation's poverty rate has continued its increase, from its 13 percent high in 2001 to over 15 percent in 2011. By that date, over 47 million Americans lived below the poverty line—defined by the U.S. Census Bureau as a family of four with an accumulated income of less than $21,000. As had been the case historically, African Americans have suffered the worst. By 2011, over 26 percent of African Americans lived below the poverty line, and the unemployment rate for African Americans stood at over 15 percent, with estimates of well above 50 percent for young African American males.

The United States, however, remains the world's richest nation, and (perhaps more importantly) the world's most innovative nation. A vast majority of the world's products are conceptualized in the United States, manufactured elsewhere, and then sold throughout the world by American companies. Despite its many flaws and weaknesses, the United States remains a world leader in many areas. And the world still looks to the United States for leadership.

Reading: Condoleezza Rice

There are fewer aspirations that are distinctly American than the basic ability to climb through the levels of society to the very top. America counts itself as a meritocracy, a nation that allows the best and the brightest to rise to the surface to become the leaders of our society, our economy, and our government. Not surprisingly, there are those who see this as one of many American myths, a wrongheaded belief that somehow the United States is run by those who are best able to run it.

Perhaps one of the best examples of what an American can be, or should be, is Condoleezza Rice. Few Americans have overcome such diversity to break through several glass ceilings to rise to the very top of the nation's government and become one of the most influential figures in modern American history.

Rice, an African American, was born in Birmingham, Alabama, at the nascence of the civil rights movement. She grew up in Titusville, a segregated neighborhood on the south side of the city. As a young girl, she attended segregated schools, ate with her family at segregated restaurants, and (at her parents' insistence) avoided using segregated public bathrooms. By anyone's account, Birmingham in the late 1950s and into the 1960s was the most segregated city in the South, under the thumb of Bull Connor and his racist reign of terror. Instead of jumping into the violent mix of the growing civil rights movement, racial segregation in Birmingham instead offered (what she called in her 2011 memoir) "a kind of buffer" that allowed her family to experience "a relatively placid cocoon of family, church, community, and school."

Her parents, however, doted on their only child. At age three, she began French lessons, music lessons, figure skating, and ballet. At age thirteen the family left their southern roots for Denver. There, at age fifteen, she began intensive classes in classical piano. She studied piano at the Aspen Institute, and then enrolled at the University of Denver (where her father was serving as assistant dean) and where she planned to study the piano with an outlook toward a career as a classical pianist. It was at Denver that Rice attended an international politics course taught by Josef Korbel, the father of future secretary of state Madeleine Albright. She changed her major, turned the piano into a pleasant pastime, and headed off on a career in political science and international studies to become one of the nation's foremost experts in Soviet and East European affairs. At age twenty-six, she received a PhD from the Korbel School of International Studies at the University of Denver. Her dissertation explored the relationship between military and political policy in postwar Czechoslovakia.

Rice's political journey is complicated. She was an early supporter of Colorado Senator Gary Hart, a generally perceived left-leaning Democrat, but in 1980 she saw the flaws in the foreign policy of Jimmy Carter. "The draining away of American power was troubling to me," she later said. In 1982 she registered Republican, the party of her father; although two years later she again worked for Hart, this time on his presidential campaign. In 1987, when Madeline Albright asked Rice to join her in working for Democratic presidential candidate Michael Dukakis, Rice revealed that she was, in fact, a Republican. "Condi," Albright responded, "how could that be? We had the same father." The reference was, of course, to Albright's biological father and Rice's international relations mentor, Josef Korbel.

In 1976 she began her tenure on the faculty at Stanford. By 1993 she had pushed her way up to provost, the first female, first minority, and the youngest provost in Stanford history. In between those years, she had caught the eye of Brent Scowcroft who served as National Security Advisor under both Gerald Ford and George H.W. Bush. In 1989 she became the Soviet expert on the National Security Council and an insider on the Bush foreign policy team. Her official title was Senior Director of Soviet and East European Affairs in the National Security Council, and Special Assistant to the President for National Security Affairs.

During the two Clinton administrations, Rice returned to her position at Stanford. In 2000, she became George W. Bush's foreign policy advisor. In the younger Bush's first term, Rice was named National Security Advisor. In that position she made an aggressive argument that the Iraqis were developing weapons of mass destruction, and she was an important proponent in the Bush administration for the 2003 invasion of Iraq.

Just following the 2004 election, Bush nominated Rice to be his Secretary of State. Since the earliest days in the nation's history, the Senate has readily confirmed the President's choice for his most prestigious and important cabinet post. But in 2004, thirteen senators opposed the appointment, most on the grounds that Rice had been at least partly responsible for the administration's failures in Iraq. Barbara Boxer, California senator and a chief critic of Rice, has argued often that Rice took on the Bush administration's job of selling the Iraq war to the American people, and that her salesmanship bordered on a flagrant disrespect for the truth.

As Secretary of State, Rice is known mostly for her "transformation diplomacy," a policy that is often described as "democracy building." The United States will, Rice has said, work to "sustain well-governed states that will respond to the needs of their people and conduct themselves responsibly in the international system."

In 2009, Rice returned to Stanford and was named the Thomas and Barbara Stephenson Senior Fellow on Public Policy at the Hoover Institute. She is also a faculty member at the Stanford Graduate School of Business. In the late summer of 2011 she published her memoir, *No Higher Honor: A Memoir of My Years in Washington*. She was the last of the primary Bush figures to publish a memoir.

·*Selected Bibliography*·

Alexander, Charles. *Holding the Line: The Eisenhower Era, 1952–1961.* Bloomington: Indiana University Press, 1975.

Allison, Graham, and Philip Zelikow. *Essence of Decision: Explaining the Cuban Missile Crisis.* New York: Longman, 1991.

Ambrose, Stephen. *Nixon: The Triumph of a Politician, 1962–1972.* New York: Simon & Schuster, 1989.

———. *Rise to Globalism.* New York: Penguin, 1983.

Andrew, John A., III. *Lyndon Johnson and the Great Society.* Chicago: Ivan Dee, 1998.

Barnouw, Erik. *Tube of Plenty: The Evolution of American Television.* New York: Oxford University Press, 1990.

Benjamin, Daniel, and Steven Simon. *The Age of Sacred Terror: Radical Islam's War Against America.* New York: Random House, 2002.

Berman, Larry. *No Peace, No Honor: Nixon, Kissinger, and Betrayal in Vietnam.* New York: Simon & Schuster, 2002.

———. *Lyndon Johnson's War: The Road to Stalemate in Vietnam.* New York: Norton, 1989.

Berman, William C. *From the Center to the Edge: The Politics and Policies of the Clinton Administration.* Lanham, MD: Rowman & Littlefield, 2001.

———. *America's Right Turn: From Nixon to Bush.* Baltimore: Johns Hopkins University Press, 1994.

———. *Politics of Civil Rights in the Truman Administration.* Columbus: Ohio State University Press, 1970.

Bernstein, Richard. *Out of the Blue: A Narrative of September 11, 2001.* New York: Time Books, 2003.

Beschloss, Michael. *The Crisis Years: Kennedy and Khrushchev, 1960–1963.* New York: HarperCollins, 1991.

Bird, Kai, and Martin J. Sherwin. *American Prometheus.* New York: Knopf, 2005.

Biven, W. Carl. *Jimmy Carter's Economy: Politics in the Age of Limits.* Chapel Hill: University of North Carolina Press, 2002.

Black, Earl, and Merle Black. *The Rise of Southern Republicans.* Cambridge, MA: Harvard University Press, 2002.

Borrelli, Peter, ed. *Crossroads: Environmental Priorities for the Future.* Washington, DC: Island Press, 1988.

Branch, Taylor. *Parting the Waters: America in the King Years, 1954–1963.* New York: Simon & Schuster, 1988.

Brinkley, Douglas. *Unfinished Presidency: Jimmy Carter's Journey Beyond the White House.* New York: Penguin, 1998.

Bruce, Steve. *The Rise and Fall of the New Christian Right: Conservative Protestant Politics in America, 1978–1988.* New York: Oxford University Press, 1990.

Bruni, Frank. *Ambling into History: The Unlikely Odyssey of George W. Bush.* New York: Harper, 2003.

Burner, David. *Making Peace with the Sixties.* Princeton, NJ: Princeton University Press, 1996.

Busby, Robert. *Defending the American Presidency: Clinton and the Lewinsky Scandal.* New York: Palgrave, 2001.

Bush, George H. W., and Brent Scowcroft. *A World Transformed.* New York: Vintage, 1998.

Cannon, James. *Time and Chance: Gerald Ford's Appointment with History.* Ann Arbor: University of Michigan Press, 1994.

Cannon, Lou. *President Reagan: A Role of a Lifetime.* New York: Simon & Schuster, 1991.

Carter, Jimmy. *Keeping Faith: Memoirs of a President.* New York: Bantam, 1982.

Cassidy, John. *dot.com: How America Lost Its Mind and Its Money in the Internet Era.* New York: Harper, 2002.

Clinton, Bill. *My Life.* New York: Knopf, 2004.

Cohen, Lizabeth. *A Consumer's Republic: The Politics of Mass Consumption in Postwar America.* New York: Vintage, 2003.

Cohen, Michael J. *Truman and Israel.* Berkeley: University of California Press, 1990.

Cohen, Warren I., and Akira Iriye. *The Great Powers in Asia, 1953–1960.* New York: Columbia University Press, 1990.

Coll, Steve. *Ghost Wars: The Secret History of the CIA, Afghanistan, and Bin Laden, from the Soviet Invasion to September 10, 2001.* New York: Penguin, 2004.

Dallek, Robert. *Flawed Giant: Lyndon Johnson and His Times, 1961–1973.* New York: Oxford University Press, 1998.

Dionne, E. J. *Why Americans Hate Politics.* New York: Simon & Schuster, 1991.

Divine, Robert. *The Sputnik Challenge.* New York: Oxford University Press, 1993.

Donaldson, Gary. *The First Modern Campaign: Kennedy, Nixon, and the Election of 1960.* Lanham, MD: Rowman & Littlefield, 2007.

———. *Liberalism's Last Hurrah: The Presidential Campaign of 1964.* Armonk, NY: M.E. Sharpe, 2003.

———. *Truman Defeats Dewey.* Lexington: University of Kentucky Press, 2000.

Dowd, Maureen. *Bushworld: Enter at Your Own Risk.* New York: Putnam, 2004.

Draper, Theodore. *A Very Thin Line: The Iran-Contra Affair.* New York: Hill and Wang, 1991.

Drew, Elizabeth. *Showdown: The Struggle between the Gingrich Congress and the Clinton White House.* New York: Simon & Schuster, 1996.

Echols, Alice. *Daring to Be Bad: Radical Feminism in American Society.* Minneapolis: University of Minnesota Press, 1989.

Edsall, Thomas Byrne, and Mary D. Edsall. *Chain Reaction: The Impact of Race, Right, and Taxes on American Politics.* New York: Norton, 1991.

Fairclough, Adam. *To Redeem the Soul of America: The Southern Christian Leadership Conference and Martin Luther King, Jr.* Athens: University of Georgia Press, 1987.

Faludi, Susan. *Backlash: The Undeclared War against American Women.* New York: Crown, 1992.

Farber, David. *Chicago '68.* Chicago: University of Chicago Press, 1988.

Ferrell, Robert H. *Harry S. Truman: A Life.* Columbia: University of Missouri Press, 1994.

Fitzgerald, Francis. *Way Out There in the Blue: Reagan, Star Wars, and the End of the Cold War.* New York: Simon & Schuster, 2000.

Freeman, Jo. *The Politics of Women's Liberation.* New York: Longman, 1975.

Fried, Richard M. *Nightmare in Red: The McCarthy Era in Perspective.* New York: Oxford University Press, 1990.

Friedman, Thomas. *The World Is Flat: A Brief History of the Twenty-First Century.* New York: Farrar, Straus, and Giroux, 2005.

Frum, David. *How We Got Here: The '70s, the Decade That Brought You Modern Life (for Better or Worse).* New York: Basic Books, 2000.

Gaddis, John Lewis. *We Now Know: Rethinking Cold War History.* New York: Oxford University Press, 1998.

———. *The United States and the End of the Cold War: Implications, Reconsiderations, Provocations.* New York: Oxford University Press, 1992.

Garrow, David J. *Protest at Selma: Martin Luther King, Jr., and the Voting Rights Act of 1965.* New Haven, CT: Yale University Press, 1978.

Gillon, Steven. *The Democrats' Dilemma: Walter Mondale and the Liberal Legacy.* New York: Columbia University Press, 1992.

Gordon, Michael R., and Bernard F. Trainor. *The Generals' War: The Inside Story of the Conflict in the Gulf.* Boston: Back Bay Books, 1995.

Gould, Lewis L. *1968: The Election That Changed America.* Chicago: Ivan R. Dee, 1993.

Greene, John Robert. *The Presidency of George Bush.* Lawrence: University of Kansas Press, 2000.

Greenstein, Fred. *The Hidden-Hand Presidency: Eisenhower as Leader.* Baltimore: Johns Hopkins University Press, 1982.

Halberstam, David. *The Fifties.* New York: Villard, 1993.

———. *The Best and the Brightest.* New York: Penguin, 1972.

Hamby, Alonzo L. *Man of the People: A Life of Harry S. Truman.* New York: Oxford University Press, 1995.

Harrison, Cynthia. *On Account of Sex: The Politics of Women's Issues, 1945–1968.* Berkeley: University of California Press, 1988.

Hartman, Susan M. *Truman and the 80th Congress.* Columbia: University of Missouri Press, 1971.

Hayes, Samuel. *Beauty, Health, and Permanence: Environmental Politics in the United States.* New York: Cambridge University Press, 1989.

Hoff, Joan. *Nixon Reconsidered.* New York: Basic Books, 1994.

Hollinger, David A. *Postethnic America: Beyond Multiculturalism.* New York: Basic Books, 1995.

Horne, Gerald. *The Fire This Time: The Watts Uprising and the 1960s.* Cambridge, MA: DaCapo, 1995.

Isaacson, Walter. *Kissinger.* New York: Simon & Schuster, 1992.

———. *Steven Jobs.* New York: Simon & Schuster, 2011.

Jackson, Kenneth A. *Crabgrass Frontier: The Suburbanization of the United States.* New York: Oxford University Press, 1986.

Johnson, Haynes. *Sleepwalking through History: America and the Reagan Years.* New York: Norton, 1992.

Karnow, Stanley. *Vietnam: A History.* New York: Penguin, 1983.

Kaufman, Barton I., and Scott Kaufman. *The Presidency of James Earl Carter.* Lawrence: University of Kansas Press, 2006.

Kearns, Doris. *Lyndon Johnson and the American Dream.* New York: St. Martin's, 1976.

Klarman, Michael. *From Jim Crow to Civil Rights: The Supreme Court and the Struggle for Racial Equality.* New York: Oxford University Press, 2004.

Klein, Joe. *The Natural: The Misunderstood Presidency of Bill Clinton.* New York: Doubleday, 2003.

Kutler, Stanley I. *The Wars of Watergate: The Last Crisis of Richard Nixon.* New York: Norton, 1990.

Lawson, Steven F. *Running for Freedom: Civil Rights and Black Politics in America since 1941.* New York: McGraw-Hill, 1991.

Lee, Chana Kai. *For Freedom's Sake: The Life of Fannie Lou Hamer.* Champaign: University of Illinois Press, 1999.

Leffler, Melvyn. *A Preponderance of Power: National Security, the Truman Administration, and the Cold War.* Palo Alto, CA: Stanford University Press, 1994.

Levering, Ralph. *The Cold War: A Post–Cold War History.* Arlington Heights, IL: Harland Davidson, 1982.

Lewis, Tom. *Divided Highways: Building the Interstate Highways, Transforming American Life.* New York: Viking/Penguin, 1997.

Marling, Karal Ann. *As Seen on TV: The Visual Culture of Everyday Life in the 1950s.* Cambridge, MA: Harvard University Press, 1998.

Mathew, Chris. *Jack Kennedy: Elusive Hero.* New York: Simon & Schuster, 2011.

May, Elaine Tyler. *Homeward Bound: American Families in the Cold War Era.* New York: Basic Books, 1988.

McAdam, Doug. *Freedom Summer.* New York: Oxford University Press, 1988.

McDougall, Walter. *"The Heavens and the Earth": The Political History of the Space Age.* Baltimore: Johns Hopkins University Press, 1997.

McGirr, Lisa. *Suburban Warriors: The Origins of the New American Right.* Princeton, NJ: Princeton University Press, 2001.

McNamara, Robert. *In Retrospect: The Tragedy and Lessons of Vietnam.* New York: Random House, 1995.

Miller, James. *Democracy in the Streets: From Port Huron to the Siege of Chicago.* Cambridge, MA: Harvard University Press, 1987.

Morris, Roger. *Uncertain Greatness: Henry Kissinger and American Foreign Policy.* New York: Harper, 1977.

Nixon, Richard. *RN.* New York: Grosset & Dunlap, 1978.

Oates, Stephen B. *Let the Trumpet Sound: A Life of Martin Luther King, Jr.* New York: Harper, 1982.

Offner, Arnold A. *Another Such Victory: President Truman and the Cold War.* Palo Alto, CA: Stanford University Press, 2002.

O'Neill, William. *American High: The Years of Confidence, 1945–1960.* New York: Free Press, 1986.

———. *Coming Apart: An Informal History of America in the 1960s.* New York: Random House, 1971.

Oshinsky, David. *A Conspiracy So Immense: The World of Joe McCarthy.* New York: Free Press, 1983.

Packer, George. *The Assassin's Gate: America in Iraq*. New York: Farrar, Straus, and Giroux, 2006.

Parmet, Herbert. *George Bush: The Life of a Lone Star Yankee*. New York: Penguin, 1997.

Patterson, James T. *Brown v. Board of Education: A Civil Rights Milestone and Its Troubled Legacy*. New York: Oxford University Press, 2001.

Pemberton, William. *Exit with Honor: The Life and Presidency of Ronald Reagan*. Armonk, NY: M. E. Sharpe, 1997.

Perlstein, Rick. *Nixonland: The Rise of a President and the Fracturing of America*. New York: Scribner, 2008.

Phillips, Kevin. *Wealth and Democracy: A Political History of the American Rich*. New York: Broadway Books, 2003.

Pollack, Kenneth. *The Threatening Storm: The Case for Invading Iraq*. New York: Random House, 2002.

Reeves, Richard. *President Reagan*. New York: Simon & Schuster, 2005.

———. *President Nixon: Alone in the White House*. New York: Simon & Schuster, 2001.

Reeves, Thomas C. *The Life and Times of Joe McCarthy*. New York: Stein and Day, 1982.

Rice, Condoleeza. *No Higher Honor: A Memoir of My Years in Washington*. New York: Crown, 2011.

Rich, Frank. *The Greatest Story Ever Told: The Decline and Fall of Truth from 9/11 to Katrina*. New York: Penguin, 2006.

Richards, David A. J. *Identity and the Case for Gay Rights: Race, Gender, Religion as Analogies*. Chicago: University of Chicago Press, 2000.

Roszak, Theodore. *The Making of a Counter Culture: Reflections on the Technocratic Society and Its Youthful Opposition*. Berkeley: University of California Press, 1995.

Rubin, Barry. *Paved with Good Intentions: The American Experience in Iran*. New York: Oxford University Press, 1980.

Sammon, Bill. *Fighting Back: The War on Terrorism—From Inside the Bush White House*. Washington, DC: Regnery, 2003.

Schoenwald, Jonathan. *A Time for Choosing: The Rise of Modern American Conservatism*. New York: Oxford University Press, 2002.

Schulman, Bruce. *The Seventies: The Great Shift in American Culture, Society, and Politics*. Boston: DaCapo, 2002.

Shilts, Randy. *And the Band Played On: Politics, People, and the AIDS Epidemic*. New York: St. Martin's, 1987.

Skocpol, Theda. *Boomerang: Clinton's Health Security Effort and the Turn against Government in U.S. Politics*. New York: Norton, 1998.

Sloan, John. *The Reagan Effect: Economics and Presidential Leadership*. Lawrence: University of Kansas Press, 2000.

Smith, Gaddis. *Morality, Reason, and Power: American Diplomacy in the Carter Years*. New York: Hill and Wang, 1987.

Stern, Sheldon. *The Week the World Stood Still: Inside the Cuban Missile Crisis*. Palo Alto, CA: Stanford University Press, 2005.

Stobaugh, Robert, and Daniel Yergin. *Energy Future: Report of the Energy Project at the Harvard Business School*. New York: Random House, 1979.

Ward, Ed, et al. *Rock of Ages: The Rolling Stone History of Rock and Roll*. New York: Simon & Schuster, 1987.

Wilcox, Clyde. *Onward Christian Soldiers? The Rise of the Religious Right in American Politics.* Boulder, CO: Westview, 1996.

Wills, Gary. *Nixon Agonistes.* New York: Signet, 1969.

Wolfe, Alan. *Is There a Culture War? A Dialogue on Values and American Public Life.* Washington, DC: Brookings Institution, 2006.

Woodward, Bob. *Plan of Attack.* New York: Simon & Schuster, 2004.

———. *Bush at War.* New York: Simon & Schuster, 2002.

———. *The Commanders.* New York: Simon & Schuster, 1991.

Woodward, Bob, and Carl Bernstein. *All the President's Men.* New York: Simon & Schuster, 1974.

Wyden, Peter. *The Bay of Pigs: The Untold Story.* New York: Simon & Schuster, 1980.

·About the Author·

Gary A. Donaldson is the Keller Foundation Chair in American History at Xavier University in New Orleans. He is also his university's director of undergraduate research. His other books include *The First Modern Campaign: Kennedy, Nixon, and the Election of 1960*; *Liberalism's Last Hurrah: The Presidential Campaign of 1964*; *Truman Defeats Dewey*; and *America at War since 1945*, among others. He lives in Mandeville, Louisiana.